D1534705

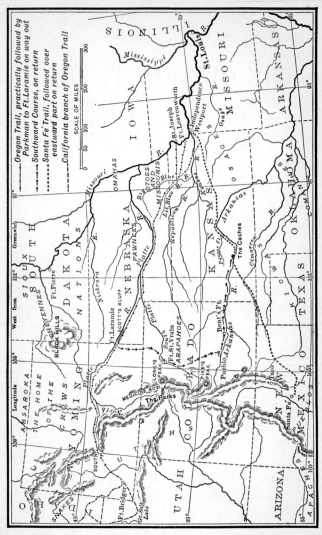

The Country of Parkman's "Oregon Trail"

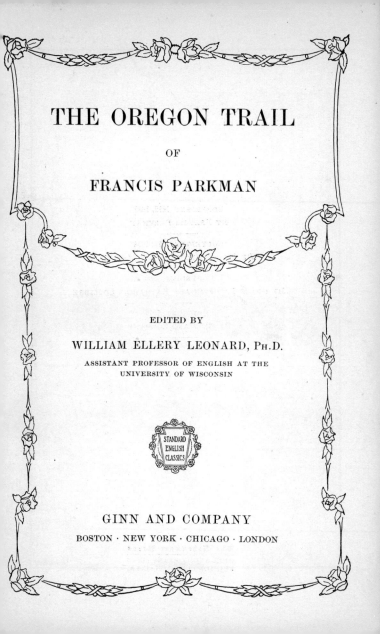

THE OREGON TRAIL

OF

FRANCIS PARKMAN

EDITED BY

WILLIAM ELLERY LEONARD, Ph.D.

ASSISTANT PROFESSOR OF ENGLISH AT THE
UNIVERSITY OF WISCONSIN

STANDARD
ENGLISH
CLASSICS

GINN AND COMPANY

BOSTON · NEW YORK · CHICAGO · LONDON

𝕿𝖍𝖊 𝕬𝖙𝖍𝖊𝖓𝖆𝖊𝖚𝖒 𝕻𝖗𝖊𝖘𝖘
GINN AND COMPANY · PRO-
PRIETORS · BOSTON · U.S.A.

INSCRIBED
TO
MY FRIEND AND TEACHER
WILLIAM PETERFIELD TRENT

PREFATORY NOTE

This edition of *The Oregon Trail* has been prepared for the teacher, the schoolroom, and the general reader, not for the technical student of the Old West. Thus from the Notes much collateral information has been excluded, and in the Introduction the attempt has been to emphasize only the intellectual outlines and the philosophic significance of the subjects broached.

The editor is indebted to Dr. Frederick Jackson Turner, Professor of American History at the University of Wisconsin, to Dr. Reuben Gold Thwaites, Secretary of the Wisconsin Historical Library, and especially to Louise Phelps Kellogg, of the same library, for useful information, and to his wife for much clerical assistance.

W. E. L.

UNIVERSITY OF WISCONSIN,
    MADISON, APRIL 30, 1910

CONTENTS

INTRODUCTION

FRANCIS PARKMAN: A GREAT WRITER IN THE GREAT WEST

I. BIOGRAPHICAL MEMORANDA

Francis Parkman, the historian of the Indians, French, and English in early North America, was born in Boston on September 16, 1823, the son of a prominent New England clergyman. After a delicate but significant childhood, spent somewhat in reading Cooper, but more in roaming the out-of-doors, his little world of wilderness, now collecting birds' eggs, now trapping woodchucks, now creeping along with juvenile bow and arrow after a blue jay or robin, he entered Harvard College in 1840, where, like Emerson before him, he profited more by devotion to his own devices than to the narrow curriculum then in vogue, reading during term time in Gibbon, Sismondi, Robertson, and other historians, cultivating his English style with his eye on the pages of Burke, and indulging in slight social relaxation with college chums. So too it was during his next two years at the Harvard Law School.

His vacations were passed in tramps through the forests and wilds of New England and New York, in visits to the Indians, to ruined forts, or other objects identified with American history before the Revolution, and in filling many notebooks with comments and data that betray the scholar's instinct for original sources and historic method long before history was taught in our universities as a science.

In 1843 ill health, which was to pursue him forever, drove him for some months abroad, chiefly to Italy, where he observed not so much the ruins and art as the Church and its priesthood, which, as he already knew, had played such an imposing part in the founding and building of the American continent. In 1846, after leaving the Law School, he went off on the Oregon trail for a study of the red man in his primeval state.

Before he was twenty, the plan of his life work lay distinct as a mountain before him, an arduous peak, clear and far, its sure path seen by the visionary eye, yet soon to be more arduous than even he could guess. His youth is the story of his preparation; his subsequent years the story of the ascent; and he died at the top in the cool sunshine of a mountain afternoon. It took him fifty years to climb that mountain, a half century of conflict, perhaps no less momentous to our appreciation of the human spirit than the conflicts of nations he so splendidly recorded. For, if the mysterious lifelong infirmities of his body are a problem to the scientific physician, what the man achieved in despite of them is a problem and an inspiration to the student of the mysterious resources of the human mind.

Full of high aims and a lover of action, from the time of his return as a lad of twenty-three out of the Far West he was beset by inflamed and weak eyes that kept him often in a dark chamber, by rheumatic gout that often prevented the small boon of a walk around its walls, by bad digestion, by insomnia, and at times by a strange perturbation and heaviness in the brain that made it perilous even to think. Yet, with unmurmuring patience and iron self-confidence, watching for the moments of some easement, which now and then mercifully extended into hours and days and weeks, he accomplished his task: sometimes through the mechanical device of a frame, with parallel wires for guiding the pencil, that enabled him to write with shut eyes; sometimes through assistants, paid out of the small competence left him by his father; sometimes through the help of a good sister, who read to him or took his dictation. Even when he was well enough in middle life to journey to Paris, it was as much to consult the physicians for his body as the archives for his history. Only rarely could he work as ordinary men; and during one period of many years he could not work at all.

It was then, with the resourcefulness of a versatile and indomitable spirit, that he began at his home on the borders of Jamaica Pond his successful cultivation of exquisite flowers; and Parkman's gardens of lilies and roses, which, with his book on the subject, won him such fame as a horticulturist, furnished the one genial resting place amid the stern victories of his mountain road. And even the gardens, we remember, were saddened by the death of his wife and boy (1857–1858).

He died with serene dignity at the homestead in Jamaica Plain, November 8, 1893. The life work, planned in boyhood, he had completed a year before. His career has thus something of that entirety which so satisfies us in contemplating the career of Goethe or of Emerson, as opposed to the pathetic fragmentariness, so puzzling and solemn, in that of Byron, or Shelley, or Keats, or Coleridge.

Parkman had kindliness, modesty, sociability, humor, besides those other traits so manfully witnessed by his books. As a man, however, he is impressive as a simple yet difficult nature,—simple in the dominance of two clearly defined characteristics, difficult in view of their baffling and extraordinary development: his singleness of purpose, almost coincident with his life, and his silent and unconquerable strength in putting it through, though the very stars fought against him. His singleness of purpose can be paralleled by many names, as by the author of *Faust* and by the first Napoleon, to mention two of the greatest; but for a parallel to that grim heroism of elemental manhood, so distinct from the resignation acquired by a mystic philosophy or the martyrdom sustained by a devout faith, I know not where to seek. Milton was blind and Poe was poor; yet neither was in chains. It seems there is left us but Prometheus himself on the bleak rock with the vulture; yet the Titan merely endured, his tasks already done. Parkman endured and — worked. The point is just that. There is something here for those of us who chafe and whine and give up.

II. Parkman's Writings

Parkman's writings are listed in Whitcomb's *Chronological Outlines* as follows:

1. *The California and Oregon Trail*, 1849.[1]
2. *History of the Conspiracy of Pontiac*, 1851.
3. *Vassall Morton*, 1856.
4. *Pioneers of France in the New World*, 1865.
5. *Book of Roses*, 1866.
6. *The Jesuits in North America*, 1867.
7. *La Salle*, 1869.[2]
8. *The Old Régime in Canada*, 1874.
9. *Count Frontenac and New France*, 1877.
10. *Montcalm and Wolfe*, 1884.
11. *Historic Handbook of the Northern Tour*, 1885.
12. *A Half-Century of Conflict*, 1892.

With the exception of 1 (the present volume), of 3 (an indifferent novel of some interest as autobiography),[3] of 5 (a work on horticulture), and of 11 (a mere compilation from his histories), the publications make one story, of which

---

[1] Originally published serially in the *Knickerbocker Magazine*.

[2] Later revised and enlarged.

[3] The novel is absurdly conventional in the plot and personages. Vassall is betrothed. His Friend, loving the lady too, gets Vassall imprisoned on false suspicion in an Austrian dungeon. After four years Vassall escapes, and, on returning to America, finds his betrothed married to the Friend. Friend is unmasked — goes to sea — is washed overboard. Vassall then marries the widow. But we get glimpses of Harvard College and the woods, and there is a reminiscence of Parkman's own captivity in the fate of the title character, who, like Parkman, "loved action and loved study" (Chapter VI).

Pontiac, though written first, is the last tragic event. That story is the epic of the American forest, the long struggle of the French and English for the possession of a continent about whose streams and valleys and cliffs still roamed the implacable savage of the age of stone. The issues fought for have an epic simplicity and grandeur of outline : here is Catholic against Protestant, Latin against Germanic, Feudalism against Democracy, and, from another point of view, Savagery against Civilization. The hero is the Anglo-Saxon Genius warring by destiny for its new home, —

> dum conderet urbem
> inferretque deos —

whence the American people and the lofty towers of these states ; Parkman fully realized the significance of his theme as the first chapter in the history of our country. But, like the *Iliad* and the *Æneid*, it has many minor heroes on either side, all men of simple and large natures : Pontiac, fighting fiercer than Mezentius for an hereditary domain ; indomitable La Salle and loyal Tonty of the iron hand ; courteous Champlain and stern and fractious Frontenac ; Marquette, discoverer of the great inland river ; Wolfe, sturdy soul in feeble frame, victor on the Plains of Abraham ; the young Washington on the Susquehanna. Out of the heroism of his own life came to Parkman the power to paint heroes, and out of his own unsatisfied craving for action came the epic verve of his fascinating style. Again, like an epic this story strikes the note of religion, — here is the Protestant farmer at prayer in his Deerfield home, the Jesuit missionary saying mass on the borders of Lake Huron in a bark chapel before the naked and astonished heathen. It is varied by episodes almost as stirring as ever were sung by epic poet : the vengeance of Gourgue, the slaughter of the Long Saut, the siege of Louisburg, the defeat of Braddock. And, as we read, nature is around us in the silence of curving streams and fragrant woods, in the majesty of her sunsets, in the terror of her thunder and rain, in her infinitudes of sea and sky — nature as she is, not as she is seen by some cult of symbolists or mystics.[1]

But in thus bearing witness to Parkman's skill in artistic choice and grouping of materials, and Parkman's power of imaginative portrayal of nature and man and action, I would not forget that he is the scientific historian as well. His work is based on a minute and painstaking research, the admiration of later scholars. The points of dramatic emphasis are also the points of historic emphasis. The vision of art and the vision of fact coincide. Every question and individual is, I believe, presented without prejudice. And though the pageant and the conflict itself dominate his pages, he has the critical mind which can, unobtrusively but effectively, analyze human character and historic cause and effect.

Thus in Parkman the writer we see, as in Parkman the man, again two qualities of chief note : that of the imagination and that of truth. And in the all but perfect fusion of the two consists his literary fame. Few European historians from Thucydides to Gibbon, down to Macaulay and Carlyle, have equaled him in this; and of American historians there is no second. Our historians of yesterday—Motley, Bancroft, Irving, Prescott, Fiske — had the literary gift; but their facts and their judgments are too often unreliable. Our historians of to-day, it seems, have accuracy, method, and philosophic understanding; but they do not produce literature.

---

[1] Yet the student must not forget that "the vision and the faculty divine" of the poets can reveal to him deeper meanings, richer passions, and a higher loveliness than any historian. Parkman, great as he is, is still neither a Homer, a Vergil, nor a Dante.

III. Parkman's *Oregon Trail*

1. *Parkman's Narrative*

The Oregon Trail is the classic of travel and adventure in the Far West. Irving, who had, to be sure, once spent a few weeks in that country, writes a charming narrative in his *Captain Bonneville*, full of people, pictures, and information; but it fails to stir the blood like the buoyant and exuberant life communicated to us by the lad Parkman. We not only see the young horseman out on the Platte, and the Oglala in their tepees near the Medicine Bow, and the dirty bourgeois at the gates of the trading post, but we mingle among them ourselves. And we thrill with a sense of danger, and laugh at absurd situations and absurd people. Primeval nature is here in all her picturesqueness and charm and terror. We are in reality; it is as if we too left our books and went afar at the call of the wild. It is for youth to have such adventures; and it is for youth to record them. Perhaps, too, it is for youth to read them.

But, after all, in some matters of fact, it is a confusing world; and, unless we are already familiar with the Far West as it was at that time, we will sometimes lose the pleasure of the imagination in a moment of intellectual bewilderment. Hence the map and the notes to this edition, and the explanatory remarks to follow.

2. *The Itinerary*

Parkman went out in the spring from Westport on the Missouri, through what is now northeastern Kansas, and, striking the Platte, followed it across the present state of Nebraska to Fort Laramie. He then spent some weeks ranging with the Oglala between the Medicine Bow Mountains and the Black Hills. Back at Fort Laramie again, he rode south along the foot of the Rocky Mountains through what is now Colorado, then eastward to the settlements through central Kansas, part of the way along the Arkansas. In a letter to his mother on October 7 he speaks of "gaining a great deal of sport and a cartload of experience."

It was an entirely uncivilized region, visited only by trappers, United States dragoons, and occasional explorers and travelers and missionaries, Oregon and California emigrants, and the caravans of the Santa Fé traders. But it was a wilderness only from the white man's point of view. The Indian knew it as an open book; the trails and watercourses, the hills, the boundaries between tribes, all were well known and all had their legends and traditions. An immemorial world of man passed away when the Anglo-Saxon set Europe on the Plains.

3. *The Indians*

Some of the tribes near the settlements, like the Delawares and Shawnee, had been deported from the east. The western Indians of the Plains and the Rockies were still in their aboriginal state: chiefly, (1) the Siouan stock [1] (including the Sioux or Dakota, of which Parkman's Oglala were a band, the Crow, the Iowa, the Mandan); (2) the Caddoan (including the Pawnee); (3) the Shoshonean (including the Shoshone, Comanche, Ute); (4) the Algonquian (including the Blackfeet, Chippewa, Cheyenne, Arapaho); (5) the Athapascan (including the Apache and the Navajo, and the large tribes far off in Alaska). Space forbids anything but these general facts: the reader must turn to *The Oregon Trail* itself. But he must remember that Parkman, even with

---

[1] The classification of the Indian tribes, begun by Gallatin (1836) and developed by Powell (1885–1886), is by languages, which, if not absolutely scientific ethnology, is the best working basis for study. The spelling of Indian names throughout the Introduction and Notes to this edition is that agreed on by the Bureau of American Ethnology and the Indian Bureau.

his keen eye for Indian character and customs, yet wrote before the days of Indian ethnology or of comparative anthropology.

4. *The Trappers*

The trappers that so frequently turn up in Parkman's narrative were the product of the great fur trade. From the earliest days of French Canada the trappers had gone out into the wilderness far beyond even the small protection of a frontier post. England, and then, especially in the person of John Jacob Astor, the United States had entered the field. Companies were formed, abandoned, amalgamated, — a complex history. But the individual trapper, whether a Frenchman from Canada or the settlements of the old régime along the Mississippi, or a restless Yankee from the border, continued year after year in the same hunt for beaver or bear or buffalo. The trapper it was who first knew the Indians, the Indian trails, their fords, their mountain passes; who prepared the way for the government explorers (Lewis and Clark, Pike, Long, and Frémont), and for the missionaries (Marcus Whitman, Father De Smet, etc.). He built, privately or for the fur company, the first defenses. His trading posts, usually called forts, sometimes became government stations, sometimes hamlets, and have more than once bequeathed their names to modern cities, where the factory whistle blows, the newsboy cries the paper, and the smug citizen visits art museum and music hall or votes for a president of the United States.

5. *The Army of the West in the Mexican War*

Every now and then, as we read *The Oregon Trail*, we are reminded of the march of events at home. General Kearney's dragoons gallop over the prairie, or the commissary wagons with their white tops shine along the river. Away out in

the deserts of peace we hear of war and rumors of war. It
seems that no place is far enough away for escape from the
brutal facts of civilization. What is General Kearney doing
here? The conflict with Mexico was on. "One of the earliest steps in the strategy of the war," says Paxson, "was
the organization of an Army of the West at Fort Leavenworth." On June 3, 1846, Kearney was appointed to lead
an expedition to Upper California by way of Santa Fé. He
left Fort Leavenworth, June 26, about the time when Parkman was out among the Oglala. His eighteen hundred dragoons were at Bent's Fort by the end of July, where a
subsidiary branch of the Santa Fé trail crossed the Arkansas River. He took Santa Fé on August 18. On September 25
he left for California, soon sending back most of his small
band, as he heard California was already in possession of
the American naval forces (Monterey, in California, taken
July 9, 1846).

6. *The Oregon Emigrants*

One may ask, too, What are those emigrant farmers and
families doing here? This is not the place to explain the
"Oregon question"; suffice it that American jealousy of
the British fur trade in the Northwest, American missionary
zeal, and the narrative of Lewis and Clark, distributed
widely as a government document, had by the thirties aroused
a very practical interest in that remote region. By treaty with
Great Britian it was opened for squatter privileges. The
first emigration of any size was that of 1843. In 1844 about
seven hundred, in 1846 about three thousand, went forth;
and the numbers swelled. Some, especially from Missouri
and Kentucky, went to avoid living with the institution of
slavery; some to avoid the fever and ague of the Mississippi
valley or the cholera of the forties and fifties; some impelled
by the hard times of 1837–1841; many again, in the words of
one of them, "because the thing was n't fenced in, and nobody

dared to keep 'em out." The last explanation goes deepest — but who shall explain in turn the age-old roving impulse of the race? Early every spring, with as little prearrangement as birds flocking together for a migration, they collected at Independence or some nearby town on the Missouri, buying there much of their outfit, and organizing themselves, with the Anglo-Saxon's genius for government, into a company with pilot, captain, lieutenant and subalterns, sergeants and judges, either there or at the camping place on the first day out. There was one large annual migration, but sometimes small parties, like those met by Parkman, arriving too late, set out alone. It was a journey of four months. The white-covered wagons, "the prairie schooners," were drawn by mules or oxen. Huge droves of cattle plodded on beside. The caravans made from five to thirty miles a day, with reg-ular encampments by night and occasional longer halts for hunting and washing. There were quarrels to be settled by due process of improvised law, newborn babes to be swathed, young couples to be married, and many of young and old to be laid in mother earth. It was civilization en route. It was the last great migration of the Aryan race; when it was accomplished, the Völkerwanderungen were over forever.

Parkman, primarily interested in the Indian, seems not to have appreciated its significance. Moreover, he seems to have been unlucky in the emigrant types he met. A reader of the contemporary diaries or the reminiscences of the old pioneers comes to respect the sturdy manhood and native intelligence of those people. Nor were they all uncouth. One young man during a prairie halt passed off the time in reading Shakespeare's *Merry Wives of Windsor*. Palmer ad-vised that "every family should lay in [i.e. on fitting out] a good supply of school-books for their children." The ear-lier parties had not been more than two or three years in the Willamette valley before they had organized themselves into a temporary government with a constitution modeled on that of Iowa. A great state is to-day what she is by virtue of those who sixty and seventy years ago took the Oregon trail.

A few sometimes left the main caravan, when west of the Rockies, for the fertile farm lands of California; but what is famous as the California migration had its inception later, and in a far different motive — more exciting perhaps, more easily defined, but not more earnest and brave.

7. *The Oregon Trail*

Parkman named his narrative after the old highway from the settlements through South Pass, which he followed in the main to his stopping point at Fort Laramie. Beyond the portion shown on our map, it wound through the present state of Idaho, near the Snake River, across the modern Oregon, down the banks of the Columbia to the Willamette valley; while the California trail originally branched off at Fort Bridger, rounded Salt Lake on the east and north, and passed through the modern Nevada, on into the valley of the Sacramento.

For some little distance, as indicated by the map, the Oregon trail was identical with the road to New Mexico; indeed its few traces in the fields and golf grounds near Kansas City are still known as the Santa Fé trail. At about the site of the present town of Gardner, Kansas, the traveler came to the fork. Here stood a guidepost pointing west. "Road to Oregon" it said, with an eloquence as simple and full as in that word "Italia" which the Alpine tourist may read to-day on a certain roadside stone in the mountains just south of the Swiss border.

The Oregon trail was already historic. Originally, like many of the main traveled roads of the west, it was made by the Indians with man's primitive instinct for the shortest or most convenient thoroughfares. The trappers had found and followed it. Over a portion of approximately the same course came the land party sent out by Astor in his fur-company enterprise of 1811. The explorers and dragoons had helped to beat it deeper. The Mormons were soon to furrow it on their hegira to the Great Salt Lake. Now it began to grow broader under the rolling wagons of the emigrant caravaneers. Year by year saw it deeper and broader. In 1849 came the rush for the gold of California. Some flung along on horseback; some crept in ox teams; some trudged afoot, each pushing a wheelbarrow. An army of forty thousand. Five thousand died of cholera on the way. Then the rumor of wealth in the Rockies brought the hordes bound for Denver, on the canvas sides of whose wagons stood scrawled "Pike's Peak or Bust," now an American proverb of some pith. The pony express of 1860–1861, from St. Joseph, Missouri, to Sacramento, swept along the entire course in eight days. The eastern part was soon traversed by the Overland Mail, bearing to the Pacific news of Gettysburg and Appomattox; and we think what a pother, after all, De Quincey made of his suburban coach rides down the inland lanes of England a half century before. The Indians gazing upon the graven wheel tracks stretching, in parallel lines a hundred feet wide, a dusty and grassless ribbon of bare earth, interminably toward the sunset, called it "the great medicine road of the white men" — in the days when it belonged to their fathers it had been no more than a footpath or a buffalo run.

To-day, west of the Rockies, much of its course is marked by the railroads. But eastward, out on the prairies it lies, overgrown with grass and flowers, distinct, yet desolate and untraveled, a relic which, though it lifts no broken column or ivied arch to the winds, and throws no solemn shadows along the silent plain, abides a while longer, with the annual revolution of earth, as one of her most vast and impressive witnesses to the Endeavor and Achievement of Man.

The human race has girdled the globe with paths for many feet. We look at a map of the Roman Empire and trace them, Appian and Flaminian and all the rest, radiating from the Eternal City through western Europe. Others cross the Russian steppes, and others pass through the wall of China. Still others thread the Andes of the vanished Incas. Now they bind together all the nations, all the cities, all the isles. And, as long as the stars arise, we shall pass from place to place.

8. *The Santa Fé Trail*

On his return Parkman encountered the Santa Fé trail (see map). For two hundred years trade with Santa Fé had been upward through the mountains by pack train and ox cart, from Vera Cruz, the Spanish-Mexican port of entry, two thousand miles below. By 1822 it surrendered to the enterprise of the north — not that of the French-American trapper and traveler, be it remarked, but that of the incorrigible Yankee. In 1825 the United States, more watchful of her commerce then than now, commissioned its civil engineers to mark a road from the Missouri frontier to the Mexican. The annual caravan of the Yankee traders, well-appointed wagons drawn by teams of eight or ten mules or oxen, laden with portable manufactures of the cities of the young republic, accompanied part way sometimes by military escort of the United States, usually set out, like the Oregon emigrants, from Independence, and organized itself, with captains, pilot, etc., when it got to Council Grove, one hundred and fifty miles away. It had then some six hundred and fifty miles to go. Its arrival became the event of the year for the Santa Féans. After barter and social excitement it returned with animals, robes, furs, and the silver of the Mexican mines, sometimes escorted to the frontier by a guard of native soldiery. In 1843 the caravan numbered two hundred and fifty wagons; but that same year Mexico forbade the trade, and it was thereafter sporadic and unimportant. A "commerce of the prairies" extending merely over a score of years, and of little ulterior importance, save as it helped to make the United States familiar with the region in the Mexican War a few years later, it nevertheless has to our imagination to-day something of the romance of the immemorial traffic over the beaten routes in the Orient — of the Arab camels crossing the Sahara, of the caravaneers, with the silks of China and India, winding along through Syria to the Midland Sea.

IV. Epilogue

Such is the man, and such is the country through which he passed and of which he has something to tell. We go with a great writer into the great West.

SUGGESTIVE BIBLIOGRAPHY

The editor has found the following works of especial interest in preparing this edition:

Adventures of Captain Bonneville (entitled in the first edition *The Rocky Mountains*), 1837, Washington Irving. Accessible in the Riverside Edition, J. B. Lippincott. It takes us into the region traversed somewhat later by Parkman, and beyond, amid trappers, traders, and Indians.

The American Fur Trade of the Far West, 3 vols., H. M. Chittenden, New York, Francis P. Harper, 1902. It furnishes exhaustive information on the old trading posts, the itineraries of the Oregon and Santa Fé travel, and (in Vol. III) a detailed map, drawn by Paul Burgoldt, of the trans-Mississippi territory as it was between 1807 and 1843.

The American Nation, edited by Albert B. Hart, especially Vol. XIV, *Rise of the New West 1819–1829*, Frederick J. Turner, and Vol. XVII, *Westward Extension 1841–1850*, George P. Garrison, New York, Harper and Brothers, 1906.

Breaking the Wilderness, Frederick S. Dellenbaugh, New York, G. P. Putnam's Sons, 1905. "The story of the conquest of the far west from the wanderings of Cabeza de Vaca to . . . the completion of the Union Pacific Railway." Copiously illustrated; "a good story," both popular and reliable.

Early Western Travels 1748–1846, Vols. I–XXXII, edited with great learning and skill by R. G. Thwaites, Cleveland, Arthur H. Clark Co., 1904–1907. This is "a series of annotated reprints of some of the best and rarest contemporary volumes of travel, descriptive of the aborigines and social and economic conditions of the middle and far west, during the period of early American settlement." It is referred to in the notes as *E. W. T.*

The volumes of *E. W. T.* most interesting to the student of Parkman's *Oregon Trail* are presumably the following:

Vols. XIX–XX, *Commerce of the Prairies* (1831–1839), J. Gregg. This is the classic of the Santa Fé trade.

Vol. XXV, "Comprising the series of original paintings by Charles Bodmer to illustrate Maximilian, Prince of Wied's, Travels in the Interior of North America, 1832–1834." Indians, landscapes, historic spots, a treasure-trove for the enthusiast.

Vols. XXVIII–XXIX, *Travels in the Great Western Prairies* (1839), T. J. Farnham. It was published in London, 1843.

Vol. XXIX, *Oregon Missions and Travels over the Rocky Mountains, 1845–1846*, Father P. J. De Smet of the Society of Jesus.

Vol. XXX, *Journal of Travels over the Rocky Mountains, 1845–1846*, Joel Palmer. "The most complete description of the Oregon trail we now possess" (Thwaites, Introduction, p. 18). It was intended, when published in 1847, for use as an emigrant's guidebook.

Vols. XXXI–XXXII, *Analytical Index to the Series.* Prepared with a staff of assistants. Remarkably thorough, ingenious, and practical, perhaps the best piece of indexing ever done in America. By its means may be found in the various volumes references throwing light on many details (especially of individuals and places) not explained in our notes.

The Last American Frontier, F. L. Paxson, New York, Macmillan, 1910. The latest and best brief popular treatment.

Our Wild Indians, Col. Richard I. Dodge, Hartford, A. D. Worthington and Co., 1883. It records thirty-three years' experience among the Plains Indians; invaluable to the mature student, and a genuine "boy's book" too.

The Plains of the Great West, Col. Richard I. Dodge, New York, G. P. Putnam's Sons, 1877.

Francis Parkman, Charles H. Farnham, Boston, Little, Brown, and Co., 1901. The most complete in biographical facts and the most thoughtful in criticism of the man and the writer of all the studies about Parkman.

Francis Parkman, Henry D. Sedgwick, *American Men of Letters Series*, Boston, Houghton, Mifflin and Co., 1904.

The Quarterly of the Oregon Historical Society, published at Salem, Oregon, especially Vol. I (1900), *The Oregon Trail*, F. G. Young. This gives interesting photographs and other data of the Oregon trail as it is to-day. Also:

Vol. I, *A Day with the Cow Column in 1843*, Jesse Applegate.

Vol. II, *The Oregon Trail in 1844*, John Minto.

Vol. VII, *Diary of the Emigration of 1843*, James W. Nesmith.

Vol. VII, *Route Across the Rocky Mountains*, Overton Johnson and William H. Winter of the Emigration of 1843. (Reprint of a work published in 1846.)

Reports of the Bureau of Ethnology, Washington, Government Printing Office. The most authoritative studies of the Indians.

Rocky Mountain Exploration, R. G. Thwaites, New York, D. Appleton and Co., 1904.

The Significance of the Frontier in American History, Frederick J. Turner in *Annual Report of the American Historical Association for 1893*, pp. 199–227.

Sources of the History of Oregon, published at Eugene, Oregon, especially Vol. I, *The Correspondence and Journals of Captain Nathaniel J. Wyeth*, *1831–1836*. Also:

Vol. I, *Journal of Medorem Crawford*. An account of his trip across the plains with the Oregon pioneers of 1842.

The Winning of the West, Theodore Roosevelt, in *The Sagamore Series*, New York, G. P. Putnam's Sons, 1900 (first published in 1889). This familiar work deals of course with an earlier period and a more easterly territory than *The Oregon Trail*, but is invaluable as a historic background to the days of the last frontier and the Far West.

Parkman's works are published by Little, Brown, and Co., Library Edition, 1909.

PREFACE TO THE FOURTH EDITION

The following sketches first appeared in 1847.[1] A summer's adventures of two youths just out of college might well enough be allowed to fall into oblivion, were it not that a certain interest will always attach to the record of that which has passed away never to return. This book is the reflection of forms and conditions of life which have ceased, in great measure, to exist. It mirrors the image of an irrevocable past.

I remember that, as we rode by the foot of Pike's Peak, when for a fortnight we met no face of man, my companion remarked, in a tone anything but complacent, that a time would come when those plains would be a grazing country, the buffalo give place to tame cattle, farmhouses be scattered along the water-courses, and wolves, bears, and Indians be numbered among the things that were. We condoled with each other on so melancholy a prospect, but we little thought what the future had in store. We knew that there was more or less gold in the seams of those untrodden mountains; but we did not foresee that it would build cities in the waste and plant hotels and gambling-houses among the haunts of the grizzly bear. We knew that a few fanatical outcasts were groping their way across the plains to

---

[1] Parkman inserted the following memorandum in the later editions :
The " Oregon Trail " is the title under which this book first appeared. It was afterwards changed by the publisher, and is now restored to the form in which it originally stood in the Knickerbocker Magazine. As the early editions were printed in my absence, I did not correct the proofs, — a process doubly necessary, since the book was written from dictation. The necessary corrections have been made in the present edition.

seek an asylum from Gentile persecution ; but we did not imagine that the polygamous hordes of Mormon would rear a swarming Jerusalem in the bosom of solitude itself. We knew that, more and more, year after year, the trains of emigrant wagons would creep in slow procession towards barbarous Oregon or wild and distant California ; but we did not dream how Commerce and Gold would breed nations along the Pacific, the disenchanting screech of the locomotive break the spell of weird mysterious mountains, woman's rights invade the fastnesses of the Arapahoes, and despairing savagery, assailed in front and rear, vail its scalp-locks and feathers before triumphant commonplace. We were no prophets to foresee all this ; and, had we foreseen it, perhaps some perverse regrets might have tempered the ardor of our rejoicing.

The wild cavalcade that defiled with me down the gorges of the Black Hills, with its paint and war-plumes, fluttering trophies and savage embroidery, bows, arrows, lances, and shields, will never be seen again. Those who formed it have found bloody graves, or a ghastlier burial in the maws of wolves. The Indian of to-day, armed with a revolver and crowned with an old hat ; cased, possibly, in trousers or muffled in a tawdry shirt, — is an Indian still, but an Indian shorn of the picturesqueness which was his most conspicuous merit.

The mountain trapper is no more, and the grim romance of his wild, hard life is a memory of the past.

As regards the motives which sent us to the mountains, our liking for them would have sufficed ; but, in my case, another incentive was added. I went in great measure as a student, to prepare for a literary undertaking of which the plan was already formed, but which, from the force of inexorable circumstances, is still but half accomplished. It was this that prompted some proceedings on my part, which, without a fixed purpose in view, might be charged with youthful rashness. My business was observation, and I was willing to pay dearly for the opportunity of exercising it.

Two or three years ago, I made a visit to our guide, the brave and true-hearted Henry Chatillon, at the town of Carondelet, near St. Louis. It was more than twenty years since we had met. Time hung heavy on his hands, as usual with old mountain-men married and established; his hair was touched with gray, and his face and figure showed tokens of early hardship; but the manly simplicity of his character was unchanged. He told me that the Indians with whom I had been domesticated, a band of the hated Sioux, had nearly all been killed in fights with the white men.

The faithful Deslauriers is, I believe, still living on the frontier of the Missouri. The hunter Raymond perished in the snow during Fremont's disastrous passage of the mountains in the winter of 1848.

Boston, March 30, 1872

PREFACE TO THE EDITION OF 1892

In the preface to the fourth edition of this book, printed in 1872, I spoke of the changes that had already come over the Far West. Since that time change has grown to metamorphosis. For Indian tepees, with their trophies of bow, lance, shield, and dangling scalp-locks, we have towns and cities, resorts of health and pleasure seekers, with an agreeable society, Paris fashions, the magazines, the latest poem, and the last new novel. The sons of civilization, drawn by the fascinations of a fresher and bolder life, thronged to the western wilds in multitudes which blighted the charm that had lured them.

The buffalo is gone, and of all his millions nothing is left but bones. Tame cattle and fences of barbed wire have supplanted his vast herds and boundless grazing grounds. Those discordant serenaders, the wolves that howled at evening about the traveller's camp-fire, have succumbed to arsenic and hushed their savage music. The wild Indian is turned into an ugly caricature of his conqueror; and that which made him romantic, terrible, and hateful, is in large measure scourged out of him. The slow cavalcade of horsemen armed to the teeth has disappeared before parlor cars and the effeminate comforts of modern travel.

The rattlesnakes have grown bashful and retiring. The mountain lion shrinks from the face of man, and even grim "Old Ephraim," [1] the grizzly bear, seeks the seclusion of his dens and caverns. It is said that he is no longer his former self, having found, by an intelligence not hitherto

_____
[1] Alias "Old Caleb" and "Old Enoch."

set to his credit, that his ferocious strength is no match for
a repeating rifle; with which discovery he is reported to have
grown diffident, and abated the truculence of his more pros-
perous days. One may be permitted to doubt if the blood-
thirsty old savage has really experienced a change of heart;
and before inviting him to single combat, the ambitious
tenderfoot, though the proud possessor of a Winchester
with sixteen cartridges in the magazine, would do well to
consider not only the quality of his weapon, but also that
of his own nerves.

He who feared neither bear, Indian, nor devil, the all-
daring and all-enduring trapper, belongs to the past, or lives
only in a few gray-bearded survivals. In his stead we have
the cowboy, and even his star begins to wane.

The Wild West is tamed, and its savage charms have
withered. If this book can help to keep their memory alive,
it will have done its part. It has found a powerful helper
in the pencil of Mr. Remington, whose pictures are as full of
truth as of spirit, for they are the work of one who knew
the prairies and the mountains before irresistible commonplace had subdued them.

BOSTON, 16 September, 1892

THE OREGON TRAIL

CHAPTER I

THE FRONTIER

Last spring, 1846, was a busy season in the city of St. Louis. Not only were emigrants from every part of the country preparing for the journey to Oregon and California, but an unusual number of traders were making ready their wagons and outfits for Santa Fé. The hotels were crowded, and the 5
gunsmiths and saddlers were kept constantly at work in providing arms and equipments for the different parties of travellers. Steamboats were leaving the levee and passing up the Missouri, crowded with passengers on their way to the frontier. 10

In one of these, the "Radnor," since snagged and lost, my friend and relative, Quincy Adams Shaw, and myself, left St. Louis on the twenty-eighth of April, on a tour of curiosity and amusement to the Rocky Mountains. The boat was loaded until the water broke alternately over her guards. 15
Her upper-deck was covered with large wagons of a peculiar form, for the Santa Fé trade, and her hold was crammed with goods for the same destination. There were also the equipments and provisions of a party of Oregon emigrants, a band of mules and horses, piles of saddles and harness, 20
and a multitude of nondescript articles, indispensable on the prairies. Almost hidden in this medley was a small French cart, of the sort very appropriately called a "mule-killer," beyond the frontiers, and not far distant a tent, together with a miscellaneous assortment of boxes and barrels. The whole

equipage was far from prepossessing in its appearance; yet, such as it was, it was destined to a long and arduous journey on which the persevering reader will accompany it.

The passengers on board the "Radnor" corresponded with her freight. In her cabin were Santa Fé traders, gamblers, speculators, and adventurers of various descriptions, and her steerage was crowded with Oregon emigrants, "mountain men," negroes, and a party of Kanzas Indians, who had been on a visit to St. Louis.

Thus laden, the boat struggled upward for seven or eight days against the rapid current of the Missouri, grating upon snags, and hanging for two or three hours at a time upon sand-bars. We entered the mouth of the Missouri in a drizzling rain, but the weather soon became clear, and showed distinctly the broad and turbid river, with its eddies, its sand-bars, its ragged islands and forest-covered shores. The Missouri is constantly changing its course, wearing away its banks on one side, while it forms new ones on the other. Its channel is continually shifting. Islands are formed, and then washed away, and while the old forests on one side are undermined and swept off, a young growth springs up from the new soil upon the other. With all these changes, the water is so charged with mud and sand that, in spring, it is perfectly opaque, and in a few minutes deposits a sediment an inch thick in the bottom of a tumbler. The river was now high; but when we descended in the autumn it was fallen very low, and all the secrets of its treacherous shallows were exposed to view. It was frightful to see the dead and broken trees, thick-set as a military abattis, firmly imbedded in the sand, and all pointing down stream, ready to impale any unhappy steamboat that at high water should pass over them.

In five or six days we began to see signs of the great western movement that was taking place. Parties of emigrants, with their tents and wagons, were encamped on open

spots near the bank, on their way to the common rendezvous
at Independence. On a rainy day, near sunset, we reached
the landing of this place, which is some miles from the
river on the extreme frontier of Missouri. The scene was
characteristic, for here were represented at one view the
most remarkable features of this wild and enterprising
region. On the muddy shore stood some thirty or forty
dark slavish-looking Spaniards, gazing stupidly out from
beneath their broad hats. They were attached to one of the
Santa Fé companies, whose wagons were crowded together
on the banks above. In the midst of these, crouching over a
smouldering fire, was a group of Indians, belonging to a remote Mexican tribe. One or two French hunters from the
mountains, with their long hair and buckskin dresses, were
looking at the boat; and seated on a log close at hand were
three men, with rifles lying across their knees. The foremost of these, a tall, strong figure, with a clear blue eye and
an open, intelligent face, might very well represent that
race of restless and intrepid pioneers whose axes and rifles
have opened a path from the Alleghanies to the western
prairies. He was on his way to Oregon, probably a more
congenial field to him than any that now remained on this
side of the great plains.

Early on the next morning we reached Kanzas, about
five hundred miles from the mouth of the Missouri. Here
we landed, and leaving our equipments in charge of Colonel
Chick, whose log-house was the substitute for a tavern, we
set out in a wagon for Westport, where we hoped to procure
mules and horses for the journey.

It was a remarkably fresh and beautiful May morning.
The woods, through which the miserable road conducted us,
were lighted by the bright sunshine and enlivened by a
multitude of birds. We overtook on the way our late fellow-
travellers, the Kanzas Indians, who, adorned with all their
finery, were proceeding homeward at a round pace; and

whatever they might have seemed on board the boat, they
made a very striking and picturesque feature in the forest
landscape.

Westport was full of Indians, whose little shaggy ponies
5 were tied by dozens along the houses and fences. Sacs and
Foxes, with shaved heads and painted faces, Shawanoes
and Delawares, fluttering in calico frocks and turbans,
Wyandots dressed like white men, and a few wretched
Kanzas wrapped in old blankets, were strolling about the
10 streets, or lounging in and out of the shops and houses.

As I stood at the door of the tavern, I saw a remarkable-
looking personage coming up the street. He had a ruddy
face, garnished with the stumps of a bristly red beard and
moustache ; on one side of his head was a round cap with a
15 knob at the top, such as Scottish laborers sometimes wear ; his
coat was of a nondescript form, and made of a gray Scotch
plaid, with the fringes hanging all about it ; he wore trousers
of coarse homespun, and hob-nailed shoes ; and to complete
his equipment, a little black pipe was stuck in one corner of
20 his mouth. In this curious attire, I recognized Captain
C——, of the British army, who, with his brother, and Mr.
R——, an English gentleman, was bound on a hunting expedition across the continent. I had seen the captain and
his companions at St. Louis. They had now been for some
25 time at Westport, making preparations for their departure,
and waiting for a reinforcement, since they were too few in
number to attempt it alone. They might, it is true, have
joined some of the parties of emigrants who were on the
point of setting out for Oregon and California ; but they
30 professed great disinclination to have any connection with
the " Kentucky fellows."

The captain now urged it upon us that we should join
forces and proceed to the mountains in company. Feeling
no greater partiality for the society of the emigrants than
they did, we thought the arrangement a good one, and

consented to it. Our future fellow-travellers had installed
themselves in a little log-house, where we found them surrounded by saddles, harness, guns, pistols, telescopes, knives,
and, in short, their complete appointments for the prairie.
R——, who had a taste for natural history, sat at a table
stuffing a woodpecker; the brother of the captain, who was
an Irishman, was splicing a trail-rope on the floor. The
captain pointed out, with much complacency, the different
articles of their outfit. "You see," said he, "that we are
all old travellers. I am convinced that no party ever went
upon the prairie better provided." The hunter whom they
had employed, a surly-looking Canadian, named Sorel, and
their muleteer, an American ruffian from St. Louis, were
lounging about the building. In a little log stable close at
hand were their horses and mules, selected with excellent
judgment by the captain.

We left them to complete their arrangements, while we
pushed our own to all convenient speed. The emigrants,
for whom our friends professed such contempt, were encamped on the prairie about eight or ten miles distant, to
the number of a thousand or more, and new parties were
constantly passing out from Independence to join them.
They were in great confusion, holding meetings, passing
resolutions, and drawing up regulations, but unable to unite
in the choice of leaders to conduct them across the prairie.
Being at leisure one day, I rode over to Independence. The
town was crowded. A multitude of shops had sprung up to
furnish the emigrants and Santa Fé traders with necessaries
for their journey; and there was an incessant hammering
and banging from a dozen blacksmiths' sheds, where the
heavy wagons were being repaired, and the horses and oxen
shod. The streets were thronged with men, horses, and
mules. While I was in the town, a train of emigrant wagons
from Illinois passed through, to join the camp on the prairie,
and stopped in the principal street. A multitude of healthy

children's faces were peeping out from under the covers of
the wagons. Here and there a buxom damsel was seated
on horseback, holding over her sunburnt face an old
umbrella or a parasol, once gaudy enough, but now miser-
5 ably faded. The men, very sober-looking countrymen, stood
about their oxen; and as I passed I noticed three old fellows, who, with their long whips in their hands, were
zealously discussing the doctrine of regeneration. The
emigrants, however, are not all of this stamp. Among
10 them are some of the vilest outcasts in the country. I have
often perplexed myself to divine the various motives that
give impulse to this migration; but whatever they may be,
whether an insane hope of a better condition in life, or a
desire of shaking off restraints of law and society, or mere
15 restlessness, certain it is, that multitudes bitterly repent the
journey, and, after they have reached the land of promise,
are happy enough to escape from it.

In the course of seven or eight days we had brought our
preparations nearly to a close. Meanwhile our friends had
20 completed theirs, and, becoming tired of Westport, they told
us that they would set out in advance, and wait at the
crossing of the Kanzas till we should come up. Accordingly
R—— and the muleteer went forward with the wagon and
tent, while the captain and his brother, together with Sorel,
25 and a trapper named Boisverd, who had joined them, followed with the band of horses. The commencement of the
journey was ominous, for the captain was scarcely a mile
from Westport, riding along in state at the head of his
party, leading his intended buffalo horse by a rope, when a
30 tremendous thunder-storm came on and drenched them all to
the skin. They hurried on to reach the place, about seven
miles off, where R—— was to have had the camp in readiness to receive them. But this prudent person, when he
saw the storm approaching, had selected a sheltered glade
in the woods where he pitched his tent, and was sipping a

comfortable cup of coffee while the captain galloped for miles beyond through the rain to look for him. At length the storm cleared away, and the sharp-eyed trapper succeeded in discovering his tent; R—— had by this time finished his coffee, and was seated on a buffalo-robe smoking his pipe. The captain was one of the most easy-tempered men in existence, so he bore his ill-luck with great composure, shared the dregs of the coffee with his brother, and lay down to sleep in his wet clothes.

We ourselves had our share of the deluge. We were leading a pair of mules to Kanzas when the storm broke. Such sharp and incessant flashes of lightning, such stunning and continuous thunder, I had never known before. The woods were completely obscured by the diagonal sheets of rain that fell with a heavy roar, and rose in spray from the ground, and the streams swelled so rapidly that we could hardly ford them. At length, looming through the rain, we saw the log-house of Colonel Chick, who received us with his usual bland hospitality; while his wife, who, though a little soured and stiffened by a long course of camp-meetings, was not behind him in goodwill, supplied us with the means of bettering our drenched and bedraggled condition. The storm clearing away at about sunset opened a noble prospect from the porch of the colonel's house, which stands upon a high hill. The sun streamed from the breaking clouds upon the swift and angry Missouri, and on the vast expanse of forest that stretched from its banks back to the distant bluffs.

Returning on the next day to Westport, we received a message from the captain, who had ridden back to deliver it in person, but finding that we were in Kanzas, had intrusted it with an acquaintance of his named Vogel, who kept a small grocery and liquor shop. Whiskey, by the way, circulates more freely in Westport than is altogether safe in a place where every man carries a loaded pistol in his

pocket. As we passed this establishment we saw Vogel's broad German face thrust from his door. He said he had something to tell us, and invited us to take a dram. Neither his liquor nor his message was very palatable. The captain
5 had returned to give us notice that R——, who assumed the direction of his party, had determined upon another route from that agreed upon between us; and instead of taking the course of the traders, had resolved to pass northward by Fort Leavenworth, and follow the path marked out by
10 the dragoons in their expedition of last summer. To adopt such a plan without consulting us, we looked upon as a high-handed proceeding; but suppressing our dissatisfaction as well as we could, we made up our minds to join them at Fort Leavenworth, where they were to wait for us.

15   Accordingly, our preparation being now complete, we attempted one fine morning to begin our journey. The first step was an unfortunate one. No sooner were our animals put in harness than the shaft-mule reared and plunged, burst ropes and straps, and nearly flung the cart into the
20 Missouri. Finding her wholly uncontrollable, we exchanged her for another, with which we were furnished by our friend Mr. Boone, of Westport, a grandson of Daniel Boone, the pioneer. This foretaste of prairie experience was very soon followed by another. Westport was scarcely out of
25 sight when we encountered a deep muddy gully, of a species that afterward became but too familiar to us, and here for the space of an hour or more the cart stuck fast.

CHAPTER II

BREAKING THE ICE

Emerging from the mud-holes of Westport, we pursued our way for some time along the narrow track, in the checkered sunshine and shadow of the woods, till at length, issuing into the broad light, we left behind us the farthest outskirts of the great forest, that once spread from the western plains to the shore of the Atlantic. Looking over an intervening belt of bushes, we saw the green, ocean-like expanse of prairie, stretching swell beyond swell to the horizon.

It was a mild, calm spring day; a day when one is more disposed to musing and revery than to action, and the softest part of his nature is apt to gain the upper hand. I rode in advance of the party, as we passed through the bushes, and, as a nook of green grass offered a strong temptation, I dismounted and lay down there. All the trees and saplings were in flower, or budding into fresh leaf; the red clusters of the maple-blossoms and the rich flowers of the Indian apple were there in profusion; and I was half inclined to regret leaving behind the land of gardens for the rude and stern scenes of the prairie and the mountains.

Meanwhile the party came in sight out of the bushes. Foremost rode Henry Chatillon, our guide and hunter, a fine athletic figure, mounted on a hardy gray Wyandot pony. He wore a white blanket-coat, a broad hat of felt, moccasons, and trousers of deer-skin, ornamented along the seams with rows of long fringes. His knife was stuck in his belt; his bullet-pouch and powder-horn hung at his side, and his rifle lay before him, resting against the high pommel of his saddle, which, like all his equipments, had seen hard service,

and was much the worse for wear. Shaw followed close, mounted on a little sorrel horse, and leading a larger animal by a rope. His outfit, which resembled mine, had been pro-vided with a view to use rather than ornament. It consisted
5 of a plain, black Spanish saddle, with holsters of heavy pis-tols, a blanket rolled up behind, and the trail-rope attached to his horse's neck hanging coiled in front. He carried a double-barrelled smooth-bore, while I had a rifle of some fifteen pounds' weight. At that time our attire, though far
10 from elegant, bore some marks of civilization, and offered a very favorable contrast to the inimitable shabbiness of our appearance on the return journey. A red flannel shirt, belted around the waist like a frock, then constituted our upper garment; moccasons had supplanted our failing boots;
15 and the remaining essential portion of our attire consisted of an extraordinary article, manufactured by a squaw out of smoked buckskin. Our muleteer, Deslauriers, brought up the rear with his cart, wading ankle-deep in the mud, alter-nately puffing at his pipe, and ejaculating in his prairie
20 patois, *"Sacré enfant de garce!"* as one of the mules would seem to recoil before some abyss of unusual profundity. The cart was of the kind that one may see by scores around the market-place at Quebec, and had a white covering to pro-tect the articles within. These were our provisions and a tent,
25 with ammunition, blankets, and presents for the Indians.

We were in all four men with eight animals; for besides the spare horses led by Shaw and myself, an additional mule was driven along with us as a reserve in case of accident.

After this summing up of our forces, it may not be amiss
30 to glance at the characters of the two men who accom-panied us.

Deslauriers was a Canadian, with all the characteristics of the true Jean Baptiste. Neither fatigue, exposure, nor hard labor could ever impair his cheerfulness and gayety, or his politeness to his *bourgeois;* and when night came, he would sit down by the fire, smoke his pipe, and tell stories with the utmost contentment. The prairie was his element. Henry Chatillon was of a different stamp. When we were at St. Louis, several gentlemen of the Fur Company had kindly offered to procure for us a hunter and guide suited for our purposes, and on coming one afternoon to the office, we found there a tall and exceedingly well-dressed man, with a face so open and frank that it attracted our notice at once. We were surprised at being told that it was he who wished to guide us to the mountains. He was born in a little French town near St. Louis, and from the age of fifteen years had been constantly in the neighborhood of the Rocky Mountains, employed for the most part by the company, to supply their forts with buffalo meat. As a hunter, he had but one rival in the whole region, a man named Simoneau, with whom, to the honor of both of them, he was on terms of the closest friendship. He had arrived at St. Louis the day before, from the mountains, where he had been for four years; and he now asked only to go and spend a day with his mother, before setting out on another expedition. His age was about thirty; he was six feet high, and very powerfully and gracefully moulded. The prairies had been his school; he could neither read nor write, but he had a natural refinement and delicacy of mind, such as is rare even in women. His manly face was a mirror of uprightness, simplicity, and kindness of heart; he had, moreover, a keen perception of character, and a tact that would preserve him from flagrant error in any society. Henry had not the restless energy of an Anglo-American. He was content to take things as he found them; and his chief fault arose from an excess of easy generosity, not conducive to thriving in the world. Yet it was commonly remarked of him, that whatever he might choose to do with what belonged to himself, the property of others was always safe in his hands. His bravery was as much celebrated in the

mountains as his skill in hunting; but it is characteristic of
him that in a country where the rifle is the chief arbiter between man and man, he was very seldom involved in
quarrels. Once or twice, indeed, his quiet good-nature had
5 been mistaken and presumed upon, but the consequences of
the error were such that no one was ever known to repeat
it. No better evidence of the intrepidity of his temper
could be asked, than the common report that he had killed
more than thirty grizzly bears. He was a proof of what
10 unaided nature will sometimes do. I have never, in the
city or in the wilderness, met a better man than my true-
hearted friend, Henry Chatillon.

We were soon free of the woods and bushes, and fairly
upon the broad prairie. Now and then a Shawanoe passed
15 us, riding his little shaggy pony at a "lope"; his calico
shirt, his gaudy sash, and the gay handkerchief bound
around his snaky hair, fluttering in the wind. At noon
we stopped to rest not far from a little creek, replete with
frogs and young turtles. There had been an Indian encamp-
20 ment at the place, and the framework of the lodges still remained, enabling us very easily to gain a shelter from the sun,
by merely spreading one or two blankets over them. Thus
shaded, we sat upon our saddles, and Shaw for the first time
lighted his favorite Indian pipe; while Deslauriers was
25 squatted over a hot bed of coals, shading his eyes with one
hand, and holding a little stick in the other, with which he
regulated the hissing contents of the frying-pan. The horses
were turned to feed among the scattered bushes of a low
oozy meadow. A drowsy spring-like sultriness pervaded the
30 air, and the voices of ten thousand young frogs and insects,
just awakened into life, rose in varied chorus from the creek
and the meadows.

Scarcely were we seated when a visitor approached. This
was an old Kanzas Indian; a man of distinction, if one
might judge from his dress. His head was shaved and

painted red, and from the tuft of hair remaining on the
crown dangled several eagle's feathers, and the tails of two
or three rattlesnakes. His cheeks, too, were daubed with
vermilion; his ears were adorned with green glass pendants; a collar of grizzly bears' claws surrounded his neck, 5
and several large necklaces of wampum hung on his breast.
Having shaken us by the hand with a grunt of salutation,
the old man, dropping his red blanket from his shoulders,
sat down cross-legged on the ground. We offered him a cup
of sweetened water, at which he ejaculated "Good!" and 10
was beginning to tell us how great a man he was, and how
many Pawnees he had killed, when suddenly a motley concourse appeared wading across the creek towards us. They
filed past in rapid succession, men, women, and children:
some were on horseback, some on foot, but all were alike 15
squalid and wretched. Old squaws, mounted astride of
shaggy, meagre little ponies, with perhaps one or two snake-
eyed children seated behind them, clinging to their tattered
blankets; tall lank young men on foot, with bows and arrows
in their hands; and girls whose native ugliness not all the 20
charms of glass beads and scarlet cloth could disguise, made
up the procession; although here and there was a man who,
like our visitor, seemed to hold some rank in this respectable community. They were the dregs of the Kanzas nation,
who, while their betters were gone to hunt the buffalo, had 25
left the village on a begging expedition to Westport.

When this ragamuffin horde had passed, we caught our
horses, saddled, harnessed, and resumed our journey. Fording the creek, the low roofs of a number of rude buildings
appeared, rising from a cluster of groves and woods on the 30
left; and riding up through a long lane amid a profusion
of wild roses and early spring flowers, we found the log-
church and schoolhouses belonging to the Methodist Shawanoe Mission. The Indians were on the point of gathering
to a religious meeting. Some scores of them, tall men in

half-civilized dress, were seated on wooden benches under the trees ; while their horses were tied to the sheds and fences. Their chief, Parks, a remarkably large and athletic man, had just arrived from Westport, where he owns a trading estab-
5 lishment. Besides this, he has a large farm and a consider-able number of slaves. Indeed, the Shawanoes have made greater progress in agriculture than any other tribe on the Missouri frontier, and both in appearance and in character form a marked contrast to our late acquaintance, the Kanzas.
10   A few hours' ride brought us to the banks of the river Kanzas. Traversing the woods that lined it, and ploughing through the deep sand, we encamped not far from the bank, at the Lower Delaware crossing. Our tent was erected for the first time, on a meadow close to the woods, and the camp
15 preparations being complete, we began to think of supper. An old Delaware woman, of some three hundred pounds' weight, sat in the porch of a little log-house, close to the water, and a very pretty half-breed girl was engaged, under her superintendence, in feeding a large flock of turkeys that
20 were fluttering and gobbling about the door. But no offers of money, or even of tobacco, could induce her to part with one of her favorites : so I took my rifle, to see if the woods or the river could furnish us anything. A multitude of quails were plaintively whistling in the meadows ; but noth-
25 ing appropriate to the rifle was to be seen, except three buzzards, seated on the spectral limbs of an old dead syca-more, that thrust itself out over the river from the dense sunny wall of fresh foliage. Their ugly heads were drawn down between their shoulders, and they seemed to luxuriate
30 in the soft sunshine that was pouring from the west. As they offered no epicurean temptations, I refrained from dis-turbing their enjoyment ; but contented myself with admir-ing the calm beauty of the sunset, — for the river, eddying swiftly in deep purple shadows between the impending woods, formed a wild but tranquillizing scene.

When I returned to the camp, I found Shaw and an old Indian seated on the ground in close conference passing the pipe between them. The old man was explaining that he loved the whites, and had an especial partiality for tobacco. Deslauriers was arranging upon the ground our service of tin cups and plates; and as other viands were not to be had, he set before us a repast of biscuit and bacon, and a large pot of coffee. Unsheathing our knives, we attacked it, disposed of the greater part, and tossed the residue to the Indian. Meanwhile our horses, now hobbled for the first time, stood among the trees, with their fore-legs tied together, in great disgust and astonishment. They seemed by no means to relish this foretaste of what awaited them. Mine, in particular, had conceived a mortal aversion to the prairie life. One of them, christened Hendrick, an animal whose strength and hardihood were his only merits, and who yielded to nothing but the cogent arguments of the whip, looked toward us with an indignant countenance, as if he meditated avenging his wrongs with a kick. The other, Pontiac, a good horse, though of plebeian lineage, stood with his head drooping and his mane hanging about his eyes, with the grieved and sulky air of a lubberly boy sent off to school. His forebodings were but too just; for when I last heard from him, he was under the lash of an Ogillallah brave, on a war-party against the Crows.

As it grew dark and the voices of the whippoorwills succeeded the whistle of the quails, we removed our saddles to the tent to serve as pillows, spread our blankets upon the ground, and prepared to bivouac for the first time that season. Each man selected the place in the tent which he was to occupy for the journey. To Deslauriers, however, was assigned the cart into which he could creep in wet weather, and find a much better shelter than his *bourgeois* enjoyed in the tent.

The river Kanzas at this point forms the boundary-line between the country of the Shawanoes and that of the

Delawares. We crossed it on the following day, rafting over
our horses and equipments with much difficulty, and un-
lading our cart in order to make our way up the steep ascent
on the farther bank. It was a Sunday morning; warm,
5 tranquil, and bright; and a perfect stillness reigned over
the rough enclosures and neglected fields of the Delawares,
except the ceaseless hum and chirruping of myriads of insects. Now and then an Indian rode past on his way to the
meeting-house, or, through the dilapidated entrance of some
10 shattered log-house, an old woman might be discerned enjoying all the luxury of idleness. There was no village bell,
for the Delawares have none; and yet upon that forlorn
and rude settlement was the same spirit of Sabbath repose
and tranquillity as in some New England village among the
15 mountains of New Hampshire, or the Vermont woods.

A military road led from this point to Fort Leavenworth,
and for many miles the farms and cabins of the Delawares
were scattered at short intervals on either hand. The little
rude structures of logs erected usually on the borders of a
20 tract of woods made a picturesque feature in the landscape.
But the scenery needed no foreign aid. Nature had done
enough for it; and the alternation of rich green prairies and
groves that stood in clusters, or lined the banks of the
numerous little streams, had all the softened and polished
25 beauty of a region that has been for centuries under the hand
of man. At that early season, too, it was in the height of
its freshness. The woods were flushed with the red buds of
the maple; there were frequent flowering shrubs unknown
in the east; and the green swells of the prairie were
30 thickly studded with blossoms.

Encamping near a spring, by the side of a hill, we resumed our journey in the morning, and early in the afternoon were within a few miles of Fort Leavenworth. The
road crossed a stream densely bordered with trees, and running in the bottom of a deep woody hollow. We were about

to descend into it when a wild and confused procession appeared, passing through the water below, and coming up the steep ascent towards us. We stopped to let them pass. They were Delawares, just returned from a hunting expedition. All, both men and women, were mounted on horseback, and drove along with them a considerable number of pack-mules, laden with the furs they had taken, together with the buffalo-robes, kettles, and other articles of their travelling equipment, which, as well as their clothing and their weapons, had a worn and dingy look, as if they had seen hard service of late. At the rear of the party was an old man, who, as he came up, stopped his horse to speak to us. He rode a tough shaggy pony, with mane and tail well knotted with burrs, and a rusty Spanish bit in its mouth, to which, by way of reins, was attached a string of raw hide. His saddle, robbed probably from a Mexican, had no covering, being merely a tree of the Spanish form, with a piece of grizzly bear's skin laid over it, a pair of rude wooden stirrups attached, and, in the absence of girth, a thong of hide passing around the horse's belly. The rider's dark features and keen snaky eye were unequivocally Indian. He wore a buckskin frock, which, like his fringed leggins, was well polished and blackened by grease and long service, and an old handkerchief was tied around his head. Resting on the saddle before him lay his rifle, a weapon in the use of which the Delawares are skilful, though, from its weight, the distant prairie Indians are too lazy to carry it.

"Who's your chief?" he immediately inquired.

Henry Chatillon pointed to us. The old Delaware fixed his eyes intently upon us for a moment, and then sententiously remarked, —

"No good! Too young!" With this flattering comment he left us and rode after his people.

This tribe, the Delawares, once the peaceful allies of William Penn, the tributaries of the conquering Iroquois,

are now the most adventurous and dreaded warriors upon
the prairies. They make war upon remote tribes, the very
names of which were unknown to their fathers in their
ancient seats in Pennsylvania, and they push these new
5 quarrels with true Indian rancor, sending out their war-
parties as far as the Rocky Mountains, and into the Mexican territories. Their neighbors and former confederates,
the Shawanoes, who are tolerable farmers, are in a prosper-
ous condition; but the Delawares dwindle every year, from
10 the number of men lost in their warlike expeditions.

Soon after leaving this party we saw, stretching on the
right, the forests that follow the course of the Missouri, and
the deep woody channel through which at this point it runs.
At a distance in front were the white barracks of Fort
15 Leavenworth, just visible through the trees upon an eminence above a bend of the river. A wide green meadow, as
level as a lake, lay between us and the Missouri, and upon
this, close to a line of trees that bordered a little brook,
stood the tent of the captain and his companions, with their
20 horses feeding around it; but they themselves were invisible. Wright, their muleteer, was there, seated on the tongue
of the wagon, repairing his harness. Boisverd stood cleaning his rifle at the door of the tent, and Sorel lounged idly
about. On closer examination, however, we discovered the
25 captain's brother, Jack, sitting in the tent, at his old occupation of splicing trail-ropes. He welcomed us in his broad
Irish brogue, and said that his brother was fishing in the
river, and R—— gone to the garrison. They returned before sunset. Meanwhile we pitched our own tent not far
30 off, and after supper a council was held, in which it was resolved to remain one day at Fort Leavenworth, and on the
next to bid a final adieu to the frontier, or, in the phrase-
ology of the region, to "jump off." Our deliberations were
conducted by the ruddy light from a distant swell of the
prairie where the long dry grass of last summer was on fire.

CHAPTER III

FORT LEAVENWORTH

On the next morning we rode to Fort Leavenworth. Colonel, now General Kearney, to whom I had had the honor of an introduction when at St. Louis, was just arrived, and received us at his quarters with the courtesy habitual to him. Fort Leavenworth is in fact no fort, being without defensive works, except two blockhouses. No rumors of war had as yet disturbed its tranquillity. In the square grassy area, surrounded by barracks and the quarters of the officers, the men were passing and repassing, or lounging among the trees; although not many weeks afterwards it presented a different scene, for here the offscourings of the frontier were congregated for the expedition against Santa Fé.

Passing through the garrison, we rode toward the Kickapoo village, five or six miles beyond. The path, a rather dubious and uncertain one, led us along the ridge of high bluffs that border the Missouri; and, by looking to the right or to the left, we could enjoy a strange contrast of scenery. On the left stretched the prairie, rising into swells and undulations, thickly sprinkled with groves, or gracefully expanding into wide grassy basins, of miles in extent; while its curvatures, swelling against the horizon, were often surmounted by lines of sunny woods; a scene to which the freshness of the season and the peculiar mellowness of the atmosphere gave additional softness. Below us, on the right, was a tract of ragged and broken woods. We could look down on the tops of the trees, some living and some dead; some erect, others leaning at every angle, and others piled in masses together by the passage of a hurricane. Beyond

their extreme verge the turbid waters of the Missouri were
discernible through the boughs, rolling powerfully along at
the foot of the woody declivities on its farther bank.

The path soon after led inland; and, as we crossed an open
5 meadow, we saw a cluster of buildings on a rising ground
before us, with a crowd of people surrounding them. They
were the storehouse, cottage, and stables of the Kickapoo
trader's establishment. Just at that moment, as it chanced,
he was beset with half the Indians of the settlement. They
10 had tied their wretched, neglected little ponies by dozens
along the fences and out-houses, and were either lounging
about the place, or crowding into the trading-house. Here
were faces of various colors: red, green, white, and black,
curiously intermingled and disposed over the visage in a
15 variety of patterns. Calico shirts, red and blue blankets,
brass ear-rings, wampum necklaces, appeared in profusion.
The trader was a blue-eyed, open-faced man, who neither in
his manners nor his appearance betrayed any of the rough-
ness of the frontier; though just at present he was obliged
20 to keep a lynx eye on his customers, who, men and women,
were climbing on his counter, and seating themselves among
his boxes and bales.

The village itself was not far off, and sufficiently illustrated the condition of its unfortunate and self-abandoned
25 occupants. Fancy to yourself a little swift stream, working
its devious way down a woody valley; sometimes wholly
hidden under logs and fallen trees, sometimes spreading
into a broad, clear pool; and on its banks, in little nooks
cleared away among the trees, miniature log-houses, in
30 utter ruin and neglect. A labyrinth of narrow, obstructed
paths connected these habitations one with another. Sometimes we met a stray calf, a pig, or a pony, belonging to
some of the villagers, who usually lay in the sun in front of
their dwellings, and looked on us with cold, suspicious eyes
as we approached. Farther on, in place of the log-huts of

the Kickapoos, we found the *pukwi* lodges of their neighbors, the Pottawattamies, whose condition seemed no better than theirs.

Growing tired at last, and exhausted by the excessive heat and sultriness of the day, we returned to our friend, the trader. By this time the crowd around him had dispersed, and left him at leisure. He invited us to his cottage, a little white-and-green building, in the style of the old French settlements, and ushered us into a neat, well-furnished room. The blinds were closed, and the heat and glare of the sun excluded; the room was as cool as a cavern. It was neatly carpeted, too, and furnished in a manner that we hardly expected on the frontier. The sofas, chairs, tables, and a well-filled bookcase would not have disgraced an eastern city, though there were one or two little tokens that indicated the rather questionable civilization of the region. A pistol, loaded and capped, lay on the mantelpiece; and through the glass of the bookcase, peeping above the works of John Milton, glittered the handle of a very mischievous-looking knife.

Our host went out, and returned with iced water, glasses, and a bottle of excellent claret, — a refreshment most welcome in the extreme heat of the day; and soon after appeared a merry, laughing woman, who must have been, a year or two before, a very rich specimen of creole beauty. She came to say that lunch was ready in the next room. Our hostess evidently lived on the sunny side of life, and troubled herself with none of its cares. She sat down and entertained us while we were at table with anecdotes of fishing-parties, frolics, and the officers at the fort. Taking leave at length of the hospitable trader and his friend, we rode back to the garrison.

Shaw passed on to the camp, while I remained to call upon Colonel Kearney. I found him still at table. There sat our friend the captain, in the same remarkable habiliments in

which we saw him at Westport; the black pipe, however, being for the present laid aside. He dangled his little cap in his hand, and talked of steeple-chases, touching occasionally upon his anticipated exploits in buffalo-hunting. There,
5 too, was R——, somewhat more elegantly attired. For the last time, we tasted the luxuries of civilization, and drank adieus to it in wine good enough to make us regret the leave-taking. Then, mounting, we rode together to the camp, where everything was in readiness for departure on
10 the morrow.

CHAPTER IV

"JUMPING OFF"

Our transatlantic companions were well equipped for the journey. They had a wagon drawn by six mules, and crammed with provisions for six months, besides ammunition enough for a regiment; spare rifles and fowling-pieces, ropes and harness, personal baggage, and a miscellaneous assortment of articles, which produced infinite embarrassment. They had also decorated their persons with telescopes and portable compasses, and carried English double-barrelled rifles of sixteen to the pound calibre, slung to their saddles in dragoon fashion.

By sunrise on the twenty-third of May we had breakfasted; the tents were levelled, the animals saddled and harnessed, and all was prepared. "*Avance donc! get up!*" cried Deslauriers to his mule. Wright, our friends' muleteer, after some swearing and lashing, got his insubordinate train in motion, and then the whole party filed from the ground. Thus we bade a long adieu to bed and board, and the principles of Blackstone's Commentaries. The day was a most auspicious one; and yet Shaw and I felt certain misgivings, which in the sequel proved but too well founded. We had just learned that though R—— had taken it upon him to adopt this course without consulting us, not a single man in the party knew the way; and the absurdity of the proceeding soon became manifest. His plan was to strike the trail of several companies of dragoons, who last summer had made an expedition under Colonel Kearney to Fort Laramie, and by this means to reach the grand trail of the Oregon emigrants up the Platte.

We rode for an hour or two, when a familiar cluster of buildings appeared on a little hill. "Hallo!" shouted the Kickapoo trader from over his fence, "where are you going?" A few rather emphatic exclamations might have been heard 5 among us, when we found that we had gone miles out of our way, and were not advanced an inch toward the Rocky Mountains. So we turned in the direction the trader indicated; and with the sun for a guide, began to trace a "bee-line" across the prairies. We struggled through copses and lines of wood; 10 we waded brooks and pools of water; we traversed prairies as green as an emerald, expanding before us mile after mile, wider and more wild than the wastes Mazeppa rode over.

> "Man nor brute,
> Nor dint of hoof, nor print of foot,
> 15   Lay in the wild luxuriant soil;
> No sign of travel; none of toil;
> The very air was mute."

Riding in advance, as we passed over one of these great plains, we looked back and saw the line of scattered horse- 20 men stretching for a mile or more; and, far in the rear, against the horizon, the white wagons creeping slowly along. "Here we are at last!" shouted the captain. And, in truth, we had struck upon the traces of a large body of horse. We turned joyfully and followed this new course, with tempers 25 somewhat improved; and towards sunset encamped on a high swell of the prairie, at the foot of which a lazy stream soaked along through clumps of rank grass. It was getting dark. We turned the horses loose to feed. "Drive down the tent-pickets hard," said Henry Chatillon; "it is going 30 to blow." We did so, and secured the tent as well as we could; for the sky had changed totally, and a fresh damp smell in the wind warned us that a stormy night was likely to succeed the hot, clear day. The prairie also wore a new aspect, and its vast swells had grown black and sombre under the shadow of the clouds. The thunder soon began to growl at a distance. Picketing and hobbling the horses among the rich grass at the foot of the slope where we encamped, we gained a shelter just as the rain began to fall; and sat at the opening of the tent, watching the proceedings of the captain. In defiance of the rain, he was 5 stalking among the horses, wrapped in an old Scotch plaid. An extreme solicitude tormented him, lest some of his favorites should escape, or some accident should befall them; and he cast an anxious eye towards three wolves who were sneaking along over the dreary surface of the plain, as if 10 he dreaded some hostile demonstration on their part.

On the next morning we had gone but a mile or two when we came to an extensive belt of woods, through the midst of which ran a stream, wide, deep, and of an appearance particularly muddy and treacherous. Deslauriers was in ad- 15 vance with his cart; he jerked his pipe from his mouth, lashed his mules, and poured forth a volley of Canadian ejaculations. In plunged the cart, but midway it stuck fast. He leaped out knee-deep in water, and, by dint of *sacrés* and a vigorous application of the whip, urged the mules out 20 of the slough. Then approached the long team and heavy wagon of our friends; but it paused on the brink.

"Now my advice is — " began the captain, who had been anxiously contemplating the muddy gulf.

"Drive on!" cried R——. 25

But Wright, the muleteer, apparently had not as yet decided the point in his own mind; and he sat still in his seat, on one of the shaft-mules, whistling in a low contemplative strain to himself.

"My advice is," resumed the captain, "that we unload; for 30 I'll bet any man five pounds that if we try to go through we shall stick fast."

"By the powers, we shall stick fast!" echoed Jack, the captain's brother, shaking his large head with an air of firm conviction.

"Drive on! drive on!" cried R——, petulantly.

"Well," observed the captain, turning to us as we sat looking on, much edified by this by-play among our confederates, "I can only give my advice, and if people won't
5 be reasonable, why, they won't, that's all!"

Meanwhile Wright had apparently made up his mind; for he suddenly began to shout forth a volley of oaths and curses, that, compared with the French imprecations of Deslauriers, sounded like the roaring of heavy cannon after the
10 popping and sputtering of a bunch of Chinese crackers. At the same time he discharged a shower of blows upon his mules, who hastily dived into the mud, and drew the wagon lumbering after them. For a moment the issue was doubtful. Wright writhed about in his saddle, and swore and
15 lashed like a madman; but who can count on a team of half-broken mules? At the most critical point, when all should have been harmony and combined effort, the perverse brutes fell into disorder, and huddled together in confusion on the farther bank. There was the wagon up to the hub
20 in mud, and visibly settling every instant. There was nothing for it but to unload; then to dig away the mud from before the wheels with a spade, and lay a causeway of bushes and branches. This agreeable labor accomplished, the wagon at length emerged; but as some interruption of this sort
25 occurred at least four or five times a day for a fortnight, our progress towards the Platte was not without its obstacles.

We travelled six or seven miles farther, and "nooned" near a brook. On the point of resuming our journey, when the horses were all driven down to water, my homesick
30 charger, Pontiac, made a sudden leap across, and set off at a round trot for the settlements. I mounted my remaining horse and started in pursuit. Making a circuit, I headed the runaway, hoping to drive him back to camp, but he instantly broke into a gallop, made a wide tour on the prairie, and got by me again. I tried this plan repeatedly with the same

result; Pontiac was evidently disgusted with the prairie, so I
abandoned it and tried another, trotting along gently behind
him, in hopes that I might quietly get near enough to seize
the trail-rope which was fastened to his neck, and dragged
about a dozen feet behind him. The chase grew interesting.   5
For mile after mile I followed the rascal with the utmost
care not to alarm him, and gradually got nearer, until at
length old Hendrick's nose was fairly brushed by the whisking tail of the unsuspecting Pontiac. Without drawing rein
I slid softly to the ground; but my long heavy rifle encum- 10
bered me, and the low sound it made in striking the horn
of the saddle startled him, he pricked up his ears and sprang
off at a run. "My friend," thought I, remounting, "do that
again and I will shoot you!"

Fort Leavenworth was about forty miles distant, and   15
thither I determined to follow him. I made up my mind to
spend a solitary and supperless night, and then set out again
in the morning. One hope, however, remained. The creek
where the wagon had stuck was just before us; Pontiac
might be thirsty with his run and stop there to drink. I   20
kept as near him as possible, taking every precaution not to
alarm him again; and the result proved as I had hoped, for
he walked deliberately among the trees and stooped down
to the water. I alighted, dragged old Hendrick through the
mud, and with a feeling of infinite satisfaction picked up   25
the slimy trail-rope, and twisted it three times round my
hand. "Now let me see you get away again!" I thought,
as I remounted. But Pontiac was exceedingly reluctant to
turn back; Hendrick, too, who had evidently flattered himself with vain hopes, showed the utmost repugnance, and   30
grumbled in a manner peculiar to himself at being compelled to face about. A smart cut of the whip restored his
cheerfulness; and, dragging the recovered truant behind, I
set out in search of the camp. An hour or two elapsed,
when, near sunset, I saw the tents, standing on a swell of

the prairie, beyond a line of woods, while the bands of
horses were feeding in a low meadow close at hand. There
sat Jack C——, cross-legged, in the sun, splicing a trail-
rope; and the rest were lying on the grass, smoking and
5 telling stories. That night we enjoyed a serenade from the
wolves, more lively than any with which they had yet favored us; and in the morning one of the musicians appeared,
not many rods from the tents, quietly seated among the
horses, looking at us with a pair of large gray eyes; but
10 perceiving a rifle levelled at him, he leaped up and made
off in hot haste.

I pass by the following day or two of our journey, for
nothing occurred worthy of record. Should any one of my
readers ever be impelled to visit the prairies, and should he
15 choose the route of the Platte (the best, perhaps, that can
be adopted), I can assure him that he need not think to enter at once upon the paradise of his imagination. A dreary
preliminary, a protracted crossing of the threshold, awaits
him before he finds himself fairly upon the verge of the
20 "great American desert," — those barren wastes, the haunts
of the buffalo and the Indian, where the very shadow of
civilization lies a hundred leagues behind him. The intervening country, the wide and fertile belt that extends for
several hundred miles beyond the extreme frontier, will
25 probably answer tolerably well to his preconceived ideas of
the prairie; for this it is from which picturesque tourists,
painters, poets, and novelists, who have seldom penetrated
farther, have derived their conceptions of the whole region.
If he has a painter's eye, he may find his period of proba-
30 tion not wholly void of interest. The scenery, though tame,
is graceful and pleasing. Here are level plains, too wide
for the eye to measure; green undulations, like motionless
swells of the ocean; abundance of streams, followed through
all their windings by lines of woods and scattered groves.
But let him be as enthusiastic as he may, he will find

enough to damp his ardor. His wagons will stick in the
mud; his horses will break loose; harness will give way;
and axle-trees prove unsound. His bed will be a soft one,
consisting often of black mud of the richest consistency. As
for food, he must content himself with biscuit and salt provisions; for, strange as it may seem, this tract of country
produces very little game. As he advances, indeed, he will
see, mouldering in the grass by his path, the vast antlers of
the eik, and farther on the whitened skulls of the buffalo,
once swarming over this now deserted region. Perhaps, like
us, he may journey for a fortnight, and see not so much as
the hoof-print of a deer; in the spring, not even a prairie-
hen is to be had.

Yet, to compensate him for this unlooked-for deficiency
of game, he will find himself beset with "varmints" innumerable. The wolves will entertain him with a concert at
night, and skulk around him by day, just beyond rifle-shot;
his horse will step into badger-holes; from every marsh and
mud-puddle will arise the bellowing, croaking, and trilling
of legions of frogs, infinitely various in color, shape, and
dimensions. A profusion of snakes will glide away from
under his horse's feet, or quietly visit him in his tent at
night; while the pertinacious humming of unnumbered
mosquitoes will banish sleep from his eyelids. When, thirsty
with a long ride in the scorching sun over some boundless
reach of prairie, he comes at length to a pool of water, and
alights to drink, he discovers a troop of young tadpoles
sporting in the bottom of his cup. Add to this, that, all the
morning, the sun beats upon him with a sultry, penetrating
heat, and that, with provoking regularity, at about four
o'clock in the afternoon, a thunderstorm rises and drenches
him to the skin.

One day, after a protracted morning's ride, we stopped to
rest at noon upon the open prairie. No trees were in sight;
but close at hand a little dribbling brook was twisting from

side to side through a hollow; now forming holes of stagnant water, and now gliding over the mud in a scarcely perceptible current, among a growth of sickly bushes, and great
clumps of tall rank grass. The day was excessively hot and
5 oppressive. The horses and mules were rolling on the prairie
to refresh themselves, or feeding among the bushes in the
hollow. We had dined; and Deslauriers, puffing at his pipe,
knelt on the grass, scrubbing our service of tin-plate. Shaw
lay in the shade, under the cart, to rest for a while before
10 the word should be given to "catch up." Henry Chatillon,
before lying down, was looking about for signs of snakes, the
only living things that he feared, and uttering various ejaculations of disgust at finding several suspicious-looking holes
close to the cart. I sat leaning against the wheel in a scanty
15 strip of shade, making a pair of hobbles to replace those
which my contumacious steed Pontiac had broken the night
before. The camp of our friends, a rod or two distant, presented the same scene of lazy tranquillity.

"Hallo!" cried Henry, looking up from his inspection of
20 the snake-holes, "here comes the old captain."

The captain approached, and stood for a moment contemplating us in silence.

"I say, Parkman," he began, "look at Shaw there, asleep
under the cart, with the tar dripping off the hub of the
25 wheel on his shoulder."

At this Shaw got up, with his eyes half opened, and feeling the part indicated, found his hand glued fast to his red
flannel shirt.

"He'll look well, when he gets among the squaws, won't
30 he?" observed the captain, with a grin.

He then crawled under the cart, and began to tell stories,
of which his stock was inexhaustible. Yet every moment
he would glance nervously at the horses. At last he jumped
up in great excitement. "See that horse! There — that
fellow just walking over the hill! By Jove! he's off. It's

your big horse, Shaw; no, it is n't, it's Jack's. Jack! Jack!
hallo, Jack!'" Jack, thus invoked, jumped up and stared
vacantly at us.

"Go and catch your horse, if you don't want to lose him,"
roared the captain. 5

Jack instantly set off at a run through the grass, his broad
trousers flapping about his feet. The captain gazed anxiously
till he saw that the horse was caught; then he sat down,
with a countenance of thoughtfulness and care.

"I tell you what it is," he said, "this will never do at all. 10
We shall lose every horse in the band some day or other,
and then a pretty plight we should be in! Now I am convinced that the only way for us is to have every man in the
camp stand horse-guard in rotation whenever we stop. Supposing a hundred Pawnees should jump up out of that ravine, 15
all yelling and flapping their buffalo robes, in the way they
do! Why, in two minutes, not a hoof would be in sight."
We reminded the captain that a hundred Pawnees would
probably demolish the horse-guard if he were to resist their
depredations. 20

"At any rate," pursued the captain, evading the point,
"our whole system is wrong; I'm convinced of it; it is totally unmilitary. Why, the way we travel, strung out
over the prairie for a mile, an enemy might attack the foremost men, and cut them off before the rest could come up." 25

"We are not in an enemy's country yet," said Shaw;
"when we are, we'll travel together."

"Then," said the captain, "we might be attacked in camp.
We've no sentinels; we 'camp in disorder; no precautions
at all to guard against surprise. My own convictions are, 30
that we ought to 'camp in a hollow-square, with the fires in
the centre; and have sentinels, and a regular password appointed for every night. Beside, there should be videttes,
riding in advance, to find a place for the camp and give
warning of an enemy. These are my convictions. I don't

want to dictate to any man. I give advice to the best of
my judgment, that's all; and then let people do as they
please."

His plan of sending out videttes seemed particularly dear
5 to him; and as no one else was disposed to second his views
on this point, he took it into his head to ride forward that
afternoon himself.

"Come, Parkman," said he, "will you go with me?"

We set out together, and rode a mile or two in advance.
10 The captain, in the course of twenty years' service in the
British army, had seen something of life; and being natu-
rally a pleasant fellow, he was a very entertaining companion.
He cracked jokes and told stories for an hour or two; until,
looking back, we saw the prairie behind us stretching away
15 to the horizon, without a horseman or a wagon in sight.

"Now," said the captain, "I think the videttes had better
stop till the main body comes up."

I was of the same opinion. There was a thick growth of
woods just before us, with a stream running through them.
20 Having crossed this, we found on the other side a level
meadow, half encircled by the trees; and, fastening our
horses to some bushes, we sat down on the grass, while,
with an old stump of a tree for a target, I began to display
the superiority of the renowned rifle of the backwoods
25 over the foreign innovation borne by the captain. At length
voices could be heard in the distance, behind the trees.

"There they come," said the captain; "let's go and see
how they get through the creek."

We mounted and rode to the bank of the stream, where
30 the trail crossed it. It ran in a deep hollow, full of trees.
As we looked down, we saw a confused crowd of horsemen
riding through the water; and among the dingy habiliments
of our party glittered the uniforms of four dragoons.

Shaw came whipping his horse up the bank, in advance of
the rest, with a somewhat indignant countenance. The first

word he spoke was a blessing fervently invoked on the head
of R——, who was riding, with a crestfallen air, in the rear.
Thanks to the ingenious devices of this gentleman, we had
missed the track entirely, and wandered, not towards the
Platte, but to the village of the Iowa Indians. This we 5
learned from the dragoons, who had lately deserted from
Fort Leavenworth. They told us that our best plan now
was to keep to the northward until we should strike the
trail formed by several parties of Oregon emigrants, who had
that season set out from St. Joseph, in Missouri.   10

In extremely bad temper, we encamped on this ill-starred
spot, while the deserters, whose case admitted of no delay,
rode rapidly forward. On the day following, striking the
St. Joseph's trail, we turned our horses' heads towards Fort
Laramie, then about seven hundred miles to the westward. 15

CHAPTER V

THE "BIG BLUE"

The great medley of Oregon and California emigrants at their camps around Independence had heard reports that several additional parties were on the point of setting out from St. Joseph farther to the northward. The prevailing impression was that these were Mormons, twenty-three hundred in number; and a great alarm was excited in consequence. The people of Illinois and Missouri, who composed by far the greater part of the emigrants, have never been on the best terms with the "Latter Day Saints"; and it is notorious throughout the country how much blood has been spilt in their feuds, even far within the limits of the settlements. No one could predict what would be the result, when large armed bodies of these fanatics should encounter the most impetuous and reckless of their old enemies on the broad prairie, far beyond the reach of law or military force. The women and children at Independence raised a great outcry; the men themselves were seriously alarmed; and, as I learned, they sent to Colonel Kearney, requesting an escort of dragoons as far as the Platte. This was refused; and, as the sequel proved, there was no occasion for it. The St. Joseph emigrants were as good Christians and as zealous Mormon-haters as the rest; and the very few families of the "Saints" who passed out this season by the route of the Platte remained behind until the great tide of emigration had gone by, standing in quite as much awe of the "gentiles" as the latter did of them.

We were now upon this St. Joseph trail. It was evident, by the traces, that large parties were a few days in advance of us; and as we too supposed them to be Mormons, we had some apprehension of interruption.

The journey was monotonous. One day we rode on for hours, without seeing a tree or a bush: before, behind, and on either side, stretched the vast expanse, rolling in a succession of graceful swells, covered with the unbroken carpet of fresh green grass. Here and there a crow, a raven, or a turkey-buzzard, relieved the uniformity.

"What shall we do to-night for wood and water?" we began to ask of each other; for the sun was within an hour of setting. At length a dark green speck appeared, far off on the right: it was the top of a tree, peering over a swell of the prairie; and, leaving the trail, we made all haste towards it. It proved to be the vanguard of a cluster of bushes and low trees, that surrounded some pools of water in an extensive hollow; so we encamped on the rising ground near it.

Shaw and I were sitting in the tent, when Deslauriers thrust his brown face and old felt hat into the opening, and, dilating his eyes to their utmost extent, announced supper. There were the tin cups and the iron spoons, arranged in order on the grass, and the coffee-pot predominant in the midst. The meal was soon despatched; but Henry Chatillon still sat cross-legged, dallying with the remnant of his coffee, the beverage in universal use upon the prairie, and an especial favorite with him. He preferred it in its virgin flavor, unimpaired by sugar or cream; and on the present occasion it met his entire approval, being exceedingly strong, or, as he expressed it, "right black."

It was a gorgeous sunset; and the ruddy glow of the sky was reflected from some extensive pools of water among the shadowy copses in the meadow below.

"I must have a bath to-night," said Shaw. "How is it, Deslauriers? Any chance for a swim down there?"

"Ah! I cannot tell; just as you please, Monsieur," replied Deslauriers, shrugging his shoulders, perplexed by his ignorance of English, and extremely anxious to conform in all respects to the opinions and wishes of his *bourgeois*.

"Look at his moccason," said I. It had evidently been lately immersed in a profound abyss of black mud.

5 "Come," said Shaw; "at any rate we can see for ourselves."

We set out together; and as we approached the bushes, which were at some distance, we found the ground becoming rather treacherous. We could only get along by step-10 ping upon large clumps of tall rank grass, with fathomless gulfs between, like innumerable little quaking islands in an ocean of mud, where a false step would have involved our boots in a catastrophe like that which had befallen Deslaurier's moccasons. The thing looked desperate; we separated, 15 to search in different directions, Shaw going off to the right, while I kept straight forward. At last I came to the edge of the bushes, — they were young water-willows, covered with their caterpillar-like blossoms, but intervening between them and the last grass-clump was a black and deep slough, over 20 which, by a vigorous exertion, I contrived to jump. Then I shouldered my way through the willows, trampling them down by main force, till I came to a wide stream of water, three inches deep, languidly creeping along over a bottom of sleek mud. My arrival produced a great commotion. 25 A huge green bull-frog uttered an indignant croak, and jumped off the bank with a loud splash; his webbed feet twinkled above the surface, as he jerked them energetically upward, and I could see him ensconcing himself in the unresisting slime at the bottom, whence several large air-bubbles 30 struggled lazily to the top. Some little spotted frogs followed the patriarch's example; and then three turtles, not larger than a dollar, tumbled themselves off a broad "lily pad," where they had been reposing. At the same time a snake, gayly striped with black and yellow, glided out from the bank, and writhed across to the other side; and a small

stagnant pool into which my foot had inadvertently pushed a
stone was instantly alive with a congregation of black tadpoles.

"Any chance for a bath where you are?" called out
Shaw, from a distance.

The answer was not encouraging. I retreated through the
willows, and rejoining my companion, we proceeded to push
our researches in company. Not far on the right, a rising
ground, covered with trees and bushes, seemed to sink down
abruptly to the water, and give hope of better success; so
towards this we directed our steps. When we reached the
place we found it no easy matter to get along between the
hill and the water, impeded as we were by a growth of stiff,
obstinate young birch-trees, laced together by grape-vines.
In the twilight we now and then, to support ourselves,
snatched at the touch-me-not stem of some ancient sweet-
brier. Shaw, who was in advance, suddenly uttered an emphatic monosyllable; and, looking up, I saw him with one
hand grasping a sapling, and one foot immersed in the
water, from which he had forgotten to withdraw it, his
whole attention being engaged in contemplating the movements of a water-snake, about five feet long, curiously checkered with black and green, who was deliberately swimming
across the pool. There being no stick or stone at hand to
pelt him with, we looked at him for a time in silent disgust,
and then pushed forward. Our perseverance was at last re-
warded; for, several rods farther on, we emerged upon a
little level grassy nook among the brushwood, and by an
extraordinary dispensation of fortune, the weeds and floating sticks, which elsewhere covered the pool, seemed to have
drawn apart, and left a few yards of clear water just in front
of this favored spot. We sounded it with a stick; it was
four feet deep: we lifted a specimen in our closed hands; it
seemed reasonably transparent, so we decided that the time
for action was arrived. But our ablutions were suddenly

interrupted by ten thousand punctures, like poisoned needles, and the humming of myriads of overgrown mosquitoes, rising in all directions from their native mud and swarming to the feast. We were fain to beat a retreat with all
5 possible speed.

We made towards the tents, much refreshed by the bath, which the heat of the weather, joined to our prejudices, had rendered very desirable.

"What's the matter with the captain? look at him!"
10 said Shaw. The captain stood alone on the prairie, swinging his hat violently around his head, and lifting first one foot and then the other, without moving from the spot. First he looked down to the ground with an air of supreme abhorrence; then he gazed upward with a perplexed and indig-
15 nant countenance, as if trying to trace the flight of an unseen enemy. We called to know what was the matter; but he replied only by execrations directed against some unknown object. We approached, when our ears were saluted by a droning sound, as if twenty bee-hives had been overturned
20 at once. The air above was full of large black insects, in a state of great commotion, and multitudes were flying about just above the tops of the grass-blades.

"Don't be afraid," called the captain, observing us recoil. "The brutes won't sting."
25 At this I knocked one down with my hat, and discovered him to be no other than a "dor-bug"; and, looking closer, we found the ground thickly perforated with their holes.

We took a hasty leave of this flourishing colony, and walking up the rising ground to the tents, found Deslau-
30 riers's fire still glowing brightly. We sat down around it, and Shaw began to expatiate on the admirable facilities for bathing that we had discovered, recommending the captain by all means to go down there before breakfast in the morning. The captain was in the act of remarking that he couldn't have believed it possible, when he suddenly interrupted

himself, and clapped his hand to his cheek, exclaiming that
"those infernal humbugs were at him again." In fact, we
began to hear sounds as if bullets were humming over our
heads. In a moment something rapped me sharply on the
forehead, then upon the neck, and immediately I felt an in-
definite number of sharp wiry claws in active motion, as if
their owner were bent on pushing his explorations farther.
I seized him, and dropped him into the fire. Our party
speedily broke up, and we adjourned to our respective tents,
where, closing the opening fast, we hoped to be exempt from
invasion. But all precaution was fruitless. The dor-bugs
hummed through the tent, and marched over our faces until
daylight; when, opening our blankets, we found several
dozen clinging there with the utmost tenacity. The first object that met our eyes in the morning was Deslauriers, who
seemed to be apostrophizing his frying-pan, which he held
by the handle, at arm's length. It appeared that he had
left it at night by the fire; and the bottom was now covered
with dor-bugs, firmly imbedded. Hundreds of others, curiously parched and shrivelled, lay scattered among the ashes.

The horses and mules were turned loose to feed. We had
just taken our seats at breakfast, or rather reclined in the
classic mode, when an exclamation from Henry Chatillon,
and a shout of alarm from the captain, gave warning of
some casualty, and looking up, we saw the whole band of
animals, twenty-three in number, filing off for the settlements, the incorrigible Pontiac at their head, jumping along
with hobbled feet, at a gait much more rapid than graceful.
Three or four of us ran to cut them off, dashing as best we
might through the tall grass, which was glittering with dewdrops. After a race of a mile or more, Shaw caught a horse.
Tying the trail-rope by way of bridle round the animal's
jaw, and leaping upon his back, he got in advance of the
remaining fugitives, while we, soon bringing them together,
drove them in a crowd up to the tents, where each man

caught and saddled his own. Then were heard lamentations
and curses; for half the horses had broken their hobbles,
and many were seriously galled by attempting to run in
fetters.

5   It was late that morning before we were on the march;
and early in the afternoon we were compelled to encamp, for
a thunder-gust came up and suddenly enveloped us in whirl-
ing sheets of rain. With much ado we pitched our tents
amid the tempest, and all night long the thunder bellowed
10 and growled over our heads. In the morning light peaceful
showers succeeded the cataracts of rain, that had been
drenching us through the canvas of our tents. About noon,
when there were some treacherous indications of fair weather,
we got in motion again.

15 Not a breath of air stirred over the free and open prairie;
the clouds were like light piles of cotton; and where the
blue sky was visible, it wore a hazy and languid aspect.
The sun beat down upon us with a sultry, penetrating heat
almost insupportable, and as our party crept slowly along
20 over the interminable level, the horses hung their heads as
they waded fetlock deep through the mud, and the men
slouched into the easiest position upon the saddle. At last,
towards evening, the old familiar black heads of thunder-
clouds rose fast above the horizon, and the same deep mut-
25 tering of distant thunder that had become the ordinary
accompaniment of our afternoon's journey began to roll
hoarsely over the prairie. Only a few minutes elapsed before the whole sky was densely shrouded, and the prairie
and some clusters of woods in front assumed a purple hue
30 beneath the inky shadows. Suddenly from the densest fold
of the cloud the flash leaped out, quivering again and again
down to the edge of the prairie; and at the same instant
came the sharp burst and the long rolling peal of the thunder. A cool wind, filled with the smell of rain, just then
overtook us, levelling the tall grass by the side of the path.

"Come on; we must ride for it!" shouted Shaw, rushing by at full speed, his led horse snorting at his side. The whole party broke into full gallop, and made for the trees in front. Passing these, we found beyond them a meadow which they half enclosed. We rode pell-mell upon the ground, leaped from horseback, tore off our saddles; and in a moment each man was kneeling at his horse's feet. The hobbles were adjusted, and the animals turned loose; then, as the wagons came wheeling rapidly to the spot, we seized upon the tent-poles, and just as the storm broke, we were prepared to receive it. It came upon us almost with the darkness of night: the trees, which were close at hand, were completely shrouded by the roaring torrents of rain.

We were sitting in the tent when Deslauriers, with his broad felt hat hanging about his ears, and his shoulders glistening with rain, thrust in his head.

"Voulez-vous du souper, tout de suite? I can make fire, sous la charette — I b'lieve so — I try."

"Never mind supper, man; come in out of the rain."

Deslauriers accordingly crouched in the entrance, for modesty would not permit him to intrude farther.

Our tent was none of the best defence against such a cataract. The rain could not enter bodily, but it beat through the canvas in a fine drizzle, that wetted us just as effectually. We sat upon our saddles with faces of the utmost surliness, while the water dropped from the visors of our caps, and trickled down our cheeks. My india-rubber cloak conducted twenty little rapid streamlets to the ground; and Shaw's blanket coat was saturated like a sponge. But what most concerned us was the sight of several puddles of water rapidly accumulating; one, in particular, that was gathering around the tent-pole, threatened to overspread the whole area within the tent, holding forth but an indifferent promise of a comfortable night's rest. Towards sunset, however, the storm ceased as suddenly as it began. A bright streak of

clear red sky appeared above the western verge of the
prairie, the horizontal rays of the sinking sun streamed
through it, and glittered in a thousand prismatic colors
upon the dripping groves and the prostrate grass. The pools
5 in the tent dwindled and sunk into the saturated soil.

But all our hopes were delusive. Scarcely had night set
in when the tumult broke forth anew. The thunder here is
not like the tame thunder of the Atlantic coast. Bursting
with a terrific crash directly above our heads, it roared over
10 the boundless waste of prairie, seeming to roll around the
whole circle of the firmament with a peculiar and awful re-
verberation. The lightning flashed all night, playing with
its livid glare upon the neighboring trees, revealing the vast
expanse of the plain, and then leaving us shut in as if by a
15 palpable wall of darkness.

It did not disturb us much. Now and then a peal awakened us, and made us conscious of the electric battle that
was raging, and of the floods that dashed upon the stanch
canvas over our heads. We lay upon india-rubber cloths,
20 placed between our blankets and the soil. For a while they
excluded the water to admiration; but when at length it accumulated and began to run over the edges, they served
equally well to retain it, so that towards the end of the night
we were unconsciously reposing in small pools of rain.

25 On finally awakening in the morning the prospect was
not a cheerful one. The rain no longer poured in torrents;
but it pattered with a quiet pertinacity upon the strained and
saturated canvas. We disengaged ourselves from our blankets, every fibre of which glistened with little bead-like
30 drops of water, and looked out in the vain hope of discovering some token of fair weather. The clouds, in lead-colored
volumes, rested upon the dismal verge of the prairie, or hung
sluggishly overhead, while the earth wore an aspect no more
attractive than the heavens, exhibiting nothing but pools of
water, grass beaten down, and mud well trampled by our

mules and horses. Our companions' tent, with an air of forlorn and passive misery, and their wagons in like manner
drenched and woe-begone, stood not far off. The captain
was just returning from his morning's inspection of the
horses. He stalked through the mist and rain, with his   5
plaid around his shoulders, his little pipe, dingy as an
antiquarian relic, projecting from beneath his moustache,
and his brother Jack at his heels.

At noon the sky was clear, and we set out, trailing through
mud and slime six inches deep. That night we were spared 10
the customary infliction of the shower-bath.

On the next afternoon we were moving slowly along, not
far from a patch of woods which lay on the right. Jack
C—— rode a little in advance, —

"The livelong day he had not spoke";   15

when suddenly he faced about, pointed to the woods, and
roared out to his brother, —

"O Bill! here's a cow."

The captain instantly galloped forward, and he and Jack
made a vain attempt to capture the prize; but the cow, with 20
a well-grounded distrust of their intentions, took refuge
among the trees. R—— joined them, and they soon drove
her out. We watched their evolutions as they galloped
around her, trying in vain to noose her with their trail-
ropes, which they had converted into *lariettes* for the occa- 25
sion. At length they resorted to milder measures, and the
cow was driven along with the party. Soon after the usual
thunder-storm came up, the wind blowing with such fury
that the streams of rain flew almost horizontally along the
prairie, roaring like a cataract. The horses turned tail to 30
the storm, and stood hanging their heads, bearing the infliction with an air of meekness and resignation; while we
drew our heads between our shoulders, and crouched forward, so as to make our backs serve as a pent-house for the

rest of our persons. Meanwhile the cow, taking advantage of the tumult, ran off, to the great discomfiture of the captain. In defiance of the storm, he pulled his cap tight over his brows, jerked a huge buffalo-pistol from his holster, and
5 set out at full speed after her. This was the last we saw of them for some time, the mist and rain making an impenetrable veil, but at length we heard the captain's shout, and saw him looming through the tempest, the picture of a Hibernian cavalier, with his cocked pistol held aloft for
10 safety's sake, and a countenance of anxiety and excitement. The cow trotted before him, but exhibited evident signs of an intention to run off again, and the captain was roaring to us to head her. But the rain had got in behind our coat-collars, and was travelling over our necks in numerous little
15 streamlets, and being afraid to move our heads, for fear of admitting more, we sat stiff and immovable, looking at the captain askance, and laughing at his frantic movements. At last the cow made a sudden plunge and ran off; the captain grasped his pistol firmly, spurred his horse, and galloped
20 after, with evident designs of mischief. In a moment we heard the faint report, deadened by the rain, and then the conqueror and his victim reappeared, the latter shot through the body, and quite helpless. Not long after, the storm moderated, and we advanced again. The cow walked pain-
25 fully along under the charge of Jack, to whom the captain had committed her, while he himself rode forward in his old capacity of vidette. We were approaching a long line of trees, that followed a stream stretching across our path, far in front, when we beheld the vidette galloping towards
30 us apparently much excited, but with a broad grin on his face.

"Let that cow drop behind!" he shouted to us; "here's her owners."

And, in fact, as we approached the line of trees, a large white object, like a tent, was visible behind them. On approaching, however, we found, instead of the expected Mormon camp, nothing but the lonely prairie, and a large white rock standing by the path. The cow, therefore, resumed her place in our procession. She walked on until we encamped, when R——, approaching with his English double-barrelled rifle, took aim at her heart, and discharged into it first one bullet and then the other. She was then butchered on the most approved principles of woodcraft, and furnished a very welcome item to our somewhat limited bill of fare.

In a day or two more we reached the river called the "Big Blue." By titles equally elegant, almost all the streams of this region are designated. We had struggled through ditches and little brooks all that morning; but on traversing the dense woods that lined the banks of the Blue, we found that more formidable difficulties awaited us, for the stream, swollen by the rains, was wide, deep, and rapid.

No sooner were we on the spot than R—— flung off his clothes, and swam across, or splashed through the shallows, with the end of a rope between his teeth. We all looked on in admiration, wondering what might be the object of this energetic preparation; but soon we heard him shouting: "Give that rope a turn round that stump. You, Sorel; do you hear? Look sharp, now, Boisverd. Come over to this side, some of you, and help me." The men to whom these orders were directed paid not the least attention to them, though they were poured out without pause or intermission. Henry Chatillon directed the work, and it proceeded quietly and rapidly. R——'s sharp brattling voice might have been heard incessantly; and he was leaping about with the utmost activity. His commands were rather amusingly inconsistent; for when he saw that the men would not do as he told them, he accommodated himself to circumstances, and with the utmost vehemence ordered them to do precisely that which they were at the time engaged upon, no doubt recollecting the story of Mahomet and the refractory mountain.

Shaw smiled; R—— observed it, and, approaching with a countenance of indignation, began to vapor a little, but was instantly reduced to silence.

The raft was at length complete. We piled our goods
5 upon it, with the exception of our guns, which each man chose to retain in his own keeping. Sorel, Boisverd, Wright, and Deslauriers took their stations at the four corners, to hold it together, and swim across with it; and in a moment more all our earthly possessions were floating on the turbid
10 waters of the Big Blue. We sat on the bank, anxiously watching the result, until we saw the raft safe landed in a little cove far down on the opposite bank. The empty wagons were easily passed across; and then, each man mounting a horse, we rode through the stream, the stray
15 animals following of their own accord.

CHAPTER VI

THE PLATTE AND THE DESERT

We were now at the end of our solitary journeyings along the St. Joseph trail. On the evening of the twenty-third of May we encamped near its junction with the old legitimate trail of the Oregon emigrants. We had ridden long that afternoon, trying in vain to find wood and water, until at length we saw the sunset sky reflected from a pool encircled by bushes and rocks. The water lay in the bottom of a hollow, the smooth prairie gracefully rising in ocean-like swells on every side. We pitched our tents by it; not, however, before the keen eye of Henry Chatillon had discerned some unusual object upon the faintly-defined outline of the distant swell. But in the moist, hazy atmosphere of the evening, nothing could be clearly distinguished. As we lay around the fire after supper, a low and distant sound, strange enough amid the loneliness of the prairie, reached our ears, — peals of laughter, and the faint voices of men and women. For eight days we had not encountered a human being, and this singular warning of their vicinity had an effect extremely impressive.

About dark a sallow-faced fellow descended the hill on horseback, and splashing through the pool, rode up to the tents. He was enveloped in a huge cloak, and his broad felt hat was weeping about his ears with the drizzling moisture of the evening. Another followed, a stout, square-built, intelligent-looking man, who announced himself as leader of an emigrant party, encamped a mile in advance of us. About twenty wagons, he said, were with him; the rest of his party were on the other side of the Big Blue, waiting for a woman

47

who was in the pains of childbirth, and quarrelling meanwhile among themselves.

These were the first emigrants that we had overtaken, although we had found abundant and melancholy traces of
their progress throughout the course of the journey. Sometimes we passed the grave of one who had sickened and died
on the way. The earth was usually torn up, and covered
thickly with wolf-tracks. Some had escaped this violation.
One morning, a piece of plank, standing upright on the summit of a grassy hill, attracted our notice, and riding up to it,
we found the following words very roughly traced upon it,
apparently with a red-hot piece of iron: —

MARY ELLIS

DIED MAY 7th, 1845

AGED TWO MONTHS

Such tokens were of common occurrence.

We were late in breaking up our camp on the following
morning, and scarcely had we ridden a mile when we saw,
far in advance of us, drawn against the horizon, a line of objects stretching at regular intervals along the level edge of
the prairie. An intervening swell soon hid them from sight,
until, ascending it a quarter of an hour after, we saw close
before us the emigrant caravan, with its heavy white wagons
creeping on in slow procession, and a large drove of cattle
following behind. Half a dozen yellow-visaged Missourians,
mounted on horseback, were cursing and shouting among
them, their lank angular proportions enveloped in brown
homespun, evidently cut and adjusted by the hands of a
domestic female tailor. As we approached, they called out
to us: "How are ye, boys? Are ye for Oregon or California?"

As we pushed rapidly by the wagons, children's faces
were thrust out from the white coverings to look at us;

while the care-worn, thin-featured matron, or the buxom girl, seated in front, suspended the knitting on which most of them were engaged to stare at us with wondering curiosity. By the side of each wagon stalked the proprietor, urging on his patient oxen, who shouldered heavily along, inch by inch, on their interminable journey. It was easy to see that fear and dissension prevailed among them; some of the men — but these, with one exception, were bachelors — looked wistfully upon us as we rode lightly and swiftly by, and then impatiently at their own lumbering wagons and heavy-gaited oxen. Others were unwilling to advance at all, until the party they had left behind should have rejoined them. Many were murmuring against the leader they had chosen, and wished to depose him; and this discontent was fomented by some ambitious spirits, who had hopes of succeeding in his place. The women were divided between regrets for the homes they had left and fear of the deserts and savages before them.

We soon left them far behind, and hoped that we had taken a final leave; but our companions' wagon stuck so long in a deep muddy ditch that before it was extricated the van of the emigrant caravan appeared again, descending a ridge close at hand. Wagon after wagon plunged through the mud; and as it was nearly noon, and the place promised shade and water, we saw with satisfaction that they were resolved to encamp. Soon the wagons were wheeled into a circle: the cattle were grazing over the meadow, and the men, with sour, sullen faces, were looking about for wood and water. They seemed to meet but indifferent success. As we left the ground, I saw a tall, slouching fellow, with the nasal accent of "down east," contemplating the contents of his tin cup, which he had just filled with water.

"Look here, you," said he; "it's chock-full of animals!"

The cup, as he held it out, exhibited in fact an extraordinary variety and profusion of animal and vegetable life.

Riding up the little hill, and looking back on the meadow, we could easily see that all was not right in the camp of the emigrants. The men were crowded together, and an angry discussion seemed to be going forward. R—— was missing
5 from his wonted place in the line, and the captain told us that he had remained behind to get his horse shod by a blacksmith attached to the emigrant party. Something whispered in our ears that mischief was on foot; we kept on, however, and coming soon to a stream of tolerable water,
10 we stopped to rest and dine. Still the absentee lingered behind. At last, at the distance of a mile, he and his horse suddenly appeared, sharply defined against the sky on the summit of a hill; and close behind, a huge white object rose slowly into view.

15   "What is that blockhead bringing with him now?"

A moment dispelled the mystery. Slowly and solemnly, one behind the other, four long trains of oxen and four emigrant wagons rolled over the crest of the hill and gravely descended, while R—— rode in state in the van. It seems
20 that, during the process of shoeing the horse, the smothered dissensions among the emigrants suddenly broke into open rupture. Some insisted on pushing forward, some on remaining where they were, and some on going back. Kearsley, their captain, threw up his command in disgust. "And now,
25 boys," said he, "if any of you are for going ahead, just you come along with me."

Four wagons, with ten men, one woman, and one small child, made up the force of the "go-ahead" faction, and R——, with his usual proclivity toward mischief, invited them
30 to join our party. Fear of the Indians — for I can conceive no other motive — must have induced him to court so burdensome an alliance. At all events, the proceeding was a cool one. The men who joined us, it is true, were all that could be desired; rude indeed in manners, but frank, manly, and intelligent. To tell them we could not travel with them was

out of the question. I merely reminded Kearsley that if his
oxen could not keep up with our mules he must expect to be
left behind, as we could not consent to be farther delayed on
the journey; but he immediately replied, that his oxen
"*should* keep up; and if they could n't, why, he allowed,   5
he 'd find out how to make 'em."

On the next day, as it chanced, our English companions
broke the axle-tree of their wagon, and down came the whole
cumbrous machine lumbering into the bed of a brook. Here
was a day's work cut out for us. Meanwhile our emigrant   10
associates kept on their way, and so vigorously did they urge
forward their powerful oxen, that, what with the broken
axle-tree and other mishaps, it was full a week before we
overtook them; when at length we discovered them, one
afternoon, crawling quietly along the sandy brink of the   15
Platte. But meanwhile various incidents occurred to ourselves.

It was probable that at this stage of our journey the
Pawnees would attempt to rob us. We began therefore to
stand guard in turn, dividing the night into three watches,   20
and appointing two men for each. Deslauriers and I held
guard together. We did not march with military precision
to and fro before the tents: our discipline was by no means
so strict. We wrapped ourselves in our blankets, and sat
down by the fire; and Deslauriers, combining his culinary   25
functions with his duties as sentinel, employed himself in
boiling the head of an antelope for our breakfast. Yet we
were models of vigilance in comparison with some of the
party; for the ordinary practice of the guard was to lay his
rifle on the ground, and, enveloping his nose in his blanket,   30
meditate on his mistress, or whatever subject best pleased
him. This is all well enough when among Indians who do
not habitually proceed further in their hostility than robbing
travellers of their horses and mules, though, indeed, a Pawnee's forbearance is not always to be trusted; but in certain

regions farther to the west, the guard must beware how he
exposes his person to the light of the fire, lest some keen-
eyed skulking marksman should let fly a bullet or an arrow
from the darkness.

5   Among various tales that circulated around our camp-fire
was one told by Boisverd, and not inappropriate here. He
was trapping with several companions on the skirts of the
Blackfoot country. The man on guard, knowing that it be-
hooved him to put forth his utmost precaution, kept aloof
10   from the fire-light, and sat watching intently on all sides.
At length he was aware of a dark, crouching figure, stealing noiselessly into the circle of the light. He hastily cocked
his rifle, but the sharp click of the lock caught the ear of the
Blackfoot, whose senses were all on the alert. Raising his
15   arrow, already fitted to the string, he shot it in the direction
of the sound. So sure was his aim, that he drove it through
the throat of the unfortunate guard, and then, with a loud
yell, bounded from the camp.

As I looked at the partner of my watch, puffing and blow-
20   ing over his fire, it occurred to me that he might not prove
the most efficient auxiliary in time of trouble.

"Deslauriers," said I, "would you run away if the Pawnees should fire at us?"

"Ah! oui, oui, Monsieur!" he replied very decisively.

25   At this instant a whimsical variety of voices, — barks,
howls, yelps, and whines, — all mingled together, sounded
from the prairie, not far off, as if a conclave of wolves of
every age and sex were assembled there. Deslauriers looked
up from his work with a laugh, and began to imitate this
30   medley of sounds with a ludicrous accuracy. At this they
were repeated with redoubled emphasis, the musician being
apparently indignant at the successful efforts of a rival.
They all proceeded from the throat of one little wolf, not
larger than a spaniel, seated by himself at some distance. He
was of the species called the prairie-wolf: a grim-visaged,

but harmless little brute, whose worst propensity is creeping among horses and gnawing the ropes of raw hide by which they are picketed around the camp. Other beasts roam the prairies, far more formidable in aspect and in character. These are the large white and gray wolves, whose deep howl we heard at intervals from far and near.

At last I fell into a doze, and awaking from it, found Deslauriers fast asleep. Scandalized by this breach of discipline, I was about to stimulate his vigilance by stirring him with the stock of my rifle; but, compassion prevailing, I determined to let him sleep awhile, and then arouse him to administer a suitable reproof for such forgetfulness of duty. Now and then I walked the rounds among the silent horses, to see that all was right. The night was chill, damp, and dark, the dank grass bending under the icy dewdrops. At the distance of a rod or two the tents were invisible, and nothing could be seen but the obscure figures of the horses, deeply breathing, and restlessly starting as they slept, or still slowly champing the grass. Far off, beyond the black outline of the prairie, there was a ruddy light, gradually increasing, like the glow of a conflagration; until at length the broad disk of the moon, blood-red, and vastly magnified by the vapors, rose slowly upon the darkness, flecked by one or two little clouds, and as the light poured over the gloomy plain, a fierce and stern howl, close at hand, seemed to greet it as an unwelcome intruder. There was something impressive and awful in the place and the hour; for I and the beasts were all that had consciousness for many a league around.

Some days elapsed, and brought us near the Platte. Two men on horseback approached us one morning, and we watched them with the curiosity and interest that, upon the solitude of the plains, such an encounter always excites. They were evidently whites, from their mode of riding, though, contrary to the usage of that region, neither of them carried a rifle.

" Fools ! " remarked Henry Chatillon, " to ride that way
on the prairie ; Pawnee find them — then they catch it."

Pawnee *had* found them, and they had come very near
" catching it "; indeed, nothing saved them but the approach
5 of our party. Shaw and I knew one of them, — a man named
Turner, whom we had seen at Westport. He and his companion belonged to an emigrant party encamped a few miles
in advance, and had returned to look for some stray oxen,
leaving their rifles, with characteristic rashness or ignorance,
10 behind them. Their neglect had nearly cost them dear ; for,
just before we came up, half-a-dozen Indians approached,
and, seeing them apparently defenceless, one of the rascals
seized the bridle of Turner's horse and ordered him to dismount. Turner was wholly unarmed ; but the other jerked
15 a pistol out of his pocket, at which the Pawnee recoiled ;
and just then some of our men appearing in the distance, the
whole party whipped their rugged little horses and made off.
In no way daunted, Turner foolishly persisted in going forward.

20   Long after leaving him, and late that afternoon, in the
midst of a gloomy and barren prairie, we came suddenly
upon the great trail of the Pawnees, leading from their villages on the Platte to their war and hunting grounds to the
southward. Here every summer passes the motley con-
25 course : thousands of savages, men, women, and children,
horses and mules, laden with their weapons and implements,
and an innumerable multitude of unruly wolfish dogs, who
have not acquired the civilized accomplishment of barking,
but howl like their wild cousins of the prairie.

30   The permanent winter villages of the Pawnees stand on
the lower Platte, but throughout the summer the greater
part of the inhabitants are wandering over the plains, — a
treacherous, cowardly banditti, who, by a thousand acts of
pillage and murder, have deserved chastisement at the hands
of government. Last year a Dahcotah warrior performed a

notable exploit at one of these villages. He approached it alone, in the middle of a dark night, and clambering up the outside of one of the lodges, which are in the form of a half-sphere, looked in at the round hole made at the top for the escape of smoke. The dusky light from the embers showed him the forms of the sleeping inmates; and dropping lightly through the opening, he unsheathed his knife, and, stirring the fire, coolly selected his victims. One by one, he stabbed and scalped them; when a child suddenly awoke and screamed. He rushed from the lodge, yelled a Sioux war-cry, shouted his name in triumph and defiance, and darted out upon the dark prairie, leaving the whole village behind him in a tumult, with the howling and baying of dogs, the screams of women, and the yells of the enraged warriors.

Our friend Kearsley, as we learned on rejoining him, signalized himself by a less bloody achievement. He and his men were good woodsmen, well skilled in the use of the rifle, but found themselves wholly out of their element on the prairie. None of them had ever seen a buffalo; and they had very vague conceptions of his nature and appearance. On the day after they reached the Platte, looking towards a distant swell, they beheld a multitude of little black specks in motion upon its surface.

"Take your rifles, boys," said Kearsley, "and we'll have fresh meat for supper." This inducement was quite sufficient. The ten men left their wagons, and set out in hot haste, some on horseback and some on foot, in pursuit of the supposed buffalo. Meanwhile a high, grassy ridge shut the game from view; but mounting it after half an hour's running and riding, they found themselves suddenly confronted by about thirty mounted Pawnees. Amazement and consternation were mutual. Having nothing but their bows and arrows, the Indians thought their hour was come, and the fate that they were conscious of richly deserving about to

overtake them. So they began, one and all, to shout forth
the most cordial salutations, running up with extreme ear-
nestness to shake hands with the Missourians, who were
as much rejoiced as they were to escape the expected
5 conflict.

A low, undulating line of sand-hills bounded the horizon
before us. That day we rode ten hours, and it was dusk before we entered the hollows and gorges of these gloomy
little hills. At length we gained the summit, and the long-
10 expected valley of the Platte lay before us. We all drew
rein, and sat joyfully looking down upon the prospect. It
was right welcome; strange, too, and striking to the imagination, and yet it had not one picturesque or beautiful
feature; nor had it any of the features of grandeur, other
15 than its vast extent, its solitude, and its wildness. For
league after league, a plain as level as a lake was outspread
beneath us; here and there the Platte, divided into a dozen
thread-like sluices, was traversing it, and an occasional clump
of wood, rising in the midst like a shadowy island, relieved
20 the monotony of the waste. No living thing was moving
throughout the vast landscape, except the lizards that darted
over the sand and through the rank grass and prickly pears
at our feet.

We had passed the more tedious part of the journey; but
25 four hundred miles still intervened between us and Fort
Laramie; and to reach that point cost us the travel of three
more weeks. During the whole of this time we were passing
up the middle of a long, narrow, sandy plain, reaching like
an outstretched belt nearly to the Rocky Mountains. Two
30 lines of sand-hills, broken often into the wildest and most
fantastic forms, flanked the valley at the distance of a mile
or two on the right and left; while beyond them lay a
barren, trackless waste, extending for hundreds of miles to
the Arkansas on the one side, and the Missouri on the other.
Before and behind us, the level monotony of the plain was

unbroken as far as the eye could reach. Sometimes it glared
in the sun, an expanse of hot, bare sand, sometimes it was
veiled by long coarse grass. Skulls and whitening bones of
buffalo were scattered everywhere; the ground was tracked
by myriads of them, and often covered with the circular in-   5
dentations where the bulls had wallowed in the hot weather.
From every gorge and ravine, opening from the hills, descended deep, well-worn paths, where the buffalo issue twice
a day in regular procession to drink in the Platte. The river
itself runs through the midst, a thin sheet of rapid, turbid   10
water, half a mile wide, and scarcely two feet deep. Its low
banks, for the most part without a bush or a tree, are of
loose sand, with which the stream is so charged that it grates
on the teeth in drinking. The naked landscape is, of itself,
dreary and monotonous enough; and yet the wild beasts and   15
wild men that frequent the valley of the Platte make it a
scene of interest and excitement to the traveller. Of those
who have journeyed there, scarcely one, perhaps, fails to
look back with fond regret to his horse and his rifle.

Early in the morning after we reached the Platte, a long   20
procession of squalid savages approached our camp. Each
was on foot, leading his horse by a rope of bull-hide. His
attire consisted merely of a scanty cincture, and an old
buffalo robe, tattered and begrimed by use, which hung
over his shoulders. His head was close shaven, except a   25
ridge of hair reaching over the crown from the middle of the
forehead, very much like the long bristles on the back of a
hyena, and he carried his bow and arrows in his hand, while
his meagre little horse was laden with dried buffalo meat,
the produce of his hunting. Such were the first specimens   30
that we met — and very indifferent ones they were — of the
genuine savages of the prairie.

They were the Pawnees whom Kearsley had encountered
the day before, and belonged to a large hunting-party, known
to be ranging the prairie in the vicinity. They strode rapidly

by, within a furlong of our tents, not pausing or looking towards us, after the manner of Indians when meditating mischief, or conscious of ill desert. I went out to meet them, and had an amicable conference with the chief, presenting 5 him with half a pound of tobacco, at which unmerited bounty he expressed much gratification. These fellows, or some of their companions, had committed a dastardly outrage upon an emigrant party in advance of us. Two men, at a distance from the rest, were seized by them, but, lashing their horses, 10 they broke away and fled. At this the Pawnees raised the yell and shot at them, transfixing the hindmost through the back with several arrows, while his companion galloped away and brought in the news to his party. The panic-stricken emigrants remained for several days in camp, not 15 daring even to send out in quest of the dead body.

Our New-England climate is mild and equable compared with that of the Platte. This very morning, for instance, was close and sultry, the sun rising with a faint oppressive heat; when suddenly darkness gathered in the west, and a 20 furious blast of sleet and hail drove full in our faces, icy cold, and urged with such demoniac vehemence that it felt like a storm of needles. It was curious to see the horses; they faced about in extreme displeasure, holding their tails like whipped dogs, and shivering as the angry gusts, howling 25 louder than a concert of wolves, swept over us. Wright's long train of mules came sweeping round before the storm, like a flight of snow-birds driven by a winter tempest. Thus we all remained stationary for some minutes, crouching close to our horses' necks, much too surly to speak, though once 30 the captain looked up from between the collars of his coat, his face blood-red, and the muscles of his mouth contracted by the cold into a most ludicrous grin of agony. He grumbled something that sounded like a curse, directed, as we believed, against the unhappy hour when he had first thought of leaving home. The thing was too good to last long; and the instant the puffs of wind subsided we pitched our tents, and remained in camp for the rest of a gloomy and lowering day. The emigrants also encamped near at hand. We being first on the ground, had appropriated all the wood within reach; so that our fire alone blazed cheerily. Around it soon 5 gathered a group of uncouth figures, shivering in the drizzling rain. Conspicuous among them were two or three of the half-savage men who spend their reckless lives in trapping among the Rocky Mountains, or in trading for the Fur Company in the Indian villages. They were all of Canadian 10 extraction; their hard, weather-beaten faces and bushy moustaches looked out from beneath the hoods of their white capotes with a bad and brutish expression, as if their owners might be the willing agents of any villany. And such in fact is the character of many of these men. 15

On the day following we overtook Kearsley's wagons, and thenceforward, for a week or two, we were fellow-travellers. One good effect, at least, resulted from the alliance; it materially diminished the fatigues of standing guard; for the party being now more numerous, there were longer in- 20 tervals between each man's turns of duty.

CHAPTER VII

THE BUFFALO

Four days on the Platte, and yet no buffalo! Last year's signs of them were provokingly abundant; and wood being extremely scarce, we found an admirable substitute in the *bois de vache*, which burns like peat, producing no unpleasant effects. The wagons one morning had left the camp; Shaw and I were already on horseback, but Henry Chatillon still sat cross-legged by the dead embers of the fire, playing pensively with the lock of his rifle, while his sturdy Wyandot pony stood quietly behind him, looking over his head. At last he got up, patted the neck of the pony (which, from an exaggerated appreciation of his merits, he had christened "Five Hundred Dollar"), and then mounted, with a melancholy air.

"What is it, Henry?"

"Ah, I feel lonesome; I never been here before but I see away yonder over the buttes, and down there on the prairie, black — all black with buffalo."

In the afternoon he and I left the party in search of an antelope, until, at the distance of a mile or two on the right, the tall white wagons and the little black specks of horsemen were just visible, so slowly advancing that they seemed motionless; and far on the left rose the broken line of scorched, desolate sand-hills. The vast plain waved with tall rank grass, that swept our horses' bellies; it swayed to and fro in billows with the light breeze, and far and near antelope and wolves were moving through it, the hairy backs of the latter alternately appearing and disappearing as they bounded awkwardly along; while the antelope, with the

60

simple curiosity peculiar to them, would often approach us closely, their little horns and white throats just visible above the grass-tops, as they gazed eagerly at us with their round black eyes.

I dismounted, and amused myself with firing at the wolves. Henry attentively scrutinized the surrounding landscape; at length he gave a shout, and called on me to mount again, pointing in the direction of the sand-hills. A mile and a half from us two black specks slowly traversed the bare glaring face of one of them, and disappeared behind the summit. "Let us go!" cried Henry, belaboring the sides of "Five Hundred Dollar"; and I following in his wake, we galloped rapidly through the rank grass toward the base of the hills.

From one of their openings descended a deep ravine, widening as it issued on the prairie. We entered it, and galloping up, in a moment were surrounded by the bleak sand-hills. Half of their steep sides were bare; the rest were scantily clothed with clumps of grass, and various uncouth plants, conspicuous among which appeared the reptile-like prickly-pear. They were gashed with numberless ravines; and as the sky had suddenly darkened, and a cold gusty wind arisen, the strange shrubs and the dreary hills looked doubly wild and desolate. But Henry's face was all eagerness. He tore off a little hair from the piece of buffalo-robe under his saddle, and threw it up, to show the course of the wind. It blew directly before us. The game were therefore to leeward, and it was necessary to make our best speed to get round them.

We scrambled from this ravine, and, galloping away through the hollows, soon found another, winding like a snake among the hills, and so deep that it completely concealed us. We rode up the bottom of it, glancing through the bushes at its edge, till Henry abruptly jerked his rein, and slid out of his saddle. Full a quarter of a mile distant, on

the outline of the farthest hill, a long procession of buffalo
were walking, in Indian file, with the utmost gravity and
deliberation; then more appeared, clambering from a hollow not far off, and ascending, one behind the other, the
5 grassy slope of another hill; then a shaggy head and a pair
of short broken horns issued out of a ravine close at hand,
and with a slow, stately step, one by one, the enormous
brutes came into view, taking their way across the valley,
wholly unconscious of an enemy. In a moment Henry was
10 worming his way, lying flat on the ground, through grass
and prickly-pears, towards his unsuspecting victims. He
had with him both my rifle and his own. He was soon out of
sight, and still the buffalo kept issuing into the valley. For
a long time all was silent; I sat holding his horse, and won-
15 dering what he was about, when suddenly, in rapid succession, came the sharp reports of the two rifles, and the whole
line of buffalo, quickening their pace into a clumsy trot,
gradually disappeared over the ridge of the hill. Henry
rose to his feet, and stood looking after them.

20   "You have missed them," said I.

"Yes," said Henry; "let us go." He descended into the
ravine, loaded the rifles, and mounted his horse.

We rode up the hill after the buffalo. The herd was out
of sight when we reached the top, but lying on the grass, not
25 far off, was one quite lifeless, and another violently strug-
gling in the death-agony.

"You see I miss him!" remarked Henry. He had fired
from a distance of more than a hundred and fifty yards, and
both balls had passed through the lungs, the true mark in
30 shooting buffalo.

The darkness increased, and a driving storm came on.
Tying our horses to the horns of the victims, Henry began
the bloody work of dissection, slashing away with the science
of a connoisseur, while I vainly tried to imitate him. Old
Hendrick recoiled with horror and indignation when I

endeavored to tie the meat to the strings of raw hide, always carried for this purpose, dangling at the back of the saddle. After some difficulty we overcame his scruples; and, heavily burdened with the more eligible portions of the buffalo, we set out on our return. Scarcely had we emerged from the labyrinth of gorges and ravines, and issued upon the open prairie, when the prickling sleet came driving, gust upon gust, directly in our faces. It was strangely dark, though wanting still an hour of sunset. The freezing storm soon penetrated to the skin, but the uneasy trot of our heavy-gaited horses kept us warm enough, as we forced them unwillingly in the teeth of the sleet and rain, by the powerful suasion of our Indian whips. The prairie in this place was hard and level. A flourishing colony of prairie-dogs had burrowed into it in every direction, and the little mounds of fresh earth around their holes were about as numerous as the hills in a cornfield; but not a yelp was to be heard; not the nose of a single citizen was visible; all had retired to the depths of their burrows, and we envied them their dry and comfortable habitations. An hour's hard riding showed us our tent dimly looming through the storm, one side puffed out by the force of the wind, and the other collapsed in proportion, while the disconsolate horses stood shivering close around, and the wind kept up a dismal whistling in the boughs of three old half-dead trees above. Shaw, like a patriarch, sat on his saddle in the entrance, with a pipe in his mouth and his arms folded, contemplating, with cool satisfaction, the piles of meat that we flung on the ground before him. A dark and dreary night succeeded; but the sun rose, with a heat so sultry and languid that the captain excused himself on that account from waylaying an old buffalo bull, who with stupid gravity was walking over the prairie to drink at the river. So much for the climate of the Platte.

But it was not the weather alone that had produced this sudden abatement of the sportsman-like zeal which the

captain had always professed. He had been out on the afternoon before, together with several members of his party;
but their hunting was attended with no other result than the
loss of one of their best horses, severely injured by Sorel, in
5 vainly chasing a wounded bull. The captain, whose ideas of
hard riding were all derived from transatlantic sources, expressed the utmost amazement at the feats of Sorel, who
went leaping ravines, and dashing at full speed up and down
the sides of precipitous hills, lashing his horse with the
10 recklessness of a Rocky Mountain rider. Unfortunately for
the poor animal, he was the property of R——, against whom
Sorel entertained an unbounded aversion. The captain himself, it seemed, had also attempted to "run" a buffalo, but
though a good and practised horseman, he had soon given
15 over the attempt, being astonished and utterly disgusted at
the nature of the ground he was required to ride over.

"Here's old Papin and Frederic, down from Fort Laramie," shouted Henry, as we returned from a reconnoitring
tour on the next morning. We had for some days expected
20 this encounter. Papin was the *bourgeois*, or "boss," of Fort
Laramie. He had come down the river with the buffalo-robes
and the beaver, the produce of the last winter's trading. I
had among our baggage a letter which I wished to commit
to their hands; so requesting Henry to detain the boats if
25 he could until my return, I set out after the wagons. They
were about four miles in advance. In half an hour I overtook them, got the letter, trotted back upon the trail, and
looking carefully, as I rode, saw a patch of broken storm-
blasted trees, and, moving near them, some little black specks
30 like men and horses. Arriving at the place, I found a
strange assembly. The boats, eleven in number, deep-laden
with the skins, hugged close to the shore, to escape being
borne down by the swift current. The rowers, swarthy ignoble Mexicans, turned their brutish faces upwards to look,
as I reached the bank. Papin sat in the middle of one of the

boats, upon the canvas covering that protected the cargo.
He was a stout, robust fellow, with a little gray eye, that
had a peculiarly sly twinkle. "Frederic," also, stretched
his tall raw-boned proportions close by the *bourgeois*, and
"mountain men" completed the group: some lounging in
the boats, some strolling on shore; some attired in gayly-
painted buffalo robes, like Indian dandies; some with hair
saturated with red paint, and plastered with glue to their
temples; and one bedaubed with vermilion upon the forehead and each cheek. They were a mongrel race; yet the
French blood seemed to predominate: in a few, indeed,
might be seen the black snaky eye of the Indian half-breed,
and, one and all, they seemed to aim at assimilating themselves to their red associates.

I shook hands with the *bourgeois*, and delivered the letter;
then the boats swung round into the stream and floated
away. They had reason for haste, for already the voyage
from Fort Laramie had occupied a full month, and the river
was growing daily more shallow. Fifty times a day the
boats had been aground; indeed, those who navigate the
Platte invariably spend half their time upon sand-bars. Two
of these boats, the property of private traders, afterwards
separating from the rest, got hopelessly involved in the
shallows, not very far from the Pawnee villages, and were
soon surrounded by a swarm of the inhabitants. They carried
off everything that they thought valuable, including most of
the robes; and amused themselves by tying up the men left
on guard, and soundly whipping them with sticks.

We encamped that night upon the bank of the river.
Among the emigrants was an overgrown boy, some eighteen
years old, with a head as round and about as large as a
pumpkin, and fever-and-ague fits had dyed his face of a
corresponding color. He wore an old white hat, tied under
his chin with a handkerchief; his body was short and stout,
but his legs were of disproportioned and appalling length.

I observed him at sunset, breasting the hill with gigantic strides, and standing against the sky on the summit, like a colossal pair of tongs. In a moment after we heard him screaming frantically behind the ridge, and nothing doubt-
5 ing that he was in the clutches of Indians or grizzly bears, some of the party caught up their rifles and ran to the res-cue. His outcries, however, were but an ebullition of joyous excitement; he had chased two wolf pups to their burrow, and was on his knees, grubbing away like a dog at the mouth
10 of the hole, to get at them.

Before morning he caused more serious disquiet in the camp. It was his turn to hold the middle-guard; but no sooner was he called up than he coolly arranged a pair of saddle-bags under a wagon, laid his head upon them, closed
15 his eyes, opened his mouth, and fell asleep. The guard on our side of the camp, thinking it no part of his duty to look after the cattle of the emigrants, contented himself with watching our own horses and mules; the wolves, he said, were unusually noisy; but still no mischief was anticipated
20 until the sun rose, when not a hoof or horn was in sight. The cattle were gone. While Tom was quietly slumbering, the wolves had driven them away.

Then we reaped the fruits of R——'s precious plan of travelling in company with emigrants. To leave them in
25 their distress was not to be thought of, and we felt bound to wait until the cattle could be searched for, and, if possible, recovered. But the reader may be curious to know what punishment awaited the faithless Tom. By the wholesome law of the prairie, he who falls asleep on guard is condemned
30 to walk all day, leading his horse by the bridle; and we found much fault with our companions for not enforcing such a sentence on the offender. Nevertheless, had he been of our own party, I have no doubt that he would in like manner have escaped scot-free. But the emigrants went farther than mere forbearance: they decreed that since Tom

could n't stand guard without falling asleep, he should n't stand guard at all, and henceforward his slumbers were unbroken. Establishing such a premium on drowsiness could have no very beneficial effect upon the vigilance of our sentinels; for it is far from agreeable, after riding from sunrise to sunset, to feel your slumbers interrupted by the butt of a rifle nudging your side, and a sleepy voice growling in your ear that you must get up, to shiver and freeze for three weary hours at midnight.

"Buffalo! buffalo!" It was but a grim old bull, roaming the prairie by himself in misanthropic seclusion; but there might be more behind the hills. Dreading the monotony and languor of the camp, Shaw and I saddled our horses, buckled our holsters in their places, and set out with Henry Chatillon in search of the game. Henry, not intending to take part in the chase, but merely conducting us, carried his rifle with him, while we left ours behind as encumbrances. We rode for some five or six miles, and saw no living thing but wolves, snakes, and prairie-dogs.

"This won't do at all," said Shaw.

"What won't do?"

"There's no wood about here to make a litter for the wounded man: I have an idea that one of us will need something of the sort before the day is over."

There was some foundation for such an idea, for the ground was none of the best for a race, and grew worse continually as we proceeded; indeed, it soon became desperately bad, consisting of abrupt hills and deep hollows, cut by frequent ravines not easy to pass. At length, a mile in advance, we saw a band of bulls. Some were scattered grazing over a green declivity, while the rest were crowded together in the wide hollow below. Making a circuit, to keep out of sight, we rode towards them, until we ascended a hill, within a furlong of them, beyond which nothing intervened that could possibly screen us from their view. We

dismounted behind the ridge, just out of sight, drew our
saddle-girths, examined our pistols, and mounting again,
rode over the hill, and descended at a canter towards them,
bending close to our horses' necks. Instantly they took the
5 alarm: those on the hill descended, those below gathered
into a mass, and the whole got into motion, shouldering each
other along at a clumsy gallop. We followed, spurring our
horses to full speed; and as the herd rushed, crowding
and trampling in terror through an opening in the hills, we
10 were close at their heels, half suffocated by the clouds of
dust. But as we drew near, their alarm and speed increased;
our horses, being new to the work, showed signs of the utmost fear, bounding violently aside as we approached, and
refusing to enter among the herd. The buffalo now broke
15 into several small bodies, scampering over the hills in different directions, and I lost sight of Shaw; neither of us
knew where the other had gone. Old Pontiac ran like a
frantic elephant up hill and down hill, his ponderous hoofs
striking the prairie like sledge-hammers. He showed a
20 curious mixture of eagerness and terror, straining to overtake the panic-stricken herd, but constantly recoiling in dis-
may as we drew near. The fugitives, indeed, offered no very
attractive spectacle, with their shaggy manes and the tattered remnants of their last winter's hair covering their
25 backs in irregular shreds and patches, and flying off in the
wind as they ran. At length I urged my horse close behind
a bull, and after trying in vain, by blows and spurring, to
bring him alongside, I fired from this disadvantageous position. At the report Pontiac swerved so much that I was
30 again thrown a little behind the game. The bullet, entering
too much in the rear, failed to disable the bull; for a buffalo
requires to be shot at particular points, or he will certainly
escape. The herd ran up a hill, and I followed in pursuit.
As Pontiac rushed headlong down on the other side, I saw
Shaw and Henry descending the hollow on the right, at a

leisurely gallop; and in front, the buffalo were just disappearing behind the crest of the next hill, their short tails erect, and their hoofs twinkling through a cloud of dust.

At that moment I heard Shaw and Henry shouting to me; but the muscles of a stronger arm than mine could not have checked at once the furious course of Pontiac, whose mouth was as insensible as leather. Added to this, I rode him that morning with a snaffle, having the day before, for the benefit of my other horse, unbuckled from my bridle the curb which I commonly used. A stronger and hardier brute never trod the prairie; but the novel sight of the buffalo filled him with terror, and when at full speed he was almost incontrollable. Gaining the top of the ridge, I saw nothing of the buffalo; they had all vanished amid the intricacies of the hills and hollows. Reloading my pistols, in the best way I could, I galloped on until I saw them again scuttling along at the base of the hill, their panic somewhat abated. Down went old Pontiac among them, scattering them to the right and left; and then we had another long chase. About a dozen bulls were before us, scouring over the hills, rushing down the declivities with tremendous weight and impetuosity, and then laboring with a weary gallop upward. Still Pontiac, in spite of spurring and beating, would not close with them. One bull at length fell a little behind the rest, and by dint of much effort, I urged my horse within six or eight yards of his side. His back was darkened with sweat: he was panting heavily, while his tongue lolled out a foot from his jaws. Gradually I came up abreast of him, urging Pontiac with leg and rein nearer to his side, when suddenly he did what buffalo in such circumstances will always do: he slackened his gallop, and turning towards us, with an aspect of mingled rage and distress, lowered his huge, shaggy head for a charge. Pontiac, with a snort, leaped aside in terror, nearly throwing me to the ground, as I was wholly unprepared for such an evolution. I raised my pistol in a

passion to strike him on the head, but thinking better of it,
fired the bullet after the bull, who had resumed his flight;
then drew rein, and determined to rejoin my companions. It
was high time. The breath blew hard from Pontiac's nos-
5 trils, and the sweat rolled in big drops down his sides; I
myself felt as if drenched in warm water. Pledging myself
to take my revenge at a future opportunity, I looked about
for some indications to show me where I was, and what
course I ought to pursue; I might as well have looked for
10 landmarks in the midst of the ocean. How many miles I
had run, or in what direction, I had no idea; and around
me the prairie was rolling in steep swells and pitches, without a single distinctive feature to guide me. I had a little
compass hung at my neck; and, ignorant that the Platte at
15 this point diverged considerably from its easterly course, I
thought that by keeping to the northward I should certainly
reach it. So I turned and rode about two hours in that
direction. The prairie changed as I advanced, softening
away into easier undulations, but nothing like the Platte ap-
20 peared, nor any sign of a human being: the same wild endless expanse lay around me still; and to all appearance I
was as far from my object as ever. I began now to think
myself in danger of being lost, and, reining in my horse,
summoned the scanty share of woodcraft that I possessed
25 (if that term is applicable upon the prairie) to extricate me.
It occurred to me that the buffalo might prove my best
guides. I soon found one of the paths made by them in their
passage to the river: it ran nearly at right angles to my
course; but turning my horse's head in the direction it
30 indicated, his freer gait and erected ears assured me that I
was right.

But in the mean time my ride had been by no means a
solitary one. The face of the country was dotted far and
wide with countless hundreds of buffalo. They trooped
along in files and columns, bulls, cows, and calves, on the

green faces of the declivities in front. They scrambled away
over the hills to the right and left; and far off, the pale
blue swells in the extreme distance were dotted with innumerable specks. Sometimes I surprised shaggy old bulls grazing alone, or sleeping behind the ridges I ascended. They
would leap up at my approach, stare stupidly at me through
their tangled manes, and then gallop heavily away. The
antelope were very numerous; and as they are always bold
when in the neighborhood of buffalo, they would approach
to look at me, gaze intently with their great round eyes, then
suddenly leap aside, and stretch lightly away over the
prairie, as swiftly as a race-horse. Squalid, ruffian-like
wolves sneaked through the hollows and sandy ravines. Several times I passed through villages of prairie-dogs, who sat,
each at the mouth of his burrow, holding his paws before
him in a supplicating attitude, and yelping away most vehemently, whisking his little tail with every squeaking cry
he uttered. Prairie-dogs are not fastidious in their choice of
companions; various long checkered snakes were sunning
themselves in the midst of the village, and demure little gray
owls, with a large white ring around each eye, were perched
side by side with the rightful inhabitants. The prairie
teemed with life. Again and again I looked toward the
crowded hillsides, and was sure I saw horsemen; and riding
near, with a mixture of hope and dread, for Indians were
abroad, I found them transformed into a group of buffalo.
There was nothing in human shape amid all this vast congregation of brute forms.

When I turned down the buffalo path, the prairie seemed
changed; only a wolf or two glided by at intervals, like
conscious felons, never looking to the right or left. Being
now free from anxiety, I was at leisure to observe minutely
the objects around me; and here, for the first time, I noticed
insects wholly different from any of the varieties found
farther to the eastward. Gaudy butterflies fluttered about

my horse's head; strangely formed beetles, glittering with
metallic lustre, were crawling upon plants that I had never
seen before; multitudes of lizards, too, were darting like
lightning over the sand.

5   I had run to a great distance from the river. It cost me
a long ride on the buffalo path, before I saw, from the ridge
of a sand-hill, the pale surface of the Platte glistening in the
midst of its desert valley, and the faint outline of the hills
beyond waving along the sky. From where I stood, not a
10 tree nor a bush nor a living thing was visible throughout the
whole extent of the sun-scorched landscape. In half an hour
I came upon the trail, not far from the river; and seeing
that the party had not yet passed, I turned eastward to meet
them, old Pontiac's long swinging trot again assuring me
15 that I was right in doing so. Having been slightly ill on
leaving camp in the morning, six or seven hours of rough
riding had fatigued me extremely. I soon stopped, therefore,
flung my saddle on the ground, and with my head resting
on it, and my horse's trail-rope tied loosely to my arm, lay
20 waiting the arrival of the party, speculating meanwhile on
the extent of the injuries Pontiac had received. At length
the white wagon coverings rose from the verge of the plain.
By a singular coincidence, almost at the same moment two
horsemen appeared coming down from the hills. They were
25 Shaw and Henry, who had searched for me awhile in the
morning, but well knowing the futility of the attempt in
such a broken country, had placed themselves on the top of
the highest hill they could find, and picketing their horses
near them, as a signal to me, had lain down and fallen asleep.
30 The stray cattle had been recovered, as the emigrants told
us, about noon. Before sunset, we pushed forward eight
miles farther.

JUNE 7, 1846. — Four men are missing: R——, Sorel, and two
emigrants. They set out this morning after buffalo, and have not
yet made their appearance; whether killed or lost, we cannot tell.

I find the above in my note-book, and well remember the council held on the occasion. Our fire was the scene of it; for the superiority of Henry Chatillon's experience and skill made him the resort of the whole camp upon every question of difficulty. He was moulding bullets at the fire, when the captain drew near, with a perturbed and careworn expression of countenance, faithfully reflected on the heavy features of Jack, who followed close behind. Then the emigrants came straggling from their wagons towards the common centre. Various suggestions were made, to account for the absence of the four men, and one or two of the emigrants declared that, when out after the cattle, they had seen Indians dogging them, and crawling like wolves along the ridges of the hills. At this the captain slowly shook his head with double gravity, and solemnly remarked,—

"It's a serious thing to be travelling through this cursed wilderness;" an opinion in which Jack immediately expressed a thorough coincidence. Henry would not commit himself by declaring any positive opinion.

"Maybe he only followed the buffalo too far; maybe Indian kill him; maybe he got lost; I cannot tell."

With this the auditors were obliged to rest content; the emigrants, not in the least alarmed, though curious to know what had become of their comrades, walked back to their wagons, and the captain betook himself pensively to his tent. Shaw and I followed his example.

CHAPTER VIII

TAKING FRENCH LEAVE

On the eighth of June, at eleven o'clock, we reached the South Fork of the Platte, at the usual fording-place. For league upon league the desert uniformity of the prospect was almost unbroken; the hills were dotted with little tufts of shrivelled grass, but betwixt these the white sand was glaring in the sun; and the channel of the river, almost on a level with the plain, was but one great sand-bed, about half a mile wide. It was covered with water, but so scantily that the bottom was scarcely hidden; for, wide as it is, the average depth of the Platte does not at this point exceed a foot and a half. Stopping near its bank, we gathered *bois de vache*, and made a meal of buffalo-meat. Far off, on the other side, was a green meadow, where we could see the white tents and wagons of an emigrant camp; and just opposite to us we could discern a group of men and animals at the water's edge. Four or five horsemen soon entered the river, and in ten minutes had waded across and clambered up the loose sand-bank. They were ill-looking fellows, thin and swarthy, with careworn anxious faces, and lips rigidly compressed. They had good cause for anxiety; it was three days since they first encamped here, and on the night of their arrival they had lost a hundred and twenty-three of their best cattle, driven off by the wolves, through the neglect of the man on guard. This discouraging and alarming calamity was not the first that had overtaken them. Since leaving the settlements they had met with nothing but misfortune. Some of their party had died; one man had been killed by the Pawnees; and about a week before they had

74

been plundered by the Dahcotahs of all their best horses, the wretched animals on which our visitors were mounted being the only ones that were left. They had encamped, they told us, near sunset, by the side of the Platte, and their oxen were scattered over the meadow, while the horses were feed-ing a little farther off. Suddenly the ridges of the hills were alive with a swarm of mounted Indians, at least six hundred in number, who came pouring with a yell down towards the camp, rushing up within a few rods, to the great terror of the emigrants; when, suddenly wheeling, they swept around the band of horses, and in five minutes disappeared with their prey through the openings of the hills.

As these emigrants were telling their story, we saw four other men approaching. They proved to be R—— and his companions, who had encountered no mischance of any kind, but had only wandered too far in pursuit of the game. They said they had seen no Indians, but only "millions of buf-falo"; and both R—— and Sorel had meat dangling behind their saddles.

The emigrants recrossed the river, and we prepared to follow. First the heavy ox-wagons plunged down the bank, and dragged slowly over the sand-beds; sometimes the hoofs of the oxen were scarcely wet by the thin sheet of water; and the next moment the river would be boiling against their sides, and eddying around the wheels. Inch by inch they receded from the shore, dwindling every moment, until at length they seemed to be floating far out in the middle of the river. A more critical experiment awaited us; for our little mule-cart was ill fitted for the passage of so swift a stream. We watched it with anxiety, till it seemed a motionless white speck in the midst of the waters; and it was motionless, for it had stuck fast in a quicksand. The mules were losing their footing, the wheels were sinking deeper and deeper, and the water began to rise through the bottom and drench the goods within. All of us who had remained on the hither bank galloped to the rescue; the men jumped into the water, adding their strength to that of the mules, until by much effort the cart was extricated, and conveyed in safety across.

5   As we gained the other bank, a rough group of men surrounded us. They were not robust, nor large of frame, yet they had an aspect of hardy endurance. Finding at home no scope for their energies, they had betaken themselves to the prairie: and in them seemed to be revived, with re-

10 doubled force, that fierce spirit which impelled their ancestors, scarcely more lawless than themselves, from the German forests, to inundate Europe, and overwhelm the Roman empire. A fortnight afterwards this unfortunate party passed Fort Laramie, while we were there. Not one of their miss-

15 ing oxen had been recovered, though they had remained encamped a week in search of them; and they had been compelled to abandon a great part of their baggage and provisions, and yoke cows and heifers to their wagons to carry them forward upon their journey, the most toilsome

20 and hazardous part of which lay still before them.

    It is worth noticing that on the Platte one may sometimes see the shattered wrecks of ancient claw-footed tables, well waxed and rubbed, or massive bureaus of carved oak. These, some of them no doubt the relics of ancestral prosperity in

25 the colonial time, must have encountered strange vicissitudes. Brought, perhaps, originally from England; then, with the declining fortunes of their owners, borne across the Alleghanies to the wilderness of Ohio or Kentucky; then to Illinois or Missouri; and now at last fondly stowed away

30 in the family wagon for the interminable journey to Oregon. But the stern privations of the way are little anticipated. The cherished relic is soon flung out to scorch and crack upon the hot prairie.

    We resumed our journey; but we had gone scarcely a mile when R—— called out from the rear, —

" We 'll 'camp here."

" Why do you want to 'camp? Look at the sun. It is not three o'clock yet."

" We 'll 'camp here ! "

This was the only reply vouchsafed. Deslauriers was in advance with his cart. Seeing the mule-wagon wheeling from the track, he began to turn his own team in the same direction.

" Go on, Deslauriers ; " and the little cart advanced again. As we rode on, we soon heard the wagon of our confederates creaking and jolting behind us, and the driver, Wright, discharging a furious volley of oaths against his mules ; no doubt venting upon them the wrath which he dared not direct against a more appropriate object.

Something of this sort had frequently occurred. Our English companion was by no means partial to us, and we thought we discovered in his conduct an intention to thwart and annoy us, especially by retarding the movements of the party, which he knew that we were anxious to quicken. Therefore he would insist on encamping at all unseasonable hours, saying that fifteen miles was a sufficient day's journey. Finding our wishes disregarded, we took the direction of affairs into our own hands. Keeping always in advance, to the inexpressible indignation of R——, we encamped at what time and place we thought proper, not much caring whether the rest chose to follow or not. They always did so, however, pitching their tent near ours, with sullen and wrathful countenances.

Travelling together on these terms did not suit our tastes, and for some time we had meditated a separation. We resolved to leave camp early in the morning, and push forward as rapidly as possible for Fort Laramie, which we hoped to reach, by hard travelling, in four or five days. The captain soon trotted up between us, and we explained our intentions.

"A very extraordinary proceeding, upon my word!" he remarked. The most prominent impression in his mind evidently was that we were deserting his party, in what he regarded as a very dangerous stage of the journey. We ventured to suggest that we were only four in number, while his party still included sixteen men; and as we were to go forward and they were to follow, a full proportion of the perils he apprehended would fall upon us. But the austerity of the captain's features would not relax. "A very extraordinary proceeding, gentlemen!" and repeating this, he rode off to confer with his principal.

Before sunrise on the next morning our tent was down; we harnessed our best horses to the cart and left the camp. But first we shook hands with our friends the emigrants, who sincerely wished us a safe journey, though some others of the party might easily have been consoled had we encountered an Indian war-party on the way. The captain and his brother were standing on the top of a hill, wrapped in their plaids, like spirits of the mist, keeping an anxious eye on the band of horses below. We waved adieu to them as we rode off the ground. The captain replied with a salutation of the utmost dignity, which Jack tried to imitate, though not with perfect success.

In five minutes we had gained the foot of the hills, but here we came to a stop. Hendrick was in the shafts, and being the incarnation of perverse and brutish obstinacy, he utterly refused to move. Deslauriers lashed and swore till he was tired, but Hendrick stood like a rock, grumbling to himself and looking askance at his enemy, until he saw a favorable opportunity to take his revenge, when he struck out under the shaft with such cool malignity of intention that Deslauriers only escaped the blow by a sudden skip into the air, such as no one but a Frenchman could achieve. Shaw and he then joined forces, and lashed on both sides at once. The brute stood still for a while, till he could bear it no longer, when he began to kick and plunge till he threatened the utter demolition of the cart and harness. We glanced back at the camp, which was in full sight. Our companions, inspired by emulation, were levelling their tents and driving in their cattle and horses.

"Take the horse out," said I.

I took the saddle from Pontiac and put it upon Hendrick; the former was harnessed to the cart in an instant. "*Avance donc!*" cried Deslauriers. Pontiac strode up the hill, twitching the little cart after him as if it were a feather's weight; and though, as we gained the top, we saw the wagons of our deserted comrades just getting into motion, we had little fear that they could overtake us.

Leaving the trail, we struck directly across the country, and took the shortest cut to reach the main stream of the Platte. A deep ravine suddenly intercepted us. We skirted its sides until we found them less abrupt, and then plunged through in the best way we could. Passing behind the sandy ravines called "Ash Hollow," we stopped for a short nooning at the side of a pool of rain-water; but soon resumed our journey, and some hours before sunset descended the ravines and gorges opening downward upon the Platte west of Ash Hollow. Our horses waded to the fetlock in sand; the sun scorched like fire, and the air swarmed with sand-flies and mosquitoes.

At last we gained the Platte. Following it for about five miles, we saw, just as the sun was sinking, a great meadow, dotted with hundreds of cattle, and beyond them an encampment of emigrants. A party of them came out to meet us, looking upon us at first with cold and suspicious faces. Seeing four men, different in appearance and equipment from themselves, emerging from the hills, they had taken us for the van of the much-dreaded Mormons, whom they were very apprehensive of encountering. We made known our true character, and then they greeted us cordially. They

expressed much surprise that so small a party should venture to traverse that region, though in fact such attempts
are often made by trappers and Indian traders. We rode
with them to their camp. The wagons, some fifty in number,
5 with here and there a tent intervening, were arranged as
usual in a circle; the best horses were picketed in the area
within, and the whole circumference was glowing with the
dusky light of fires, displaying the forms of the women and
children who were crowded around them. This patriarchal
10 scene was curious and striking enough; but we made our
escape from the place with all possible despatch, being tormented by the intrusive questioning of the men who thronged
about us. Yankee curiosity was nothing to theirs. They
demanded our names, whence we came, whither we were
15 going, and what was our business. The last query was particularly embarrassing; since travelling in that country, or
indeed anywhere, from any other motive than gain, was an
idea of which they took no cognizance. Yet they were fine-
looking fellows, with an air of frankness, generosity, and
20 even courtesy, having come from one of the least barbarous
of the frontier counties.

We passed about a mile beyond them, and encamped.
Being too few in number to stand guard without excessive
fatigue, we extinguished our fire, lest it should attract the
25 notice of wandering Indians; and, picketing our horses close
around us, slept undisturbed till morning. For three days
we travelled without interruption, and on the evening of the
third encamped by the well-known spring on Scott's Bluff.

Henry Chatillon and I rode out in the morning, and, de-
30 scending the western side of the Bluff, were crossing the
plain beyond. Something that seemed to me a file of buffalo
came into view, descending the hills several miles before us.
But Henry reined in his horse, and, peering across the
prairie with a better and more practised eye, soon discovered
its real nature. "Indians!" he said. "Old Smoke's lodges,

I b'lieve. Come; let us go! Wah! get up, now, 'Five Hundred Dollar.'" And laying on the lash with good will, he
galloped forward, and I rode by his side. Not long after, a
black speck became visible on the prairie, full two miles off.
It grew larger and larger; it assumed the form of a man 5
and horse; and soon we could discern a naked Indian,
careering at full gallop towards us. When within a furlong
he wheeled his horse in a wide circle, and made him describe
various mystic figures upon the prairie; Henry immediately
compelled "Five Hundred Dollar" to execute similar evo- 10
lutions. "It *is* Old Smoke's village," said he, interpreting
these signals; "did n't I say so?"

As the Indian approached we stopped to wait for him,
when suddenly he vanished, sinking, as it were, into the
earth. He had come upon one of the deep ravines that every- 15
where intersect these prairies. In an instant the rough head
of his horse stretched upward from the edge, and the rider
and steed came scrambling out, and bounded up to us; a
sudden jerk of the rein brought the wild panting horse to a
full stop. Then followed the needful formality of shaking 20
hands. I forget our visitor's name. He was a young fellow,
of no note in his nation; yet in his person and equipments
he was a good specimen of a Dahcotah warrior in his ordinary travelling dress. Like most of his people, he was
nearly six feet high; lithely and gracefully, yet strongly 25
proportioned; and with a skin singularly clear and delicate.
He wore no paint; his head was bare; and his long hair
was gathered in a clump behind, to the top of which was attached transversely, both by way of ornament and of talis-
man, the mystic whistle, made of the wingbone of the war- 30
eagle, and endowed with various magic virtues. From the
back of his head descended a line of glittering brass plates,
tapering from the size of a doubloon to that of a half-dime,
a cumbrous ornament, in high vogue among the Dahcotahs,
and for which they pay the traders a most extravagant price;

his chest and arms were naked, the buffalo-robe, worn over
them when at rest, had fallen about his waist, and was confined there by a belt. This, with the gay moccasons on his
feet, completed his attire. For arms he carried a quiver of
5 dogskin at his back, and a rude but powerful bow in his hand.
His horse had no bridle; a cord of hair, lashed around his
jaw, served in place of one. The saddle was made of wood
covered with raw hide, and both pommel and cantle rose
perpendicularly full eighteen inches, so that the warrior was
10 wedged firmly in his seat, whence nothing could dislodge
him but the bursting of the girths.

Advancing with our new companion, we found more of
his people, seated in a circle on the top of a hill; while a
rude procession came straggling down the neighboring hol-
15 low, men, women, and children, with horses dragging the
lodge-poles behind them. All that morning, as we moved
forward, tall savages were stalking silently about us. At
noon we reached Horse Creek. The main body of the Indians had arrived before us. On the farther bank stood a
20 large and strong man, nearly naked, holding a white horse
by a long cord, and eying us as we approached. This was the
chief, whom Henry called "Old Smoke." Just behind him,
his youngest and favorite squaw sat astride a fine mule,
covered with caparisons of whitened skins, garnished with
25 blue and white beads, and fringed with little ornaments of
metal that tinkled with every movement of the animal. The
girl had a light clear complexion, enlivened by a spot of
vermilion on each cheek; she smiled, not to say grinned,
upon us, showing two gleaming rows of white teeth. In her
30 hand she carried the tall lance of her unchivalrous lord,
fluttering with feathers; his round white shield hung at the
side of her mule; and his pipe was slung at her back. Her
dress was a tunic of deer-skin, made beautifully white by
means of a species of clay found on the prairie, ornamented
with beads, arranged in figures more gay than tasteful, and

with long fringes at all the seams. Not far from the chief stood a group of stately figures, their white buffalo-robes thrown over their shoulders, gazing coldly upon us; and in the rear, for several acres, the ground was covered with a temporary encampment. Warriors, women, and children swarmed like bees; hundreds of dogs, of all sizes and colors, ran restlessly about; and, close at hand, the wide shallow stream was alive with boys, girls, and young squaws, splashing, screaming, and laughing in the water. At the same time a long train of emigrants with their heavy wagons was crossing the creek, and dragging on in slow procession by the encampment of the people whom they and their descendants, in the space of a century, are to sweep from the face of the earth.

The encampment itself was merely a temporary one during the heat of the day. None of the lodges were pitched; but their heavy leather coverings, and the long poles used to support them, were scattered everywhere, among weapons, domestic utensils, and the rude harness of mules and horses. The squaws of each lazy warrior had made him a shelter from the sun, by stretching a few buffalo-robes, or the corner of a lodge-covering, upon poles; and here he sat in the shade, with a favorite young squaw, perhaps, at his side, glittering with all imaginable trinkets. Before him stood the insignia of his rank as a warrior, his white shield of bull-hide, his medicine-bag, his bow and quiver, his lance and his pipe, raised aloft on a tripod of poles. Except the dogs, the most active and noisy tenants of the camp were the old women, ugly as Macbeth's witches, with hair streaming loose in the wind, and nothing but the tattered fragment of an old buffalo-robe to hide their shrivelled limbs. The day of their favoritism passed two generations ago; now the heaviest labors of the camp devolved upon them; they must harness the horses, pitch the lodges, dress the buffalo-robes, and bring in meat for the hunters. With the cracked voices of these hags, the clamor of dogs, the shouting and laughing

of children and girls, and the listless tranquillity of the warriors, the whole scene had an effect too lively and picturesque to be forgotten.

We stopped not far from the Indian camp, and having
5 invited some of the chiefs and warriors to dinner, placed
before them a repast of biscuit and coffee. Squatted in a
half-circle on the ground, they soon disposed of it. As we
rode forward on the afternoon journey, several of our late
guests accompanied us. Among the rest was a bloated savage,
10 of more than three hundred pounds' weight, christened *Le
Cochon*, in consideration of his preposterous dimensions, and
certain corresponding traits of his character. "The Hog"
bestrode a little white pony, scarcely able to bear up under
the enormous burden, though, by way of keeping up the
15 necessary stimulus, the rider kept both feet in constant
motion, playing alternately against his ribs. The old man
was not a chief; he never had ambition enough to become
one; he was not a warrior nor a hunter, for he was too fat
and lazy; but he was the richest man in the village. Riches
20 among the Dahcotahs consist in horses, and of these "The
Hog" had accumulated more than thirty. He had already
ten times as many as he wanted, yet still his appetite for
horses was insatiable. Trotting up to me, he shook me by
the hand, and gave me to understand that he was my de-
25 voted friend; then he began a series of signs and gesticulation, his oily countenance radiant with smiles, and his little
eyes peeping out with a cunning twinkle from between the
masses of flesh that almost obscured them. Knowing nothing
at that time of the sign-language of the Indians, I could
30 only guess at his meaning. So I called on Henry to explain it.

"The Hog," it seems, was anxious to conclude a matri-
monial bargain, and barter one of his daughters for my
horse. These overtures I chose to reject; at which "The
Hog," still laughing with undiminished good humor, gathered
his robe about his shoulders, and rode away.

Where we encamped that night, an arm of the Platte ran between high bluffs; it was turbid and swift as heretofore, but trees were growing on its crumbling banks, and there was a nook of grass between the water and the hill. Just before entering this place, we saw the emigrants encamping 5 two or three miles distant on the right; while the whole Indian rabble were pouring down the neighboring hill in hope of the same sort of entertainment which they had experienced from us. In the savage landscape before our camp, nothing but the rushing of the Platte broke the 10 silence. Through the ragged boughs of the trees, dilapidated and half dead, we saw the sun setting in crimson behind the peaks of the Black Hills; the restless bosom of the river was suffused with red; our white tent was tinged with it, and the sterile bluffs, up to the rocks that crowned 15 them, partook of the same fiery hue. It soon passed away; no light remained but that from our fire, blazing high among the dusky trees and bushes, while we lay around it wrapped in our blankets, smoking and conversing through half the night.

We crossed a sun-scorched plain on the next morning; the 20 line of old cotton-wood trees that fringed the bank of the Platte forming its extreme verge. Nestled close beneath them, we could discern in the distance something like a building. As we came nearer, it assumed form and dimensions, and proved to be a rough structure of logs. It was a 25 little trading fort, belonging to two private traders; and originally intended, like all the forts of the country, to form a hollow square, with rooms for lodging and storage opening upon the area within. Only two sides of it had been completed; the place was now as ill-fitted for the purposes 30 of defence as any of those little log-houses which upon our constantly-shifting frontier have been so often successfully held against overwhelming odds of Indians. Two lodges were pitched close to the fort; the sun beat scorching upon the logs; no living thing was stirring except one old squaw,

who thrust her round head from the opening of the nearest
lodge, and three or four stout young puppies, who were
peeping with looks of eager inquiry from under the covering.
In a moment a door opened, and a little, swarthy, black-
5 eyed Frenchman came out. His dress was rather singular;
his black curling hair was parted in the middle of his head,
and fell below his shoulders; he wore a tight frock of smoked
deer-skin, gayly ornamented with figures worked in dyed por-
cupine-quills. His moccasons and leggins were also gaudily
10 adorned in the same manner; and the latter had in addition
a line of long fringes, reaching down the seams. The small
frame of Richard, for by this name Henry made him known
to us, was in the highest degree athletic and vigorous. There
was no superfluity, and indeed there seldom is among the
15 white men of this country, but every limb was compact and
hard; every sinew had its full tone and elasticity, and the
whole man wore an air of mingled hardihood and buoyancy.

Richard committed our horses to a Navaho slave, a mean-
looking fellow, taken prisoner on the Mexican frontier; and,
20 relieving us of our rifles with ready politeness, led the way
into the principal apartment of his establishment. This was
a room ten feet square. The walls and floor were of black
mud, and the roof of rough timber; there was a huge fire-
place made of four flat rocks, picked up on the prairie. An
25 Indian bow and otter-skin quiver, several gaudy articles of
Rocky Mountain finery, an Indian medicine-bag, and a pipe
and tobacco-pouch, garnished the walls, and rifles rested in
a corner. There was no furniture except a sort of rough
settle, covered with buffalo-robes, upon which lolled a tall
30 half-breed with his hair glued in masses upon each temple,
and saturated with vermilion. Two or three more "mountain men" sat cross-legged on the floor. Their attire was
not unlike that of Richard himself; but the most striking
figure of the group was a naked Indian boy of sixteen, with
a handsome face, and light, active proportions, who sat in

an easy posture in the corner near the door. Not one of his limbs moved the breadth of a hair; his eye was fixed immovably, not on any person present, but, as it appeared, on the projecting corner of the fireplace opposite to him.

On the prairie the custom of smoking with friends is seldom omitted, whether among Indians or whites. The pipe, therefore, was taken from the wall, and its red bowl crammed with the tobacco and *shongsasha*, mixed in suitable proportions. Then it passed round the circle, each man inhaling a few whiffs and handing it to his neighbor. Having spent half an hour here, we took our leave; first inviting our new friends to drink a cup of coffee with us at our camp a mile farther up the river.

By this time we had grown rather shabby; our clothes had burst into rags and tatters; and, what was worse, we had little means of renovation. Fort Laramie was but seven miles before us. Being averse to appearing in such a plight among any society that could boast an approximation to the civilized, we stopped by the river to make our toilet in the best way we could. We hung up small looking-glasses against the trees and shaved, an operation neglected for six weeks; we performed our ablutions in the Platte, though the utility of such a proceeding was questionable, the water looking exactly like a cup of chocolate, and the banks consisting of the softest and richest yellow mud, so that we were obliged, as a preliminary, to build a causeway of branches and twigs. Having also put on radiant moccasons, procured from a squaw of Richard's establishment, and made what other improvements our narrow circumstances allowed, we took our seats on the grass with a feeling of greatly increased respectability, to await the arrival of our guests. They came; the banquet was concluded, and the pipe smoked. Bidding them adieu, we turned our horses' heads towards the fort.

An hour elapsed. The barren hills closed across our front, and we could see no farther; until, having surmounted them,

a rapid stream appeared at the foot of the descent, running
into the Platte; beyond was a green meadow, dotted with
bushes, and in the midst of these, at the point where the two
rivers joined, were the low clay walls of a fort. This was not
5 Fort Laramie, but another post, of less recent date, which
having sunk before its successful competitor, was now deserted and ruinous. A moment after, the hills seeming to
draw apart as we advanced, disclosed Fort Laramie itself, its
high bastions and perpendicular walls of clay crowning an
10 eminence on the left beyond the stream, while behind stretched
a line of arid and desolate ridges, and behind these again,
towering seven thousand feet aloft, rose the grim Black Hills.

We tried to ford Laramie Creek at a point nearly opposite
the fort, but the stream, swollen with rains, was too rapid.
15 We passed up along its bank to find a better crossing-place.
Men gathered on the wall to look at us. "There's Bordeaux!" called Henry, his face brightening as he recognized his acquaintance; "him there with the spy-glass;
and there's old Vaskiss, and Tucker, and May; and, by
20 George! there's Simoneau." This Simoneau was Henry's
fast friend, and the only man in the country who could
rival him in hunting.

We soon found a ford. Henry led the way, the pony approaching the bank with a countenance of cool indifference,
25 bracing his feet and sliding into the stream with the most
unmoved composure. We followed; the water boiled against
our saddles, but our horses bore us easily through. The unfortunate little mules were near going down with the current,
cart and all; and we watched them with some solicitude
30 scrambling over the loose round stones at the bottom, and
bracing stoutly against the stream. All landed safely at
last; we crossed a little plain, descended a hollow, and, riding
up a steep bank, found ourselves before the gateway of Fort
Laramie, under the impending blockhouse erected above it
to defend the entrance.

CHAPTER IX

SCENES AT FORT LARAMIE

Looking back, after the expiration of a year, upon Fort Laramie and its inmates, they seem less like a reality than like some fanciful picture of the olden time; so different was the scene from any which this tamer side of the world can present. Tall Indians, enveloped in their white buffalo-robes, were striding across the area or reclining at full length on the low roofs of the buildings which enclosed it. Numerous squaws, gayly bedizened, sat grouped in front of the rooms they occupied; their mongrel offspring, restless and vociferous, rambled in every direction through the fort; and the trappers, traders, and *engagés* of the establishment were busy at their labor or their amusements.

We were met at the gate, but by no means cordially welcomed. Indeed, we seemed objects of some distrust and suspicion, until Henry Chatillon explained that we were not traders, and we, in confirmation, handed to the *bourgeois* a letter of introduction from his principals. He took it, turned it upside down, and tried hard to read it; but his literary attainments not being adequate to the task, he applied for relief to the clerk, a sleek, smiling Frenchman, named Monthalon. The letter read, Bordeaux (the *bourgeois*) seemed gradually to awaken to a sense of what was expected of him. Though not deficient in hospitable intentions, he was wholly unaccustomed to act as master of ceremonies. Discarding all formalities of reception, he did not honor us with a single word, but walked swiftly across the area, while we followed in some admiration to a railing and a flight of steps opposite the entrance. He signed to us that we had

better fasten our horses to the railing; then he walked up
the steps, tramped along a rude balcony, and, kicking open
a door, displayed a large room, rather more elaborately furnished than a barn. For furniture it had a rough bedstead,
5 but no bed; two chairs, a chest of drawers, a tin pail to hold
water, and a board to cut tobacco upon. A brass crucifix
hung on the wall, and close at hand a recent scalp, with hair
full a yard long, was suspended from a nail. I shall again
have occasion to mention this dismal trophy, its history be-
10 ing connected with that of our subsequent proceedings.

This apartment, the best in Fort Laramie, was that usually
occupied by the legitimate *bourgeois*, Papin, in whose absence
the command devolved upon Bordeaux. The latter, a stout,
bluff little fellow, much inflated by a sense of his new au-
15 thority, began to roar for buffalo-robes. These being brought
and spread upon the floor, formed our beds; much better
ones than we had of late been accustomed to. Our arrangements made, we stepped out to the balcony to take a more
leisurely survey of the long-looked-for haven at which we
20 had arrived at last. Beneath us was the square area surrounded by little rooms, or rather cells, which opened upon
it. These were devoted to various purposes, but served
chiefly for the accommodation of the men employed at the
fort, or of the equally numerous squaws whom they were
25 allowed to maintain in it. Opposite to us rose the blockhouse
above the gateway; it was adorned with the figure of a
horse at full speed, daubed upon the boards with red paint,
and exhibiting a degree of skill which might rival that displayed by the Indians in executing similar designs upon
30 their robes and lodges. A busy scene was enacting in the
area. The wagons of Vaskiss, an old trader, were about to
set out for a remote post in the mountains, and the Canadians were going through their preparations with all possible
bustle, while here and there an Indian stood looking on with
imperturbable gravity.

Fort Laramie is one of the posts established by the "American Fur Company," which wellnigh monopolizes the Indian trade of this region. Here its officials rule with an absolute sway; the arm of the United States has little force; for when we were there, the extreme outposts of her troops were about seven hundred miles to the eastward. The little fort is built of bricks dried in the sun, and externally is of an oblong form, with bastions of clay, in the form of ordinary blockhouses, at two of the corners. The walls are about fifteen feet high, and surmounted by a slender palisade. The roofs of the apartments within, which are built close against the walls, serve the purpose of a banquette. Within, the fort is divided by a partition: on one side is the square area, surrounded by the store-rooms, offices, and apartments of the inmates; on the other is the *corral*, a narrow place, encompassed by the high clay walls, where at night, or in presence of dangerous Indians, the horses and mules of the fort are crowded for safe keeping. The main entrance has two gates, with an arched passage intervening. A little square window, high above the ground, opens laterally from an adjoining chamber into this passage; so that when the inner gate is closed and barred, a person without may still hold communication with those within, through this narrow aperture. This obviates the necessity of admitting suspicious Indians, for purposes of trading, into the body of the fort; for when danger is apprehended, the inner gate is shut fast, and all traffic is carried on by means of the window. This precaution, though necessary at some of the company's posts, is seldom resorted to at Fort Laramie; where, though men are frequently killed in the neighborhood, no apprehensions are felt of any general designs of hostility from the Indians.

We did not long enjoy our new quarters undisturbed. The door was silently pushed open, and two eyeballs and a visage as black as night looked in upon us; then a red arm and shoulder intruded themselves, and a tall Indian, gliding

in, shook us by the hand, grunted his salutation, and sat
down on the floor. Others followed, with faces of the
natural hue, and letting fall their heavy robes from their
shoulders, took their seats, quite at ease, in a semicircle be-
5 fore us. The pipe was now to be lighted and passed
from one to another; and this was the only entertainment
that at present they expected from us. These visitors were
fathers, brothers, or other relatives of the squaws in the
fort, where they were permitted to remain, loitering about
10 in perfect idleness. All those who smoked with us were men
of standing and repute. Two or three others dropped in also;
young fellows who neither by their years nor their exploits
were entitled to rank with the old men and warriors, and
who, abashed in the presence of their superiors, stood aloof,
15 never withdrawing their eyes from us. Their cheeks were
adorned with vermilion, their ears with pendants of shell,
and their necks with beads. Never yet having signalized
themselves as hunters, or performed the honorable exploit
of killing a man, they were held in slight esteem, and were
20 diffident and bashful in proportion. Certain formidable in-
conveniences attended this influx of visitors. They were
bent on inspecting everything in the room; our equipments
and our dress alike underwent their scrutiny; for though
the contrary has been asserted, few beings have more curi-
25 osity than Indians in regard to subjects within their ordinary range of thought. As to other matters, indeed, they
seem utterly indifferent. They will not trouble themselves
to inquire into what they cannot comprehend, but are quite
contented to place their hands over their mouths in token
30 of wonder, and exclaim that it is "great medicine." With
this comprehensive solution, an Indian never is at a loss. He
never launches into speculation and conjecture; his reason
moves in its beaten track. His soul is dormant; and no
exertions of the missionaries, Jesuit or Puritan, of the old
world or of the new, have as yet availed to arouse it.

As we were looking, at sunset, from the wall, upon the desolate plains that surround the fort, we observed a cluster of strange objects, like scaffolds, rising in the distance against the red western sky. They bore aloft some singular-looking burdens; and at their foot glimmered something white, like 5 bones. This was the place of sepulture of some Dahcotah chiefs, whose remains their people are fond of placing in the vicinity of the fort, in the hope that they may thus be protected from violation at the hands of their enemies. Yet it has happened more than once, and quite recently, that 10 war-parties of the Crow Indians, ranging through the country, have thrown the bodies from the scaffolds, and broken them to pieces, amid the yells of the Dahcotah, who remained pent up in the fort, too few to defend the honored relics from insult. The white objects upon the ground were 15 buffalo skulls, arranged in the mystic circle commonly seen at Indian places of sepulture upon the prairie.

We soon discovered, in the twilight, a band of fifty or sixty horses approaching the fort. These were the animals belonging to the establishment; who, having been sent out 20 to feed, under the care of armed guards, in the meadows below, were now being driven into the *corral* for the night. A gate opened into this enclosure: by the side of it stood one of the guards, an old Canadian, with gray bushy eyebrows, and a dragoon-pistol stuck into his belt; while his comrade, 25 mounted on horseback, his rifle laid across the saddle in front, and his long hair blowing before his swarthy face, rode at the rear of the disorderly troop, urging them up the ascent. In a moment the narrow *corral* was thronged with the half-wild horses, kicking, biting, and crowding restlessly together. 30

The discordant jingling of a bell, rung by a Canadian in the area, summoned us to supper. The repast was served on a rough table in one of the lower apartments of the fort, and consisted of cakes of bread and dried buffalo-meat, — an excellent thing for strengthening the teeth. At this meal were seated the *bourgeois* and superior dignitaries of the establishment, among whom Henry Chatillon was worthily included. No sooner was it finished, than the table was spread a second time (the luxury of bread being now, how-ever, omitted), for the benefit of certain hunters and trappers of an inferior standing; while the ordinary Canadian *engagés* were regaled on dried meat in one of their lodging-rooms. By way of illustrating the domestic economy of Fort Laramie, it may not be amiss to introduce in this place a story current among the men when we were there.

There was an old man named Pierre, whose duty it was to bring the meat from the store-room for the men. Old Pierre, in the kindness of his heart, used to select the fattest and the best pieces for his companions. This did not long escape the keen-eyed *bourgeois*, who was greatly disturbed at such improvidence, and cast about for some means to stop it. At last he hit on a plan that exactly suited him. At the side of the meat-room, and separated from it by a clay partition, was another apartment, used for the storage of furs. It had no communication with the fort, except through a square hole in the partition; and of course it was perfectly dark. One evening the *bourgeois*, watching for a moment when no one observed him, dodged into the meat-room, clambered through the hole, and ensconced himself among the furs and buffalo-robes. Soon after, old Pierre came in with his lantern, and, muttering to himself, began to pull over the bales of meat, and select the best pieces, as usual. But suddenly a hollow and sepulchral voice proceeded from the inner room: "Pierre, Pierre! Let that fat meat alone. Take nothing but lean." Pierre dropped his lantern, and bolted out into the fort, screaming, in an agony of terror, that the devil was in the store-room; but tripping on the threshold, he pitched over upon the gravel, and lay senseless, stunned by the fall. The Canadians ran out to the rescue. Some lifted the unlucky Pierre; and others, making

an extempore crucifix of two sticks, were proceeding to attack the devil in his stronghold, when the *bourgeois*, with a
crestfallen countenance, appeared at the door. To add to
his mortification, he was obliged to explain the whole strata-
gem to Pierre, in order to bring him to his senses. 5

We were sitting, on the following morning, in the passage-
way between the gates, conversing with the traders Vaskiss
and May. These two men, together with our sleek friend,
the clerk Monthalon, were, I believe, the only persons then
in the fort who could read and write. May was telling a 10
curious story about the traveller Catlin, when an ugly, diminutive Indian, wretchedly mounted, came up at a gallop,
and rode by us into the fort. On being questioned, he said
that Smoke's village was close at hand. Accordingly only a
few minutes elapsed before the hills beyond the river were 15
covered with a disorderly swarm of savages, on horseback
and on foot. May finished his story; and by that time the
whole array had descended to Laramie Creek, and begun to
cross it in a mass. I walked down to the bank. The stream
is wide, and was then between three and four feet deep, 20
with a very swift current. For several rods the water was
alive with dogs, horses, and Indians. The long poles used
in pitching the lodges are carried by the horses, fastened by
the heavier end, two or three on each side, to a rude sort
of pack-saddle, while the other end drags on the ground. 25
About a foot behind the horse, a kind of large basket or
pannier is suspended between the poles, and firmly lashed
in its place. On the back of the horse are piled various
articles of luggage; the basket also is well filled with domestic utensils, or, quite as often, with a litter of puppies, a 30
brood of small children, or a superannuated old man. Numbers of these curious vehicles, *traineaux*, or, as the Canadians
called them, *travaux*, were now splashing together through
the stream. Among them swam countless dogs, often burdened with miniature *traineaux*; and dashing forward on

horseback through the throng came the warriors, the slender
figure of some lynx-eyed boy clinging fast behind them.
The women sat perched on the pack-saddles, adding not a
little to the load of the already overburdened horses. The
confusion was prodigious. The dogs yelled and howled in
chorus; the puppies in the *traineaux* set up a dismal whine,
as the water invaded their comfortable retreat; the little
black-eyed children, from one year of age upward, clung
fast with both hands to the edge of their basket, and looked
over in alarm at the water rushing so near them, sputtering
and making wry mouths as it splashed against their faces.
Some of the dogs, encumbered by their load, were carried
down by the current, yelping piteously; and the old squaws
would rush into the water, seize their favorites by the neck,
and drag them out. As each horse gained the bank, he
scrambled up as he could. Stray horses and colts came
among the rest, often breaking away at full speed through
the crowd, followed by the old hags, screaming after their
fashion on all occasions of excitement. Buxom young
squaws, blooming in all the charms of vermilion, stood here
and there on the bank, holding aloft their master's lance, as
a signal to collect the scattered portions of his houshold. In
a few moments the crowd melted away; each family, with
its horses and equipage, filing off to the plain at the rear of
the fort; and here, in the space of half an hour, arose sixty
or seventy of their tapering lodges. Their horses were feeding by hundreds over the surrounding prairie, and their
dogs were roaming everywhere. The fort was full of
warriors, and the children were whooping and yelling incessantly under the walls.

These new-comers were scarcely arrived, when Bordeaux
ran across the fort, shouting to his squaw to bring him his
spy-glass. The obedient Marie, the very model of a squaw,
produced the instrument, and Bordeaux hurried with it to
the wall. Pointing it eastward, he exclaimed, with an oath,

that the families were coming. But a few moments elapsed before the heavy caravan of the emigrant wagons could be seen, steadily advancing from the hills. They gained the river, and, without turning or pausing, plunged in, passed through, and slowly ascending the opposing bank, kept directly on their way by the fort and the Indian village, until, gaining a spot a quarter of a mile distant, they wheeled into a circle. For some time our tranquillity was undisturbed. The emigrants were preparing their encampment; but no sooner was this accomplished, than Fort Laramie was taken by storm. A crowd of broad-brimmed hats, thin visages, and staring eyes, appeared suddenly at the gate. Tall, awkward men, in brown homespun; women, with cadaverous faces and long lank figures, came thronging in together, and, as if inspired by the very demon of curiosity, ransacked every nook and corner of the fort. Dismayed at this invasion, we withdrew in all speed to our chamber, vainly hoping that it might prove a sanctuary. The emigrants prosecuted their investigations with untiring vigor. They penetrated the rooms, or rather dens, inhabited by the astonished squaws. Resolved to search every mystery to the bottom, they explored the apartments of the men, and even that of Marie and the *bourgeois*. At last a numerous deputation appeared at our door, but found no encouragement to remain.

Having at length satisfied their curiosity, they next proceeded to business. The men occupied themselves in procuring supplies for their onward journey; either buying them, or giving in exchange superfluous articles of their own.

The emigrants felt a violent prejudice against the French Indians, as they called the trappers and traders. They thought, and with some reason, that these men bore them no goodwill. Many of them were firmly persuaded that the French were instigating the Indians to attack and cut them off. On visiting the encampment we were at once struck with the extraordinary perplexity and indecision that prevailed among them. They seemed like men totally out of their element; bewildered and amazed, like a troop of schoolboys lost in the woods. It was impossible to be long 5 among them without being conscious of the bold spirit with which most of them were animated. But the *forest* is the home of the backwoodsman. On the remote prairie he is totally at a loss. He differs as much from the genuine "mountain-man" as a Canadian *voyageur*, paddling his canoe on 10 the rapids of the Ottawa, differs from an American sailor among the storms of Cape Horn. Still my companion and I were somewhat at a loss to account for this perturbed state of mind. It could not be cowardice: these men were of the same stock with the volunteers of Monterey and Buena 15 Vista. Yet, for the most part, they were the rudest and most ignorant of the frontier population; they knew absolutely nothing of the country and its inhabitants; they had already experienced much misfortune, and apprehended more; they had seen nothing of mankind, and had never 20 put their own resources to the test.

A full share of suspicion fell upon us. Being strangers, we were looked upon as enemies. Having occasion for a supply of lead and a few other necessary articles, we used to go over to the emigrant camps to obtain them. After 25 some hesitation, some dubious glances, and fumbling of the hands in the pockets, the terms would be agreed upon, the price tendered, and the emigrant would go off to bring the article in question. After waiting until our patience gave out, we would go in search of him, and find him 30 seated on the tongue of his wagon.

"Well, stranger," he would observe, as he saw us approach, "I reckon I won't trade."

Some friend of his had followed him from the scene of the bargain, and whispered in his ear that clearly we meant to cheat him, and he had better have nothing to do with us.

This timorous mood of the emigrants was doubly unfortunate, as it exposed them to real danger. Assume, in the presence of Indians, a bold bearing, self-confident yet vigilant, and you will find them tolerably safe neighbors. But your safety depends on the respect and fear you are able to inspire. If you betray timidity or indecision, you convert them from that moment into insidious and dangerous enemies. The Dahcotah saw clearly enough the perturbation of the emigrants, and instantly availed themselves of it. They became extremely insolent and exacting in their demands. It has become an established custom with them to go to the camp of every party, as it arrives in succession at the fort, and demand a feast. Smoke's village had come with this express design, having made several days' journey with no other object than that of enjoying a cup of coffee and two or three biscuit. So the "feast" was demanded, and the emigrants dared not refuse it.

One evening, about sunset, the village was deserted. We met old men, warriors, squaws, and children in gay attire, trooping off to the encampment, with faces of anticipation; and, arriving here, they seated themselves in a semicircle. Smoke occupied the centre, with his warriors on either hand; the young men and boys came next, the squaws and children formed the horns of the crescent. The biscuit and coffee were promptly despatched, the emigrants staring open-mouthed at their savage guests. With each emigrant party that arrived at Fort Laramie this scene was renewed; and every day the Indians grew more rapacious and presumptuous. One evening they broke in pieces, out of mere wantonness, the cups from which they had been feasted; and this so exasperated the emigrants that many of them seized their rifles and could scarcely be restrained from firing on the insolent mob of Indians. Before we left the country this dangerous spirit on the part of the Dahcotah had mounted to a yet higher pitch. They began openly to

threaten the emigrants with destruction, and actually fired
upon one or two parties of them. A military force and
military law are urgently called for in that perilous region;
and unless troops are speedily stationed at Fort Laramie,
or elsewhere in the neighborhood, both emigrants and other
travellers will be exposed to most imminent risks.

The Ogillallah, the Brulé, and the other western bands of
the Dahcotah or Sioux, are thorough savages, unchanged by
any contact with civilization. Not one of them can speak
a European tongue, or has ever visited an American settlement. Until within a year or two, when the emigrants
began to pass through their country on the way to Oregon,
they had seen no whites, except the few employed about
the Fur Company's posts. They thought them a wise people,
inferior only to themselves, living in leather lodges, like
their own, and subsisting on buffalo. But when the swarm
of *Meneaska*, with their oxen and wagons, began to invade
them, their astonishment was unbounded. They could
scarcely believe that the earth contained such a multitude
of white men. Their wonder is now giving way to indignation; and the result, unless vigilantly guarded against,
may be lamentable in the extreme.

But to glance at the interior of a lodge. Shaw and I
used often to visit them. Indeed, we spent most of our
evenings in the Indian village, Shaw's assumption of the
medical character giving us a fair pretext. As a sample of
the rest I will describe one of these visits. The sun had
just set, and the horses were driven into the *corral*. The
Prairie Cock, a noted beau, came in at the gate with a bevy
of young girls, with whom he began a dance in the area,
leading them round and round in a circle, while he jerked
up from his chest a succession of monotonous sounds, to
which they kept time in a rueful chant. Outside the gate
boys and young men were idly frolicking; and close by,
looking grimly upon them, stood a warrior in his robe, with

his face painted jet-black, in token that he had lately taken a Pawnee scalp. Passing these, the tall dark lodges rose between us and the red western sky. We repaired at once to the lodge of Old Smoke himself. It was by no means better than the others; indeed, it was rather shabby; for in this democratic community the chief never assumes superior state. Smoke sat cross-legged on a buffalo-robe, and his grunt of salutation as we entered was unusually cordial, out of respect no doubt to Shaw's medical character. Seated around the lodge were several squaws, and an abundance of children. The complaint of Shaw's patients was, for the most part, a severe inflammation of the eyes, occasioned by exposure to the sun, a species of disorder which he treated with some success. He had brought with him a homœopathic medicine-chest, and was, I presume, the first who introduced that harmless system of treatment among the Ogillallah. No sooner had a robe been spread at the head of the lodge for our accommodation, and we had seated ourselves upon it, than a patient made her appearance: the chief's daughter herself, who, to do her justice, was the best-looking girl in the village. Being on excellent terms with the physician, she placed herself readily under his hands, and submitted with a good grace to his applications, laughing in his face during the whole process, for a squaw hardly knows how to smile. This case despatched, another of a different kind succeeded. A hideous, emaciated old woman sat in the darkest corner of the lodge, rocking to and fro with pain, and hiding her eyes from the light by pressing the palms of both hands against her face. At Smoke's command she came forward, very unwillingly, and exhibited a pair of eyes that had nearly disappeared from excess of inflammation. No sooner had the doctor fastened his grip upon her, than she set up a dismal moaning, and writhed so in his grasp that he lost all patience; but being resolved to carry his point, he succeeded at last in applying his favorite remedies.

"It is strange," he said, when the operation was finished, "that I forgot to bring any Spanish flies with me; we must have something here to answer for a counter-irritant."

So, in the absence of better, he seized upon a red-hot brand from the fire, and clapped it against the temple of the old squaw, who set up an unearthly howl, at which the rest of the family broke into a laugh.

During these medical operations Smoke's eldest squaw entered the lodge, with a mallet in her hand, the stone head of which, precisely like those sometimes ploughed up in the fields of New England, was made fast to the handle by a covering of raw hide. I had observed some time before a litter of well-grown black puppies, comfortably nestled among some buffalo-robes at one side; but this new-comer speedily disturbed their enjoyment; for seizing one of them by the hind paw, she dragged him out, and carrying him to the entrance of the lodge, hammered him on the head till she killed him. Conscious to what this preparation tended, I looked through a hole in the back of the lodge to see the next steps of the process. The squaw, holding the puppy by the legs, was swinging him to and fro through the blaze of a fire, until the hair was singed off. This done, she unsheathed her knife and cut him into small pieces, which she dropped into a kettle to boil. In a few moments a large wooden dish was set before us, filled with this delicate preparation. A dog-feast is the greatest compliment a Dahcotah can offer to his guest; and, knowing that to refuse eating would be an affront, we attacked the little dog, and devoured him before the eyes of his unconscious parent. Smoke in the mean time was preparing his great pipe. It was lighted when we had finished our repast, and we passed it from one to another till the bowl was empty. This done, we took our leave without farther ceremony, knocked at the gate of the fort, and, after making ourselves known, were admitted.

CHAPTER X

THE WAR-PARTIES

The summer of 1846 was a season of warlike excitement among all the western bands of the Dahcotah. In 1845 they encountered great reverses. Many war-parties had been sent out; some of them had been cut off, and others had returned broken and disheartened; so that the whole nation was in mourning. Among the rest, ten warriors had gone to the Snake country, led by the son of a prominent Ogillallah chief, called The Whirlwind. In passing over Laramie Plains they encountered a superior number of their enemies, were surrounded, and killed to a man. Having performed this exploit, the Snakes became alarmed, dreading the resentment of the Dahcotah; and they hastened therefore to signify their wish for peace by sending the scalp of the slain partisan, with a small parcel of tobacco attached, to his tribesmen and relations. They had employed old Vaskiss, the trader, as their messenger, and the scalp was the same that hung in our room at the fort. But The Whirlwind proved inexorable. Though his character hardly corresponds with his name, he is nevertheless an Indian, and hates the Snakes with his whole soul. Long before the scalp arrived, he had made his preparations for revenge. He sent messengers with presents and tobacco to all the Dahcotah within three hundred miles, proposing a grand combination to chastise the Snakes, and naming a place and time of rendezvous. The plan was readily adopted, and at this moment many villages, probably embracing in the whole five or six thousand souls, were slowly creeping over the prairies and tending towards the common centre at "La Bonté's camp," on the Platte. Here their warlike rites were to be celebrated with more than ordinary solemnity, and a thousand warriors, as it was said, were to set out for the enemy's country. The characteristic result of this preparation will appear in 5 the sequel.

I was greatly rejoiced to hear of it. I had come into the country chiefly with a view of observing the Indian character. To accomplish my purpose it was necessary to live in the midst of them, and become, as it were, one of them. I 10 proposed to join a village, and make myself an inmate of one of their lodges; and henceforward this narrative, so far as I am concerned, will be chiefly a record of the progress of this design, and the unexpected impediments that opposed it.

15 We resolved on no account to miss the rendezvous at "La Bonté's camp." Our plan was to leave Deslauriers at the fort, in charge of our equipage and the better part of our horses, while we took with us nothing but our weapons and the worst animals we had. In all probability, jealousies 20 and quarrels would arise among so many hordes of fierce impulsive savages, congregated together under no common head, and many of them strangers from remote prairies and mountains. We were bound in common prudence to be cautious how we excited any feeling of cupidity. This was 25 our plan; but unhappily we were not destined to visit "La Bonté's camp" in this manner, for one morning a young Indian came to the fort and brought us evil tidings. The new-comer was an arrant dandy. His ugly face was painted with vermilion; on his head fluttered the tail of a prairie-30 cock (a large species of pheasant, not found, as I have heard, eastward of the Rocky Mountains); in his ears were hung pendants of shell, and a flaming red blanket was wrapped around him. He carried a dragoon-sword in his hand, solely for display, since the knife, the arrow, and the rifle are the arbiters of every prairie fight; but as no one in this country

goes abroad unarmed, the dandy carried a bow and arrows in an otter-skin quiver at his back. In this guise, and bestriding his yellow horse with an air of extreme dignity, "The Horse," for that was his name, rode in at the gate, turning neither to the right nor the left, but casting glances askance at the groups of squaws who, with their mongrel progeny, were sitting in the sun before their doors. The evil tidings brought by "The Horse" were of the following import: The squaw of Henry Chatillon, a woman with whom he had been connected for years by the strongest ties which in that country exist between the sexes, was dangerously ill. She and her children were in the village of The Whirlwind, at the distance of a few days' journey. Henry was anxious to see the woman before she died, and provide for the safety and support of his children, of whom he was extremely fond. To have refused him this would have been inhumanity. We abandoned our plan of joining Smoke's village and proceeding with it to the rendezvous, and determined to meet The Whirlwind, and go in his company.

I had been slightly ill for several weeks, but on the third night after reaching Fort Laramie a violent pain awoke me, and I found myself attacked by the same disorder that occasioned such heavy losses to the army on the Rio Grande. In a day and a half I was reduced to extreme weakness, so that I could not walk without pain and effort. Having no medical adviser, nor any choice of diet, I resolved to throw myself upon Providence for recovery, using, without regard to the disorder, any portion of strength that might remain to me. So on the twentieth of June we set out from Fort Laramie to meet The Whirlwind's village. Though aided by the high-bowed "mountain-saddle," I could scarcely keep my seat on horseback. Before we left the fort we hired another man, a long-haired Canadian, named Raymond, with a face like an owl's, contrasting oddly enough with

Deslauriers's mercurial countenance. This was not the only
reinforcement to our party. A vagrant Indian trader,
named Reynal, joined us, together with his squaw, Margot,
and her two nephews, our dandy friend, " The Horse," and
5 his younger brother, " The Hail-Storm." Thus accompanied,
we betook ourselves to the prairie, leaving the beaten trail,
and passing over the desolate hills that flank the valley of
Laramie Creek. In all, Indians and whites, we counted
eight men and one woman.

10   Reynal, the trader, the image of sleek and selfish complacency, carried " The Horse's " dragoon-sword in his hand,
delighting apparently in this useless parade; for, from
spending half his life among Indians, he had caught not
only their habits but their ideas. Margot, a female animal of
15 more than two hundred pounds' weight, was couched in the
basket of a *traineau*, such as I have before described; besides her ponderous bulk, various domestic utensils were
attached to the vehicle, and she led by a trail-rope a pack-
horse, which carried the covering of Reynal's lodge. Des-
20 lauriers walked briskly by the side of the cart, and Raymond
came behind, swearing at the spare horses which it was his
business to drive. The restless young Indians, their quivers
at their backs and their bows in their hands, galloped over
the hills, often starting a wolf or an antelope from the
25 thick growth of wild-sage bushes. Shaw and I were in
keeping with the rest of the rude cavalcade, having in the
failure of other clothing adopted the buckskin attire of the
trappers. Henry Chatillon rode in advance of the whole.
Thus we passed hill after hill and hollow after hollow, a
30 country arid, broken and so parched by the sun that none
of the plants familiar to our more favored soil wou l flourish
upon it, though there were multitudes of strange medicinal
herbs, more especially the absinth, which covered every
declivity, while cacti were hanging like reptiles at the edges
of every ravine. At length we ascended a high hill, our

horses treading upon pebbles of flint, agate, and rough jasper, until, gaining the top, we looked down on the wild bottoms of Laramie Creek, which far below us wound like a writhing snake from side to side of the narrow interval, amid a growth of shattered cotton-wood and ash-trees. 5
Lines of tall cliffs, white as chalk, shut in this green strip of woods and meadow-land, into which we descended and encamped for the night. In the morning we passed a wide grassy plain by the river; there was a grove in front, and beneath its shadows the ruins of an old trading fort of logs. 10
The grove bloomed with myriads of wild roses, with their sweet perfume fraught with recollections of home. As we emerged from the trees, a rattlesnake, as large as a man's arm, and more than four feet long, lay coiled on a rock, fiercely rattling and hissing at us; a gray hare, twice as large as 15 those of New England, leaped up from the tall ferns; curlew flew screaming over our heads, and a host of little prairie-dogs sat yelping at us at the mouths of their burrows on the dry plain beyond. Suddenly an antelope leaped up from the wild-sage bushes, gazed eagerly at us, and then, erecting his 20 white tail, stretched away like a greyhound. The two Indian boys found a white wolf, as large as a calf, in a hollow, and, giving a sharp yell, they galloped after him; but the wolf leaped into the stream and swam across. Then came the crack of a rifle, the bullet whistling harmlessly over his 25 head, as he scrambled up the steep declivity, rattling down stones and earth into the water below. Advancing a little, we beheld, on the farther bank of the stream, a spectacle not common even in that region; for, emerging from among the trees, a herd of some two hundred elk came out upon 30 the meadow, their antlers clattering as they walked forward in a dense throng. Seeing us, they broke into a run, rushing across the opening and disappearing among the trees and scattered groves. On our left was a barren prairie, stretching to the horizon; on our right, a deep gulf, with Laramie

Creek at the bottom. We found ourselves at length at the
edge of a steep descent; a narrow valley, with long rank
grass and scattered trees stretching before us for a mile or
more along the course of the stream. Reaching the farther
5 end, we stopped and encamped. A huge old cotton-wood
tree spread its branches horizontally over our tent. Laramie
Creek, circling before our camp, half enclosed us; it swept
along the bottom of a line of tall white cliffs that looked
down on us from the farther bank. There were dense copses
10 on our right; the cliffs, too, were half hidden by bushes,
though behind us a few cotton-wood trees, dotting the green
prairie, alone impeded the view, and friend or enemy could
be discerned in that direction at a mile's distance. Here we
resolved to remain and await the arrival of The Whirlwind,
15 who would certainly pass this way in his progress towards
La Bonté's camp. To go in search of him was not expedient,
both on account of the broken and impracticable nature of
the country, and the uncertainty of his position and movements; besides, our horses were almost worn out, and I was
20 in no condition to travel. We had good grass, good water,
tolerable fish from the stream, and plenty of small game,
such as antelope and deer, though no buffalo. There was
one little drawback to our satisfaction: a certain extensive
tract of bushes and dried grass, just behind us, which it
25 was by no means advisable to enter, since it sheltered a
numerous brood of rattlesnakes. Henry Chatillon again
despatched "The Horse" to the village, with a message to
his squaw that she and her relatives should leave the rest
and push on as rapidly as possible to our camp.
30   Our daily routine soon became as regular as that of a
well-ordered household. The weather-beaten old tree was in
the centre; our rifles generally rested against its vast trunk,
and our saddles were flung on the ground around it; its
distorted roots were so twisted as to form one or two convenient armchairs, where we could sit in the shade and read

or smoke; but meal-times became, on the whole, the most
interesting hours of the day, and a bountiful provision was
made for them. An antelope or a deer usually swung from
a bough, and haunches were suspended against the trunk.
The camp is daguerreotyped on my memory: the old tree, 5
the white tent, with Shaw sleeping in the shadow of it, and
Reynal's miserable lodge close by the bank of the stream.
It was a wretched oven-shaped structure, made of begrimed
and tattered buffalo-hides stretched over a frame of poles;
one side was open, and at the side of the opening hung the 10
powder-horn and bullet-pouch of the owner, together with
his long red pipe, and a rich quiver of otter-skin, with a
bow and arrows; for Reynal, an Indian in most things but
color, chose to hunt buffalo with these primitive weapons.
In the darkness of this cavern-like habitation might be dis- 15
cerned Madame Margot, her overgrown bulk stowed away
among her domestic implements, furs, robes, blankets, and
painted cases of raw hide, in which dried meat is kept.
Here she sat from sunrise to sunset, an impersonation of
gluttony and laziness, while her affectionate proprietor was 20
smoking, or begging petty gifts from us, or telling lies concerning his own achievements, or perchance engaged in the
more profitable occupation of cooking some preparation of
prairie delicacies. Reynal was an adept at this work; he
and Deslauriers have joined forces, and are hard at work 25
together over the fire, while Raymond spreads, by way of
table-cloth, a buffalo-hide carefully whitened with pipe-clay,
on the grass before the tent. Here he arranges the teacups
and plates; and then, creeping on all fours, like a dog,
thrusts his head in at the opening of the tent. For a mo- 30
ment we see his round owlish eyes rolling wildly, as if
the idea he came to communicate had suddenly escaped
him; then collecting his scattered thoughts, as if by an
effort, he informs us that supper is ready, and instantly
withdraws.

When sunset came, and at that hour the wild and desolate
scene would assume a new aspect, the horses were driven
in. They had been grazing all day in the neighboring
meadow, but now they were picketed close about the camp.
5 As the prairie darkened we sat and conversed around the
fire, until, becoming drowsy, we spread our saddles on the
ground, wrapped our blankets around us, and lay down.
We never placed a guard, having by this time become too
indolent; but Henry Chatillon folded his loaded rifle in the
10 same blanket with himself, observing that he always took it
to bed with him when he 'camped in that place. Henry was
too bold a man to use such a precaution without good cause.
We had a hint now and then that our situation was none of
the safest; several Crow war-parties were known to be in
15 the vicinity, and one of them, that passed here some time
before, had peeled the bark from a neighboring tree, and
engraved upon the white wood certain hieroglyphics, to
signify that they had invaded the territories of their enemies,
the Dahcotah, and set them at defiance. One morning a
20 thick mist covered the whole country. Shaw and Henry
went out to ride, and soon came back with a startling piece
of intelligence; they had found within rifle-shot of our
camp the recent trail of about thirty horsemen. They could
not be whites, and they could not be Dahcotah, since we
25 knew no such parties to be in the neighborhood; therefore
they must be Crows. Thanks to that friendly mist, we
had escaped a hard battle; they would inevitably have
attacked us and our Indian companions had they seen our
camp. Whatever doubts we might have entertained, were
30 removed a day or two after, by two or three Dahcotah, who
came to us with an account of having hidden in a ravine on
that very morning, from whence they saw and counted the
Crows; they said that they followed them, carefully keeping out of sight, as they passed up Chugwater; that here
the Crows discovered five dead bodies of Dahcotah, placed,

according to custom, in trees, and flinging them to the ground, held their guns against them and blew them to atoms.

If our camp were not altogether safe, still it was comfortable enough; at least it was so to Shaw, for I was tormented with illness and vexed by the delay in the accomplishment of my designs. When a respite in my disorder gave me some returning strength, I rode out well armed upon the prairie, or bathed with Shaw in the stream, or waged a petty warfare with the inhabitants of a neighboring prairie-dog village. Around our fire at night we employed ourselves in inveighing against the fickleness and inconstancy of Indians, and execrating The Whirlwind and all his crew. At last the thing grew insufferable.

"To-morrow morning," said I, "I will start for the fort, and see if I can hear any news there." Late that evening, when the fire had sunk low, and all the camp were asleep, a loud cry sounded from the darkness. Henry leaped up, recognized the voice, replied to it, and our dandy friend, "The Horse," rode in among us, just returned from his mission to the village. He coolly picketed his mare, without saying a word, sat down by the fire and began to eat, but his imperturbable philosophy was too much for our patience. Where was the village? — about fifty miles south of us; it was moving slowly, and would not arrive in less than a week. And where was Henry's squaw? — coming as fast as she could with Mahto-Tatonka, and the rest of her brothers, but she would never reach us, for she was dying, and asking every moment for Henry. Henry's manly face became clouded and downcast; he said that if we were willing he would go in the morning to find her, at which Shaw offered to accompany him.

We saddled our horses at sunrise. Reynal protested vehemently against being left alone, with nobody but the two Canadians and the young Indians, when enemies were in the neighborhood. Disregarding his complaints, we left him,

and, coming to the mouth of Chugwater, separated, Shaw
and Henry turning to the right, up the bank of the stream,
while I made for the fort.

Taking leave for a while of my friend and the unfortunate squaw, I will relate by way of episode what I saw and
did at Fort Laramie. It was not more than eighteen miles
distant, and I reached it in three hours. A shrivelled little
figure, wrapped from head to foot in a dingy white Canadian
capote, stood in the gateway, holding by a cord of bull-hide
a shaggy wild-horse, which he had lately caught. His sharp
prominent features, and his keen snake-like eyes, looked out
from beneath the shadowy hood of the capote, which was
drawn over his head like the cowl of a Capuchin friar. His
face was like an old piece of leather, and his mouth spread
from ear to ear. Extending his long wiry hand, he welcomed
me with something more cordial than the ordinary cold sa-
lute of an Indian, for we were excellent friends. We had
made an exchange of horses to our mutual advantage; and
Paul, thinking himself well treated, had declared everywhere
that the white man had a good heart. He was a Dahcotah
from the Missouri, a reputed son of the half-breed inter-
preter, Pierre Dorion, so often mentioned in Irving's
"Astoria." He said that he was going to Richard's trading-
house to sell his horse to some emigrants, who were encamped there, and asked me to go with him. We forded the
stream together, Paul dragging his wild charge behind him.
As we passed over the sandy plains beyond, he grew com-
municative. Paul was a cosmopolitan in his way; he had
been to the settlements of the whites, and visited in peace
and war most of the tribes within the range of a thousand
miles. He spoke a jargon of French and another of English,
yet nevertheless he was a thorough Indian; and as he told
of the bloody deeds of his own people against their enemies,
his little eyes would glitter with a fierce lustre. He told
how the Dahcotah exterminated a village of the Hohays on

the Upper Missouri, slaughtering men, women, and children; and how, in overwhelming force, they cut off sixteen of the brave Delawares, who fought like wolves to the last, amid the throng of their enemies. He told me also another story, which I did not believe until I had heard it confirmed from so many independent sources that my scepticism was almost overcome.

Six years ago, a fellow named Jim Beckworth, a mongrel of French, American, and negro blood, was trading for the Fur Company, in a large village of the Crows. Jim Beckworth was last summer at St. Louis. He is a ruffian of the worst stamp; bloody and treacherous, without honor or honesty; such at least is the character he bears upon the prairie. Yet in his case the standard rules of character fail, for though he will stab a man in his sleep, he will also perform most desperate acts of daring; such, for instance, as the following: While he was in the Crow village, a Blackfoot war-party, between thirty and forty in number, came stealing through the country, killing stragglers and carrying off horses. The Crow warriors got upon their trail and pressed them so closely that they could not escape, at which the Blackfeet, throwing up a semi-circular breastwork of logs at the foot of a precipice, coolly awaited their approach. The logs and sticks, piled four or five feet high, protected them in front. The Crows might have swept over the breastwork and exterminated their enemies; but though outnumbering them tenfold, they did not dream of storming the little fortification. Such a proceeding would be altogether repugnant to their notions of warfare. Whooping and yelling, and jumping from side to side like devils incarnate, they showered bullets and arrows upon the logs; not a Blackfoot was hurt, but several Crows, in spite of their leaping and dodging, were shot down. In this childish manner, the fight went on for an hour or two. Now and then a Crow warrior in an ecstasy of valor and vainglory would scream forth his

war-song, boast himself the bravest and greatest of mankind, grasp his hatchet, rush up, strike it upon the breastwork, and then, as he retreated to his companions, fall dead under a shower of arrows; yet no combined attack was made. The
5 Blackfeet remained secure in their intrenchment. At last Jim Beckworth lost patience.

" You are all fools and old women," he said to the Crows; " come with me, if any of you are brave enough, and I will show you how to fight."

10 He threw off his trapper's frock of buckskin and stripped himself naked, like the Indians themselves. He left his rifle on the ground, took in his hand a small light hatchet, and ran over the prairie to the right, concealed by a hollow from the eyes of the Blackfeet. Then climbing up the rocks, he
15 gained the top of the precipice behind them. Forty or fifty young Crow warriors followed him. By the cries and whoops that rose from below he knew that the Blackfeet were just beneath him; and running forward, he leaped down the rock into the midst of them. As he fell he caught one by
20 the long loose hair, and dragging him down, tomahawked him; then grasping another by the belt at his waist, he struck him also a stunning blow, and, gaining his feet, shouted the Crow war-cry. He swung his hatchet so fiercely around him that the astonished Blackfeet bore back and gave
25 him room. He might, had he chosen, have leaped over the breastwork and escaped; but this was not necessary, for with devilish yells the Crow warriors came dropping in quick succession over the rock among their enemies. The main body of the Crows, too, answered the cry from the
30 front, and rushed up simultaneously. The convulsive struggle within the breastwork was frightful; for an instant the Blackfeet fought and yelled like pent-up tigers; but the butchery was soon complete, and the mangled bodies lay piled together under the precipice. Not a Blackfoot made his escape.

As Paul finished his story we came in sight of Richard's Fort, a disorderly crowd of men around it, and an emigrant camp a little in front.

"Now, Paul," said I, "where are your Minnicongew lodges?"

"Not come yet," said Paul; "maybe come to-morrow."

Two large villages of a band of Dahcotah had come three hundred miles from the Missouri, to join in the war, and they were expected to reach Richard's that morning. There was as yet no sign of their approach; so pushing through a noisy, drunken crowd, I entered an apartment of logs and mud, the largest in the fort: it was full of men of various races and complexions, all more or less drunk. A company of California emigrants, it seemed, had made the discovery at this late day that they had encumbered themselves with too many supplies for their journey. A part, therefore, they had thrown away, or sold at great loss to the traders; but had determined to get rid of their very copious stock of Missouri whiskey, by drinking it on the spot. Here were maudlin squaws stretched on piles of buffalo-robes; squalid Mexicans, armed with bows and arrows; Indians sedately drunk; long-haired Canadians and trappers, and American backwoodsmen in brown homespun, the well-beloved pistol and bowie-knife displayed openly at their sides. In the middle of the room a tall, lank man, with a dingy broadcloth coat, was haranguing the company in the style of the stump orator. With one hand he sawed the air, and with the other clutched firmly a brown jug of whiskey, which he applied every moment to his lips, forgetting that he had drained the contents long ago. Richard formally introduced me to this personage, who was no less a man than Colonel R——, once the leader of the party. Instantly the colonel, seizing me, in the absence of buttons, by the leather fringes of my frock, began to define his position. His men, he said, had mutinied and deposed him; but still he exercised over them the

influence of a superior mind; in all but the name he was yet
their chief. As the colonel spoke, I looked round on the wild
assemblage, and could not help thinking that he was but ill
fitted to conduct such men across the deserts to California.
5 Conspicuous among the rest stood three tall young men,
grandsons of Daniel Boone. They had clearly inherited the
adventurous character of that prince of pioneers; but I saw
no signs of the quiet and tranquil spirit that so remarkably
distinguished him.

10   Fearful was the fate that, months after, overtook some of
the members of that party. General Kearney, on his late
return from California, brought back their story. They were
interrupted by the deep snows among the mountains, and,
maddened by cold and hunger, fed upon each other's flesh!

15   I got tired of the confusion. "Come, Paul," said I, "we
will be off." Paul sat in the sun, under the wall of the fort.
He jumped up, mounted, and we rode towards Fort Laramie.
When we reached it, a man came out of the gate with a
pack at his back and a rifle on his shoulder; others were
20 gathering about him, shaking him by the hand, as if taking
leave. I thought it a strange thing that a man should set
out alone and on foot for the prairie. I soon got an explanation. Perrault — this, if I recollect right, was the Canadian's name — had quarrelled with the *bourgeois*, and the
25 fort was too hot to hold him. Bordeaux, inflated with his
transient authority, had abused him, and received a blow in
return. The men then sprang at each other, and grappled in
the middle of the fort. Bordeaux was down in an instant,
at the mercy of the incensed Canadian; had not an old
30 Indian, the brother of his squaw, seized hold of his antagonist it would have fared ill with him. Perrault broke loose
from the old Indian, and both the white men ran to their
rooms for their guns; but when Bordeaux, looking from his
door, saw the Canadian, gun in hand, standing in the area
and calling on him to come out and fight, his heart failed

him; he chose to remain where he was. In vain the old Indian, scandalized by his brother-in-law's cowardice, called upon him to go to the prairie and fight it out in the white man's manner; and Bordeaux's own squaw, equally incensed, screamed to her lord and master that he was a dog and an old woman. It all availed nothing. Bordeaux's prudence got the better of his valor, and he would not stir. Perrault stood showering opprobrious epithets at the recreant *bourgeois*, till, growing tired of this, he made up a pack of dried meat, and, slinging it at his back, set out alone for Fort Pierre, on the Missouri, a distance of three hundred miles, over a desert country, full of hostile Indians.

I remained in the fort that night. In the morning, as I was coming out from breakfast, talking with a trader named McCluskey, I saw a strange Indian leaning against the side of the gate. He was a tall, strong man, with heavy features.

"Who is he?" I asked.

"That's The Whirlwind," said McCluskey. "He is the fellow that made all this stir about the war. It's always the way with the Sioux; they never stop cutting each other's throats; it's all they are fit for; instead of sitting in their lodges, and getting robes to trade with us in the winter. If this war goes on, we'll make a poor trade of it next season, I reckon."

And this was the opinion of all the traders, who were vehemently opposed to the war, from the injury that it must occasion to their interests. The Whirlwind left his village the day before to make a visit to the fort. His warlike ardor had abated not a little since he first conceived the design of avenging his son's death. The long and complicated preparations for the expedition were too much for his fickle disposition. That morning Bordeaux fastened upon him, made him presents, and told him that if he went to war he would destroy his horses and kill no buffalo to trade with the white men; in short, that he was a fool to think of such a thing,

and had better make up his mind to sit quietly in his lodge
and smoke his pipe, like a wise man. The Whirlwind's
purpose was evidently shaken; he had become tired, like a
child, of his favorite plan. Bordeaux exultingly predicted
5 that he would not go to war. My philanthropy was no match
for my curiosity, and I was vexed at the possibility that
after all I might lose the rare opportunity of seeing the ceremonies of war. The Whirlwind, however, had merely thrown
the firebrand; the conflagration was become general. All
10 the western bands of the Dahcotah were bent on war; and,
as I heard from McCluskey, six large villages were already
gathered on a little stream, forty miles distant, and were
daily calling to the Great Spirit to aid them in their enterprise. McCluskey had just left them, and represented them
15 as on their way to La Bonté's camp, which they would
reach in a week, *unless they should learn that there were no
buffalo there.* I did not like this condition, for buffalo this
season were rare in the neighborhood. There were also the
two Minnicongew villages that I mentioned before; but
20 about noon, an Indian came from Richard's Fort with the
news that they were quarrelling, breaking up, and dispersing.
So much for the whiskey of the emigrants! Finding themselves unable to drink the whole, they had sold the residue
to these Indians, and it needed no prophet to foretell the
25 result; a spark dropped into a powder-magazine would not
have produced a quicker effect. Instantly the old jealousies
and rivalries and smothered feuds that exist in an Indian
village broke out into furious quarrels. They forgot the warlike enterprise that had already brought them three hundred
30 miles. They seemed like ungoverned children inflamed
with the fiercest passions of men. Several of them were
stabbed in the drunken tumult; and in the morning they
scattered and moved back towards the Missouri in small
parties. I feared that, after all, the long-projected meeting
and the ceremonies that were to attend it might never take

place, and I should lose so admirable an opportunity of seeing the Indian under his most fearful and characteristic
aspect; however, in foregoing this, I should avoid a very
fair probability of being plundered and stripped, and it
might be, stabbed or shot into the bargain. Consoling myself with this reflection, I prepared to carry the news, such
as it was, to the camp.

I caught my horse, and to my vexation found that he had
lost a shoe and broken his hoof against the rocks. Horses
are shod at Fort Laramie at the moderate rate of three dollars a foot; so I tied Hendrick to a beam in the *corral*, and
summoned Roubidou, the blacksmith. Roubidou, with the
hoof between his knees, was at work with hammer and file,
and I was inspecting the process, when a strange voice addressed me.

"Two more gone under! Well, there's more of us left yet.
Here's Gingras and me off to the mountains to-morrow. Our
turn will come next, I suppose. It's a hard life, anyhow!"

I looked up and saw a man, not much more than five feet
high, but of very square and strong proportions. In appearance he was particularly dingy; for his old buckskin frock
was black and polished with time and grease, and his belt,
knife, pouch, and powder-horn appeared to have seen the
roughest service. The first joint of each foot was entirely
gone, having been frozen off several winters before, and his
moccasons were curtailed in proportion. His whole appearance and equipment bespoke the "free trapper." He had a
round, ruddy face, animated with a spirit of carelessness
and gayety not at all in accordance with the words he had
just spoken.

"'Two more gone,'" said I; "what do you mean by that?"

"Oh, the Arapahoes have just killed two of us in the
mountains. Old Bull-Tail has come to tell us. They stabbed
one behind his back, and shot the other with his own rifle.
That's the way we live here! I mean to give up trapping

after this year. My squaw says she wants a pacing horse and some red ribbons: I'll make enough beaver to get them for her, and then I'm done! I'll go below and live on a farm."

"Your bones will dry on the prairie, Rouleau!" said another trapper, who was standing by; a strong, brutal-looking fellow, with a face as surly as a bull-dog's.

Rouleau only laughed, and began to hum a tune and shuffle a dance on his stumps of feet.

"You'll see us, before long, passing up your way," said the other man.

"Well," said I, "stop and take a cup of coffee with us;" and, as it was late in the afternoon, I prepared to leave the fort at once.

As I rode out, a train of emigrant wagons was passing across the stream. "Whar are ye goin', stranger?" Thus I was saluted by two or three voices at once.

"About eighteen miles up the creek."

"It's mighty late to be going that far! Make haste, ye'd better, and keep a bright look-out for Indians!"

I thought the advice too good to be neglected. Fording the stream, I passed at a round trot over the plains beyond. But "the more haste, the worse speed." I proved the truth of the proverb by the time I reached the hills three miles from the fort. The trail was faintly marked, and, riding forward with more rapidity than caution, I lost sight of it. I kept on in a direct line, guided by Laramie Creek, which I could see at intervals darkly glistening in the evening sun, at the bottom of the woody gulf on my right. Half an hour before sunset I came upon its banks. There was something exciting in the wild solitude of the place. An antelope sprang suddenly from the sage-bushes before me. As he leaped gracefully not thirty yards before my horse, I fired, and instantly he spun round and fell. Quite sure of him, I walked my horse towards him, leisurely reloading my rifle, when, to my surprise, he sprang up and trotted rapidly away on three legs into the dark recesses of the hills, whither I had no time to follow. Ten minutes after, I was passing along the bottom of a deep valley, and, chancing to look behind me, I saw in the dim light that something was following. Supposing it to be a wolf, I slid from my seat and sat down behind my horse to shoot it; but as it came up, I saw by its motions that it was another antelope. It approached within a hundred yards, arched its neck, and gazed intently. I levelled at the white spot on its chest, and was about to fire, when it started off, ran first to one side and then to the other, like a vessel tacking against the wind, and at last stretched away at full speed. Then it stopped again, looked curiously behind it, and trotted up as before; but not so boldly, for it soon paused and stood gazing at me. I fired; it leaped upward and fell upon its tracks. Measuring the distance, I found it two hundred and four paces. When I stood by his side, the antelope turned his expiring eye upward. It was like a beautiful woman's, dark and bright. " Fortunate that I am in a hurry," thought I; " I might be troubled with remorse, if I had time for it."

Cutting the animal up, not in the most skilful manner, I hung the meat at the back of my saddle, and rode on again. The hills (I could not remember one of them) closed around me. " It is too late," thought I, " to go forward. I will stay here to-night, and look for the path in the morning." As a last effort, however, I ascended a high hill, from which, to my great satisfaction, I could see Laramie Creek stretching before me, twisting from side to side amid ragged patches of timber; and far off, close beneath the shadows of the trees, the ruins of the old trading-fort were visible. I reached them at twilight. It was far from pleasant, in that uncertain light, to be pushing through the dense trees and bushes of the grove beyond. I listened anxiously for the footfall of man or beast. Nothing was stirring but one harmless brown bird, chirping among the branches. I was glad when I gained

the open prairie once more, where I could see if anything approached. When I came to the mouth of Chugwater, it was totally dark. Slackening the reins, I let my horse take his own course. He trotted on with unerring instinct, and
5 by nine o'clock was scrambling down the steep descent into the meadows where we were encamped. While I was looking in vain for the light of the fire, Hendrick, with keener perceptions, gave a loud neigh, which was immediately answered by another neigh from the distance. In a moment
10 I was hailed from the darkness by the voice of Reynal, who had come out, rifle in hand, to see who was approaching.

He, with his squaw, the two Canadians, and the Indian boys, were the sole inmates of the camp, Shaw and Henry Chatillon being still absent. At noon of the following day
15 they came back, their horses looking none the better for the journey. Henry seemed dejected. The woman was dead, and his children must henceforward be exposed, without a protector, to the hardships and vicissitudes of Indian life. Even in the midst of his grief he had not forgotten his
20 attachment to his *bourgeois*, for he had procured among his Indian relatives two beautifully ornamented buffalo-robes, which he spread on the ground as a present to us.

Shaw lighted his pipe, and told me in a few words the history of his journey. When I went to the fort they left
25 me, as I mentioned, at the mouth of Chugwater. They followed the course of the little stream all day, traversing a desolate and barren country. Several times they came upon the fresh traces of a large war-party, the same, no doubt, from whom we had so narrowly escaped an attack. At an
30 hour before sunset, without encountering a human being by the way, they came upon the lodges of the squaw and her brothers, who, in compliance with Henry's message, had left the Indian village, in order to join us at our camp. The lodges were already pitched, five in number, by the side of the stream. The woman lay in one of them, reduced to a

mere skeleton. For some time she had been unable to move
or speak. Indeed, nothing had kept her alive but the hope
of seeing Henry, to whom she was strongly and faithfully
attached. No sooner did he enter the lodge than she revived,
and conversed with him the greater part of the night. Early 5
in the morning she was lifted into a *traineau,* and the whole
party set out towards our camp. There were but five warriors ; the rest were women and children. The whole were
in great alarm at the proximity of the Crow war-party, who
would certainly have killed them without mercy had they 10
met. They had advanced only a mile or two, when they discerned a horseman, far off, on the edge of the horizon. They
all stopped, gathering together in the greatest anxiety, from
which they did not recover until long after the horseman
disappeared ; then they set out again. Henry was riding 15
with Shaw a few rods in advance of the Indians, when
Mahto-Tatonka, a younger brother of the woman, hastily
called after them. Turning back, they found all the Indians
crowded around the *traineau* in which the woman was lying.
They reached her just in time to hear the death-rattle in her 20
throat. In a moment she lay dead in the basket of the
vehicle. A complete stillness succeeded ; then the Indians
raised in concert their cries of lamentation over the corpse,
and among them Shaw clearly distinguished those strange
sounds resembling the word "Halleluyah," which, together 25
with some other accidental coincidences, has given rise to
the absurd notion that the Indians are descended from the
ten lost tribes of Israel.

The Indian usage required that Henry, as well as the
other relatives of the woman, should make valuable presents, 30
to be placed by the side of the body at its last resting-place.
Leaving the Indians, he and Shaw set out for the camp,
and reached it, as we have seen, by hard pushing, at about
noon. Having obtained the necessary articles, they immediately returned. It was very late and quite dark when they

again reached the lodges. They were all placed in a deep
hollow among dreary hills. Four of them were just visible
through the gloom, but the fifth and largest was illumined
by the blaze of a fire within, glowing through the half-
5 transparent covering of raw hides. There was a perfect
stillness as they approached. The lodges seemed without a
tenant. Not a living thing was stirring; there was something awful in the scene. They rode up to the entrance of
the lodge, and there was no sound but the tramp of their
10 horses. A squaw came out and took charge of the animals,
without speaking a word. Entering, they found the lodge
crowded with Indians; a fire was burning in the midst, and
the mourners encircled it in a triple row. Room was made
for the new-comers at the head of the lodge, a robe spread
15 for them to sit upon, and a pipe lighted and handed to them
in perfect silence. Thus they passed the greater part of the
night. At times the fire would subside into a heap of embers, until the dark figures seated around it were scarcely
visible; then a squaw would drop upon it a piece of buffalo-
20 fat, and a bright flame, instantly springing up, would reveal
the crowd of wild faces, motionless as bronze. The silence
continued unbroken. It was a relief to Shaw when daylight
returned and he could escape from this house of mourning.
He and Henry prepared to return homeward; first, how-
25 ever, they placed the presents they had brought near the
body of the squaw, which, gaudily attired, remained in a
sitting posture in one of the lodges. A fine horse was picketed not far off, destined to be killed that morning for the
service of her spirit; for the woman was lame, and could
30 not travel on foot over the dismal prairies to the villages of
the dead. Food, too, was provided, and household implements, for her use upon this last journey.

Henry left her to the care of her relatives, and came
immediately with Shaw to the camp. It was some time
before he entirely recovered from his dejection.

CHAPTER XI

SCENES AT THE CAMP

Reynal heard guns fired one day, at the distance of a mile or two from the camp. He grew nervous instantly. Visions of Crow war-parties began to haunt his imagination; and when we returned (for we were all absent), he renewed his complaints about being left alone with the Canadians and the squaw. The day after, the cause of the alarm appeared. Four trappers, called Morin, Saraphin, Rouleau, and Gingras came to our camp and joined us. They it was who fired the guns and disturbed the dreams of our confederate Reynal. They soon encamped by our side. Their rifles, dingy and battered with hard service, rested with ours against the old tree; their strong rude saddles, their buffalo-robes, their traps, and the few rough and simple articles of their travelling equipment were piled near our tent. Their mountain-horses were turned to graze in the meadow among our own; and the men themselves, no less rough and hardy, used to lie half the day in the shade of our tree, lolling on the grass, lazily smoking, and telling stories of their adventures; and I defy the annals of chivalry to furnish the record of a life more wild and perilous than that of a Rocky Mountain trapper.

With this efficient reinforcement the agitation of Reynal's nerves subsided. We began to conceive a sort of attachment to our old camping-ground; yet it was time to change our quarters, since remaining too long on one spot must lead to unpleasant results, not to be borne unless in case of dire necessity. The grass no longer presented a smooth surface of turf; it was trampled into mud and clay. So we removed

to another old tree, larger yet, that grew by the side of the
river a furlong distant. Its trunk was full six feet in diameter; on one side it was marked by a party of Indians
with various inexplicable hieroglyphics, commemorating
5 some warlike enterprise, and aloft among the branches were
the remains of a scaffold, where dead bodies had once been
deposited, after the Indian manner.

"There comes Bull-Bear," said Henry Chatillon, as we
sat on the grass at dinner. Looking up, we saw several
10 horsemen coming over the neighboring hill, and in a moment
four stately young men rode up and dismounted. One of
them was Bull-Bear, or Mahto-Tatonka, a compound name
which he inherited from his father, the principal chief in the
Ogillallah band. One of his brothers and two other young
15 men accompanied him. We shook hands with the visitors,
and when we had finished our meal — for this is the approved manner of entertaining Indians, even the best of
them — we handed to each a tin cup of coffee and a biscuit, at which they ejaculated from the bottom of their
20 throats, "How! how!" a monosyllable by which an Indian
contrives to express half the emotions of which he is sus-
ceptible. Then we lighted the pipe, and passed it to them
as they squatted on the ground.

"Where is the village?"

25 "There," said Mahto-Tatonka, pointing southward; "it
will come in two days."

"Will they go to the war?"

"Yes."

No man is a philanthropist on the prairie. We welcomed
30 this news cordially, and congratulated ourselves that Bordeaux's interested efforts to divert The Whirlwind from
his congenial vocation of bloodshed had failed of success,
and that no further obstacles would interpose between us
and our plan of repairing to the rendezvous at La Bonté's
camp.

For that and several succeeding days, Mahto-Tatonka and his friends remained our guests. They devoured the relics of our meals; they filled the pipe for us, and also helped us to smoke it. Sometimes they stretched themselves side by side in the shade, indulging in raillery and equivocal jokes, ill becoming the dignity of brave and aspiring warriors, such as two of them in reality were.

Two days dragged away, and on the morning of the third we hoped confidently to see the Indian village. It did not come; so we rode out to look for it. In place of the eight hundred Indians we expected, we met one solitary savage riding towards us over the prairie, who told us that the Indians had changed their plan, and would not come within three days. Taking along with us this messenger of evil tidings, we retraced our footsteps to the camp, amusing ourselves by the way with execrating Indian inconstancy. When we came in sight of our little white tent under the big tree, we saw that it no longer stood alone. A huge old lodge was erected by its side, discolored by rain and storms, rotten with age, with the uncouth figures of horses and men and outstretched hands that were painted upon it wellnigh obliterated. The long poles which supported this squalid habitation thrust themselves rakishly out from its pointed top, and over its entrance were suspended a " medicine-pipe " and various other implements of the magic art. While we were yet at a distance, we observed a greatly increased population of various colors and dimensions, swarming about our quiet encampment. Morin, the trapper, having been absent for a day or two, had returned, it seemed, bringing all his family with him. He had taken to himself a wife, for whom he had paid the established price of one horse. This looks cheap at first sight, but in truth the purchase of a squaw is a transaction which no man should enter into without mature deliberation, since it involves not only the payment of the price, but the burden of feeding and supporting a rapacious

horde of the bride's relatives, who hold themselves entitled
to feed upon the indiscreet white man. They gather about
him like leeches, and drain him of all he has.

Morin had not made an aristocratic match. His bride's
relatives occupied but a contemptible position in Ogillallah
society; for among these democrats of the prairie, as among
others more civilized, there are virtual distinctions of rank
and place. Morin's partner was not the most beautiful of
her sex, and he had the bad taste to array her in an old
calico gown, bought from an emigrant woman, instead of the
neat tunic of whitened deer-skin usually worn by the squaws.
The moving spirit of the establishment was an old hag of
eighty. Human imagination never conceived hobgoblin or
witch more ugly than she. You could count all her ribs
through the wrinkles of her leathery skin. Her withered
face more resembled an old skull than the countenance of a
living being, even to the hollow, darkened sockets, at the
bottom of which glittered her little black eyes. Her arms
had dwindled into nothing but whip-cord and wire. Her hair,
half black, half gray, hung in total neglect nearly to the
ground, and her sole garment consisted of the remnant of a
discarded buffalo-robe tied round her waist with a string of
hide. Yet the old squaw's meagre anatomy was wonderfully
strong. She pitched the lodge, packed the horses, and did
the hardest labor of the camp. From morning till night she
bustled about the lodge, screaming like a screech-owl when
anything displeased her. Her brother, a "medicine-man,"
or magician, was equally gaunt and sinewy with herself.
His mouth spread from ear to ear, and his appetite, as we
had occasion to learn, was ravenous in proportion. The other
inmates of the lodge were a young bride and bridegroom,
the latter one of those idle, good-for-nothing fellows who
infest an Indian village as well as more civilized communities. He was fit neither for hunting nor war, as one might
see from the stolid unmeaning expression of his face. The

happy pair had just entered upon the honeymoon. They would stretch a buffalo-robe upon poles, to protect them from the rays of the sun, and spreading under it a couch of furs, would sit affectionately side by side for half the day, though I could not discover that much conversation passed between them. Probably they had nothing to say; for an Indian's supply of topics for conversation is far from being copious. There were half a dozen children, too, playing and whooping about the camp, shooting birds with little bows and arrows, or making miniature lodges of sticks, as children of a different complexion build houses of blocks.

A day passed, and Indians began rapidly to come in. Parties of two, three, or more would ride up and silently seat themselves on the grass. The fourth day came at last, when about noon horsemen appeared in view on the summit of the neighboring ridge. Behind followed a wild procession, hurrying in haste and disorder down the hill and over the plain below; horses, mules, and dogs; heavily-burdened *traineaux*, mounted warriors, squaws walking amid the throng, and a host of children. For a full half-hour they continued to pour down; and keeping directly to the bend of the stream, within a furlong of us, they soon assembled there, a dark and confused throng, until, as if by magic, a hundred and fifty tall lodges sprang up. The lonely plain was transformed into the site of a swarming encampment. Countless horses were soon grazing over the meadows around us, and the prairie was animated by restless figures careering on horseback, or sedately stalking in their long white robes. The Whirlwind was come at last. One question yet remained to be answered: "Will he go to the war in order that we, with so respectable an escort, may pass over to the somewhat perilous rendezvous at La Bonté's camp?"

This still remained in doubt. Characteristic indecision perplexed their councils. Indians cannot act in large bodies. Though their object be of the highest importance, they

cannot combine to attain it by a series of connected efforts.
King Philip, Pontiac, and Tecumseh, all felt this to their
cost. The Ogillallah once had a war-chief who could con-
trol them; but he was dead, and now they were left to the
5 sway of their own unsteady impulses.

As this Indian village and its inhabitants will hold a
prominent place in the rest of the story, perhaps it may not
be amiss to glance for an instant at the savage people of
which they form a part. The Dahcotah or Sioux range over
10 a vast territory, from the river St. Peter to the Rocky
Mountains. They are divided into several independent
bands, united under no central government, and acknowledging no common head. The same language, usages, and
superstitions form the sole bond between them. They do
15 not unite even in their wars. The bands of the east fight
the Ojibwas on the Upper Lakes; those of the west make
incessant war upon the Snake Indians in the Rocky Mountains. As the whole people is divided into bands, so each
band is divided into villages. Each village has a chief, who
20 is honored and obeyed only so far as his personal qualities
may command respect and fear. Sometimes he is a mere
nominal chief; sometimes his authority is little short of
absolute, and his fame and influence reach beyond his
own village, so that the whole band to which he belongs
25 is ready to acknowledge him as their head. This was, a
few years since, the case with the Ogillallah. Courage, address, and enterprise may raise any warrior to the highest
honor, especially if he be the son of a former chief, or a
member of a numerous family, to support him and avenge
30 his quarrels; but when he has reached the dignity of
chief, and the old men and warriors, by a peculiar ceremony, have formally installed him, let it not be imagined
that he assumes any of the outward signs of rank and honor.
He knows too well on how frail a tenure he holds his station.
He must conciliate his uncertain subjects. Many a man in

the village lives better, owns more squaws and more horses, and goes better clad than he. Like the Teutonic chiefs of old, he ingratiates himself with his young men by making them presents, thereby often impoverishing himself. If he fails to gain their favor, they will set his authority at naught, and may desert him at any moment; for the usages of his people have provided no means of enforcing his authority. Very seldom does it happen, at least among these western bands, that a chief attains to much power, unless he is the head of a numerous family. Frequently the village is principally made up of his relatives and descendants, and the wandering community assumes much of the patriarchal character.

The western Dahcotah have no fixed habitations. Hunting and fighting, they wander incessantly, through summer and winter. Some follow the herds of buffalo over the waste of prairie; others traverse the Black Hills, thronging, on horseback and on foot, through the dark gulfs and sombre gorges, and emerging at last upon the "Parks," those beautiful but most perilous hunting-grounds. The buffalo supplies them with the necessaries of life; with habitations, food, clothing, beds, and fuel; strings for their bows, glue, thread, cordage, trail-ropes for their horses, coverings for their saddles, vessels to hold water, boats to cross streams, and the means of purchasing all that they want from the traders. When the buffalo are extinct, they too must dwindle away.

War is the breath of their nostrils. Against most of the neighboring tribes they cherish a rancorous hatred, transmitted from father to son, and inflamed by constant aggression and retaliation. Many times a year, in every village, the Great Spirit is called upon, fasts are made, the war-parade is celebrated, and the warriors go out by handfuls at a time against the enemy. This fierce spirit awakens their most eager aspirations, and calls forth their greatest energies. It is chiefly this that saves them from lethargy and utter abasement. Without its powerful stimulus they would be like the unwarlike tribes beyond the mountains, scattered among the caves and rocks like beasts, and living on roots and reptiles. These latter have little of humanity except 5 the form; but the proud and ambitious Dahcotah warrior can sometimes boast heroic virtues. It is seldom that distinction and influence are attained among them by any other course than that of arms. Their superstition, however, sometimes gives great power to those among them 10 who pretend to the character of magicians; and their orators, such as they are, have their share of honor.

But to return. Look into our tent, or enter, if you can bear the stifling smoke and the close air. There, wedged close together, you will see a circle of stout warriors, pass-15 ing the pipe around, joking, telling stories, and making themselves merry after their fashion. We were also infested by little copper-colored naked boys and snake-eyed girls. They would come up to us, muttering certain words, which being interpreted conveyed the concise invitation, 20 "Come and eat." Then we would rise, cursing the pertinacity of Dahcotah hospitality, which allowed scarcely an hour of rest between sun and sun, and to which we were bound to do honor, unless we would offend our entertainers. This necessity was particularly burdensome to me, as I was 25 scarcely able to walk, from the effects of illness, and was poorly qualified to dispose of twenty meals a day. So bounteous an entertainment looks like an outgushing of goodwill; but, doubtless, half at least of our kind hosts, had they met us alone and unarmed on the prairie, would have 30 robbed us of our horses, and perhaps have bestowed an arrow upon us besides.

One morning we were summoned to the lodge of an old man, the Nestor of his tribe. We found him half sitting, half reclining, on a pile of buffalo-robes; his long hair, jet-black, though he had seen some eighty winters, hung on either side of his thin features. His gaunt but symmetrical frame did not more clearly exhibit the wreck of bygone strength, than did his dark, wasted features, still prominent and commanding, bear the stamp of mental energies. Opposite the patriarch was his nephew, the young aspirant Mahto-Tatonka; and besides these, there were one or two women in the lodge.

The old man's story is peculiar, and illustrative of a superstition that prevails in full force among many of the Indian tribes. He was one of a powerful family, renowned for warlike exploits. When a very young man, he submitted to the singular rite to which most of the tribe subject themselves before entering upon life. He painted his face black; then seeking out a cavern in a sequestered part of the Black Hills, he lay for several days, fasting, and praying to the spirits. In the dreams and visions produced by his weakened and excited state, he fancied, like all Indians, that he saw supernatural revelations. Again and again the form of an antelope appeared before him. The antelope is the graceful peace spirit of the Ogillallah; but seldom is it that such a gentle visitor presents itself during the initiatory fasts of their young men. The terrible grizzly bear, the divinity of war, usually appears to fire them with martial ardor and thirst for renown. At length the antelope spoke. It told the young dreamer that he was not to follow the path of war; that a life of peace and tranquillity was marked out for him; that thenceforward he was to guide the people by his counsels, and protect them from the evils of their own feuds and dissensions. Others were to gain renown by fighting the enemy; but greatness of a different kind was in store for him.

The visions beheld during the period of this fast usually determine the whole course of the dreamer's life. From that time, Le Borgne, which was the only name by which we knew him, abandoned all thoughts of war, and devoted himself to the labors of peace. He told his vision to the people. They honored his commission and respected him in his novel capacity.

A far different man was his brother, Mahto-Tatonka, who had left his name, his features, and many of his qualities, to his son. He was the father of Henry Chatillon's squaw, a circumstance which proved of some advantage to us, as it secured the friendship of a family perhaps the most noted and influential in the whole Ogillallah band; Mahto-Tatonka, in his way, was a hero. No chief could vie with him in war-like renown, or in power over his people. He had a fearless spirit, and an impetuous and inflexible resolution. His will was law. He was politic and sagacious, and with true Indian craft, always befriended the whites, knowing that he might thus reap great advantages for himself and his adherents. When he had resolved on any course of conduct, he would pay to the warriors the compliment of calling them together to deliberate upon it, and when their debates were over, quietly state his own opinion, which no one ever disputed. It fared hard with those who incurred his displeasure. He would strike them or stab them on the spot; and this act, which, if attempted by any other chief would have cost him his life, the awe inspired by his name enabled him to repeat again and again with impunity. In a community where, from immemorial time, no man has acknowledged any law but his own will, Mahto-Tatonka raised himself to power little short of despotic. His career came at last to an end. He had a host of enemies patiently biding their time; and our old friend Smoke in particular, together with all his kinsmen, hated him cordially. Smoke sat one day in his lodge, in the midst of his own village, when Mahto-Tatonka entered it alone, and approaching the dwelling of his enemy, challenged him in a loud voice to come out, and fight. Smoke would not move. At this, Mahto-Tatonka proclaimed him a coward and an old woman, and, striding to the entrance

of the lodge, stabbed the chief's best horse, which was picketed there. Smoke was daunted, and even this insult failed
to bring him out. Mahto-Tatonka moved haughtily away;
all made way for him; but his hour of reckoning was near.

One hot day, five or six years ago, numerous lodges of
Smoke's kinsmen were gathered about some of the Fur Company's men, who were trading in various articles with them,
whiskey among the rest. Mahto-Tatonka was also there with
a few of his people. As he lay in his own lodge, a fray
arose between his adherents and the kinsmen of his enemy.
The war-whoop was raised, bullets and arrows began to fly,
and the camp was in confusion. The chief sprang up, and
rushing in a fury from the lodge, shouted to the combatants
on both sides to cease. Instantly — for the attack was pre-
concerted — came the reports of two or three guns, and the
twanging of a dozen bows, and the savage hero, mortally
wounded, pitched forward headlong to the ground. Rouleau
was present, and told me the particulars. The tumult became general, and was not quelled until several had fallen
on both sides. When we were in the country the feud between the two families was still rankling.

Thus died Mahto-Tatonka; but he left behind him a
goodly army of descendants, to perpetuate his renown and
avenge his fate. Besides daughters, he had thirty sons, a
number which need not stagger the credulity of those acquainted with Indian usages and practices. We saw many
of them, all marked by the same dark complexion, and the
same peculiar cast of features. Of these, our visitor, young
Mahto-Tatonka, was the eldest, and some reported him as
likely to succeed to his father's honors. Though he appeared
not more than twenty-one years old, he had oftener struck
the enemy, and stolen more horses and more squaws, than
any young man in the village. Horse-stealing is well known
as an avenue to distinction on the prairies, and the other
kind of depredation is esteemed equally meritorious. Not

that the act can confer fame from its own intrinsic merits.
Any one can steal a squaw, and if he chooses afterwards to
make an adequate present to her rightful proprietor, the easy
husband for the most part rests content, his vengeance falls
5 asleep, and all danger from that quarter is averted. Yet this
is regarded as a pitiful and mean-spirited transaction. The
danger is averted, but the glory of the achievement also is
lost. Mahto-Tatonka proceeded after a more dashing fashion.
Out of several dozen squaws whom he had stolen, he could
10 boast that he had never paid for one, but snapping his
fingers in the face of the injured husband, had defied the
extremity of his indignation, and no one yet had dared to
lay the finger of violence upon him. He was following close
in the footsteps of his father. The young men and the
15 young squaws, each in their way, admired him. The former
would always follow him to war, and he was esteemed to
have an unrivalled charm in the eyes of the latter. Perhaps
his impunity may excite some wonder. An arrow-shot from
a ravine, or a stab given in the dark, require no great valor,
20 and are especially suited to the Indian genius; but Mahto-
Tatonka had a strong protection. It was not alone his courage and audacious will that enabled him to career so dashingly
among his compeers. His enemies did not forget that he
was one of thirty warlike brethren, all growing up to man-
25 hood. Should they wreak their anger upon him, many keen
eyes would be ever upon them, and many fierce hearts thirst
for their blood. The avenger would dog their footsteps
everywhere. To kill Mahto-Tatonka would be an act of
suicide.

30   Though he found such favor in the eyes of the fair, he
was no dandy. He was indifferent to the gaudy trappings
and ornaments of his companions, and was content to rest
his chances of success upon his own warlike merits. He
never arrayed himself in gaudy blanket and glittering necklaces, but left his statue-like form, limbed like an Apollo

of bronze, to win its way to favor. His voice was singularly
deep and strong, and sounded from his chest like the deep
notes of an organ. Yet, after all, he was but an Indian. See
him as he lies there in the sun before our tent, kicking his
heels in the air and cracking jokes with his brother. Does   5
he look like a hero? See him now in the hour of his glory,
when at sunset the whole village empties itself to behold
him, for to-morrow their favorite young partisan goes out
against the enemy. His head-dress is adorned with a crest
of the war-eagle's feathers, rising in a waving ridge above   10
his brow, and sweeping far behind him. His round white
shield hangs at his breast, with feathers radiating from the
centre like a star. His quiver is at his back; his tall lance
in his hand, the iron point flashing against the declining
sun, while the long scalp-locks of his enemies flutter from   15
the shaft. Thus, gorgeous as a champion in panoply, he
rides round and round within the great circle of lodges, bal-
ancing with a graceful buoyancy to the free movements of
his war-horse, while with a sedate brow he sings his song to
the Great Spirit. Young rival warriors look askance at him;   20
vermilion-cheeked girls gaze in admiration; boys whoop and
scream in a thrill of delight, and old women yell forth his
name and proclaim his praises from lodge to lodge.

Mahto-Tatonka was the best of all our Indian friends.
Hour after hour, and day after day, when swarms of savages   25
of every age, sex, and degree beset our camp, he would lie
in our tent, his lynx-eye ever open to guard our property
from pillage.

The Whirlwind invited us one day to his lodge. The feast
was finished, and the pipe began to circulate. It was a re-   30
markably large and fine one, and I expressed admiration of it.

"If the Meneaska likes the pipe," asked The Whirlwind,
"why does he not keep it?"

Such a pipe among the Ogillallah is valued at the price
of a horse. The gift seemed worthy of a chieftain and a

warrior; but The Whirlwind's generosity rose to no such pitch. He gave me the pipe, confidently expecting that I in return would make him a present of equal or superior value. This is the implied condition of every gift among the In-
5 dians, and should it not be complied with, the present is usually reclaimed. So I arranged upon a gaudy calico hand-kerchief, an assortment of vermilion, tobacco, knives, and gunpowder, and summoning the chief to camp, assured him of my friendship, and begged his acceptance of a slight
10 token of it. Ejaculating, "How! how!" he folded up the offerings and withdrew to his lodge.

Late one afternoon a party of Indians on horseback came suddenly in sight from behind some clumps of bushes that lined the bank of the stream, leading with them a mule, on
15 whose back was a wretched negro, sustained in his seat by the high pommel and cantle of the Indian saddle. His cheeks were shrunken in the hollow of his jaws; his eyes were un-naturally dilated, and his lips shrivelled and drawn back from his teeth like those of a corpse. When they brought
20 him before our tent, and lifted him from the saddle, he could not walk or stand, but crawled a short distance, and with a look of utter misery sat down on the grass. All the children and women came pouring out of the lodges, and with screams and cries made a circle about him, while he sat supporting
25 himself with his hands, and looking from side to side with a vacant stare. The wretch was starving to death. For thirty-three days he had wandered alone on the prairie, without weapon of any kind; without shoes, moccasons, or any other clothing than an old jacket and trousers; without
30 intelligence to guide his course, or any knowledge of the productions of the prairie. All this time he had subsisted on crickets and lizards, wild onions, and three eggs which he found in the nest of a prairie-dove. He had not seen a human being. Bewildered in the boundless, hopeless desert that stretched around him, he had walked on in despair, till

he could walk no longer, and then crawled on his knees, till the bone was laid bare. He chose the night for travelling, lying down by day to sleep in the glaring sun, always dreaming, as he said, of the broth and corn-cake he used to eat under his old master's shed in Missouri. Every man in the camp, both white and red, was astonished at his escape not only from starvation, but from the grizzly bears, which abound in that neighborhood, and the wolves which howled around him every night.

Reynal recognized him the moment the Indians brought him in. He had run away from his master about a year before and joined the party of Richard, who was then leaving the frontier for the mountains. He had lived with Richard until, at the end of May, he with Reynal and several other men went out in search of some stray horses, when he was separated from the rest in a storm, and had never been heard of to this time. Knowing his inexperience and helplessness, no one dreamed that he could still be living. The Indians had found him lying exhausted on the ground.

As he sat there, with the Indians gazing silently on him, his haggard face and glazed eye were disgusting to look upon. Deslauriers made him a bowl of gruel, but he suffered it to remain untasted before him. At length he languidly raised the spoon to his lips; again he did so, and again; and then his appetite seemed suddenly inflamed into madness, for he seized the bowl, swallowed all its contents in a few seconds, and eagerly demanded meat. This we refused, telling him to wait until morning; but he begged so eagerly that we gave him a small piece, which he devoured, tearing it like a dog. He said he must have more. We told him that his life was in danger if he ate so immoderately at first. He assented, and said he knew he was a fool to do so, but he must have meat. This we absolutely refused, to the great indignation of the senseless squaws, who, when we were not watching him, would slyly bring dried meat and *pommes blanches,* and place them on the ground by his side. Still this was not enough for him. When it grew dark he contrived to creep away between the legs of the horses and crawl over to the Indian camp. Here he fed to his heart's content, and was brought back again in the morning, when Gingras, the trapper, put him on horseback and carried him to the fort. He managed to survive the effects of his greediness. Though slightly deranged when we left this part of the country, he was otherwise in tolerable health, and expressed his firm conviction that nothing could ever kill him.

When the sun was yet an hour high, it was a gay scene in the village. The warriors stalked sedately among the lodges, or along the margin of the stream, or walked out to visit the bands of horses that were feeding over the prairie. Half the population deserted the close and heated lodges and betook themselves to the water; and here you might see boys and girls, and young squaws, splashing, swimming, and diving, beneath the afternoon sun, with merry screams and laughter. But when the sun was resting above the broken peaks, and the purple mountains threw their shadows for miles over the prairie; when our old tree basked peacefully in the horizontal rays, and the swelling plains and scattered groves were softened into a tranquil beauty, — then the scene around our tent was worthy of a Salvator. Savage figures, with quivers at their backs, and guns, lances, or tomahawks in their hands, sat on horseback, motionless as statues, their arms crossed on their breasts and their eyes fixed in a steady unwavering gaze upon us. Others stood erect, wrapped from head to foot in their long white robes of buffalo-hide. Others sat together on the grass, holding their shaggy horses by a rope, with their dark busts exposed to view as they suffered their robes to fall from their shoulders. Others again stood carelessly among the throng, with nothing to conceal the matchless symmetry of their forms.

There was one in particular, a ferocious fellow, named The Mad Wolf, who, with the bow in his hand and the quiver at his back, might have seemed, but for his face, the Pythian Apollo himself. Such a figure rose before the imagination of West, when, on first seeing the Belvedere in the Vatican, he exclaimed, "By God, a Mohawk!"

When the prairie grew dark, the horses were driven in and secured near the camp, and the crowd began to melt away. Fires gleamed around, duskily revealing the rough trappers and the graceful Indians. One of the families near us was always gathered about a bright fire that lighted up the interior of their lodge. Withered, witch-like hags flitted around the blaze; and here for hour after hour sat a circle of children and young girls, laughing and talking, their round merry faces glowing in the ruddy light. We could hear the monotonous notes of the drum from the Indian camp, with the chant of the war-song, deadened in the distance, and the long chorus of quavering yells, where the war-dance was going on in the largest lodge. For several nights, too, we heard wild and mournful cries, rising and dying away like the melancholy voice of a wolf. They came from the sisters and female relatives of Mahto-Tatonka, who were gashing their limbs with knives, and bewailing the death of Henry Chatillon's squaw. The hour would grow late before all went to rest in our camp. Then, while the embers of the fires glowed dimly, the men lay stretched in their blankets on the ground, and nothing could be heard but the restless motions of the crowded horses.

I recall these scenes with a mixed feeling of pleasure and pain. At this time, I was so reduced by illness that I could seldom walk without reeling like a drunken man, and when I rose from my seat upon the ground, the landscape suddenly grew dim before my eyes, the trees and lodges seemed to sway to and fro, and the prairie to rise and fall like the swells of the ocean. Such a state of things is not enviable anywhere. In a country where a man's life may at any moment depend on the strength of his arm, or it may be on the activity of his legs, it is more particularly inconvenient. Nor is sleeping on damp ground, with an occasional drenching from a shower, very beneficial in such cases. I sometimes suffered the extremity of exhaustion, and was in a tolerably fair way of atoning for my love of the prairie by resting there forever.

I tried repose and a very sparing diet. For a long time, with exemplary patience, I lounged about the camp, or at the utmost staggered over to the Indian village, and walked faint and dizzy among the lodges. It would not do; and I bethought me of starvation. During five days I sustained life on one small biscuit a day. At the end of that time I was weaker than before, but the disorder seemed shaken in its stronghold, and very gradually I began to resume a less rigid diet.

I used to lie languid and dreamy before our tent, musing on the past and the future, and when most overcome with lassitude, my eyes turned always towards the distant Black Hills. There is a spirit of energy in mountains, and they impart it to all who approach them. At that time I did not know how many dark superstitions and gloomy legends are associated with the Black Hills in the minds of the Indians, but I felt an eager desire to penetrate their hidden recesses, and explore the chasms and precipices, black torrents and silent forests, that I fancied were concealed there.

CHAPTER XII

ILL-LUCK

A Canadian came from Fort Laramie, and brought a curious piece of intelligence. A trapper, fresh from the mountains, had become enamoured of a Missouri damsel belonging to a family who with other emigrants had been for some days encamped in the neighborhood of the fort. If bravery be the most potent charm to win the favor of the fair, then no wooer could be more irresistible than a Rocky Mountain trapper. In the present instance, the suit was not urged in vain. The lovers concerted a scheme, which they proceeded to carry into effect with all possible despatch. The emigrant party left the fort, and on the next night but one encamped as usual, and placed a guard. A little after midnight, the enamoured trapper drew near, mounted on a strong horse, and leading another by the bridle. Fastening both animals to a tree, he stealthily moved towards the wagons, as if he were approaching a band of buffalo. Eluding the vigilance of the guard, who were probably half asleep, he met his mistress by appointment at the outskirts of the camp, mounted her on his spare horse, and made off with her through the darkness. The sequel of the adventure did not reach our ears, and we never learned how the imprudent fair one liked an Indian lodge for a dwelling, and a reckless trapper for a bridegroom.

At length The Whirlwind and his warriors determined to move. They had resolved after all their preparations not to go to the rendezvous at La Bonté's camp, but to pass through the Black Hills and spend a few weeks in hunting the buffalo on the other side, until they had killed enough to

143

furnish them with a stock of provisions and with hides to make their lodges for the next season. This done, they were to send out a small independent war-party against the enemy. Their final determination placed us in some embarrassment.

5 Should we go to La Bonté's camp, it was not impossible that the other villages would prove as vacillating as The Whirlwind's, and that no assembly whatever would take place. Our old companion Reynal had conceived a liking for us, or rather for our biscuit and coffee, and for the occasional small

10 presents which we made him. He was very anxious that we should go with the village which he himself intended to follow. He was certain that no Indians would meet at the rendezvous, and said, moreover, that it would be easy to convey our cart and baggage through the Black Hills. He

15 knew, however, nothing of the matter. Neither he nor any white man with us had ever seen the difficult and obscure defiles through which the Indians intended to make their way. I passed them afterwards, and had much ado to force my distressed horse along the narrow ravines, and through

20 chasms where daylight could scarcely penetrate. Our cart might as easily have been driven over the summit of Pike's Peak. But of this we were ignorant; and in view of the difficulties and uncertainties of an attempt to visit the rendezvous, we recalled the old proverb, about "A bird in the

25 hand," and decided to follow the village.

Both camps, the Indians' and our own, broke up on the morning of the first of July. I was so weak that the aid of a spoonful of whiskey, swallowed at short intervals, alone enabled me to sit my horse through the short journey of that

30 day. For half a mile before us and half a mile behind, the prairie was covered far and wide with the moving throng of savages. The barren, broken plain stretched away to the right and left, and far in front rose the precipitous ridge of the Black Hills. We pushed forward to the head of the scattered column, passing burdened *traineaux*, heavily laden

pack-horses, gaunt old women on foot, gay young squaws on horseback, restless children running among the crowd, old men striding along in their white buffalo-robes, and groups of young warriors mounted on their best horses. Henry Chatillon, looking backward over the distant prairie, exclaimed suddenly that a horseman was approaching, and in truth we could just discern a small black speck slowly moving over the face of a distant swell, like a fly creeping on a wall. It rapidly grew larger as it approached.

"White man, I b'lieve," said Henry; "look how he ride. Indian never ride that way. Yes; he got rifle on the saddle before him."

The horseman disappeared in a hollow of the prairie, but we soon saw him again, and as he came riding at a gallop towards us through the crowd of Indians, his long hair streaming in the wind behind him, we recognized the ruddy face and old buckskin frock of Gingras the trapper. He was just arrived from Fort Laramie, and said he had a message for us. A trader named Bisonette, one of Henry's friends, had lately come from the settlements, and intended to go with a party of men to La Bonté's camp, where, as Gingras assured us, ten or twelve villages of Indians would certainly assemble. Bisonette desired that we would cross over and meet him there, and promised that his men should protect our horses and baggage while we went among the Indians. Shaw and I stopped our horses, held a council, and in an evil hour resolved to go.

For the rest of that day our course and that of the Indians was the same. In less than an hour we came to where the high barren prairie terminated, sinking down abruptly in steep descent; and standing on the verge, we saw below us a great meadow. Laramie Creek bounded it on the left, sweeping along in the shadow of the heights, and passing with its shallow and rapid current just beneath us. We sat on horseback, waiting and looking on, while the whole

savage array went pouring by, hurrying down the declivity
and spreading over the meadow below. In a few moments
the plain was swarming with the moving multitude, some
just visible, like specks in the distance, others still hasten-
5 ing by and fording the stream in bustle and confusion. On
the edge of the heights sat a group of the elder warriors,
gravely smoking and looking with unmoved faces on the
wild and striking spectacle.

Up went the lodges in a circle on the margin of the
10 stream. For the sake of quiet we pitched our tent among
some trees half a mile distant. In the afternoon we were
in the village. The day was a glorious one, and the whole
camp seemed lively and animated in sympathy. Groups of
children and young girls were laughing gayly outside the
15 lodges. The shields, the lances, and the bows were removed
from the tall tripods on which they usually hung, before the
dwellings of their owners. The warriors were mounting
their horses, and one by one riding away over the prairie
towards the neighboring hills.

20 Shaw and I sat on the grass near the lodge of Reynal.
An old woman, with true Indian hospitality, brought a bowl
of boiled venison and placed it before us. We amused ourselves with watching a few young squaws who were playing
together and chasing each other in and out of one of the
25 lodges. Suddenly the wild yell of the war-whoop came pealing from the hills. A crowd of horsemen appeared, rushing
down their sides, and riding at full speed towards the village,
each warrior's long hair flying behind him in the wind like
a ship's streamer. As they approached, the confused throng
30 assumed a regular order, and entering two by two, they
circled round the area at full gallop, each warrior singing
his war-song as he rode. Some of their dresses were superb.
They wore crests of feathers, and close tunics of antelope
skins, fringed with the scalp-locks of their enemies ; many
of their shields, too, fluttered with the war-eagle's feathers.

All had bows and arrows at their backs; some carried long lances, and a few were armed with guns. The White Shield, their partisan, rode in gorgeous attire at their head, mounted on a black-and-white horse. Mahto-Tatonka and his brothers took no part in this parade, for they were in mourning for their sister, and were all sitting in their lodges, their bodies bedaubed from head to foot with white clay, and a lock of hair cut from the forehead of each.

The warriors rode three times round the village; and as each noted champion passed, the old women would scream out his name, to honor his bravery, and excite the emulation of the younger warriors. Little urchins, not two years old, followed the warlike pageant with glittering eyes, and gazed with eager admiration at the heroes of their tribe.

The procession rode out of the village as it had entered it, and in half an hour all the warriors had returned again, dropping quietly in, singly or in parties of two or three.

The parade over, we were entertained with an episode of Indian domestic life. A vicious-looking squaw, beside herself with rage, was berating her spouse, who, with a look of total unconcern, sat cross-legged in the middle of his lodge, smoking his pipe in silence. At length, maddened by his coolness, she made a rush at the lodge, seized the poles which supported it, and tugged at them, one after the other, till she brought down the whole structure, poles, hides, and all, clattering on his head, burying him in the wreck of his habitation. He pushed aside the hides with his hand, and presently his head emerged, like a turtle's from its shell. Still he sat smoking sedately as before, a wicked glitter in his eyes alone betraying the pent-up storm within. The squaw, scolding all the while, proceeded to saddle her horse, bestride him, and canter out of the camp, intending, as it seemed, to return to her father's lodge, wherever that might be. The warrior, who had not deigned even to look at her, now coolly arose, disengaged himself from the ruins, tied a cord of hair by way of bridle round the jaw of his buffalo-horse, broke a stout cudgel, about four feet long, from the butt-end of a lodge-pole, mounted, and galloped majestically over the prairie to discipline his offending helpmeet.

5   As the sun rose next morning we looked across the meadow, and could see the lodges levelled and the Indians gathering together in preparation to leave the camp. Their course lay to the westward. We turned towards the north with our three men, the four trappers following us, with the

10 Indian family of Morin. We travelled until night, and encamped among some trees by the side of a little brook, where during the whole of the next day we lay waiting for Bisonette; but no Bisonette appeared. Here two of our trapper friends left us, and set out for the Rocky Mountains. On the

15 second morning, despairing of Bisonette's arrival, we resumed our journey, traversing a forlorn and dreary monotony of sun-scorched plains, where no living thing appeared save here and there an antelope flying before us like the wind. When noon came we saw an unwonted and welcome sight; a fine growth

20 of trees, marking the course of a little stream called Horse-shoe Creek. They stood wide asunder, spreading a thick canopy of leaves above a surface of rich, tall grass. The stream ran swiftly, as clear as crystal, through the bosom of the wood, sparkling over its bed of white sand, and darkening again as

25 it entered a deep cavern of foliage. I was thoroughly exhausted, and flung myself on the ground, scarcely able to move.

In the morning, as glorious a sun rose upon us as ever animated that wilderness. We advanced, and soon were surrounded by tall bare hills, overspread from top to bottom

30 with prickly-pears and other cacti, that seemed like clinging reptiles. A plain, flat and hard, with scarcely the vestige of grass, lay before us, and a line of tall misshapen trees bounded the onward view. There was no sight or sound of man or beast, or any living thing, although behind those trees was the long-looked-for place of rendezvous, where we

hoped to have found the Indians congregated by thousands. We looked and listened anxiously. We pushed forward with our best speed, and forced our horses through the trees. There were copses of some extent beyond, with a scanty stream creeping among them; and as we pressed through the yielding branches, deer sprang up to the right and left. At length we caught a glimpse of the prairie beyond, emerged upon it, and saw, not a plain covered with encampments and swarming with life, but a vast unbroken desert stretching away before us league upon league, without bush or tree, or anything that had life. We drew rein and gave to the winds our sentiments concerning the whole aboriginal race of America. Our journey was worse than vain. For myself, I was vexed beyond measure; as I well knew that a slight aggravation of my disorder would render this false step irrevocable, and make it impossible to accomplish effectually the object which had led me an arduous journey of between three and four thousand miles.

And where were the Indians? They were mustered in great numbers at a spot about twenty miles distant, where at that very moment they were dancing their war dances. The scarcity of buffalo in the vicinity of La Bonté's camp, which would render their supply of provisions scanty and precarious, had probably prevented them from assembling there; but of all this we knew nothing until some weeks after.

Shaw lashed his horse and galloped forward. I, though much more vexed than he, was not strong enough to adopt this convenient vent to my feelings; so I followed at a quiet pace. We rode up to a solitary old tree, which seemed the only place fit for encampment. Half its branches were dead, and the rest were so scantily furnished with leaves that they cast but a meagre and wretched shade. We threw down our saddles in the strip of shadow cast by the old twisted trunk, and sat down upon them. In silent indignation we remained smoking for an hour or more, shifting our saddles with the shifting shadow, for the sun was intolerably hot.

CHAPTER XIII

HUNTING INDIANS

At last we had reached La Bonté's camp, towards which our eyes had turned so long. Of all weary hours, those that passed between noon and sunset of that day may bear away the palm of exquisite discomfort. I lay under the tree reflecting on what course to pursue, watching the shadows which seemed never to move, and the sun which seemed fixed in the sky, and hoping every moment to see the men and horses of Bisonette emerging from the woods. Shaw and Henry had ridden out on a scouting expedition, and did not return till the sun was setting. There was nothing very cheering in their faces or in the news they brought.

"We have been ten miles from here," said Shaw. "We climbed the highest butte we could find, and could not see a buffalo or an Indian; nothing but prairie for twenty miles around us." Henry's horse was disabled by clambering up and down the sides of ravines, and Shaw's was greatly fatigued.

After supper that evening, as we sat around the fire, I proposed to Shaw to wait one day longer, in hopes of Bisonette's arrival, and if he should not come, to send Deslauriers with the cart and baggage back to Fort Laramie, while we ourselves followed The Whirlwind's village, and attempted to overtake it as it passed the mountains. Shaw, not having the same motive for hunting Indians that I had, was averse to the plan; I therefore resolved to go alone. This design I adopted very unwillingly, for I knew that in the present state of my health the attempt would be painful and hazardous. I hoped that Bisonette would

150

appear in the course of the following day, and bring us some information by which to direct our course, thus enabling me to accomplish my purpose by means less objectionable.

The rifle of Henry Chatillon was necessary for the subsistence of the party in my absence; so I called Raymond, and ordered him to prepare to set out with me. Raymond rolled his eyes vacantly about, but at length, having succeeded in grappling with the idea, he withdrew to his bed under the cart. He was a heavy-moulded fellow, with a broad face, expressing impenetrable stupidity and entire self-confidence. As for his good qualities, he had a sort of stubborn fidelity, an insensibility to danger, and a kind of instinct and sagacity, which sometimes led him right where better heads than his were at a loss. Besides this, he knew very well how to handle a rifle and picket a horse.

Through the following day the sun glared down upon us with a pitiless, penetrating heat. The distant blue prairie seemed quivering under it. The lodge of our Indian associates parched in the burning rays, and our rifles, as they leaned against the tree, were too hot for the touch. There was a dead silence through our camp, broken only by the hum of gnats and mosquitoes. The men, resting their foreheads on their arms, were sleeping under the cart. The Indians kept close within their lodge, except the newly-married pair, who were seated together under an awning of buffalo-robes, and the old conjurer, who, with his hard, emaciated face and gaunt ribs, was perched aloft like a turkey-buzzard, among the dead branches of an old tree, constantly on the lookout for enemies. We dined, and then Shaw saddled his horse.

"I will ride back," said he, "to Horseshoe Creek, and see if Bisonette is there."

"I would go with you," I answered, "but I must reserve all the strength I have."

The afternoon dragged away at last. I occupied myself in cleaning my rifle and pistols, and making other preparations for the journey. It was late before I wrapped myself in my blanket, and lay down for the night, with my head
5 on my saddle. Shaw had not returned, but this gave us no uneasiness, for we supposed that he had fallen in with Bisonette, and was spending the night with him. For a day or two past I had gained in strength and health, but about midnight an attack of pain awoke me, and for some hours
10 I could not sleep. The moon was quivering on the broad breast of the Platte ; nothing could be heard except those low inexplicable sounds, like whisperings and footsteps, which no one who has spent the night alone amid deserts and forests will be at a loss to understand. As I was falling
15 asleep, a familiar voice, shouting from the distance, awoke me again. A rapid step approached the camp, and Shaw, on foot, with his gun in his hand, hastily entered.

" Where 's your horse ? " said I, raising myself on my elbow.

20 " Lost ! " said Shaw. " Where 's Deslauriers ? "

" There," I replied, pointing to a confused mass of blankets and buffalo-robes.

Shaw touched them with the butt of his gun, and up sprang our faithful Canadian.

25 " Come, Deslauriers ; stir up the fire, and get me something to eat."

" Where 's Bisonette ? " asked I.

" The Lord knows ; there 's nobody at Horseshoe Creek."

Shaw had gone back to the spot where we had encamped
30 two days before, and finding nothing there but the ashes of our fires, he had tied his horse to the tree while he bathed in the stream. Something startled his horse, which broke loose, and for two hours Shaw tried in vain to catch him. Sunset approached, and it was twelve miles to camp. So he abandoned the attempt, and set out on foot to join us.

The greater part of his perilous and solitary walk was in darkness. His moccasons were worn to tatters and his feet severely lacerated. He sat down to eat, however, the usual equanimity of his temper not at all disturbed by his misfortune, and my last recollection before falling asleep was of Shaw, seated cross-legged before the fire, smoking his pipe.

When I awoke again there was a fresh damp smell in the air, a gray twilight involved the prairie, and above its eastern verge was a streak of cold red sky. I called to the men, and in a moment a fire was blazing brightly in the dim morning light, and breakfast was getting ready. We sat down together on the grass, to the last civilized meal which Raymond and I were destined to enjoy for some time.

"Now bring in the horses."

My little mare Pauline was soon standing by the fire. She was a fleet, hardy, and gentle animal, christened after Paul Dorion, from whom I had procured her in exchange for Pontiac. She did not look as if equipped for a morning pleasure-ride. In front of the black, high-bowed mountain-saddle were fastened holsters, with heavy pistols. A pair of saddle-bags, a blanket tightly rolled, a small parcel of Indian presents tied up in a buffalo-skin, a leather bag of flour, and a smaller one of tea, were all secured behind, and a long trail-rope was wound round her neck. Raymond had a strong black mule, equipped in a similar manner. We crammed our powder-horns to the throat, and mounted.

"I will meet you at Fort Laramie on the first of August," said I to Shaw.

"That is," he replied, "if we don't meet before that. I think I shall follow after you in a day or two."

This in fact he attempted, and would have succeeded if he had not encountered obstacles against which his resolute spirit was of no avail. Two days after I left him he sent Deslauriers to the fort with the cart and baggage, and set out for the mountains with Henry Chatillon; but a tremendous thunder-storm had deluged the prairie, and nearly obliterated not only our trail but that of the Indians themselves. They encamped at the base of the mountains, at a loss in what direction to go. In the morning Shaw found himself poisoned by the plant known as "poison ivy," in such a manner that it was impossible for him to travel. So they turned back reluctantly towards Fort Laramie. Shaw lay seriously ill for a week, and remained at the fort till I rejoined him some time after.

To return to my own story. Raymond and I shook hands with our friends, rode out upon the prairie, and, clambering the sandy hollows channelled in the sides of the hills, gained the high plains above. If a curse had been pronounced upon the land, it could not have worn an aspect more forlorn. There were abrupt broken hills, deep hollows, and wide plains; but all alike glared with an insupportable whiteness under the burning sun. The country, as if parched by the heat, was cracked into innumerable fissures and ravines, that not a little impeded our progress. Their steep sides were white and raw, and along the bottom we several times discovered the broad tracks of the grizzly bear, nowhere more abundant than in this region. The ridges of the hills were hard as rock, and strewn with pebbles of flint and coarse red jasper; looking from them, there was nothing to relieve the desert uniformity, save here and there a pine-tree clinging at the edge of a ravine, and stretching its rough, shaggy arms into the scorching air. Its resinous odors recalled the pine-clad mountains of New England, and, goaded as I was with a morbid thirst, I thought with a longing desire on the crystal treasure poured in such wasteful profusion from our thousand hills. I heard, in fancy, the plunging and gurgling of waters among the shaded rocks, and saw them gleaming dark and still far down amid the crevices, the cold drops trickling from the long green mosses.

When noon came we found a little stream, with a few trees and bushes; and here we rested for an hour. Then we travelled on, guided by the sun, until, just before sunset, we reached another stream, called Bitter Cotton-wood Creek. A thick growth of bushes and old storm-beaten trees grew at intervals along its bank. Near the foot of one of the trees we flung down our saddles, and hobbling our horses, turned them loose to feed. The little stream was clear and swift, and ran musically over its white sands. Small water-birds were splashing in the shallows, and filling the air with cries and flutterings. The sun was just sinking among gold and crimson clouds behind Mount Laramie. I lay upon a log by the margin of the water, and watched the restless motions of the little fish in a deep, still nook below. Strange to say, I seemed to have gained strength since the morning, and almost felt a sense of returning health.

We built our fire. Night came, and the wolves began to howl. One deep voice began, answered in awful responses from hills, plains, and woods. Such sounds do not disturb one's sleep upon the prairie. We picketed the mare and the mule, and did not awake until daylight. Then we turned them loose, still hobbled, to feed for an hour before starting. We were getting ready our breakfast when Raymond saw an antelope half a mile distant and said he would go and shoot it.

"Your business," said I, "is to look after the animals. I am too weak to do much, if anything happens to them, and you must keep within sight of the camp."

Raymond promised, and set out with his rifle in his hand. The mare and the mule had crossed the stream, and were feeding among the long grass on the other side, much tormented by the attacks of large green-headed flies. As I watched them, I saw them go down into a hollow, and as several minutes elapsed without their reappearing, I waded through the stream to look after them. To my vexation and

alarm I discovered them at a great distance, galloping away
at full speed, Pauline in advance, with her hobbles broken,
and the mule, still fettered, following with awkward leaps.
I fired my rifle and shouted to recall Raymond. In a moment
he came running through the stream, with a red handkerchief bound round his head. I pointed to the fugitives, and
ordered him to pursue them. Muttering a " Sacré " between
his teeth, he set out at full speed, still swinging his rifle in
his hand. I walked up to the top of a hill, and, looking
away over the prairie, could distinguish the runaways, still
at full gallop. Returning to the fire, I sat down at the foot
of a tree. Wearily and anxiously hour after hour passed away.
The loose bark dangling from the trunk behind me flapped
to and fro in the wind, and the mosquitoes kept up their
drowsy hum; but other than this there was no sight nor
sound of life throughout the burning landscape. The sun
rose higher and higher, until I knew that it must be noon.
It seemed scarcely possible that the animals could be recovered. If they were not, my situation was one of serious
difficulty. Shaw, when I left him, had decided to move that
morning, but whither he had not determined. To look for
him would be a vain attempt. Fort Laramie was forty miles
distant, and I could not walk a mile without great effort.
Not then having learned the philosophy of yielding to
disproportionate obstacles, I resolved, come what would, to
continue the pursuit of the Indians. Only one plan occurred
to me; this was, to send Raymond to the fort with an order
for more horses, while I remained on the spot, awaiting his
return, which might take place within three days. But to
remain stationary and alone for three days, in a country
full of dangerous Indians, was not the most flattering of
prospects; and, protracted as my Indian hunt must be by
such delay, it was not easy to foretell its result. Revolving
these matters, I grew hungry; and as our stock of provisions, except four or five pounds of flour, was by this time

exhausted, I left the camp to see what game I could find. Nothing could be seen except four or five large curlews wheeling over my head, and now and then alighting upon the prairie. I shot two of them, and was about returning, when a startling sight caught my eye. A small, dark object, like a human head, suddenly appeared, and vanished among the thick bushes along the stream below. In that country every stranger is a suspected enemy; and I threw forward the muzzle of my rifle. In a moment the bushes were violently shaken, two heads, but not human heads, protruded, and to my great joy I recognized the downcast, disconsolate countenance of the black mule and the yellow visage of Pauline. Raymond came upon the mule, pale and haggard, complaining of a fiery pain in his chest. I took charge of the animals while he kneeled down by the side of the stream to drink. He had kept the runaways in sight as far as the Side Fork of Laramie Creek, a distance of more than ten miles; and here with great difficulty he had succeeded in catching them. I saw that he was unarmed, and asked him what he had done with his rifle. It had encumbered him in his pursuit, and he had dropped it on the prairie, thinking that he could find it on his return; but in this he had failed. The loss might prove a very serious one. I was too much rejoiced, however, at the recovery of the animals, and at the fidelity of Raymond, who might easily have deserted with them, to think much about it; and having made some tea for him in a tin vessel which we had brought with us, I told him that I would give him two hours for resting before we set out again. He had eaten nothing that day; but having no appetite, he lay down immediately to sleep. I picketed the animals among the best grass that I could find, and made fires of green wood to protect them from the flies; then sitting down again by the tree, I watched the slow movements of the sun, grudging every moment that passed.

The time I had mentioned expired, and I awoke Raymond. We saddled and set out again, but first we went in search of the lost rifle, and in the course of an hour were fortunate enough to find it. Then we turned westward, and moved over the hills and hollows at a slow pace towards the Black Hills. The heat no longer tormented us, for a cloud was before the sun. The air grew fresh and cool, the distant mountains frowned more gloomily, there was a low muttering of thunder, and dense black masses of cloud rose heavily behind the broken peaks. At first they were fringed with silver by the afternoon sun; but soon thick blackness overspread the sky, and the desert around us was wrapped in gloom. There was an awful sublimity in the hoarse murmuring of the thunder, and the sombre shadows that involved the mountains and the plain. The storm broke with a zigzag blinding flash, a terrific crash of thunder, and a hurricane that howled over the prairie, dashing floods of water against us. Raymond looked about him and cursed the merciless elements. There seemed no shelter near, but we discerned at length a deep ravine gashed in the level prairie, and saw half-way down its side an old pine-tree, whose rough horizontal boughs formed a sort of pent-house against the tempest. We found a practicable passage, led our animals down, and fastened them to large loose stones at the bottom; then climbing up, we drew our blankets over our heads, and crouched close beneath the old tree. Perhaps I was no competent judge of time, but it seemed to me that we were sitting there a full hour, while around us poured a deluge of rain, through which the rocks on the opposite side of the gulf were barely visible. The first burst of the tempest soon subsided, but the rain poured in steady torrents. At length Raymond grew impatient, and scrambling out of the ravine, gained the level prairie above.

"What does the weather look like?" asked I, from my seat under the tree.

"It looks bad," he answered: "dark all round"; and again he descended and sat down by my side. Some ten minutes elapsed.

"Go up again," said I, "and take another look"; and he clambered up the precipice. "Well, how is it?" 5

"Just the same, only I see one little bright spot over the top of the mountain."

The rain by this time had begun to abate; and going down to the bottom of the ravine, we loosened the animals, who were standing up to their knees in water. Leading them up 10 the rocky throat of the ravine, we reached the plain above. All around us was obscurity; but the bright spot above the mountains grew wider and ruddier, until at length the clouds drew apart, and a flood of sunbeams poured down, streaming along the precipices, and involving them in a thin blue haze, 15 as soft as that which wraps the Apennines on an evening in spring. Rapidly the clouds were broken and scattered, like routed legions of evil spirits. The plain lay basking in sunbeams around us; a rainbow arched the desert from north to south, and far in front a line of woods seemed inviting us to 20 refreshment and repose. When we reached them, they were glistening with prismatic dewdrops, and enlivened by the songs and flutterings of birds. Strange winged insects, benumbed by the rain, were clinging to the leaves and the bark of the trees.

Raymond kindled a fire with great difficulty. The animals 25 turned eagerly to feed on the soft rich grass, while I, wrapping myself in my blanket, lay down and gazed on the evening landscape. The mountains, whose stern features had frowned upon us so gloomily, seemed lighted up with a benignant smile, and the green waving undulations of the 30 plain were gladdened with warm sunshine. Wet, ill, and wearied as I was, my heart grew lighter at the view, and I drew from it an augury of good.

When morning came, Raymond awoke, coughing violently, though I had apparently received no injury. We mounted,

crossed the little stream, pushed through the trees, and
began our journey over the plain beyond. And now, as we
rode slowly along, we looked anxiously on every hand for
traces of the Indians, not doubting that the village had
5 passed somewhere in that vicinity ; but the scanty shrivelled
grass was not more than three or four inches high, and the
ground was so hard that a host might have marched over it
and left scarcely a trace of its passage. Up hill and down
hill, and clambering through ravines, we continued our jour-
10 ney. As we were passing the foot of a hill, I saw Raymond,
who was some rods in advance, suddenly jerk the reins of
his mule, slide from his seat, and run in a crouching posture
up a hollow ; then in an instant I heard the sharp crack of
his rifle. A wounded antelope came running on three legs
15 over the hill. I lashed Pauline and made after him. My
fleet little mare soon brought me by his side, and, after leaping and bounding for a few moments in vain, he stood still,
as if despairing of escape. His glistening eyes turned up
towards my face with so piteous a look that it was with feel-
20 ings of infinite compunction that I shot him through the
head with a pistol. Raymond skinned and cut him up, and
we hung the fore-quarters to our saddles, much rejoiced
that our exhausted stock of provisions was renewed in such
good time.

25   Gaining the top of a hill, we could see along the cloudy
verge of the prairie before us the lines of trees and shadowy
groves, that marked the course of Laramie Creek. Before
noon we reached its banks, and began anxiously to search
them for footprints of the Indians. We followed the stream
30 for several miles, now on the shore and now wading
in the water, scrutinizing every sand-bar and every muddy
bank. So long was the search that we began to fear
that we had left the trail undiscovered behind us. At length
I heard Raymond shouting, and saw him jump from his
mule to examine some object under the shelving bank.

I rode up to his side. It was the impression of an Indian
moccason. Encouraged by this, we continued our search till
at last some appearances on a soft surface of earth not far
from the shore attracted my eye; and going to examine
them, I found half a dozen tracks, some made by men and   5
some by children. Just then Raymond observed across the
stream the mouth of a brook, entering it from the south.
He forded the water, rode in at the opening, and in a moment I heard him shouting again; so I passed over and
joined him. The brook had a broad sandy bed, along which   10
the water trickled in a scanty stream; and on either bank
the bushes were so close that the view was completely intercepted. I found Raymond stooping over the footprints of
three or four horses. Proceeding, we found those of a man,
then those of a child, then those of more horses; till at last   15
the bushes on each bank were beaten down and broken, and
the sand ploughed up with a multitude of footsteps, and
scored across with the furrows made by the lodge-poles that
had been dragged through. It was now certain that we had
found the trail. I pushed through the bushes, and at a   20
little distance on the prairie beyond found the ashes of
a hundred and fifty lodge-fires, with bones and pieces of
buffalo-robes scattered about, and the pickets to which horses
had been tied, still standing in the ground. Elated by our
success, we selected a convenient tree, and, turning the ani-   25
mals loose, prepared to make a meal from the haunch of the
antelope.

Hardship and exposure had thriven with me wonderfully.
I had gained both health and strength since leaving La
Bonté's camp. Raymond and I dined together, in high   30
spirits; for we rashly presumed that having found one end
of the trail we should have little difficulty in reaching the
other. But when the animals were led in, we found that our
ill-luck had not ceased to follow us. As I was saddling
Pauline, I saw that her eye was dull as lead, and the hue of

her yellow coat visibly darkened. I placed my foot in the stirrup to mount, when she staggered and fell flat on her side. Gaining her feet with an effort, she stood by the fire with a drooping head. Whether she had been bitten by a
5 snake, or poisoned by some noxious plant, or attacked by a sudden disorder, it was hard to say; but at all events, her sickness was sufficiently ill-timed and unfortunate. I succeeded in a second attempt to mount her, and with a slow pace we moved forward on the trail of the Indians. It led
10 us up a hill and over a dreary plain; and here, to our great mortification, the traces almost disappeared, for the ground was hard as adamant; and if its flinty surface had ever retained the dent of a hoof, the marks had been washed away by the deluge of yesterday. An Indian village, in its disorderly
15 march, is scattered over the prairie often to the width of half a mile; so that its trail is nowhere clearly marked, and the task of following it is made doubly wearisome and difficult. By good fortune, many large ant-hills, a yard or more in diameter, were scattered over the plain, and these were
20 frequently broken by the footprints of men and horses, and marked by traces of the lodge-poles. The succulent leaves of the prickly-pear, bruised from the same causes, also helped to guide us; so, inch by inch, we moved along. Often we lost the trail altogether, and then found it again; but late
25 in the afternoon we were totally at fault. We stood alone, without a clew to guide us. The broken plain expanded for league after league around us, and in front the long dark ridge of mountains stretched from north to south. Mount Laramie, a little on our right, towered high above the rest,
30 and from a dark valley just beyond one of its lower declivities, we discerned volumes of white smoke rising slowly.

"I think," said Raymond, "some Indians must be there. Perhaps we had better go." But this plan was not lightly to be adopted, and we determined still to continue our search after the lost trail. Our good stars prompted us to this decision, for we afterward had reason to believe, from information given us by the Indians, that the smoke was raised as a decoy by a Crow war-party.

Evening was coming on, and there was no wood or water nearer than the foot of the mountains. So thither we turned, directing our course towards the point where Laramie Creek issues upon the prairie. When we reached it, the bare tops of the mountains were still bright with sunshine. The little river was breaking, with an angry current, from its dark prison. There was something in the close vicinity of the mountains and the loud surging of the rapids, wonderfully cheering and exhilarating. There was a grass-plot by the river-bank, surrounded by low ridges, which would effectually screen us and our fire from the sight of wandering Indians. Here, among the grass, I observed numerous circles of large stones, traces of a Dahcotah winter encampment. We lay down, and did not awake till the sun was up. A large rock projected from the shore, and behind it the deep water was slowly eddying round and round. The temptation was irresistible. I threw off my clothes, leaped in, suffered myself to be borne once round with the current, and then, seizing the strong root of a water-plant, drew myself to the shore. The effect was so refreshing that I mistook it for returning health. But scarcely were we mounted and on our way, before the momentary glow passed. Again I hung as usual in my seat, scarcely able to hold myself erect.

"Look yonder," said Raymond; "you see that big hollow there; the Indians must have gone that way, if they went anywhere about here."

We reached the gap, which was like a deep notch cut into the mountain-ridge, and here we soon found an ant-hill furrowed with the mark of a lodge-pole. This was quite enough; there could be no doubt now. As we rode on, the opening growing narrower, the Indians had been compelled to march in closer order, and the traces became numerous

and distinct. The gap terminated in a rocky gateway, leading into a rough and steep defile, between two precipitous
mountains. Here grass and weeds were bruised to fragments
by the throng that had passed through. We moved slowly
5 over the rocks, up the passage; and in this toilsome manner
advanced for an hour or two, bare precipices, hundreds of
feet high, shooting up on either hand. Raymond, with his
hardy mule, was a few rods before me, when we came to the
foot of an ascent steeper than the rest, and which I trusted
10 might prove the highest point of the defile. Pauline strained
upward for a few yards, moaning and stumbling, and then
came to a dead stop, unable to proceed further. I dismounted, and attempted to lead her; but my own exhausted
strength soon gave out; so I loosened the trail-rope from
15 her neck, and tying it round my arm, crawled up on my
hands and knees. I gained the top, totally spent, the sweat-
drops trickling from my forehead. Pauline stood like a
statue by my side, her shadow falling upon the scorching
rock; and in this shade, for there was no other, I lay for
20 some time, scarcely able to move a limb. All around, the
black crags, sharp as needles at the top, stood baking in the
sun, without tree or bush or blade of grass to cover their
nakedness. The whole scene seemed parched with a pitiless,
insufferable heat.

25   After a while I could mount again, and we moved on,
descending the defile on its western side. There was something ridiculous in the situation. Man and horse were helpless alike. Pauline and I could neither fight nor run.

  Raymond's saddle-girth slipped; and while I proceeded
30 he stopped to repair the mischief. I came to the top of a
little declivity, where a welcome sight greeted my eye; a
nook of fresh green grass nestled among the cliffs, sunny
clumps of bushes on one side, and shaggy old pine-trees
leaning from the rocks on the other. A shrill, familiar voice
saluted me, and recalled me to days of boyhood; that of the

insect called the "locust" by New England schoolboys,
which was clinging among the heated boughs of the old
pine-trees. Then, too, as I passed the bushes, the low sound
of falling water reached my ear. Pauline turned of her own
accord, and pushing through the boughs, we found a black
rock, overarched by the cool green canopy. An icy stream
was pouring from its side into a wide basin of white sand,
whence it had no visible outlet, but filtered through into the
soil below. While I filled a tin cup at the spring, Pauline
was eagerly plunging her head deep in the pool. Other
visitors had been there before us. All around in the soft soil
were the footprints of elk, deer, and the Rocky-Mountain
sheep; and the grizzly bear too had left the recent prints
of his broad foot, with its frightful array of claws. Among
these mountains was his home.

Soon after leaving the spring we found a little grassy
plain, encircled by the mountains, and marked, to our great
joy, with all the traces of an Indian camp. Raymond's
practised eye detected certain signs, by which he recognized
the spot where Reynal's lodge had been pitched and his
horses picketed. I approached, and stood looking at the
place. Reynal and I had, I believe, hardly a feeling in
common, and it perplexed me a good deal to understand
why I should look with so much interest on the ashes of
his fire, when between him and me there was no other
bond of sympathy than the slender and precarious one of
a kindred race.

In half an hour from this we were free of the mountains.
There was a plain before us, totally barren and thickly
peopled in many parts with prairie-dogs, who sat at the
mouths of their burrows, and yelped at us as we passed.
The plain, as we thought, was about six miles wide; but it
cost us two hours to cross it. Then another mountain-range
rose before us. From the dense bushes that clothed the
steeps for a thousand feet shot up black crags, all leaning

one way, and shattered by storms and thunder into grim and threatening shapes. As we entered a narrow passage on the trail of the Indians, they impended frightfully above our heads.

5   Our course was through thick woods, in the shade and sunlight of overhanging boughs. As we wound from side to side of the passage, to avoid its obstructions, we could see at intervals, through the foliage, the awful forms of the gigantic cliffs, that seemed to hem us in on the right and
10 on the left, before and behind.

In an open space, fenced in by high rocks, stood two Indian forts, of a square form, rudely built of sticks and logs. They were somewhat ruinous, having probably been constructed the year before. Each might have contained
15 about twenty men. Perhaps in this gloomy spot some party had been beset by enemies, and those scowling rocks and blasted trees might not long since have looked down on a conflict, unchronicled and unknown. Yet if any traces of bloodshed remained they were hidden by the bushes and
20 tall rank weeds.

Gradually the mountains drew apart, and the passage expanded into a plain, where again we found traces of an Indian encampment. There were trees and bushes just before us, and we stopped here for an hour's rest and refresh-
25 ment. When we had finished our meal, Raymond struck fire, and, lighting his pipe, sat down at the foot of a tree to smoke. For some time I observed him puffing away with a face of unusual solemnity. Then slowly taking the pipe from his lips, he looked up and remarked that we had better
30 not go any farther.

" Why not ? " asked I.

He said that the country was become very dangerous, that we were entering the range of the Snakes, Arapahoes, and Gros-Ventre Blackfeet, and that if any of their wandering parties should meet us, it would cost us our lives; but he added with blunt fidelity that he would go anywhere I wished. I told him to bring up the animals, and mounting them we proceeded again. I confess that, as we moved forward, the prospect seemed but a doubtful one. I would have given the world for my ordinary elasticity of body and mind, and for a horse of such strength and spirit as the journey required.

Closer and closer the rocks gathered round us, growing taller and steeper, and pressing more and more upon our path. We entered at length a defile which, in its way, I never have seen rivalled. The mountain was cracked from top to bottom, and we were creeping along the bottom of the fissure, in dampness and gloom, with the clink of hoofs on the loose shingly rocks, and the hoarse murmuring of a petulant brook which kept us company. Sometimes the water, foaming among the stones, overspread the whole narrow passage; sometimes, withdrawing to one side, it gave us room to pass dry-shod. Looking up, we could see a narrow ribbon of bright blue sky between the dark edges of the opposing cliffs. This did not last long. The passage soon widened, and sunbeams found their way down, flashing upon the black waters. The defile would spread to many rods in width; bushes, trees, and flowers would spring by the side of the brook; the cliffs would be feathered with shrubbery, that clung in every crevice, and fringed with trees, that grew along their sunny edges. Then we would be moving again in darkness. The passage seemed about four miles long, and before we reached the end of it, the unshod hoofs of our animals were broken, and their legs cut by the sharp stones. Issuing from the mountain we found another plain. All around it stood a circle of precipices, that seemed the impersonation of Silence and Solitude. Here again the Indians had encamped, as well they might, after passing with their women, children, and horses, through the gulf behind us. In one day we had made a journey which it had cost them three to accomplish.

The only outlet to this amphitheatre lay over a hill some
two hundred feet high, up which we moved with difficulty.
Looking from the top, we saw that at last we were free of
the mountains. The prairie spread before us, but so wild and
5 broken that the view was everywhere obstructed. Far on
our left one tall hill swelled up against the sky, on the
smooth, pale-green surface of which four slowly moving
black specks were discernible. They were evidently buffalo,
and we hailed the sight as a good augury; for where the
10 buffalo were, there the Indians would probably be found.
We hoped on that very night to reach the village. We were
anxious to do so for a double reason, wishing to bring our
journey to an end, and knowing moreover that though to
enter the village in broad daylight would be perfectly safe,
15 yet to encamp in its vicinity would be dangerous. But as
we rode on, the sun was sinking, and soon was within half
an hour of the horizon. We ascended a hill, and looked
about us for a spot for our encampment. The prairie was
like a turbulent ocean, suddenly congealed when its waves
20 were at the highest, and it lay half in light and half in
shadow, as the rich sunshine, yellow as gold, was pouring
over it. The rough bushes of the wild sage were growing
everywhere, its dull pale-green overspreading hill and hollow. Yet a little way before us, a bright verdant line of
25 grass was winding along the plain, and here and there
throughout its course glistened pools of water. We went
down to it, kindled a fire, and turned our horses loose to
feed. It was a little trickling brook, that for some yards on
either side turned the barren prairie into fertility, and here
30 and there it spread into deep pools, where the beavers had
dammed it up.

We placed our last remaining piece of antelope before a
scanty fire, mournfully reflecting on our exhausted stock of
provisions. Just then a large gray hare, peculiar to these
prairies, came jumping along, and seated himself within

fifty yards to look at us. I thoughtlessly raised my rifle to shoot him, but Raymond called out to me not to fire for fear the report should reach the ears of the Indians. That night for the first time we considered that the danger to which we were exposed was of a somewhat serious character; and to those who are unacquainted with Indians, it may seem strange that our chief apprehensions arose from the supposed proximity of the people whom we intended to visit. Had any straggling party of these faithful friends caught sight of us from the hill-top, they would probably have returned in the night to plunder us of our horses, and perhaps of our scalps. But the prairie is unfavorable to nervousness; and I presume that neither Raymond nor I thought twice of the matter that evening.

For eight hours pillowed on our saddles, we lay insensible as logs. Pauline's yellow head was stretched over me when I awoke. I rose and examined her. Her feet were bruised and swollen by the accidents of yesterday, but her eye was brighter, her motions livelier, and her mysterious malady had visibly abated. We moved on, hoping within an hour to come in sight of the Indian village; but again disappointment awaited us. The trail disappeared upon a hard and stony plain. Raymond and I rode from side to side, scrutinizing every yard of ground, until at length I found traces of the lodge-poles, by the side of a ridge of rocks. We began again to follow them.

"What is that black spot out there on the prairie?"

"It looks like a dead buffalo," answered Raymond.

We rode to it, and found it to be the huge carcass of a bull killed by the hunters as they had passed. Tangled hair and scraps of hide were scattered on all sides, for the wolves had made merry over it, and hollowed out the entire carcass. It was covered with myriads of large black crickets, and from its appearance must have lain there four or five days. The sight was a disheartening one, and I observed to

Raymond that the Indians might still be fifty or sixty miles off. But he shook his head, and replied that they dared not go so far for fear of their enemies, the Snakes.

Soon after this we lost the trail again, and ascended a neighboring ridge, totally at a loss. Before us lay a plain perfectly flat, spreading on the right and left, without apparent limit, and bounded in front by a long broken line of hills, ten or twelve miles distant. All was open and exposed to view, yet not a buffalo nor an Indian was visible.

"Do you see that?" said Raymond: "now we had better turn round."

But as Raymond's *bourgeois* thought otherwise, we descended the hill and began to cross the plain. We had come so far that neither Pauline's limbs nor my own could carry me back to Fort Laramie. I considered that the lines of expediency and inclination tallied exactly, and that the most prudent course was to keep forward. The ground immediately around us was thickly strewn with the skulls and bones of buffalo, for here a year or two before the Indians had made a "surround"; yet no living game was in sight. At length an antelope sprang up and gazed at us. We fired together, and both missed, although the animal stood, a fair mark, within eighty yards. This ill-success might perhaps be charged to our own eagerness, for by this time we had no provisions left except a little flour. We could see several pools of water, glistening in the distance. As we approached, wolves and antelopes bounded away through the tall grass around them, and flocks of large white plover flew screaming over their surface. Having failed of the antelope, Raymond tried his hand at the birds, with the same ill-success. The water also disappointed us. Its margin was so mired by the crowd of buffalo that our timorous animals were afraid to approach. So we turned away and moved towards the hills. The rank grass where it was not trampled down by the buffalo, fairly swept our horses' necks.

Again we found the same execrable barren prairie offering
no clew by which to guide our way. As we drew near the
hills, an opening appeared, through which the Indians must
have gone if they had passed that way at all. Slowly we
began to ascend it. I felt the most dreary forebodings of   5
ill-success, when on looking round I could discover neither
dent of hoof, nor footprint, nor trace of lodge-pole, though
the passage was encumbered by the skulls of buffalo. We
heard thunder muttering; another storm was coming on.

As we gained the top of the gap, the prospect beyond   10
began to disclose itself. First, we saw a long dark line of
ragged clouds upon the horizon, while above them rose the
peaks of the Medicine Bow range, the vanguard of the
Rocky Mountains; then little by little the plain came into
view, a vast green uniformity, forlorn and tenantless, though   15
Laramie Creek glistened in a waving line over its surface,
without a bush or a tree upon its banks. As yet, the round
projecting shoulder of a hill intercepted a part of the view.
I rode in advance, when suddenly I could distinguish a few
dark spots on the prairie, along the bank of the stream.   20

"Buffalo!" said I.

"Horses, by God!" exclaimed Raymond, lashing his mule
forward as he spoke. More and more of the plain disclosed
itself, and more and more horses appeared, scattered along
the river-bank, or feeding in bands over the prairie. Then,   25
standing in a circle by the stream, swarming with their
savage inhabitants, we saw, a mile or more off, the tall
lodges of the Ogillallah. Never did the heart of wanderer
more gladden at the sight of home than did mine at the
sight of that Indian camp.   30

CHAPTER XIV

THE OGILLALLAH VILLAGE

This is hardly the place for portraying the mental features of the Indians. The same picture, slightly changed in shade and coloring, would serve with very few exceptions for all the tribes north of the Mexican territories. But with this similarity in their modes of thought, the tribes of the lake and ocean shores, of the forests and of the plains, differ greatly in their manner of life. Having been domesticated for several weeks among one of the wildest of the hordes that roam over the remote prairies, I had unusual opportunities of observing them, and flatter myself that a sketch of the scenes that passed daily before my eyes may not be devoid of interest. They were thorough savages. Neither their manners nor their ideas were in the slightest degree modified by contact with civilization. They knew nothing of the power and real character of the white men, and their children would scream in terror when they saw me. Their religion, superstitions, and prejudices were the same handed down to them from immemorial time. They fought with the weapons that their fathers fought with, and wore the same garments of skins. They were living representatives of the "stone age"; for though their lances and arrows were tipped with iron procured from the traders, they still used the rude stone mallet of the primeval world.

Great changes are at hand in that region. With the stream of emigration to Oregon and California, the buffalo will dwindle away, and the large wandering communities who depend on them for support must be broken and scattered. The Indians will soon be abased by whiskey and

overawed by military posts; so that within a few years
the traveller may pass in tolerable security through their
country. Its danger and its charm will have disappeared
together.

As soon as Raymond and I discovered the village from
the gap in the hills, we were seen in our turn; keen eyes
were constantly on the watch. As we rode down upon the
plain, the side of the village nearest us was darkened with
a crowd of naked figures. Several men came forward to
meet us. I could distinguish among them the green blanket
of the Frenchman Reynal. When we came up the ceremony
of shaking hands had to be gone through in due form, and
then all were eager to know what had become of the rest of
my party. I satisfied them on this point, and we all moved
together towards the village.

"You've missed it," said Reynal; "if you'd been here
day before yesterday, you'd have found the whole prairie
over yonder black with buffalo as far as you could see.
There were no cows, though; nothing but bulls. We made
a 'surround' every day till yesterday. See the village there;
don't that look like good living?"

In fact, I could see, even at that distance, long cords
stretched from lodge to lodge, over which the meat, cut by
the squaws into thin sheets, was hanging to dry in the sun.
I noticed too that the village was somewhat smaller than
when I had last seen it, and I asked Reynal the cause. He
said that old Le Borgne had felt too weak to pass over the
mountains, and so had remained behind with all his relations,
including Mahto-Tatonka and his brothers. The Whirlwind
too had been unwilling to come so far, because, as Reynal
said, he was afraid. Only half a dozen lodges had adhered
to him, the main body of the village setting their chief's
authority at naught, and taking the course most agreeable
to their inclinations.

"What chiefs are there in the village now?" asked I.

"Well," said Reynal, "there's old Red-Water, and the
Eagle-Feather, and the Big Crow, and the Mad Wolf, and
the Panther, and the White Shield, and — what's his name?
— the half-breed Shienne."

5   By this time we were close to the village, and I observed
that while the greater part of the lodges were very large
and neat in their appearance, there was at one side a cluster of
squalid, miserable huts. I looked towards them, and made
some remark about their wretched appearance. But I was
10 touching upon delicate ground.

"My squaw's relations live in those lodges," said Reynal,
very warmly; "and there is n't a better set in the whole
village."

"Are there any chiefs among them?"

15   "Chiefs?" said Reynal; "yes, plenty!"

"What are their names?"

"Their names? Why, there's the Arrow-Head. If he
is n't a chief, he ought to be one. And there's the Hail-
Storm. He's nothing but a boy, to be sure; but he's bound
20 to be a chief one of these days."

Just then we passed between two of the lodges, and
entered the great area of the village. Superb, naked figures
stood silently gazing on us.

"Where's the Bad Wound's lodge?" said I to Reynal.

25   "There, you've missed it again! The Bad Wound is
away with The Whirlwind. If you could have found him
here, and gone to live in his lodge, he would have treated
you better than any man in the village. But there's the
Big Crow's lodge yonder, next to old Red-Water's. He's a
30 good Indian for the whites, and I advise you to go and live
with him."

"Are there many squaws and children in his lodge?"
said I.

"No; only one squaw and two or three children. He
keeps the rest in a separate lodge by themselves."

So, still followed by a crowd of Indians, Raymond and I rode up to the entrance of the Big Crow's lodge. A squaw came out immediately and took our horses. I put aside the leather flap that covered the low opening, and stooping, entered the Big Crow's dwelling. There I could see the chief in the dim light, seated at one side, on a pile of buffalo-robes. He greeted me with a guttural "How, colà!" I requested Reynal to tell him that Raymond and I were come to live with him. The Big Crow gave another low exclamation. The announcement may seem intrusive, but, in fact, every Indian in the village would have deemed himself honored that white men should give such preference to his hospitality.

The squaw spread a buffalo-robe for us in the guest's place at the head of the lodge. Our saddles were brought in, and scarcely were we seated upon them before the place was thronged with Indians, crowding in to see us. The Big Crow produced his pipe and filled it with the mixture of tobacco and *shongsasha*, or red willow bark. Round and round it passed, and a lively conversation went forward. Meanwhile a squaw placed before the two guests a wooden bowl of boiled buffalo-meat; but unhappily this was not the only banquet destined to be inflicted on us. One after another, boys and young squaws thrust their heads in at the opening, to invite us to various feasts in different parts of the village. For half an hour or more we were actively engaged in passing from lodge to lodge, tasting in each of the bowl of meat set before us, and inhaling a whiff or two from our entertainer's pipe. A thunder-storm that had been threatening for some time now began in good earnest. We crossed over to Reynal's lodge, though it hardly deserved the name, for it consisted only of a few old buffalo-robes, supported on poles, and was quite open on one side. Here we sat down, and the Indians gathered round us.

"What is it," said I, "that makes the thunder?"

"It's my belief," said Reynal, "that it's a big stone rolling over the sky."

"Very likely," I replied; "but I want to know what the Indians think about it."

5   So he interpreted my question, which produced some debate. There was a difference of opinion. At last old Mene-Seela, or Red-Water, who sat by himself at one side, looked up with his withered face, and said he had always known what the thunder was. It was a great black bird;
10 and once he had seen it, in a dream, swooping down from the Black Hills, with its loud roaring wings; and when it flapped them over a lake, they struck lightning from the water.

"The thunder is bad," said another old man, who sat muffled in his buffalo-robe; "he killed my brother last
15 summer."

   Reynal, at my request, asked for an explanation; but the old man remained doggedly silent, and would not look up. Some time after, I learned how the accident occurred. The man who was killed belonged to an association which, among
20 other mystic functions, claimed the exclusive power and privilege of fighting the thunder. Whenever a storm which they wished to avert was threatening, the thunder-fighters would take their bows and arrows, their guns, their magic drum, and a sort of whistle, made out of the wing-bone of
25 the war-eagle, and, thus equipped, run out and fire at the rising cloud, whooping, yelling, whistling, and beating their drum, to frighten it down again. One afternoon, a heavy black cloud was coming up, and they repaired to the top of a hill, where they brought all their magic artillery into
30 play against it. But the undaunted thunder, refusing to be terrified, darted out a bright flash, which struck one of the party dead as he was in the very act of shaking his long iron-pointed lance against it. The rest scattered and ran yelling in an ecstasy of superstitious terror back to their lodges.

The lodge of my host Kongra-Tonga, or the Big Crow, presented a picturesque spectacle that evening. A score or more of Indians were seated around it in a circle, their dark naked forms just visible by the dull light of the smouldering fire in the middle. The pipe glowed brightly in the gloom as it passed from hand to hand. Then a squaw would drop a piece of buffalo-fat on the dull embers. Instantly a bright flame would leap up, darting its light to the very apex of the tall conical structure, where the tops of the slender poles that supported the covering of hide were gathered together. It gilded the features of the Indians, as with animated gestures they sat around it, telling their endless stories of war and hunting, and displayed rude garments of skins that hung around the lodge; the bow, quiver, and lance, suspended over the resting-place of the chief, and the rifles and powder-horns of the two white guests. For a moment all would be bright as day; then the flames would die out; fitful flashes from the embers would illumine the lodge, and then leave it in darkness. Then the light would wholly fade, and the lodge and all within it be involved again in obscurity.

As I left the lodge next morning, I was saluted by howling and yelping all around the village, and half its canine population rushed forth to the attack. Being as cowardly as they were clamorous, they kept jumping about me at the distance of a few yards, only one little cur, about ten inches long, having spirit enough to make a direct assault. He dashed valiantly at the leather tassel which in the Dahcotah fashion was trailing behind the heel of my moccason, and kept his hold, growling and snarling all the while, though every step I made almost jerked him over on his back. As I knew that the eyes of the whole village were on the watch to see if I showed any sign of fear, I walked forward without looking to the right or left, surrounded wherever I went by this magic circle of dogs. When I came to Reynal's lodge I

sat down by it, on which the dogs dispersed growling to
their respective quarters. Only one large white one remained,
running about before me and showing his teeth. I called him,
but he only growled the more. I looked at him well. He
5 was fat and sleek; just such a dog as I wanted. "My
friend," thought I, "you shall pay for this! I will have
you eaten this very morning!"

I intended that day to give the Indians a feast, by way of
conveying a favorable impression of my character and dig-
10 nity; and a white dog is the dish which the customs of the
Dahcotah prescribe for all occasions of formality and importance. I consulted Reynal: he soon discovered that an
old woman in the next lodge was owner of the white dog. I
took a gaudy cotton handkerchief, and, laying it on the
15 ground, arranged some vermilion, beads, and other trinkets
upon it. Then the old squaw was summoned. I pointed to
the dog and to the handkerchief. She gave a scream of delight, snatched up the prize, and vanished with it into her
lodge. For a few more trifles, I engaged the services of two
20 other squaws, each of whom took the white dog by one of
his paws, and led him away behind the lodges. Having
killed him, they threw him into a fire to singe; then chopped
him up and put him into two large kettles to boil. Meanwhile I told Raymond to fry in buffalo fat what little flour
25 we had left, and also to make a kettle of tea as an additional
luxury.

The Big Crow's squaw was briskly at work sweeping out
the lodge for the approaching festivity. I confided to my
host himself the task of inviting the guests, thinking that I
30 might thereby shift from my own shoulders the odium of
neglect and oversight.

When feasting is in question, one hour of the day serves
an Indian as well as another. My entertainment came off at
about eleven o'clock. At that hour, Reynal and Raymond
walked across the area of the village, to the admiration of

the inhabitants, carrying the two kettles of dog-meat slung on a pole between them. These they placed in the centre of the lodge, and then went back for the bread and the tea. Meanwhile I had put on a pair of brilliant moccasons, and substituted for my old buck-skin frock a coat, which I had brought with me in view of such public occasions. I also made careful use of the razor, an operation which no man will neglect who desires to gain the good opinion of Indians. Thus attired, I seated myself between Reynal and Raymond at the head of the lodge. Only a few minutes elapsed before all the guests had come in and were seated on the ground, wedged together in a close circle. Each brought with him a wooden bowl to hold his share of the repast. When all were assembled, two of the officials called "soldiers" by the white men came forward with ladles made of the horn of the Rocky Mountain sheep, and began to distribute the feast, assigning a double share to the old men and chiefs. The dog vanished with astonishing celerity, and each guest turned his dish bottom upward to show that all was gone. Then the bread was distributed in its turn, and finally the tea. As the "soldiers" poured it out into the same wooden bowls that had served for the substantial part of the meal, I thought it had a particularly curious and uninviting color.

"Oh," said Reynal, "there was not tea enough, so I stirred some soot in the kettle, to make it look strong."

Fortunately an Indian's palate is not very discriminating. The tea was well sweetened, and that was all they cared for.

Now, the feast being over, the time for speech-making was come. The Big Crow produced a flat piece of wood on which he cut up tobacco and *shongsasha*, and mixed them in due proportions. The pipes were filled and passed from hand to hand around the company. Then I began my speech, each sentence being interpreted by Reynal as I went on, and echoed by the whole audience with the usual exclamations

of assent and approval. As nearly as I can recollect, it was
as follows : —

"I had come," I told them, "from a country so far distant that at the rate they travel, they could not reach it in
5 a year."

"How! how!"

"There the Meneaska were more numerous than the blades
of grass on the prairie. The squaws were far more beautiful
than any they had ever seen, and all the men were brave
10 warriors."

"How! how! how!"

I was assailed by twinges of conscience as I uttered these
last words. But I recovered myself and began again.

"While I was living in the Meneaska lodges, I had heard
15 of the Ogillallah, how great and brave a nation they were,
how they loved the whites, and how well they could hunt
the buffalo and strike their enemies. I resolved to come and
see if all that I heard was true."

"How! how! how! how!"

20   "As I had come on horseback through the mountains, I
had been able to bring them only a very few presents."

"How!"

"But I had enough tobacco to give them all a small piece.
They might smoke it and see how much better it was than
25 the tobacco which they got from the traders."

"How! how! how!"

"I had plenty of powder, lead, knives, and tobacco at Fort
Laramie. These I was anxious to give them, and if any of
them should come to the fort before I went away, I would
30 make them handsome presents."

"How! how! how! how!"

Raymond then cut up and distributed among them two
or three pounds of tobacco, and old Mene-Seela began to
make a reply. It was long, but the following was the pith
of it.

"He had always loved the whites. They were the wisest people on earth. He believed they could do anything, and he was always glad when any of them came to live in the Ogillallah lodges. It was true I had not made them many presents, but the reason of it was plain. It was clear that I liked them, or I never should have come so far to find their village."

Several other speeches of similar import followed, and then, this more serious matter being disposed of, there was an interval of smoking, laughing, and conversation. Old Mene-Seela suddenly interrupted it with a loud voice: —

"Now is a good time," he said, "when all the old men and chiefs are here together, to decide what the people shall do. We came over the mountains to make our lodges for next year. Our old ones are good for nothing; they are rotten and worn out. But we have been disappointed. We have killed buffalo-bulls enough, but we have found no herds of cows, and the skins of bulls are too thick and heavy for our squaws to make lodges of. There must be plenty of cows about the Medicine Bow Mountain. We ought to go there. To be sure, it is farther westward than we have ever been before, and perhaps the Snakes will attack us, for those hunting-grounds belong to them. But we must have new lodges at any rate; our old ones will not serve for another year. We ought not to be afraid of the Snakes. Our warriors are brave, and they are all ready for war. Besides, we have three white men with their rifles to help us."

This speech produced a good deal of debate. As Reynal did not interpret what was said, I could only judge of the meaning by the features and gestures of the speakers. At the end of it, however, the greater number seemed to have fallen in with Mene-Seela's opinion. A short silence followed, and then the old man struck up a discordant chant, which I was told was a song of thanks for the entertainment I had given them.

"Now," said he, "let us go and give the white men a chance to breathe."

So the company all dispersed into the open air, and for some time the old chief was walking round the village, singing his
5 song in praise of the feast, after the custom of the nation.

At last the day drew to a close; and as the sun went down, the horses came trooping from the surrounding plains to be picketed before the dwellings of their respective masters. Soon within the great circle of lodges appeared another con-
10 centric circle of restless horses; and here and there fires glowed and flickered amid the gloom, on the dusky figures around them. I went over and sat by the lodge of Reynal. The Eagle-Feather, who was a son of Mene-Seela, and brother of my host the Big Crow, was seated there already, and I
15 asked him if the village would move in the morning. He shook his head, and said that nobody could tell, for since old Mahto-Tatonka had died, the people had been like children that did not know their own minds. They were no better than a body without a head. So I, as well as the Indians
20 themselves, fell asleep that night without knowing whether we should set out in the morning towards the country of the Snakes.

At daybreak, however, as I was coming up from the river after my morning's ablutions, I saw that a movement was
25 contemplated. Some of the lodges were reduced to nothing but bare skeletons of poles; the leather covering of others was flapping in the wind as the squaws pulled it off. One or two chiefs of note had resolved, it seemed, on moving; and so having set their squaws at work, the example was
30 followed by the rest of the village. One by one the lodges were sinking down in rapid succession, and where the great circle of the village had been only a few moments before, nothing now remained but a ring of horses and Indians, crowded in confusion together. The ruins of the lodges were spread over the ground, together with kettles, stone mallets,

great ladles of horn, buffalo-robes, and cases of painted hide,
filled with dried meat. Squaws bustled about in busy preparation, the old hags screaming to one another at the stretch
of their leathern lungs. The shaggy horses were patiently
standing while the lodge-poles were lashed to their sides,   5
and the baggage piled upon their backs. The dogs, with
tongues lolling out, lay lazily panting, and waiting for the
time of departure. Each warrior sat on the ground by the
decaying embers of his fire, unmoved amid the confusion,
holding in his hand the long trail-rope of his horse.   10

As their preparations were completed, each family moved
off the ground. The crowd was rapidly melting away. I
could see them crossing the river, and passing in quick succession along the profile of the hill on the farther side.
When all were gone, I mounted and set out after them,   15
followed by Raymond, and, as we gained the summit, the
whole village came in view at once, straggling away for a
mile or more over the barren plains before us. Everywhere
glittered the iron points of lances. The sun never shone
upon a more strange array. Here were the heavy-laden   20
pack-horses, some wretched old woman leading them, and two
or three children clinging to their backs. Here were mules
or ponies covered from head to tail with gaudy trappings,
and mounted by some gay young squaw, grinning bashful-
ness and pleasure as the Meneaska' looked at her. Boys with 25
miniature bows and arrows wandered over the plains, little
naked children ran along on foot, and numberless dogs
scampered among the feet of the horses. The young braves,
gaudy with paint and feathers, rode in groups among the
crowd, often galloping, two or three at once along the line, 30
to try the speed of their horses. Here and there you might
see a rank of sturdy pedestrians stalking along in their
white buffalo-robes. These were the dignitaries of the
village, the old men and warriors, to whose age and experience that wandering democracy yielded a silent deference.

With the rough prairie and the broken hills for its background, the restless scene was striking and picturesque beyond description. Days and weeks made me familiar with it, but never impaired its effect upon my fancy.

5   As we moved on, the broken column grew yet more scattered and disorderly, until, as we approached the foot of a hill, I saw the old men before mentioned seating themselves in a line upon the ground, in advance of the whole. They lighted a pipe and sat smoking, laughing, and telling
10 stories, while the people, stopping as they successively came up, were soon gathered in a crowd behind them. Then the old men rose, drew their buffalo-robes over their shoulders, and strode on as before. Gaining the top of the hill, we found a steep declivity before us. There was not a minute's
15 pause. The whole descended in a mass, amid dust and confusion. The horses braced their feet as they slid down, women and children screamed, dogs yelped as they were trodden upon, while stones and earth went rolling to the bottom. In a few moments I could see the village from the
20 summit, spreading again far and wide over the plain below.

At our encampment that afternoon I was attacked anew by my old disorder. In half an hour the strength that I had been gaining for a week past had vanished again, and I became like a man in a dream. But at sunset I lay down in the
25 Big Crow's lodge and slept, totally unconscious till the morning. The first thing that awakened me was a hoarse flapping over my head, and a sudden light that poured in upon me. The camp was breaking up, and the squaws were moving the covering from the lodge. I arose and shook off my
30 blanket with the feeling of perfect health; but scarcely had I gained my feet when a sense of my helpless condition was once more forced upon me, and I found myself scarcely able to stand. Raymond had brought up Pauline and the mule, and I stooped to raise my saddle from the ground. My strength was unequal to the task. " You must saddle her,"

said I to Raymond, as I sat down again on a pile of buffalo-robes. He did so, and with a painful effort I mounted. As we were passing over a great plain, surrounded by long broken ridges, I rode slowly in advance of the Indians with thoughts that wandered far from the time and the place. 5 Suddenly the sky darkened, and thunder began to mutter. Clouds were rising over the hills, as dark as the first fore-bodings of an approaching calamity; and in a moment all around was wrapped in shadow. I looked behind. The Indians had stopped to prepare for the approaching storm, 10 and the dense mass of savages stretched far to the right and left. Since the first attack of my disorder the effects of rain upon me had usually been injurious in the extreme. I had no strength to spare, having at that moment scarcely enough to keep my seat on horseback. Then, for the first time, it 15 pressed upon me as a strong probability that I might never leave those deserts. " Well," thought I to myself, " the prairie makes quick and sharp work. Better to die here, in the saddle to the last, than to stifle in the hot air of a sick chamber; and a thousand times better than to drag out life, as 20 many have done, in the helpless inaction of lingering disease." So, drawing the buffalo-robe on which I sat, over my head, I waited till the storm should come. It broke at last with a sudden burst of fury, and passing away as rapidly as it came, left the sky clear again. My reflections served me no 25 other purpose than to look back upon as a piece of curious experience; for the rain did not produce the ill effects that I had expected. We encamped within an hour. Having no change of clothes, I contrived to borrow a curious kind of substitute from Reynal; and this done, I went home — that 30 is, to the Big Crow's lodge — to make the entire transfer that was necessary. Half a dozen squaws were in the lodge, and one of them taking my arm held it against her own, while a general laugh and scream of admiration was raised at the contrast in the color of the skin.

Our encampment that afternoon was not far from a spur of the Black Hills, whose ridges, bristling with fir-trees, rose from the plains a mile or two on our right. That they might move more rapidly towards their proposed hunting-
5 grounds, the Indians determined to leave at this place their stock of dried meat and other superfluous articles. Some left even their lodges, and contented themselves with carrying a few hides to make a shelter from the sun and rain. Half the inhabitants set out in the afternoon, with loaded
10 pack-horses, towards the mountains. Here they suspended the dried meat upon trees, where the wolves and grizzly bears could not get at it. All returned at evening. Some of the young men declared that they had heard the reports of guns among the mountains to the eastward, and many sur-
15 mises were thrown out as to the origin of these sounds. For my part, I was in hopes that Shaw and Henry Chatillon were coming to join us. I little suspected that at that very moment my unlucky comrade was lying on a buffalo-robe at Fort Laramie, fevered with ivy poison, and solacing his
20 woes with tobacco and Shakespeare.

As we moved over the plains on the next morning, several young men rode about the country as scouts ; and at length we began to see them occasionally on the tops of the hills, shaking their robes as a signal that they saw buffalo. Soon
25 after, some bulls came in sight. Horsemen darted away in pursuit, and we could see from the distance that one or two of the buffalo were killed. Raymond suddenly became inspired.

"This is the country for me!" he said; "if I could only carry the buffalo that are killed here every month down to
30 St. Louis, I'd make my fortune in one winter; I'd grow as rich as old Papin, or Mackenzie either. I call this the poor man's market. When I'm hungry, I've only got to take my rifle and go out and get better meat than the rich folks down below can get, with all their money. You won't catch me living in St. Louis another winter."

"No," said Reynal, "you had better say that, after you and your Spanish woman almost starved to death there. What a fool you were ever to take her to the settlements!"

*   *   *   *   *   *   *   *   *

I found that my two associates, in common with other white men in that country, were as indifferent to their future welfare as men whose lives are in constant peril are apt to be. Raymond had never heard of the Pope. A certain bishop, who lived at Taos or at Santa Fé, embodied his loftiest idea of an ecclesiastical dignitary.

*   *   *   *   *   *   *   *   *

The Panther, on his black-and-white horse, one of the best in the village, came at full speed over the hill in hot pursuit of an antelope, that darted away like lightning before him. The attempt was made in mere sport and bravado, for very few are the horses that can for a moment compete in swiftness with this little animal. The antelope ran down the hill towards the main body of the Indians, who were moving over the plain below. Sharp yells were given, and horsemen galloped out to intercept his flight. At this he turned sharply to the left, and scoured away with such speed that he distanced all his pursuers, even the vaunted horse of the Panther himself. A few moments after, we witnessed a more serious sport. A shaggy buffalo-bull bounded out from a neighboring hollow, and close behind him came a slender Indian boy, riding without stirrups or saddle, and lashing his eager little horse to full speed. Yard after yard he drew closer to his gigantic victim, though the bull, with his short tail erect and his tongue lolling out a foot from his foaming jaws, was straining his unwieldy strength to the utmost. A moment more, and the boy was close alongside. It was our friend the Hail-Storm. He dropped the rein on his horse's neck, and jerked an arrow like lightning from the quiver at his shoulder.

"I tell you," said Reynal, "that in a year's time that boy will match the best hunter in the village. There, he has given it to him!—and there goes another! You feel well, now, old bull, don't you, with two arrows stuck in your lights! There, he has given him another! Hear how the Hail-Storm yells when he shoots! Yes, jump at him; try it again, old fellow! You may jump all day before you get your horns into that pony!"

The bull sprang again and again at his assailant, but the horse kept dodging with wonderful celerity. At length the bull followed up his attack with a furious rush, and the Hail-Storm was put to flight, the shaggy monster following close behind. The boy clung in his seat like a leech, and secure in the speed of his little pony, looked round towards us and laughed. In a moment he was again alongside the bull, who was now driven to desperation. His eyeballs glared through his tangled mane, and the blood flew from his mouth and nostrils. Thus, still battling with each other, the two enemies disappeared over the hill.

Many of the Indians rode at full gallop towards the spot. We followed at a more moderate pace, and soon saw the bull lying dead on the side of the hill. The Indians were gathered around him, and several knives were already at work. These little instruments were plied with such wonderful address that the twisted sinews were cut apart, the ponderous bones fell asunder as if by magic, and in a moment the vast carcass was reduced to a heap of bloody ruins. The surrounding group of savages offered no very attractive spectacle to a civilized eye. Some were cracking the huge thigh-bones and devouring the marrow within; others were cutting away pieces of the liver, and other approved morsels, and swallowing them on the spot with the appetite of wolves. The faces of most of them, besmeared with blood from ear to ear, looked grim and horrible enough. My friend the White Shield proffered me a marrow-bone, so skilfully

laid open that all the rich substance within was exposed to
view at once. Another Indian held out a large piece of the
delicate lining of the paunch; but these courteous offerings
I begged leave to decline. I noticed one little boy who was
very busy with his knife about the jaws and throat of the
buffalo, from which he extracted some morsel of peculiar
delicacy. It is but fair to say, that only certain parts of the
animal are considered eligible in these extempore banquets.

We encamped that night, and marched westward through
the greater part of the following day. On the next morning
we again resumed our journey. It was the seventeenth of
July, unless my note-book misleads me. At noon we stopped
by some pools of rain-water, and in the afternoon again set
forward. This double movement was contrary to the usual
practice of the Indians, but all were very anxious to reach
the hunting-ground, kill the necessary number of buffalo,
and retreat as soon as possible from the dangerous neighborhood. I pass by for the present some curious incidents that
occurred during these marches and encampments. Late in
the afternoon of the last-mentioned day we came upon the
banks of a little sandy stream, of which the Indians could
not tell the name; for they were very ill acquainted with
that part of the country. So parched and arid were the
prairies around, that they could not supply grass enough
for the horses to feed upon, and we were compelled to move
farther and farther up the stream in search of ground for
encampment. The country was much wilder than before.
The plains were gashed with ravines and broken into hollows and steep declivities, which flanked our course, as, in
long scattered array, the Indians advanced up the side of
the stream. Mene-Seela consulted an extraordinary oracle
to instruct him where the buffalo were to be found. When
he with the other chiefs sat down on the grass to smoke and
converse, as they often did during the march, the old man
picked up one of those enormous black and green crickets,

which the Dahcotah call by a name that signifies, "They
who point out the buffalo." The "Root-Diggers," a wretched
tribe beyond the mountains, turn them to good account
by making them into a sort of soup, pronounced by certain
5 unscrupulous trappers to be extremely rich. Holding the
bloated insect respectfully between his fingers and thumb,
the old Indian looked attentively at him and inquired,
"Tell me, my father, where must we go to-morrow to find
the buffalo?" The cricket twisted about his long horns in
10 evident embarrassment. At last he pointed, or seemed to
point, them westward. Mene-Seela, dropping him gently on
the grass, laughed with great glee, and said that if we went
that way in the morning we should be sure to kill plenty
of game.

15 Towards evening we came upon a fresh green meadow,
traversed by the stream, and deep set among tall sterile
bluffs. The Indians descended its steep bank; and as I was
at the rear, I was one of the last to reach this point. Lances
were glittering, feathers fluttering, and the water below me
20 was crowded with men and horses passing through, while
the meadow beyond swarmed with the restless crowd of
Indians. The sun was just setting, and poured its softened
light upon them through an opening in the hills.

I remarked to Reynal that at last we had found a good
25 'camping-ground.

"Oh, it's very good," replied he, ironically, "especially
if there is a Snake war-party about, and they take it into
their heads to shoot down at us from the top of these hills.
It's no plan of mine, 'camping in such a hole as this."

30 The Indians also seemed anxious. High up on the top of
the tallest bluff, conspicuous in the bright evening sunlight,
sat a naked warrior on horseback, looking around over the
neighboring country; and Raymond told me that many of
the young men had gone out in different directions as
scouts.

The shadows had reached to the very summit of the bluffs before the lodges were erected, and the village reduced again to quiet and order. A cry was suddenly raised, and men, women, and children came running out with animated faces, and looked eagerly through the opening in the hills by which the stream entered from the westward. I could discern afar off some dark, heavy masses, passing over the sides of a low hill. They disappeared, and then others followed. These were bands of buffalo-cows. The hunting-ground was reached at last, and everything promised well for the morrow's chase. Being fatigued and exhausted, I lay down in Kongra-Tonga's lodge, when Raymond thrust in his head, and called upon me to come and see some sport. A number of Indians were gathered, laughing, along the line of lodges on the western side of the village, and at some distance, I could plainly see in the twilight two huge black monsters stalking, heavily and solemnly, directly towards us. They were buffalo-bulls. The wind blew from them to the village, and such was their blindness and stupidity that they were advancing upon the enemy without the least consciousness of his presence. Raymond told me that two young men had hidden themselves with guns in a ravine about twenty yards in front of us. The two bulls walked slowly on, heavily swinging from side to side in their peculiar gait of stupid dignity. They approached within four or five rods of the ravine where the Indians lay in ambush. Here at last they seemed conscious that something was wrong, for they both stopped and stood perfectly still, without looking either to the right or to the left. Nothing of them was to be seen but two black masses of shaggy mane, with horns, eyes, and nose in the centre, and a part of hoofs visible at the bottom. At last the more intelligent of them seemed to have concluded that it was time to retire. Very slowly, and with an air of the gravest and most majestic deliberation, he began to turn round, as if he were revolving on a pivot. Little by little his ugly brown side was exposed to view. A white smoke sprang out, as it were from the ground; a sharp report came with it. The old bull gave a very undignified jump, and galloped off. At this his comrade wheeled about with considerable expedition. The other Indian shot at him from the ravine, and then both the bulls ran away at full speed, while half the juvenile population of the village raised a yell and ran after them. The first bull soon stopped, and while the crowd stood looking at him at a respectful distance, he reeled and rolled over on his side. The other, wounded in a less vital part, galloped away to the hills and escaped.

In half an hour it was totally dark. I lay down to sleep, and ill as I was, there was something very animating in the prospect of the general hunt that was to take place on the morrow.

CHAPTER XV

THE HUNTING CAMP

Long before daybreak the Indians broke up their camp. The women of Mene-Seela's lodge were as usual among the first that were ready for departure, and I found the old man himself sitting by the embers of the decayed fire, over which he was warming his withered fingers, as the morning was 5 very chill and damp. The preparations for moving were even more confused and disorderly than usual. While some families were leaving the ground, the lodges of others were still standing untouched. At this old Mene-Seela grew impatient, and walking out to the middle of the village, he stood 10 with his robe wrapped close around him, and harangued the people in a loud, sharp voice. Now, he said, when they were on an enemy's hunting-grounds, was not the time to behave like children; they ought to be more active and united than ever. His speech had some effect. The delin- 15 quents took down their lodges and loaded their pack-horses; and when the sun rose, the last of the men, women, and children had left the deserted camp.

This movement was made merely for the purpose of finding a better and safer position. So we advanced only three 20 or four miles up the little stream, when each family assumed its relative place in the great ring of the village, and the squaws set actively at work in preparing the camp. But not a single warrior dismounted from his horse. All the men that morning were mounted on inferior animals, leading 25 their best horses by a cord, or confiding them to the care of boys. In small parties they began to leave the ground and ride rapidly away over the plains to the westward. I had

taken no food, and not being at all ambitious of farther ab-
stinence, I went into my host's lodge, which his squaws had
set up with wonderful despatch, and sat down in the centre,
as a gentle hint that I was hungry. A wooden bowl was
5 soon set before me, filled with the nutritious preparation of
dried meat, called *pemmican* by the northern voyagers, and
wasna by the Dahcotah. Taking a handful to break my fast
upon, I left the lodge just in time to see the last band of
hunters disappear over the ridge of the neighboring hill. I
10 mounted Pauline and galloped in pursuit, riding rather by
the balance than by any muscular strength that remained to
me. From the top of the hill I could overlook a wide extent
of desolate prairie, over which, far and near, little parties of
naked horsemen were rapidly passing. I soon came up to
15 the nearest, and we had not ridden a mile before all were
united into one large and compact body. All was haste and
eagerness. Each hunter whipped on his horse, as if anxious
to be the first to reach the game. In such movements among
the Indians this is always more or less the case; but it was
20 especially so in the present instance, because the head chief
of the village was absent, and there were but few " soldiers,"
a sort of Indian police, who among their other functions
usually assume the direction of a buffalo hunt. No man
turned to the right hand or to the left. We rode at a swift
25 canter straight forward, up hill and down hill, and through
the stiff, obstinate growth of the endless wild-sage bushes.
For an hour and a half the same red shoulders, the same
long black hair, rose and fell with the motion of the horses
before me. Very little was said, though once I observed an
30 old man severely reproving Raymond for having left his
rifle behind him, when there was some probability of encountering an enemy before the day was over. As we galloped
across a plain thickly set with sage-bushes, the foremost
riders vanished suddenly from sight, as if diving into the
earth. The arid soil was cracked into a deep ravine. Down

we all went in succession and galloped in a line along the
bottom, until we found a point where, one by one, the horses
could scramble out. Soon after, we came upon a wide shallow stream, and as we rode swiftly over the hard sand-beds
and through the thin sheets of rippling water, many of the 5
savage horsemen threw themselves to the ground, knelt on
the sand, snatched a hasty draught, and leaping back again
to their seats, galloped on as before.

Meanwhile scouts kept in advance of the party; and now
we began to see them on the ridges of the hills, waving their 10
robes in token that buffalo were visible. These, however,
proved to be nothing more than old straggling bulls, feeding
upon the neighboring plains, who would stare for a moment
at the hostile array and then gallop clumsily off. At length
we could discern several of these scouts making their signals 15
to us at once; no longer waving their robes boldly from the
top of the hill, but standing lower down, so that they could
not be seen from the plains beyond. Game worth pursuing
had evidently been discovered. The excited Indians now
urged forward their tired horses even more rapidly than 20
before. Pauline, who was still sick and jaded, began to
groan heavily; and her yellow sides were darkened with
sweat. As we were crowding together over a lower intervening hill, I heard Reynal and Raymond shouting to me
from the left; and, looking in that direction, I saw them 25
riding away behind a party of about twenty mean-looking
Indians. These were the relatives of Reynal's squaw, Margot, who, not wishing to take part in the general hunt, were
riding towards a distant hollow, where they saw a small
band of buffalo which they meant to appropriate to them- 30
selves. I answered to the call by ordering Raymond to turn
back and follow me. He reluctantly obeyed, though Reynal,
who had relied on his assistance in skinning, cutting up,
and carrying to camp the buffalo that he and his party
should kill, loudly protested, and declared that we should

see no sport if we went with the rest of the Indians. Followed by Raymond, I pursued the main body of hunters, while Reynal, in a great rage, whipped his horse over the hill after his ragamuffin relatives. The Indians, still about
5 a hundred in number, galloped in a dense body at some distance in advance, a cloud of dust flying in the wind behind them. I could not overtake them until they had stopped on the side of the hill where the scouts were standing. Here each hunter sprang in haste from the tired animal he had
10 ridden, and leaped upon the fresh horse he had brought with him. There was not a saddle or a bridle in the whole party. A piece of buffalo-robe, girthed over the horse's back, served in the place of the one, and a cord of twisted hair, lashed round his lower jaw, answered for the other. Eagle feathers
15 dangled from every mane and tail, as marks of courage and speed. As for the rider, he wore no other clothing than a light cincture at his waist, and a pair of moccasons. He had a heavy whip, with a handle of solid elk-horn, and a lash of knotted bull-hide, fastened to his wrist by a band. His bow
20 was in his hand, and his quiver of otter or panther skin hung at his shoulder. Thus equipped, some thirty of the hunters galloped away towards the left, in order to make a circuit under cover of the hills, that the buffalo might be assailed on both sides at once. The rest impatiently waited
25 until time enough had elapsed for their companions to reach the required position. Then riding upward in a body, we gained the ridge of the hill, and for the first time came in sight of the buffalo on the plain beyond.

They were a band of cows, four or five hundred in number,
30 crowded together near the bank of a wide stream that was soaking across the sand-beds of the valley. This valley was a large circular basin, sun-scorched and broken, scantily covered with herbage, and surrounded with high barren hills, from an opening in which we could see our allies galloping out upon the plain. The wind blew from that direction.

The buffalo, aware of their approach, had begun to move, though very slowly and in a compact mass. I have no farther recollection of seeing the game until we were in the midst of them, for as we rode down the hill other objects engrossed my attention. Numerous old bulls were scattered over the plain, and, ungallantly deserting their charge at our approach, began to wade and plunge through the quicksands of the stream, and gallop away towards the hills. One old veteran was straggling behind the rest, with one of his fore-legs, which had been broken by some accident, dangling about uselessly. His appearance, as he went shambling along on three legs, was so ludicrous that I could not help pausing for a moment to look at him. As I came near, he would try to rush upon me, nearly throwing himself down at every awkward attempt. Looking up, I saw the whole body of Indians full an hundred yards in advance. I lashed Pauline in pursuit and reached them just in time; for, at that moment, each hunter, as if by a common impulse, violently struck his horse, each horse sprang forward, and, scattering in the charge in order to assail the entire herd at once, we all rushed headlong upon the buffalo. We were among them in an instant. Amid the trampling and the yells I could see their dark figures running hither and thither through clouds of dust, and the horsemen darting in pursuit. While we were charging on one side, our companions attacked the bewildered and panic-stricken herd on the other. The uproar and confusion lasted but a moment. The dust cleared away, and the buffalo could be seen scattering as from a common centre, flying over the plain singly, or in long files and small compact bodies, while behind them followed the Indians, riding at furious speed, and yelling as they launched arrow after arrow into their sides. The carcasses were strewn thickly over the ground. Here and there stood wounded buffalo, their bleeding sides feathered with arrows; and as I rode by them their eyes would glare, they

would bristle like gigantic cats, and feebly attempt to rush
up and gore my horse.

I left camp that morning with a philosophic resolution.
Neither I nor my horse were at that time fit for such sport,
and I had determined to remain a quiet spectator; but amid
the rush of horses and buffalo, the uproar and the dust, I found
it impossible to sit still; and as four or five buffalo ran past
me in a line, I lashed Pauline in pursuit. We went plunging through the water and the quicksands, and clambering
the bank, chased them through the wild-sage bushes that
covered the rising ground beyond. But neither her native
spirit nor the blows of the knotted bull-hide could supply
the place of poor Pauline's exhausted strength. We could
not gain an inch upon the fugitives. At last, however, they
came full upon a ravine too wide to leap over; and as this
compelled them to turn abruptly to the left, I contrived to
get within ten or twelve yards of the hindmost. At this she
faced about, bristled angrily, and made a show of charging.
I shot at her, and hit her somewhere in the neck. Down she
tumbled into the ravine, whither her companions had descended before her. I saw their dark backs appearing and
disappearing as they galloped along the bottom; then, one
by one, they scrambled out on the other side, and ran off as
before, the wounded animal following with the rest.

Turning back, I saw Raymond coming on his black mule
to meet me; and as we rode over the field together, we
counted scores of carcasses lying on the plain, in the ravines,
and on the sandy bed of the stream. Far away in the distance, horsemen and buffalo were still scouring along, with
clouds of dust rising behind them; and over the sides of the
hills long files of the frightened animals were rapidly ascending. The hunters began to return. The boys, who had held
the horses behind the hill, made their appearance, and the
work of flaying and cutting up began in earnest all over the
field. I noticed my host Kongra-Tonga beyond the stream,

just alighting by the side of a cow which he had killed. Riding up to him, I found him in the act of drawing out an arrow, which, with the exception of the notch at the end, had entirely disappeared in the animal. I asked him to give it to me, and I still retain it as a proof, though by no means 5 the most striking one that could be offered, of the force and dexterity with which the Indians discharge their arrows.

The hides and meat were piled upon the horses, and the hunters began to leave the ground. Raymond and I, too, getting tired of the scene, set out for the village, riding 10 straight across the intervening desert. There was no path, and as far as I could see, no landmarks sufficient to guide us; but Raymond seemed to have an instinctive perception of the point on the horizon towards which we ought to direct our course. Antelope were bounding on all sides, and as is 15 always the case in the presence of buffalo, they seemed to have lost their natural shyness. Bands of them would run lightly up the rocky declivities, and stand gazing down upon us from the summit. At length we could distinguish the tall white rocks and the old pine-trees that, as we well remem- 20 bered, were just above the site of the encampment. Still we could see nothing of the camp itself, until, mounting a grassy hill, we saw the circle of lodges, dingy with storms and smoke, standing on the plain at our feet.

I entered the lodge of my host. His squaw instantly 25 brought me food and water, and spread a buffalo-robe for me to lie upon; and being much fatigued, I lay down and fell asleep. In about an hour, the entrance of Kongra-Tonga, with his arms smeared with blood to the elbows, awoke me; he sat down in his usual seat, on the left side of the lodge. 30 His squaw gave him a vessel of water for washing, set before him a bowl of boiled meat, and, as he was eating, pulled off his bloody moccasons and placed fresh ones on his feet; then outstretching his limbs, my host composed himself to sleep.

And now the hunters, two or three at a time, came rapidly in, and each consigning his horses to the squaws, entered his lodge with the air of a man whose day's work was done. The squaws flung down the load from the burdened horses, and vast piles of meat and hides were soon gathered before every lodge. By this time it was darkening fast, and the whole village was illumined by the glare of fires. All the squaws and children were gathered about the piles of meat, exploring them in search of the daintiest portions. Some of these they roasted on sticks before the fires, but often they dispensed with this superfluous operation. Late into the night the fires were still glowing upon the groups of feasters engaged in this savage banquet around them.

Several hunters sat down by the fire in Kongra-Tonga's lodge to talk over the day's exploits. Among the rest, Mene-Seela came in. Though he must have seen full eighty winters, he had taken an active share in the day's sport. He boasted that he had killed two cows that morning, and would have killed a third if the dust had not blinded him so that he had to drop his bow and arrows and press both hands against his eyes to stop the pain. The firelight fell upon his wrinkled face and shrivelled figure as he sat telling his story with such inimitable gesticulation that every man in the lodge broke into a laugh.

Old Mene-Seela was one of the few Indians in the village with whom I would have trusted myself alone without suspicion, and the only one from whom I should have received a gift or a service without the certainty that it proceeded from an interested motive. He was a great friend to the whites. He liked to be in their society, and was very vain of the favors he had received from them. He told me one afternoon, as we were sitting together in his son's lodge, that he considered the beaver and the whites the wisest people on earth; indeed, he was convinced they were the same; and an incident which had happened to him long before had assured him of this. So he began the following story, and as the pipe passed in turn to him, Reynal availed himself of these interruptions to translate what had preceded. But the old man accompanied his words with such admirable pantomime that translation was hardly necessary. 5

He said that when he was very young, and had never yet seen a white man, he and three or four of his companions were out on a beaver hunt, and he crawled into a large beaver-lodge, to see what was there. Sometimes he crept on his hands and knees, sometimes he was obliged to swim, and 10 sometimes to lie flat on his face and drag himself along. In this way he crawled a great distance under ground. It was very dark, cold, and close, so that at last he was almost suffocated, and fell into a swoon. When he began to recover, he could just distinguish the voices of his companions out- 15 side, who had given him up for lost, and were singing his death-song. At first he could see nothing, but soon discerned something white before him, and at length plainly distinguished three people, entirely white, one man and two women, sitting at the edge of a black pool of water. He be- 20 came alarmed, and thought it high time to retreat. Having succeeded, after great trouble, in reaching daylight again, he went to the spot directly above the pool of water where he had seen the three mysterious beings. Here he beat a hole with his war-club in the ground, and sat down to watch. In 25 a moment the nose of an old male beaver appeared at the opening. Mene-Seela instantly seized him and dragged him up, when two other beavers, both females, thrust out their heads, and these he served in the same way. "These," said the old man, concluding his story, for which he was proba- 30 bly indebted to a dream, "must have been the three white people whom I saw sitting at the edge of the water."

Mene-Seela was the grand depositary of the legends and traditions of the village. I succeeded, however, in getting from him only a few fragments. Like all Indians, he was

excessively superstitious, and continually saw some reason
for withholding his stories. "It is a bad thing," he would
say, "to tell the tales in summer. Stay with us till next
winter, and I will tell you everything I know; but now our
5 war-parties are going out, and our young men will be killed
if I sit down to tell stories before the frost begins."

But to leave this digression. We remained encamped on
this spot five days, during three of which the hunters were
at work incessantly, and immense quantities of meat and
10 hides were brought in. Great alarm, however, prevailed in
the village. All were on the alert. The young men ranged
the country as scouts, and the old men paid careful attention to omens and prodigies, and especially to their dreams.
In order to convey to the enemy (who, if they were in the
15 neighborhood, must inevitably have known of our presence)
the impression that we were constantly on the watch, piles
of sticks and stones were erected on all the surrounding
hills, in such a manner as to appear at a distance like sentinels. Often, even to this hour, that scene will rise before
20 my mind like a visible reality: the tall white rocks; the old
pine-trees on their summits; the sandy stream that ran
along their bases and half encircled the village; and the
wild-sage bushes, with their dull green hue and their medicinal odor, that covered all the neighboring declivities.
25 Hour after hour the squaws would pass and repass with
their vessels of water between the stream and the lodges.
For the most part, no one was to be seen in the camp
but women and children, two or three superannuated old
men, and a few lazy and worthless young ones. These, to-
30 gether with the dogs, now grown fat and good-natured with
the abundance in the camp, were its only tenants. Still it
presented a busy and bustling scene. In all quarters the
meat, hung on cords of hide, was drying in the sun, and
around the lodges, the squaws, young and old, were laboring
on the fresh hides stretched upon the ground, scraping the

hair from one side and the still adhering flesh from the other, and rubbing into them the brains of the buffalo, in order to render them soft and pliant.

In mercy to myself and my horse, I did not go out with the hunters after the first day. Of late, however, I had been gaining strength rapidly, as was always the case upon every respite of my disorder. I was soon able to walk with ease. Raymond and I would go out upon the neighboring prairies to shoot antelope, or sometimes to assail straggling buffalo, on foot; an attempt in which we met with rather indifferent success. As I came out of Kongra-Tonga's lodge one morning, Reynal called to me from the opposite side of the village, and asked me over to breakfast. The breakfast was a substantial one. It consisted of the rich, juicy hump-ribs of a fat cow; a repast absolutely unrivalled in its way. It was roasting before the fire, impaled upon a stout stick, which Reynal took up and planted in the ground before his lodge; when he, with Raymond and myself, taking our seats around it, unsheathed our knives and assailed it with good will. In spite of all medical experience, this solid fare, without bread or salt, seemed to agree with me admirably.

" We shall have strangers here before night," said Reynal.

" How do you know that ? " I asked.

" I dreamed so. I am as good at dreaming as an Indian. There's the Hail-Storm ; he dreamed the same thing, and he and his crony, The Rabbit, have gone out on discovery."

I laughed at Reynal for his credulity, went over to my host's lodge, took down my rifle, walked out a mile or two on the prairie, saw an old bull standing alone, crawled up a ravine, shot him, and saw him escape. Then, exhausted and rather ill-humored, I walked back to the village. By a strange coincidence, Reynal's prediction had been verified ; for the first persons whom I saw were the two trappers, Rouleau and Saraphin, coming to meet me. These men, as the reader may possibly recollect, had left our party about

a fortnight before. They had been trapping among the
Black Hills, and were now on their way to the Rocky
Mountains, intending in a day or two to set out for the
neighboring Medicine Bow. They were not the most elegant
or refined of companions, yet they made a very welcome
addition to the limited society of the village. For the rest
of that day we lay smoking and talking in Reynal's lodge.
This indeed was no better than a hut, made of hides stretched
on poles, and entirely open in front. It was well carpeted
with soft buffalo-robes, and here we remained, sheltered from
the sun, surrounded by the domestic utensils of Madame
Margot's household. All was quiet in the village. Though
the hunters had not gone out that day, they lay sleeping in
their lodges, and most of the women were silently engaged
in their heavy tasks. A few young men were playing at a lazy
game of ball in the area of the village; and when they became tired, some girls supplied their place with a more
boisterous sport. At a little distance, among the lodges, some
children and half-grown squaws were playfully tossing one
of their number in a buffalo-robe, — an exact counterpart of
the ancient pastime from which Sancho Panza suffered so
much. Farther out on the prairie, a host of little naked boys
were roaming about, engaged in various rough games, or
pursuing birds and ground-squirrels with their bows and
arrows; and woe to the unhappy little animals that fell into
their merciless, torture-loving hands. A squaw from the
next lodge, a notable housewife, named Weah Washtay, or
the Good Woman, brought us a large bowl of *wasna*, and
went into an ecstasy of delight when I presented her with
a green glass ring, such as I usually wore with a view to
similar occasions.

The sun went down, and half the sky was glowing fiery
red, reflected on the little stream as it wound away among
the sage-bushes. Some young men left the village, and soon
returned, driving in before them all the horses, hundreds in

number, and of every size, age, and color. The hunters came
out, and each securing those that belonged to him, examined
their condition, and tied them fast by long cords to stakes
driven in front of his lodge. It was half an hour before the
bustle subsided and tranquillity was restored again. By this
time it was nearly dark. Kettles were hung over the fires,
around which the squaws were gathered with their children, laughing and talking merrily. A circle of a different
kind was formed in the centre of the village. This was composed of the old men and warriors of repute, who sat together with their white buffalo-robes drawn close around
their shoulders; and as the pipe passed from hand to hand,
their conversation had not a particle of the gravity and reserve usually ascribed to Indians. I sat down with them as
usual. I had in my hand half a dozen squibs and serpents,
which I had made one day when encamped upon Laramie
Creek, with gunpowder and charcoal, and the leaves of
"Fremont's Expedition," rolled round a stout lead-pen-
cil. I waited till I could get hold of the large piece of burning *bois-de-vache* which the Indians kept by them on the
ground for lighting their pipes. With this I lighted all the
fireworks at once, and tossed them whizzing and sputtering
into the air, over the heads of the company. They all
jumped up and ran off with yelps of astonishment and consternation. After a moment or two, they ventured to come
back one by one, and some of the boldest, picking up the
cases of burnt paper, examined them with eager curiosity to
discover their mysterious secret. From that time forward I
enjoyed great repute as a "fire-medicine."

The camp was filled with the low hum of cheerful voices.
There were other sounds, however, of a different kind;
for from a large lodge, lighted up like a gigantic lantern by
the blazing fire within, came a chorus of dismal cries and
wailings, long drawn out, like the howling of wolves, and a
woman, almost naked, was crouching close outside, crying

violently, and gashing her legs with a knife till they were
covered with blood. Just a year before, a young man belonging to this family had been slain by the enemy, and his
relatives were thus lamenting his loss. Still other sounds
5 might be heard; loud earnest cries often repeated from
amid the gloom, at a distance beyond the village. They proceeded from some young men who, being about to set out in
a few days on a war-party, were standing at the top of a
hill, calling on the Great Spirit to aid them in their enter-
10 prise. While I was listening, Rouleau, with a laugh on his
careless face, called me and directed my attention to another
quarter. In front of the lodge where Weah Washtay lived,
another squaw was standing, angrily scolding an old yellow
dog, who lay on the ground with his nose resting between
15 his paws, and his eyes turned sleepily up to her face, as if
pretending to give respectful attention, but resolved to fall
asleep as soon as it was all over.

"You ought to be ashamed of yourself!" said the old
woman. "I have fed you well, and taken care of you ever
20 since you were small and blind, and could only crawl about
and squeal a little, instead of howling as you do now. When
you grew old, I said you were a good dog. You were strong
and gentle when the load was put on your back, and you
never ran among the feet of the horses when we were all
25 travelling together over the prairie. But you had a bad
heart! Whenever a rabbit jumped out of the bushes, you
were always the first to run after him and lead away all the
other dogs behind you. You ought to have known that it
was very dangerous to act so. When you had got far out on
30 the prairie, and no one was near to help you, perhaps a
wolf would jump out of the ravine; and then what could
you do? You would certainly have been killed, for no dog
can fight well with a load on his back. Only three days
ago you ran off in that way, and turned over the bag
of wooden pins with which I used to fasten up the front

of the lodge. Look up there, and you will see that it is all flapping open. And now to-night you have stolen a great piece of fat meat which was roasting before the fire for my children. I tell you, you have a bad heart, and you must die!"

So saying, the squaw went into the lodge, and coming out with a large stone mallet, killed the unfortunate dog at one blow. This speech is worthy of notice, as illustrating a curious characteristic of the Indians, who ascribe intelligence and a power of understanding speech to the inferior animals; to whom, indeed, according to many of their traditions, they are linked in close affinity; and they even claim the honor of a lineal descent from bears, wolves, deer, or tortoises.

As it grew late, I walked across the village to the lodge of my host, Kongra-Tonga. As I entered I saw him, by the blaze of the fire in the middle, reclining half asleep in his usual place. His couch was by no means an uncomfortable one. It consisted of buffalo-robes, laid together on the ground, and a pillow made of whitened deer-skin, stuffed with feathers and ornamented with beads. At his back was a light framework of poles and slender reeds, against which he could lean with ease when in a sitting posture; and at the top of it, just above his head, hung his bow and quiver. His squaw, a laughing, broad-faced woman, apparently had not yet completed her domestic arrangements, for she was bustling about the lodge, pulling over the utensils and the bales of dried meat that were ranged carefully around it. Unhappily, she and her partner were not the only tenants of the dwelling; for half a dozen children were scattered about, sleeping in every imaginable posture. My saddle was in its place at the head of the lodge, and a buffalo-robe was spread on the ground before it. Wrapping myself in my blanket, I lay down; but had I not been extremely fatigued, the noise in the next lodge would have prevented my sleeping. There was the monotonous thumping of the Indian drum, mixed with occasional sharp yells, and a chorus chanted by twenty voices. A grand scene of gambling was going forward with all the appropriate formalities. The players were staking on the chances of the game their ornaments, their horses, and as the excitement rose, their garments, and even their weapons; for desperate gambling is not confined to the hells of Paris. The men of the plains and forests no less resort to it as a relief to the tedious monotony of their lives, which alternate between fierce excitement and listless inaction. I fell asleep with the dull notes of the drum still sounding on my ear; but these orgies lasted without intermission till daylight. I was soon awakened by one of the children crawling over me, while another larger one was tugging at my blanket and nestling himself in a very disagreeable proximity. I immediately repelled these advances by punching the heads of these miniature savages with a short stick which I always kept by me for the purpose; and as sleeping half the day and eating much more than is good for them makes them extremely restless, this operation usually had to be repeated four or five times in the course of the night. My host himself was the author of another formidable annoyance. All these Indians, and he among the rest, think themselves bound to the constant performance of certain acts as the condition on which their success in life depends, whether in war, love, hunting, or any other employment. These "medicines," as they are called, which are usually communicated in dreams, are often absurd enough. Some Indians will strike the butt of the pipe against the ground every time they smoke; others will insist that everything they say shall be interpreted by contraries; and Shaw once met an old man who conceived that all would be lost unless he compelled every white man he met to drink a bowl of cold water. My host was particularly unfortunate in his allotment. The spirits had told him in a

dream that he must sing a certain song in the middle of
every night; and regularly at about twelve o'clock his dismal monotonous chanting would awaken me, and I would
see him seated bolt upright on his couch, going through his
dolorous performance with a most business-like air. There
were other voices of the night, still more inharmonious.
Twice or thrice, between sunset and dawn, all the dogs in
the village, and there were hundreds of them, would bay and
yelp in chorus; a horrible clamor, resembling no sound that
I have ever heard, except perhaps the frightful howling of
wolves that we used sometimes to hear, long afterward,
when descending the Arkansas on the trail of General
Kearney's army. This canine uproar is, if possible, more
discordant than that of the wolves. Heard at a distance
slowly rising on the night, it has a strange unearthly effect,
and would fearfully haunt the dreams of a nervous man;
but when you are sleeping in the midst of it, the din is
outrageous. One long, loud howl begins it, and voice after
voice takes up the sound, till it passes around the whole circumference of the village, and the air is filled with confused
and discordant cries, at once fierce and mournful. It lasts a
few moments, and then dies away into silence.

Morning came, and Kongra-Tonga, mounting his horse,
rode out with the hunters. It may not be amiss to glance at
him for an instant in his character of husband and father.
Both he and his squaw, like most other Indians, were very
fond of their children, whom they indulged to excess, and
never punished, except in extreme cases, when they would
throw a bowl of cold water over them. Their offspring became sufficiently undutiful and disobedient under this system
of education, which tends not a little to foster that wild idea
of liberty and utter intolerance of restraint which lie at the
foundation of the Indian character. It would be hard to find
a fonder father than Kongra-Tonga. There was one urchin
in particular, rather less than two feet high, to whom he

was exceedingly attached; and sometimes spreading a
buffalo-robe in the lodge, he would seat himself upon it,
place his small favorite upright before him, and chant in a
low tone some of the words used as an accompaniment to
5 the war-dance. The little fellow, who could just manage to
balance himself by stretching out both arms, would lift his
feet and turn slowly round and round in time to his father's
music, while my host would laugh with delight, and look
smiling up into my face to see if I were admiring this preco-
10 cious performance of his offspring. In his capacity of husband he was less tender. The squaw who lived in the lodge
with him had been his partner for many years. She took
good care of his children and his household concerns. He
liked her well enough, and as far as I could see, they never
15 quarrelled; but his warmer affections were reserved for
younger and more recent favorites. Of these he had at
present only one, who lived in a lodge apart from his own.
One day while in this camp, he became displeased with her,
pushed her out, threw after her her ornaments, dresses, and
20 everything she had, and told her to go home to her father.
Having consummated this summary divorce, for which he
could show good reasons, he came back, seated himself in
his usual place, and began to smoke with an air of the utmost
tranquillity and self-satisfaction.

25   I was sitting in the lodge with him on that very afternoon,
when I felt some curiosity to learn the history of the numerous scars that appeared on his naked body. Of some of
them, however, I did not venture to inquire, for I already
understood their origin. Each of his arms was marked as if
30 deeply gashed with a knife at regular intervals, and there
were other scars also, of a different character, on his back
and on either breast. They were the traces of the tortures
which these Indians, in common with a few other tribes, inflict upon themselves at certain seasons; in part, it may be,
to gain the glory of courage and endurance, but chiefly as

an act of self-sacrifice to secure the favor of the spirits. The scars upon the breast and back were produced by running through the flesh strong splints of wood, to which heavy buffalo-skulls are fastened by cords of hide, and the wretch runs forward with all his strength, assisted by two companions, who take hold of each arm, until the flesh tears apart and the skulls are left behind. Others of Kongra-Tonga's scars were the result of accidents; but he had many received in war. He was one of the most noted warriors in the village. In the course of his life he had slain, as he boasted to me, fourteen men; and though, like other Indians, he was a braggart and liar, yet in this statement common report bore him out. Being flattered by my inquiries, he told me tale after tale, true or false, of his warlike exploits; and there was one among the rest illustrating the worst features of Indian character too well for me to omit it. Pointing out of the opening of the lodge towards the Medicine Bow Mountain, not many miles distant, he said that he was there a few summers ago with a war-party of his young men. Here they found two Snake Indians, hunting. They shot one of them with arrows, and chased the other up the side of the mountain till they surrounded him, and Kongra-Tonga himself, jumping forward among the trees, seized him by the arm. Two of his young men then ran up and held him fast while he scalped him alive. They then built a great fire, and cutting the tendons of their captive's wrists and feet, threw him in, and held him down with long poles until he was burnt to death. He garnished his story with descriptive particulars much too revolting to mention. His features were remarkably mild and open, without the fierceness of expression common among these Indians; and as he detailed these devilish cruelties, he looked up into my face with the air of earnest simplicity which a little child would wear in relating to its mother some anecdote of its youthful experience.

Old Mene-Seela's lodge could offer another illustration of the ferocity of Indian warfare. A bright-eyed, active little boy was living there who had belonged to a village of the Gros-Ventre Blackfeet, a small but bloody and treacherous
5 band, in close alliance with the Arapahoes. About a year before, Kongra-Tonga and a party of warriors had found about twenty lodges of these Indians upon the plains a little to the eastward of our present camp; and surrounding them in the night, they butchered men, women, and children, pre-
10 serving only this little boy alive. He was adopted into the old man's family, and was now fast becoming identified with the Ogillallah children, among whom he mingled on equal terms. There was also a Crow warrior in the village, a man of gigantic stature and most symmetrical proportions. Hav-
15 ing been taken prisoner many years before and adopted by a squaw in place of a son whom she had lost, he had for- gotten his old nationality, and was now both in act and inclination an Ogillallah.

It will be remembered that the scheme of the grand war-
20 party against the Snake and Crow Indians originated in this village; and though this plan had fallen to the ground, the embers of martial ardor continued to glow. Eleven young men had prepared to go out against the enemy, and the fourth day of our stay in this camp was fixed upon for their
25 departure. At the head of this party was a well-built, active little Indian, called the White Shield, whom I had always noticed for the neatness of his dress and appearance. His lodge too, though not a large one, was the best in the village, his squaw was one of the prettiest, and altogether his dwell-
30 ing was the model of an Ogillallah domestic establishment. I was often a visitor there, for the White Shield, being rather partial to white men, used to invite me to continual feasts at all hours of the day. Once, when the substantial part of the entertainment was over, and he and I were seated cross-legged on a buffalo-robe smoking together very

amicably, he took down his warlike equipments, which were hanging around the lodge, and displayed them with great pride and self-importance. Among the rest was a superb head-dress of feathers. Taking this from its case, he put it on and stood before me, perfectly conscious of the gallant air which it gave to his dark face and his vigorous, graceful figure. He told me that upon it were the feathers of three war-eagles, equal in value to the same number of good horses. He took up also a shield gayly painted and hung with feathers. The effect of these barbaric ornaments was admirable. His quiver was made of the spotted skin of a small panther, common among the Black Hills, from which the tail and distended claws were still allowed to hang. The White Shield concluded his entertainment in a manner characteristic of an Indian. He begged of me a little powder and ball, for he had a gun as well as a bow and arrows; but this I was obliged to refuse, because I had scarcely enough for my own use. Making him, however, a parting present of a paper of vermilion, I left him quite contented.

On the next morning the White Shield took cold, and was attacked with an inflammation of the throat. Immediately he seemed to lose all spirit, and though before no warrior in the village had borne himself more proudly, he now moped about from lodge to lodge with a forlorn and dejected air. At length he sat down, close wrapped in his robe, before the lodge of Reynal, but when he found that neither he nor I knew how to relieve him, he arose and stalked over to one of the medicine-men of the village. This old impostor thumped him for some time with both fists, howled and yelped over him, and beat a drum close to his ear to expel the evil spirit. This treatment failing of the desired effect, the White Shield withdrew to his own lodge, where he lay disconsolate for some hours. Making his appearance once more in the afternoon, he again took his seat on the ground before Reynal's lodge, holding his throat with his hand.

For some time he sat silent with his eyes fixed mournfully on the ground. At last he began to speak in a low tone.

"I am a brave man," he said; "all the young men think me a great warrior, and ten of them are ready to go with me to the war. I will go and show them the enemy. Last summer the Snakes killed my brother. I cannot live unless I revenge his death. To-morrow we will set out and I will take their scalps."

The White Shield, as he expressed this resolution, seemed to have lost all the accustomed fire and spirit of his look, and hung his head as if in a fit of despondency.

As I was sitting that evening at one of the fires, I saw him arrayed in his splendid war-dress, his cheeks painted with vermilion, leading his favorite war-horse to the front of his lodge. He mounted and rode round the village, singing his war-song in a loud, hoarse voice amid the shrill acclamations of the women. Then dismounting, he remained for some minutes prostrate upon the ground, as if in an act of supplication. On the following morning I looked in vain for the departure of the warriors. All was quiet in the village until late in the forenoon, when the White Shield came and seated himself in his old place before us. Reynal asked him why he had not gone out to find the enemy.

"I cannot go," he answered in a dejected voice. "I have given my war-arrows to the Meneaska."

"You have only given him two of your arrows," said Reynal. "If you ask him, he will give them back again."

For some time the White Shield said nothing. At last he spoke in a gloomy tone, —

"One of my young men has had bad dreams. The spirits of the dead came and threw stones at him in his sleep."

If such a dream had actually taken place it might have broken up this or any other war-party, but both Reynal and I were convinced at the time that it was a mere fabrication to excuse his remaining at home.

The White Shield was a warrior of noted prowess. Very probably, he would have received a mortal wound without the show of pain, and endured without flinching the worst tortures that an enemy could inflict upon him. The whole power of an Indian's nature would be summoned to encounter such a trial; every influence of his education from childhood would have prepared him for it; the cause of his suffering would have been visibly and palpably before him, and his spirit would rise to set his enemy at defiance, and gain the highest glory of a warrior by meeting death with fortitude. But when he feels himself attacked by a mysterious evil, before whose assaults his manhood is wasted, and his strength drained away, when he can see no enemy to resist and defy, the boldest warrior falls prostrate at once. He believes that a bad spirit has taken possession of him, or that he is the victim of some charm. When suffering from a protracted disorder, an Indian will often abandon himself to his supposed destiny, pine away and die, the victim of his own imagination. The same effect will often follow a series of calamities, or a long run of ill-luck, and Indians have been known to ride into the midst of an enemy's camp, or attack a grizzly bear single-handed, to get rid of a life supposed to lie under the doom of fate.

Thus, after all his fasting, dreaming, and calling upon the Great Spirit, the White Shield's war-party came to nought.

CHAPTER XVI

THE TRAPPERS

In speaking of the Indians, I have almost forgotten two bold adventurers of another race, the trappers Rouleau and Saraphin. These men were bent on a hazardous enterprise. They were on their way to the country ranged by the Arapahoes, a day's journey west of our camp. These Arapahoes, of whom Shaw and I afterwards fell in with a large number, are ferocious savages, who of late had declared themselves enemies to the whites, and threatened death to the first who should venture within their territory. The occasion of the declaration was as follows : —

In the preceding spring, 1845, Colonel Kearney left Fort Leavenworth with several companies of dragoons, marched to Fort Laramie, passed along the foot of the mountains to Bent's Fort, and then, turning eastward again, returned to the point whence he set out. While at Fort Laramie, he sent a part of his command as far westward as Sweetwater, while he himself remained at the fort, and despatched messages to the surrounding Indians to meet him there in council. Then for the first time the tribes of that vicinity saw the white warriors, and, as might have been expected, they were lost in astonishment at their regular order, their gay attire, the completeness of their martial equipment, and the size and strength of their horses. Among the rest, the Arapahoes came in considerable numbers to the fort. They had lately committed numerous murders, and Colonel Kearney threatened that if they killed any more white men he would turn loose his dragoons upon them, and annihilate their nation. In the evening, to add effect to his speech, he

ordered a howitzer to be fired and a rocket to be thrown up.
Many of the Arapahoes fell flat on the ground, while others
ran away screaming with amazement and terror. On the
following day they withdrew to their mountains, confounded
at the appearance of the dragoons, at their big gun which
went off twice at one shot, and the fiery messenger which
they had sent up to the Great Spirit. For many months
they remained quiet, and did no farther mischief. At length,
just before we came into the country, one of them, by an
act of the basest treachery, killed two white men, Boot and
May, who were trapping among the mountains. For this
act it was impossible to discover a motive. It seemed to
spring from one of those inexplicable impulses which often
possess Indians, and which appear to be mere outbreaks
of native ferocity. No sooner was the murder committed
than the whole tribe were in consternation. They expected
every day that the avenging dragoons would come, little
thinking that a desert of nine hundred miles lay between
them and their enemy. A large deputation of them came
to Fort Laramie, bringing a valuable present of horses, in
atonement. These Bordeaux refused to accept. They then
asked if he would be satisfied with their delivering up the
murderer himself; but he declined this offer also. The
Arapahoes went back more terrified than ever. Weeks
passed away, and still no dragoons appeared. A result followed which those best acquainted with Indians had predicted. They imagined that fear had prevented Bordeaux
from accepting their gifts, and that they had nothing to
apprehend from the vengeance of the whites. From terror
they rose to the height of insolence. They called the white
men cowards and old women; and a friendly Dahcotah
came to Fort Laramie with the report that they were determined to kill the first white dog they could lay hands on.

Had a military officer, with suitable powers, been stationed
at Fort Laramie; had he accepted the offer of the Arapahoes

to deliver up the murderer, and ordered him to be led out and
shot, in presence of his tribe, — they would have been awed
into tranquillity, and much danger averted; but now the
neighborhood of the Medicine Bow Mountain was perilous in
5 the extreme. Old Mene-Seela, a true friend of the whites, and
many other of the Indians, gathered about the two trappers,
and vainly endeavored to turn them from their purpose;
but Rouleau and Saraphin only laughed at the danger. On
the morning preceding that on which they were to leave the
10 camp, we could all see faint white columns of smoke rising
against the dark base of the Medicine Bow. Scouts were
sent out immediately, and reported that these proceeded
from an Arapahoe camp, abandoned only a few hours before. Still the two trappers continued their preparations
15 for departure.

Saraphin was a tall, powerful fellow, with a sullen and
sinister countenance. His rifle had very probably drawn
other blood than that of buffalo or Indians. Rouleau had
a broad ruddy face, marked with as few traces of thought
20 or care as a child's. His figure was square and strong, but
the first joints of both his feet were frozen off, and his horse
had lately thrown and trampled upon him, by which he had
been severely injured in the chest. But nothing could sub-
due his gayety. He went all day rolling about the camp
25 on his stumps of feet, talking, singing, and frolicking with
the Indian women. Rouleau had an unlucky partiality for
squaws. He always had one, whom he must needs bedizen
with beads, ribbons, and all the finery of an Indian ward-
robe; and though he was obliged to leave her behind him
30 during his expeditions, this hazardous necessity did not at
all trouble him, for his disposition was the reverse of jealous. If at any time he had not lavished the whole of the
precarious profits of his vocation upon his dark favorite, he
devoted the rest to feasting his comrades. If liquor was not
to be had — and this was usually the case — strong coffee

would be substituted. As the men of that region are by no means remarkable for providence or self-restraint, whatever was set before them on these occasions, however extravagant in price or enormous in quantity, was sure to be disposed of at one sitting. Like other trappers, Rouleau's life was one of contrast and variety. It was only at certain seasons, and for a limited time, that he was absent on his expeditions. For the rest of the year he would lounge about the fort, or encamp with his friends in its vicinity, hunting, or enjoying all the luxury of inaction; but when once in pursuit of the beaver, he was involved in extreme privations and perils. Hand and foot, eye and ear, must be always alert. Frequently he must content himself with devouring his evening meal uncooked, lest the light of his fire should attract the eyes of some wandering Indian; and sometimes having made his rude repast, he must leave his fire still blazing, and withdraw to a distance under cover of the darkness, that his disappointed enemy, drawn thither by the light, may find his victim gone, and be unable to trace his footsteps in the gloom. This is the life led by scores of men among the Rocky Mountains. I once met a trapper whose breast was marked with the scars of six bullets and arrows, one of his arms broken by a shot and one of his knees shattered; yet still, with the mettle of New England, whence he had come, he continued to follow his perilous calling.

On the last day of our stay in this camp, the trappers were ready for departure. When in the Black Hills they had caught seven beavers, and they now left their skins in charge of Reynal, to be kept until their return. Their strong, gaunt horses were equipped with rusty Spanish bits, and rude Mexican saddles, to which wooden stirrups were attached, while a buffalo-robe was rolled up behind, and a bundle of beaver-traps slung at the pommel. These, together with their rifles, knives, powder-horns, and bullet pouches,

flint and steel and a tin cup, composed their whole travelling equipment. They shook hands with us, and rode away;
Saraphin, with his grim countenance, was in advance; but
Rouleau, clambering gayly into his seat, kicked his horse's
sides, flourished his whip, and trotted briskly over the
prairie, trolling forth a Canadian song at the top of his
voice. Reynal looked after them with his face of brutal
selfishness.

"Well," he said, "if they are killed, I shall have the
beaver. They'll fetch me fifty dollars at the fort, anyhow."

This was the last I saw of them.

We had been five days in the hunting-camp, and the
meat, which all this time had hung drying in the sun, was
now fit for transportation. Buffalo-hides also had been procured in sufficient quantities for making the next season's
lodges; but it remained to provide the long poles on which
they were to be supported. These were only to be had
among the tall spruce woods of the Black Hills, and in that
direction therefore our next move was to be made. Amid
the general abundance which during this time had prevailed
in the camp, there were no instances of individual privation; for although the hide and the tongue of the buffalo
belong by exclusive right to the hunter who has killed it,
yet any one else is equally entitled to help himself from
the rest of the carcass. Thus the weak, the aged, and even
the indolent come in for a share of the spoils, and many a
helpless old woman, who would otherwise perish from starvation, is sustained in abundance.

On the twenty-fifth of July, late in the afternoon, the
camp broke up, with the usual tumult and confusion, and
we all moved once more, on horseback and on foot, over the
plains. We advanced, however, but a few miles. The old
men, who during the whole march had been stoutly striding
along on foot in front of the people, now seated themselves
in a circle on the ground, while the families, erecting their

lodges in the prescribed order around them, formed the
usual great circle of the camp; meanwhile these village
patriarchs sat smoking and talking. I threw my bridle to
Raymond, and sat down as usual along with them. There
was none of that reserve and apparent dignity which an
Indian always assumes when in council, or in the presence
of white men whom he distrusts. The party, on the contrary, was an extremely merry one, and as in a social circle
of a quite different character, " if there was not much wit,
there was at least a great deal of laughter."

When the first pipe was smoked out, I rose and withdrew
to the lodge of my host. Here I was stooping, in the act of
taking off my powder-horn and bullet-pouch, when suddenly,
and close at hand, pealing loud and shrill, and in right good
earnest, came the terrific yell of the war-whoop. Kongra-
Tonga's squaw snatched up her youngest child, and ran out
of the lodge. I followed, and found the whole village in
confusion, resounding with cries and yells. The circle of
old men in the centre had vanished. The warriors, with
glittering eyes, came darting, weapons in hand, out of the
low openings of the lodges, and running with wild yells
towards the farther end of the village. Advancing a few
rods in that direction, I saw a crowd in furious agitation.
Just then I distinguished the voices of Raymond and Reynal, shouting to me from a distance, and, looking back, I
saw the latter with his rifle in his hand, standing on the
farther bank of a little stream that ran along the outskirts
of the camp. He was calling to Raymond and me to come
over and join him, and Raymond, with his usual deliberate
gait and stolid countenance, was already moving in that
direction.

This was clearly the wisest course, unless we wished to
involve ourselves in the fray; so I turned to go, but just
then a pair of eyes, gleaming like a snake's, and an aged
familiar countenance was thrust from the opening of a

neighboring lodge, and out bolted old Mene-Seela, full of
fight, clutching his bow and arrows in one hand and his
knife in the other. At that instant he tripped and fell
sprawling on his face, while his weapons flew scattering in
5 every direction. The women with loud screams were hurrying with their children in their arms to place them out of
danger, and I observed some hastening to prevent mischief,
by carrying away all the weapons they could lay hands on.
On a rising ground close to the camp stood a line of old
10 women singing a medicine-song to allay the tumult. As I
approached the side of the brook, I heard gun-shots behind
me, and, turning back, saw that the crowd had separated
into two long lines of naked warriors confronting each other
at a respectful distance, and yelling and jumping about to
15 dodge the shot of their adversaries, while they discharged
bullets and arrows against each other. At the same time
certain sharp, humming sounds in the air over my head, like
the flight of beetles on a summer evening, warned me that
the danger was not wholly confined to the immediate scene
20 of the fray. So wading through the brook, I joined Reynal
and Raymond, and we sat down on the grass, in the posture
of an armed neutrality, to watch the result.

Happily it may be for ourselves, though contrary to our
expectation, the disturbance was quelled almost as soon as
25 it began. When I looked again, the combatants were once
more mingled together in a mass. Though yells sounded
occasionally from the throng, the firing had entirely ceased,
and I observed five or six persons moving busily about, as
if acting the part of peace-makers. One of the village her-
30 alds or criers proclaimed in a loud voice something which
my two companions were too much engrossed in their own
observations to translate for me. The crowd began to disperse, though many a deep-set black eye still glittered with
an unnatural lustre, as the warriors slowly withdrew to their
lodges. This fortunate suppression of the disturbance was

owing to a few of the old men, less pugnacious than Mene-
Seela, who boldly ran in between the combatants, and aided
by some of the "soldiers," or Indian police, succeeded in
effecting their object.

It seemed very strange to me that although many arrows 5
and bullets were discharged, no one was mortally hurt, and
I could only account for this by the fact that both the
marksman and the object of his aim were leaping about
incessantly. By far the greater part of the villagers had
joined in the fray, for although there were not more than 10
a dozen guns in the whole camp, I heard at least eight or
ten shots fired.

In a quarter of an hour all was comparatively quiet. A
group of warriors was again seated in the middle of the village, but this time I did not venture to join them, because I 15
could see that the pipe, contrary to the usual order, was
passing from the left hand to the right around the circle; a
sure sign that a "medicine-smoke" of reconciliation was
going forward, and that a white man would be an intruder.
When I again entered the still agitated camp it was nearly 20
dark, and mournful cries, howls, and wailings resounded
from many female voices. Whether these had any connection with the late disturbance, or were merely lamentations
for relatives slain in some former war expeditions, I could
not distinctly ascertain. 25

To inquire too closely into the cause of the quarrel was
by no means prudent, and it was not until some time after
that I discovered what had given rise to it. Among the
Dahcotah there are many associations or fraternities, superstitious, warlike, or social. Among them was one called 30
"The Arrow-Breakers," now in great measure disbanded
and dispersed. In the village there were, however, four men
belonging to it, distinguished by the peculiar arrangement
of their hair, which rose in a high bristling mass above
their foreheads, adding greatly to their apparent height, and

giving them a most ferocious appearance. The principal
among them was the Mad Wolf, a warrior of remarkable size
and strength, great courage, and the fierceness of a demon.
I had always looked upon him as the most dangerous man
5 in the village; and though he often invited me to feasts, I
never entered his lodge unarmed. The Mad Wolf had taken
a fancy to a fine horse belonging to another Indian, called
the Tall Bear; and anxious to get the animal into his possession, he made the owner a present of another horse nearly
10 equal in value. According to the customs of the Dahcotah,
the acceptance of this gift involved a sort of obligation to
make a return; and the Tall Bear well understood that the
other had his favorite buffalo-horse in view. He, however,
accepted the present without a word of thanks, and, having
15 picketed the horse before his lodge, suffered day after day
to pass without making the expected return. The Mad Wolf
grew impatient; and at last, seeing that his bounty was not
likely to produce the desired result, he resolved to reclaim
it. So this evening, as soon as the village was encamped, he
20 went to the lodge of the Tall Bear, seized upon the horse he
had given him, and led him away. At this the Tall Bear
broke into one of those fits of sullen rage not uncommon
among Indians, ran up to the unfortunate horse, and gave
him three mortal stabs with his knife. Quick as lightning,
25 the Mad Wolf drew his bow to its utmost tension, and held
the arrow quivering close to the breast of his adversary.
The Tall Bear, as the Indians who were near him said, stood
with his bloody knife in his hand, facing the assailant with
the utmost calmness. Some of his friends and relatives,
30 seeing his danger, ran hastily to his assistance. The remaining three Arrow-Breakers, on the other hand, came to the
aid of their associate. Their friends joined them, the war-
cry was raised, and the tumult became general.

The "soldiers," who lent their timely aid in putting it
down, are the most important executive functionaries in an

Indian village. The office is one of considerable honor, being confided only to men of courage and repute. They derive their authority from the old men and chief warriors of the village, who elect them in councils occasionally convened for the purpose, and thus can exercise a degree of authority which no one else in the village would dare to assume. While very few Ogillallah chiefs could venture without risk of their lives to strike or lay hands upon the meanest of their people, the "soldiers," in the discharge of their appropriate functions, have full license to make use of these and similar acts of coercion.

CHAPTER XVII

THE BLACK HILLS

We travelled eastward for two days, and then the gloomy ridges of the Black Hills rose up before us. The village passed along for some miles beneath their declivities, trailing out to a great length over the arid prairie, or winding among small detached hills of distorted shapes. Turning sharply to the left, we entered a wide defile of the mountains, down the bottom of which a brook came winding, lined with tall grass and dense copses, amid which were hidden many beaver-dams and lodges. We passed along between two lines of high precipices and rocks piled in disorder one upon another, with scarcely a tree, a bush, or a clump of grass. The restless Indian boys wandered along their edges and clambered up and down their rugged sides, and sometimes a group of them would stand on the verge of a cliff and look down on the procession as it passed beneath. As we advanced, the passage grew more narrow; then it suddenly expanded into a round grassy meadow, completely encompassed by mountains; and here the families stopped as they came up in turn, and the camp rose like magic.

The lodges were hardly pitched when, with their usual precipitation, the Indians set about accomplishing the object that had brought them there; that is, obtaining poles for their new lodges. Half the population, men, women, and boys, mounted their horses and set out for the depths of the mountains. It was a strange cavalcade, as they rode at full gallop over the shingly rocks and into the dark opening of the defile beyond. We passed between precipices, sharp and

splintering at the tops, their sides beetling over the defile
or descending in abrupt declivities, bristling with fir-trees.
On our left they rose close to us like a wall, but on the right
a winding brook with a narrow strip of marshy soil intervened. The stream was clogged with old beaver-dams, and 5
spread frequently into wide pools. There were thick bushes
and many dead and blasted trees along its course, though
frequently nothing remained but stumps cut close to the
ground by the beaver, and marked with the sharp chisel-
like teeth of those indefatigable laborers. Sometimes we 10
dived among trees, and then emerged upon open spots, over
which, Indian-like, all galloped at full speed. As Pauline
bounded over the rocks I felt her saddle-girth slipping, and
alighted to draw it tighter; when the whole cavalcade swept
past me in a moment, the women with their gaudy orna- 15
ments tinkling as they rode, the men whooping, laughing,
and lashing forward their horses. Two black-tailed deer
bounded away among the rocks; Raymond shot at them
from horseback; the sharp report of his rifle was answered
by another equally sharp from the opposing cliffs, and then 20
the echoes, leaping in rapid succession from side to side,
died away rattling far amid the mountains.

After having ridden in this manner six or eight miles,
the scene changed, and all the declivities were covered with
forests of tall, slender spruce-trees. The Indians began to 25
fall off to the right and left, dispersing with their hatchets
and knives to cut the poles which they had come to seek.
I was soon left almost alone; but in the stillness of those
lonely mountains, the stroke of hatchets and the sound of
voices might be heard from far and near. 30

Reynal, who imitated the Indians in their habits as well
as the worst features of their character, had killed buffalo
enough to make a lodge for himself and his squaw, and now
he was eager to get the poles necessary to complete it. He
asked me to let Raymond go with him, and assist in the

work. I assented, and the two men immediately entered
the thickest part of the wood. Having left my horse in
Raymond's keeping, I began to climb the mountain. I was
weak and weary, and made slow progress, often pausing to
5 rest, but after an hour, I gained a height whence the little
valley out of which I had climbed seemed like a deep, dark
gulf, though the inaccessible peak of the mountain was still
towering to a much greater distance above. Objects familiar
from childhood surrounded me; crags and rocks, a black
10 and sullen brook that gurgled with a hollow voice deep
among the crevices, a wood of mossy distorted trees and prostrate trunks flung down by age and storms, scattered among
the rocks, or damming the foaming waters of the brook.

Wild as they were, these mountains were thickly peopled.
15 As I climbed farther, I found the broad dusty paths made
by the elk, as they filed across the mountain-side. The grass
on all the terraces was trampled down by deer; there were
numerous tracks of wolves, and in some of the rougher and
more precipitous parts of the ascent, I found footprints dif-
20 ferent from any that I had ever seen, and which I took to
be those of the Rocky Mountain sheep. I sat down upon
a rock; there was a perfect stillness. No wind was stirring,
and not even an insect could be heard. I remembered the
danger of becoming lost in such a place, and fixed my eye
25 upon one of the tallest pinnacles of the opposite mountain.
It rose sheer upright from the woods below, and, by an extraordinary freak of nature, sustained aloft on its very summit a large loose rock. Such a landmark could never be
mistaken, and, feeling once more secure, I began again to
30 move forward. A white wolf jumped up from among some
bushes, and leaped clumsily away; but he stopped for a
moment, and turned back his keen eye and grim bristling
muzzle. I longed to take his scalp and carry it back with
me, as a trophy of the Black Hills, but before I could fire,
he was gone among the rocks. Soon after I heard a rustling

sound, with a cracking of twigs at a little distance, and saw moving above the tall bushes the branching antlers of an elk. I was in the midst of a hunter's paradise.

Such are the Black Hills, as I found them in July; but they wear a different garb when winter sets in, when the broad boughs of the fir-trees are bent to the ground by the load of snow, and the dark mountains are white with it. At that season the trappers, returned from their autumn expeditions, often build their cabins in the midst of these solitudes, and live in abundance and luxury on the game that harbors there. I have heard them tell, how with their tawny mistresses, and perhaps a few young Indian companions, they had spent months in total seclusion. They would dig pitfalls, and set traps for the white wolves, sables, and martens, and though through the whole night the awful chorus of the wolves would resound from the frozen mountains around them, yet within their massive walls of logs they would lie in careless ease before the blazing fire, and in the morning shoot the elk and deer from their very door.

CHAPTER XVIII

A MOUNTAIN HUNT

The camp was full of the newly-cut lodge-poles: some, already prepared, were stacked together, white and glistening, to dry and harden in the sun; others were lying on the ground, and the squaws, the boys, and even some of the
5 warriors, were busily at work peeling off the bark and paring them with their knives to the proper dimensions. Most of the hides obtained at the last camp were dressed and scraped thin enough for use, and many of the squaws were engaged in fitting them together and sewing them with sinews, to
10 form the coverings for the lodges. Men were wandering among the bushes that lined the brook along the margin of the camp, cutting sticks of red willow, or *shongsasha*, the bark of which, mixed with tobacco, they used for smoking. Reynal's squaw was hard at work with her awl and buffalo
15 sinews upon her lodge, while her proprietor, having just finished an enormous breakfast of meat, was smoking a social pipe with Raymond and myself. He proposed at length that we should go out on a hunt. " Go to the Big Crow's lodge," said he, " and get your rifle. I 'll bet the
20 gray Wyandot pony against your mare that we start an elk or a black-tailed deer, or likely as not, a big-horn before we are two miles out of camp. I 'll take my squaw's old yellow horse; you can't whip her more than four miles an hour, but she is as good for the mountains as a mule."

25 I mounted the black mule which Raymond usually rode. She was a powerful animal, gentle and manageable enough by nature; but of late her temper had been soured by mis-
• fortune. About a week before, I had chanced to offend some

230

one of the Indians, who out of revenge went secretly into the meadow and gave her a severe stab in the haunch with his knife. The wound, though partially healed, still galled her extremely, and made her even more perverse and obstinate than the rest of her species.

The morning was a glorious one, and I was in better health than I had been at any time for the last two months. We left the little valley and ascended a rocky hollow in the mountain. Very soon we were out of sight of the camp, and of every living thing, man, beast, bird, or insect. I had never before, except on foot, passed over such execrable ground, and I desire never to repeat the experiment. The black mule grew indignant, and even the redoubtable yellow horse stumbled every moment, and kept groaning to himself as he cut his feet and legs among the sharp rocks.

It was a scene of silence and desolation. Little was visible except beetling crags and the bare shingly sides of the mountains, relieved by scarcely a trace of vegetation. At length, however, we came upon a forest tract, and had no sooner done so than we heartily wished ourselves back among the rocks again; for we were on a steep descent, among trees so thick that we could see scarcely a rod in any direction.

If one is anxious to place himself in a situation where the hazardous and the ludicrous are combined in about equal proportions, let him get upon a vicious mule, with a snaffle bit, and try to drive her through the woods down a slope of forty-five degrees. Let him have a long rifle, a buckskin frock with long fringes, and a head of long hair. These latter appendages will be caught every moment and twitched away in small portions by the twigs, which will also whip him smartly across the face, while the large branches above thump him on the head. His mule, if she be a true one, will alternately stop short and dive violently forward, and his positions upon her back will be somewhat diversified. At one time he will clasp her affectionately, to avoid the blow of a bough overhead;

at another, he will throw himself back and fling his knee
forward against her neck, to keep it from being crushed between the rough bark of a tree and the ribs of the animal.
Reynal was cursing incessantly during the whole way down.
5 Neither of us had the remotest idea where we were going;
and though I have seen rough riding, I shall always retain
an evil recollection of that five minutes' scramble.

At last we left our troubles behind us, emerging into the
channel of a brook that circled along the foot of the descent;
10 and here, turning joyfully to the left, we rode at ease over
the white pebbles and the rippling water, shaded from the
glaring sun by an overarching green transparency. These
halcyon moments were of short duration. The friendly
brook, turning sharply to one side, went brawling and foam-
15 ing down the rocky hill into an abyss, which, as far as we
could see, had no bottom; so once more we betook ourselves
to the detested woods. When next we came out from their
shadow and sunlight, we found ourselves standing in the
broad glare of day, on a high, jutting point of the mountain.
20 Before us stretched a long, wide, desert valley, winding
away far amid the mountains. Reynal gazed intently; he
began to speak at last: —

"Many a time, when I was with the Indians, I have been
hunting for gold all through the Black Hills. There's plenty
25 of it here; you may be certain of that. I have dreamed
about it fifty times, and I never dreamed yet but what it
came out true. Look over yonder at those black rocks piled
up against that other big rock. Don't it look as if there
might be something there? It won't do for a white man to
30 be rummaging too much about these mountains; the Indians
say they are full of bad spirits; and I believe myself that
it's no good luck to be hunting about here after gold. Well,
for all that, I would like to have one of those fellows up
here, from down below, to go about with his witch-hazel rod,
and I'll guarantee that it would not be long before he would

light on a gold mine. Never mind; we'll let the gold alone for to-day. Look at those trees down below us in the hollow; we'll go down there, and I reckon we'll get a black-tailed deer."

But Reynal's predictions were not verified. We passed mountain after mountain, and valley after valley; we explored deep ravines; yet still, to my companion's vexation and evident surprise, no game could be found. So, in the absence of better, we resolved to go out on the plains and look for an antelope. With this view we began to pass down a narrow valley, the bottom of which was covered with the stiff wild-sage bushes, and marked with deep paths, made by the buffalo, who, for some inexplicable reason, are accustomed to penetrate, in their long, grave processions, deep among the gorges of these sterile mountains.

Reynal's eye ranged incessantly among the rocks and along the edges of the precipices, in hopes of discovering the mountain-sheep peering down upon us from that giddy elevation. Nothing was visible for some time. At length we both detected something in motion near the foot of one of the mountains, and a moment afterwards a black-tailed deer stood gazing at us from the top of a rock, and then, slowly turning away, disappeared behind it. In an instant Reynal was out of his saddle, and running towards the spot. I, being too weak to follow, sat holding his horse and waiting the result. I lost sight of him; then heard the report of his rifle deadened among the rocks, and finally saw him reappear, with a surly look, that plainly betrayed his ill success. Again we moved forward down the long valley, when soon after we came full upon what seemed a wide and very shallow ditch, incrusted at the bottom with white clay, dried and cracked in the sun. Under this fair outside Reynal's eye detected the signs of lurking mischief. He called to me to stop, and then alighting, picked up a stone and threw it into the ditch. To my amazement it fell with a dull splash, breaking at once through the thin crust, and spattering round the hole a yellowish creamy fluid, into which it sank and disappeared. A stick, five or six feet long, lay on the ground, and with this we sounded the insidious abyss close to its edge. It was just possible to touch the bottom. Places like this are numerous among the Rocky Mountains. The buffalo, in his blind and heedless walk, often plunges into them unawares. Down he sinks; one snort of terror, one convulsive struggle, and the slime calmly flows above his shaggy head, the languid undulations of its sleek and placid surface alone betraying how the powerful monster writhes in his death-throes below.

We found after some trouble a point where we could pass the abyss, and now the valley began to open upon plains which spread to the horizon before us. On one of their distant swells we discerned three or four black specks, which Reynal pronounced to be buffalo.

"Come," said he, "we must get one of them. My squaw wants more sinews to finish her lodge with, and I want some glue myself."

He immediately put the yellow horse to such a gallop as he was capable of executing, while I set spurs to the mule, who soon far outran her plebeian rival. When we had galloped a mile or more, a large rabbit, by ill-luck, sprang up just under the feet of the mule, who bounded violently aside in full career. Weakened as I was, I was flung forcibly to the ground, and my rifle, falling close to my head, went off with the shock. Its sharp, spiteful report rang for some moments in my ear. Being slightly stunned, I lay for an instant motionless, and Reynal, supposing me to be shot, rode up and began to curse the mule. Soon recovering myself, I arose, picked up the rifle, and anxiously examined it. It was badly injured. The stock was cracked, and the main screw broken, so that the lock had to be tied in its place with a string; yet happily it was not rendered totally unserviceable. I wiped it out, reloaded it, and handing it to Reynal, who meanwhile had caught the mule and led her up to me, I mounted again. No sooner had I done so, than the brute began to rear and plunge with extreme violence; but being now well prepared for her, and free from encumbrance, I soon reduced her to submission. Then taking the rifle again from Reynal, we galloped forward as before.

We were now free of the mountains and riding far out on the broad prairie. The buffalo were still some two miles in advance of us. When we came near them, we stopped where a gentle swell of the plain concealed us, and while I held his horse, Reynal ran forward with his rifle, till I lost sight of him beyond the rising ground. A few minutes elapsed: I heard the report of his piece, and saw the buffalo running away, at full speed on the right; immediately after, the hunter himself, unsuccessful as before, came up and mounted his horse in excessive ill-humor. He cursed the Black Hills and the buffalo, swore that he was a good hunter, which indeed was true, and that he had never been out before among those mountains without killing two or three deer at least.

We now turned towards the distant encampment. As we rode along, antelope in considerable numbers were flying lightly in all directions over the plain, but not one of them would stand and be shot at. When we reached the foot of the mountain-ridge that lay between us and the village, we were too impatient to take the smooth and circuitous route; so turning short to the left, we drove our wearied animals upward among the rocks. Still more antelope were leaping about among these flinty hillsides. Each of us shot at one, though from a great distance, and each missed his mark. At length we reached the summit of the last ridge. Looking down we saw the bustling camp in the valley at our feet, and ingloriously descended to it. As we rode among the

lodges, the Indians looked in vain for the fresh meat that
should have hung behind our saddles, and the squaws
uttered various suppressed ejaculations, to the great indignation of Reynal. Our mortification was increased when we
5 rode up to his lodge. Here we saw his young Indian relative,
the Hail-Storm, his light graceful figure reclining on the
ground in an easy attitude, while with his friend The Rabbit,
who sat by his side, he was making an abundant meal from
a wooden bowl of *wasna*, which the squaw had placed be-
10 tween them. Near him lay the fresh skin of a female elk,
which he had just killed among the mountains, only a mile
or two from the camp. No doubt the boy's heart was elated
with triumph, but he betrayed no sign of it. He even seemed
totally unconscious of our approach, and his handsome face
15 had all the tranquillity of Indian self-control,— a self-control
which prevents the exhibition of emotion without restraining the emotion itself. It was about two months since I had
known the Hail-Storm, and within that time his character
had remarkably developed. When I first saw him, he was
20 just emerging from the habits and feelings of the boy into
the ambition of the hunter and warrior. He had lately
killed his first deer, and this had excited his aspirations for
distinction. Since that time he had been continually in
search of game, and no young hunter in the village had been
25 so active or so fortunate as he. All this success had produced a marked change in his character. As I first remembered him, he always shunned the society of the young
squaws, and was extremely bashful and sheepish in their
presence ; but now, in the confidence of his new reputation,
30 be began to assume the airs and arts of a man of gallantry.
He wore his red blanket dashingly over his left shoulder,
painted his cheeks every day with vermilion, and hung pendants of shells in his ears. If I observed aright, he met with
very good success in his new pursuits ; still the Hail-Storm
had much to accomplish before he attained the full standing

of a warrior. Gallantly as he began to bear himself among
the women and girls, he was still timid and abashed in the
presence of the chiefs and old men; for he had never yet
killed a man, or stricken the dead body of an enemy in
battle. I have no doubt that the handsome, smooth-faced
boy burned with desire to flesh his maiden scalping-knife,
and I would not have encamped alone with him without
watching his movements with a suspicious eye.

His elder brother, The Horse, was of a different character.
He was nothing but a lazy dandy. He knew very well how
to hunt, but preferred to live by the hunting of others. He
had no appetite for distinction, and the Hail-Storm already
surpassed him in reputation. He had a dark and ugly face,
and passed a great part of his time in adorning it with
vermilion, and contemplating it by means of a little pocket
looking-glass which I had given him. As for the rest of the
day, he divided it between eating, sleeping, and sitting in
the sun on the outside of a lodge. Here he would remain
for hour after hour, arrayed in all his finery, with an old
dragoon's sword in his hand, evidently flattering himself
that he was the centre of attraction to the eyes of the surrounding squaws. Yet he sat looking straight forward with
a face of the utmost gravity, as if wrapped in profound med-
itation, and it was only by the occasional side-long glances
which he shot at his supposed admirers that one could
detect the true course of his thoughts.

Both he and his brother may represent classes in the
Indian community: neither should the Hail-Storm's friend,
The Rabbit, be passed by without notice. The Hail-Storm
and he were inseparable: they ate, slept, and hunted together, and shared with one another almost all that they
possessed. If there be anything that deserves to be called
romantic in the Indian character, it is to be sought for in
friendships such as this, which are common among many
of the prairie tribes.

Slowly, hour after hour, that weary afternoon dragged away. I lay in Reynal's lodge, overcome by the listless torpor that pervaded the encampment. The day's work was finished, or if it were not, the inhabitants had resolved not to finish it at all, and were dozing quietly within the shelter of the lodges. A profound lethargy, the very spirit of indolence, seemed to have sunk upon the village. Now and then I could hear the low laughter of some girl from within a neighboring lodge, or the small shrill voices of a few restless children, who alone were moving in the deserted area. The spirit of the place infected me; I could not think consecutively; I was fit only for musing and revery, when at last, like the rest, I fell asleep.

When evening came, and the fires were lighted round the lodges, a select family circle convened in the neighborhood of Reynal's domicile. It was composed entirely of his squaw's relatives, a mean and ignoble clan, among whom none but the Hail-Storm held forth any promise of future distinction. Even his prospects were rendered not a little dubious by the character of the family, less, however, from any principle of aristocratic distinction than from the want of powerful supporters to assist him in his undertakings, and help to avenge his quarrels. Raymond and I sat down along with them. There were eight or ten men gathered around the fire, together with about as many women, old and young, some of whom were tolerably good-looking. As the pipe passed round among the men, a lively conversation went forward, more merry than delicate, and at length two or three of the elder women (for the girls were somewhat diffident and bashful) began to assail Raymond with various pungent witticisms. Some of the men took part, and an old squaw concluded by bestowing on him a ludicrous and indecent nickname, at which a general laugh followed at his expense. Raymond grinned and giggled, and made several futile attempts at repartee. Knowing the impolicy and even danger of suffering myself to be placed in a ludicrous light among the Indians, I maintained a rigid, inflexible countenance, and wholly escaped their sallies.

In the morning I found, to my great disgust, that the camp was to retain its position for another day. I dreaded its languor and monotony, and, to escape it, set out to explore the surrounding mountains. I was accompanied by a faithful friend, my rifle, the only friend indeed on whose prompt assistance in time of trouble I could wholly rely. Most of the Indians in the village, it is true, professed good-will towards the whites, but the experience of others and my own observation had taught me the extreme folly of confidence, and the utter impossibility of foreseeing to what sudden acts the strange, unbridled impulses of an Indian may urge him. When among this people danger is never so near as when you are unprepared for it, never so remote as when you are armed and on the alert to meet it at any moment. Nothing offers so strong a temptation to their ferocious instincts as the appearance of timidity, weakness, or security.

Many deep and gloomy gorges, choked with trees and bushes, opened from the sides of the hills, which were shaggy with forests wherever the rocks permitted vegetation to spring. A great number of Indians were stalking along the edges of the woods, and boys were whooping and laughing on the mountains, practising eye and hand, and indulging their destructive propensities by killing birds and small animals with their little bows and arrows. There was one glen, stretching up between steep cliffs far into the bosom of the mountain. I began to ascend along its bottom, pushing my way onward among the rocks, trees, and bushes that obstructed it. A slender thread of water trickled through it, which since issuing from the heart of its native rock could scarcely have been warmed or gladdened by a ray of sunshine. After advancing for some time, I conceived myself to

be entirely alone; but coming to a part of the glen in a great measure free of trees and undergrowth, I saw at some distance the black head and red shoulders of an Indian among the bushes above. The reader need not prepare him-
5 self for a startling adventure, for I have none to relate. The head and shoulders belonged to Mene-Seela, my best friend in the village. As I had approached noiselessly with my moccasoned feet, the old man was quite unconscious of my presence; and turning to a point where I could gain an
10 unobstructed view of him, I saw him seated alone, immov-able as a statue, among the rocks and trees. His face was turned upward, and his eyes seemed riveted on a pine-tree swinging from a cleft in the precipice above. The crest of the pine was swaying to and fro in the wind, and its long
15 limbs waved slowly up and down, as if the tree had life. Looking for a while at the old man, I was satisfied that he was engaged in an act of worship, or prayer, or communion of some kind with a supernatural being. I longed to pene-trate his thoughts, but I could do nothing more than con-
20 jecture and speculate. I knew that though the intellect of an Indian can embrace the idea of an all-wise, all-powerful Spirit, the supreme Ruler of the universe, yet his mind will not always ascend into communion with a being that seems to him so vast, remote, and incomprehensible; and when dan-
25 ger threatens, when his hopes are broken, and trouble over-shadows him, he is prone to turn for relief to some inferior agency, less removed from the ordinary scope of his faculties. He has a guardian spirit, on whom he relies for succor and guidance. To him all nature is instinct with mystic influ-
30 ence. Among those mountains not a wild beast was prowl-ing, a bird singing, or a leaf fluttering, that might not tend to direct his destiny, or give warning of what was in store for him; and he watches the world of nature around him as the astrologer watches the stars. So closely is he linked with it that his guardian spirit, no unsubstantial creation of

the fancy, is usually embodied in the form of some living thing: a bear, a wolf, an eagle, or a serpent; and Mene-Seela, as he gazed intently on the old pine-tree, might believe it to enshrine the fancied guide and protector of his life. 5

Whatever was passing in the mind of the old man, it was no part of good sense to disturb him. Silently retracing my footsteps, I descended the glen until I came to a point where I could climb the precipices that shut it in, and gain the side of the mountain. Looking up, I saw a tall peak rising among 10 the woods. Something impelled me to climb; I had not felt for many a day such strength and elasticity of limb. An hour and a half of slow and often intermitted labor brought me to the very summit; and emerging from the dark shadows of the rocks and pines, I stepped forth into the light, and 15 walking along the sunny verge of a precipice, seated myself on its extreme point. Looking between the mountain-peaks to the westward, the pale blue prairie was stretching to the farthest horizon, like a serene and tranquil ocean. The surrounding mountains were in themselves sufficiently 20 striking and impressive, but this contrast gave redoubled effect to their stern features.

CHAPTER XIX

PASSAGE OF THE MOUNTAINS

When I took leave of Shaw at La Bonté's camp, I promised to meet him at Fort Laramie on the first of August. The Indians, too, intended to pass the mountains and move towards the fort. To do so at this point was impossible,
5 because there was no passage; and in order to find one, we were obliged to go twelve or fourteen miles southward. Late in the afternoon the camp got in motion. I rode in company with three or four young Indians at the rear, and the moving swarm stretched before me, in the ruddy light
10 of sunset, or the deep shadow of the mountains, far beyond my sight. It was an ill-omened spot they chose to encamp upon. When they were there just a year before, a war-party of ten men, led by The Whirlwind's son, had gone out against the enemy, and not one had ever returned. This
15 was the immediate cause of this season's warlike preparations. I was not a little astonished, when I came to the camp, at the confusion of horrible sounds with which it was filled: howls, shrieks, and wailings rose from all the women present, many of whom, not content with this exhibition of
20 grief for the loss of their friends and relatives, were gashing their legs deeply with knives. A warrior in the village, who had lost a brother in the expedition, chose another mode of displaying his sorrow. The Indians, who, though often rapacious, are devoid of avarice, will sometimes, when in
25 mourning, or on other solemn occasions, give away the whole of their possessions, and reduce themselves to nakedness and want. The warrior in question led his two best horses into the middle of the village, and gave them away

242

to his friends; upon which, songs and acclamations in praise
of his generosity mingled with the cries of the women.

On the next morning we entered again among the mountains. There was nothing in their appearance either grand
or picturesque, though they were desolate to the last degree,
being mere piles of black and broken rocks, without trees or
vegetation of any kind. As we passed among them along
a wide valley, I noticed Raymond riding by the side of a
young squaw, to whom he was addressing various compli-
ments. All the old squaws in the neighborhood watched his
proceedings in great admiration, and the girl herself would
turn aside her head and laugh. Just then his mule thought
proper to display her vicious pranks, and began to rear and
plunge most furiously. Raymond was an excellent rider,
and at first he stuck fast in his seat; but the moment after,
I saw the mule's hind-legs flourishing in the air, and my unlucky follower pitching headforemost over her ears. There
was a burst of screams and laughter from all the women,
in which his mistress herself took part, and Raymond was
assailed by such a shower of witticisms that he was glad to
ride forward out of hearing.

Not long after, as I rode near him, I heard him shouting
to me. He was pointing towards a detached rocky hill that
stood in the middle of the valley before us, and from behind
it a long file of elk came out at full speed and entered an
opening in the mountain. They had scarcely disappeared,
when whoops and exclamations came from fifty voices around
me. The young men leaped from their horses, flung down
their heavy buffalo-robes, and ran at full speed towards
the foot of the nearest mountain. Reynal also broke away
at a gallop in the same direction. "Come on! come on!"
he called to us. "Do you see that band of big-horn up
yonder? If there's one of them, there's a hundred!"

In fact, near the summit of the mountain, I could see a
large number of small white objects, moving rapidly upwards

among the precipices, while others were filing along its rocky
profile. Anxious to see the sport, I galloped forward, and
entering a passage in the side of the mountain, ascended
among the loose rocks as far as my horse could carry me.
5 Here I fastened her to an old pine-tree. At that moment
Raymond called to me from the right that another band of
sheep was close at hand in that direction. I ran up to the
top of the opening, which gave me a full view into the rocky
gorge beyond; and here I plainly saw some fifty or sixty
10 sheep, almost within rifle-shot, clattering upwards among the
rocks, and endeavoring, after their usual custom, to reach
the highest point. The naked Indians bounded up lightly
in pursuit. In a moment the game and hunters disappeared.
Nothing could be seen or heard but the occasional report of a
15 gun, more and more distant, reverberating among the rocks.

I turned to descend, and as I did so, could see the valley
below alive with Indians passing rapidly through it, on
horseback and on foot. A little farther on, all were stopping
as they came up; the camp was preparing and the lodges
20 rising. I descended to this spot, and soon after Reynal and
Raymond returned. They bore between them a sheep which
they had pelted to death with stones from the edge of a
ravine, along the bottom of which it was attempting to escape. One by one the hunters came dropping in; yet such
25 is the activity of the Rocky Mountain sheep that although
sixty or seventy men were out in pursuit, not more than half
a dozen animals were killed. Of these only one was a full-
grown male. He had a pair of horns, the dimensions of
which were almost beyond belief. I have seen among the
30 Indians ladles with long handles, capable of containing
more than a quart, cut out from such horns.

Through the whole of the next morning we were moving
forward among the hills. On the following day the heights
closed around us, and the passage of the mountains began
in earnest. Before the village left its 'camping-ground, I

set forward in company with the Eagle-Feather, a man of
powerful frame, but with a bad and sinister face. His son,
a light-limbed boy, rode with us, and another Indian, named
The Panther, was also of the party. Leaving the village out
of sight behind us, we rode together up a rocky defile. After
a while, however, the Eagle-Feather discovered in the distance some appearance of game, and set off with his son in
pursuit of it, while I went forward with The Panther. This
was a mere *nom de guerre ;* for, like many Indians, he concealed his real name out of some superstitious notion. He
was a noble-looking fellow. As he suffered his ornamented
buffalo-robe to fall in folds about his loins, his stately and
graceful figure was fully displayed; and while he sat his
horse in an easy attitude, the long feathers of the prairie-
cock fluttering from the crown of his head, he seemed the
very model of a wild prairie-rider. He had not the same
features with those of other Indians. Unless his face
greatly belied him, he was free from the jealousy, suspicion,
and malignant cunning of his people. For the most part, a
civilized white man can discover very few points of sympathy between his own nature and that of an Indian. With
every disposition to do justice to their good qualities, he
must be conscious that an impassable gulf lies between him
and his red brethren. Nay, so alien to himself do they appear, that, after breathing the air of the prairie for a few
months or weeks, he begins to look upon them as a troublesome and dangerous species of wild beast. Yet, in the countenance of The Panther, I gladly read that there were at
least some points of sympathy between him and me. We
were excellent friends, and as we rode forward together
through rocky passages, deep dells, and little barren plains,
he occupied himself very zealously in teaching me the Dahcotah language. After a while, we came to a grassy recess,
where some gooseberry-bushes were growing at the foot of a
rock: and these offered such temptation to my companion that

he gave over his instructions, and stopped so long to gather
the fruit, that before we were in motion again the van of
the village came in view. An old woman appeared, leading
down her pack-horse among the rocks above. Savage after
5 savage followed, and the little dell was soon crowded with
the throng.

That morning's march was one not to be forgotten. It
led us through a sublime waste, a wilderness of mountains
and pine-forests, over which the spirit of loneliness and
10 silence seemed brooding. Above and below, little could be
seen but the same dark green foliage. It overspread the
valleys, and enveloped the mountains, from the black rocks
that crowned their summits to the streams that circled
round their base. I rode to the top of a hill whence I could
15 look down on the savage procession as it passed beneath my
feet, and, far on the left, could see its thin and broken line,
visible only at intervals, stretching away for miles among
the mountains. On the farthest ridge, horsemen were still
descending like mere specks in the distance.

20   I remained on the hill until all had passed, and then descending followed after them. A little farther on I found a
very small meadow, set deeply among steep mountains ; and
here the whole village had encamped. The little spot was
crowded with the confused and disorderly host. Some of
25 the lodges were already set up, or the squaws perhaps were
busy in drawing the heavy coverings of skin over the bare
poles. Others were as yet mere skeletons, while others still,
poles, covering, and all, lay scattered in disorder on the
ground among buffalo-robes, bales of meat, domestic uten-
30 sils, harness, and weapons. Squaws were screaming to one
another, horses rearing and plunging, dogs yelping, eager
to be disburdened of their loads, while the fluttering of
feathers and the gleam of savage ornaments added liveliness to the scene. The small children ran about amid the
crowd, while many of the boys were scrambling among the

overhanging rocks, and standing with their little bows in
their hands, looking down upon the restless throng. In
contrast with the general confusion, a circle of old men and
warriors sat in the midst, smoking in profound indifference
and tranquillity. The disorder at length subsided. The
horses were driven away to feed along the adjacent valley,
and the camp assumed an air of listless repose. It was
scarcely past noon; a vast white canopy of smoke from a
burning forest to the eastward overhung the place, and partially obscured the rays of the sun; yet the heat was almost
insupportable. The lodges stood crowded together without
order in the narrow space. Each was a hot-house, within
which the lazy proprietor lay sleeping. The camp was silent as death. Nothing stirred except now and then an old
woman passing from lodge to lodge. The girls and young
men sat together in groups, under the pine-trees upon the
surrounding heights. The dogs lay panting on the ground,
too languid even to growl at the white man. At the entrance of the meadow, there was a cold spring among the
rocks, completely overshadowed by tall trees and dense
undergrowth. In this cool and shady retreat a number of
girls were assembled, sitting together on rocks and fallen
logs, discussing the latest gossip of the village, or laughing and throwing water with their hands at the intruding
Meneaska. The minutes seemed lengthened into hours. I lay
for a long time under a tree studying the Ogillallah tongue,
with the aid of my friend The Panther. When we were
both tired of this, I lay down by the side of a deep, clear
pool, formed by the water of the spring. A shoal of little
fishes of about a pin's length were playing in it, sporting
together, as it seemed, very amicably; but on closer observation, I saw that they were engaged in cannibal warfare
among themselves. Now and then one of the smallest
would fall a victim, and immediately disappear down the
maw of his conqueror. Every moment, however, the tyrant

of the pool, a goggle-eyed monster about three inches long, would slowly emerge with quivering fins and tail from under the shelving bank. The small fry at this would suspend their hostilities, and scatter in a panic at the appearance of
5 overwhelming force.

"Soft-hearted philanthropists," thought I, "may sigh long for their peaceful millennium; for, from minnows to men, life is incessant war."

Evening approached at last; the crests of the mountains
10 were still bright in sunshine, while our deep glen was completely shadowed. I left the camp, and climbed a neighboring hill. The sun was still glaring through the stiff pines on the ridge of the western mountain. In a moment he was gone, and, as the landscape darkened, I turned again to-
15 wards the village. As I descended, the howling of wolves and the barking of foxes came up out of the dim woods from far and near. The camp was glowing with a multitude of fires, and alive with dusky naked figures, whose tall shadows flitted, weird and ghost-like, among the surrounding crags.

20 I found a circle of smokers seated in their usual place; that is, on the ground before the lodge of a certain warrior, who seemed to be generally known for his social qualities. I sat down to smoke a parting pipe with my savage friends. That day was the first of August, on which I had promised
25 to meet Shaw at Fort Laramie. The fort was less than two days' journey distant, and that my friend need not suffer anxiety on my account, I resolved to push forward as rapidly as possible to the place of meeting. I went to look after the Hail-Storm, and having found him, I offered him
30 a handful of hawks'-bells and a paper of vermilion, on condition that he would guide me in the morning through the mountains.

The Hail-Storm ejaculated, "*How!*" and accepted the gift. Nothing more was said on either side; the matter was settled, and I lay down to sleep in Kongra-Tonga's lodge.

Long before daylight, Raymond shook me by the shoulder.

"Everything is ready," he said.

I went out. The morning was chill, damp, and dark; and the whole camp seemed asleep. The Hail-Storm sat on horseback before the lodge, and my mare Pauline and the mule which Raymond rode were picketed near it. We saddled and made our other arrangements for the journey, but before these were completed the camp began to stir, and the lodge-coverings fluttered and rustled as the squaws pulled them down in preparation for departure. Just as the light began to appear, we left the ground, passing up through a narrow opening among the rocks which led eastward out of the meadow. Gaining the top of this passage, I turned and sat looking back upon the camp, dimly visible in the gray light of morning. All was alive with the bustle of preparation. I turned away, half unwilling to take a final leave of my savage associates. We passed among rocks and pine-trees so dark that for a while we could scarcely see our way. The country in front was wild and broken, half hill, half plain, partly open and partly covered with woods of pine and oak. Barriers of lofty mountains encompassed it; the woods were fresh and cool in the early morning, the peaks of the mountains were wreathed with mist, and sluggish vapors were entangled among the forests upon their sides. At length the black pinnacle of the tallest mountain was tipped with gold by the rising sun. The Hail-Storm, who rode in front, gave a low exclamation. Some large animal leaped up from among the bushes, and an elk, as I thought, his horns thrown back over his neck, darted past us across the open space, and bounded like a mad thing away among the adjoining pines. Raymond was soon out of his saddle, but before he could fire, the animal was full two hundred yards distant. The ball struck its mark, though much too low for mortal effect. The elk, however, wheeled in his flight, and

ran at full speed among the trees, nearly at right angles to
his former course. I fired and broke his shoulder; still he
moved on, limping down into a neighboring woody hollow,
whither the young Indian followed and killed him. When
5 we reached the spot, we discovered him to be no elk, but
a black-tailed deer, an animal nearly twice as large as the
common deer, and quite unknown in the east. The reports
of the rifles had reached the ears of the Indians, and several of them came to the spot. Leaving the hide of the deer
10 to the Hail-Storm, we hung as much of the meat as we
wanted behind our saddles, left the rest to the Indians, and
resumed our journey. Meanwhile the village was on its
way, and had gone so far that to get in advance of it was
impossible. We directed our course so as to strike its line
15 of march at the nearest point. In a short time, through the
dark trunks of the pines, we could see the figures of the
Indians as they passed. Once more we were among them.
They were moving with even more than their usual precipitation, crowded together in a narrow pass between rocks
20 and old pine-trees. We were on the eastern descent of the
mountain, and soon came to a rough and difficult defile,
leading down a very steep declivity. The whole swarm
poured down together, filling the rocky passage-way like
some turbulent mountain-stream. The mountains before us
25 were on fire, and had been so for weeks. The view in front
was obscured by a vast dim sea of smoke, while on either
hand rose the tall cliffs, bearing aloft their crests of pines,
and the sharp pinnacles and broken ridges of the mountains
beyond were faintly traceable as through a veil. The scene
30 in itself was grand and imposing, but with the savage multitude, the armed warriors, the naked children, the gayly
apparelled girls, pouring impetuously down the heights,
it would have formed a noble subject for a painter, and
only the pen of a Scott could have done it justice in description.

We passed over a burnt tract where the ground was hot beneath the horses' feet, and between the blazing sides of two mountains. Before long we had descended to a softer region, where we found a succession of little valleys watered by a stream, along the borders of which grew abundance of wild gooseberries and currants, and the children and many of the men straggled from the line of march to gather them as we passed along. Descending still farther, the view changed rapidly. The burning mountains were behind us, and through the open valleys in front we could see the prairie, stretching like an ocean beyond the sight. After passing through a line of trees that skirted the brook, the Indians filed out upon the plains. I was thirsty and knelt down by the little stream to drink. As I mounted again, I very carelessly left my rifle among the grass, and, my thoughts being otherwise absorbed, I rode for some distance before discovering its absence. I lost no time in turning about and galloping back in search of it. Passing the line of Indians, I watched every warrior as he rode by me at a canter, and at length discovered my rifle in the hands of one of them, who, on my approaching to claim it, immediately gave it up. Having no other means of acknowledging the obligation, I took off one of my spurs and gave it to him. He was greatly delighted, looking upon it as a distinguished mark of favor, and immediately held out his foot for me to buckle it on. As soon as I had done so, he struck it with all his force into the side of his horse, which gave a violent leap. The Indian laughed and spurred harder than before. At this the horse shot away like an arrow, amid the screams and laughter of the squaws, and the ejaculations of the men, who exclaimed, " Washtay !— Good !" at the potent effect of my gift. The Indian had no saddle, and nothing in place of a bridle except a leather string tied around the horse's jaw. The animal was of course wholly uncontrollable, and stretched away at full

speed over the prairie, till he and his rider vanished behind a distant swell. I never saw the man again, but I
presume no harm came to him. An Indian on horseback
has more lives than a cat.

5   The village encamped on the scorching prairie, close to
the foot of the mountains. The heat was most intense and
penetrating. The coverings of the lodgings were raised a
foot or more from the ground, in order to procure some cir-
culation of air; and Reynal thought proper to lay aside his
10 trapper's dress of buckskin and assume the very scanty cos-
tume of an Indian. Thus elegantly attired, he stretched
himself in his lodge on a buffalo-robe, alternately cursing
the heat and puffing at the pipe which he and I passed between us. There was present also a select circle of Indian
15 friends and relatives. A small boiled puppy was served up
as a parting feast, to which was added, by way of dessert,
a wooden bowl of gooseberries from the mountains.

"Look there," said Reynal, pointing out of the opening
of his lodge; "do you see that line of buttes about fifteen
20 miles off? Well, now do you see that farthest one, with
the white speck on the face of it? Do you think you ever
saw it before?"

"It looks to me," said I, "like the hill that we were
'camped under when we were on Laramie Creek, six or
25 eight weeks ago."

"You've hit it," answered Reynal.

"Go and bring in the animals, Raymond," said I; "we'll
'camp there to-night, and start for the fort in the morning."

The mare and the mule were soon before the lodge. We
30 saddled them, and in the mean time a number of Indians
collected about us. The virtues of Pauline, my strong, fleet,
and hardy little mare, were well known in camp, and several
of the visitors were mounted upon good horses which they
had brought me as presents. I promptly declined their offers,
since accepting them would have involved the necessity

of transferring Pauline into their barbarous hands. We took leave of Reynal, but not of the Indians, who are accustomed to dispense with such superfluous ceremonies. Leaving the camp, we rode straight over the prairie towards the white-faced bluff, whose pale ridges swelled gently against the horizon, like a cloud. An Indian went with us, whose name I forget, though the ugliness of his face and the ghastly width of his mouth dwell vividly in my recollection. The antelope were numerous, but we did not heed them. We rode directly towards our destination, over the arid plains and barren hills; until, late in the afternoon, half spent with heat, thirst, and fatigue, we saw a gladdening sight: the long line of trees and the deep gulf that mark the course of Laramie Creek. Passing through the growth of huge dilapidated old cotton-wood trees that bordered the creek, we rode across to the other side. The rapid and foaming waters were filled with fish playing and splashing in the shallows. As we gained the farther bank, our horses turned eagerly to drink, and we, kneeling on the sand, followed their example. We had not gone far before the scene began to grow familiar.

"We are getting near home, Raymond," said I.

There stood the big tree under which we had encamped so long; there were the white cliffs that used to look down upon our tent when it stood at the bend of the creek; there was the meadow in which our horses had grazed for weeks, and a little farther on, the prairie-dog village where I had beguiled many a languid hour in shooting the unfortunate inhabitants.

"We are going to catch it now," said Raymond, turning his broad face up towards the sky.

In truth, the cliffs and the meadow, the stream and the groves, were darkening fast. Black masses of cloud were swelling up in the south, and the thunder was growling ominously.

" We will 'camp there," I said, pointing to a dense grove of trees lower down the stream. Raymond and I turned towards it, but the Indian stopped and called earnestly after us. When we demanded what was the matter, he said that
5 the ghosts of two warriors were always among those trees, and that if we slept there, they would scream and throw stones at us all night, and perhaps steal our horses before morning. Thinking it as well to humor him, we left behind us the haunt of these extraordinary ghosts, and passed on
10 towards Chugwater, riding at full gallop, for the big drops began to patter down. Soon we came in sight of the poplar saplings that grew about the mouth of the little stream. We leaped to the ground, threw off our saddles, turned our horses loose, and drawing our knives began to slash among the bushes
15 to cut twigs and branches for making a shelter against the rain. Bending down the taller saplings as they grew, we piled the young shoots upon them, and thus made a convenient pent-house; but our labor was needless. The storm scarcely touched us. Half a mile on our right the rain was pouring
20 down like a cataract, and the thunder roared over the prairie like a battery of cannon; while we by good fortune received only a few heavy drops from the skirt of the passing cloud. The weather cleared and the sun set gloriously. Sitting close under our leafy canopy, we proceeded to discuss a sub-
25 stantial meal of *wasna* which Weah Washtay had given me. The Indian had brought with him his pipe and a bag of *shongsasha;* so before lying down to sleep, we sat for some time smoking together. First, however, our wide-mouthed friend had taken the precaution of carefully examining the
30 neighborhood. He reported that eight men, counting them on his fingers, had been encamped there not long before, — Bisonette, Paul Dorion, Antoine Le Rouge, Richardson, and four others, whose names he could not tell. All this proved strictly correct. By what instinct he had arrived at such accurate conclusions, I am utterly at a loss to divine.

It was still quite dark when I awoke and called Raymond. The Indian was already gone, having chosen to go on before us to the fort. Setting out after him, we rode for some time in complete darkness, and when the sun at length rose, glowing like a fiery ball of copper, we were within ten miles of the fort. At length, from the summit of a sandy bluff, we could see Fort Laramie, miles before us, standing by the side of the stream like a little gray speck, in the midst of the boundless desolation. I stopped my horse, and sat for a moment looking down upon it. It seemed to me the very centre of comfort and civilization. We were not long in approaching it, for we rode at speed the greater part of the way. Laramie Creek still intervened between us and the friendly walls. Entering the water at the point where we had struck upon the bank, we raised our feet to the saddle behind us, and thus kneeling as it were on horseback, passed dry-shod through the swift current. As we rode up the bank, a number of men appeared in the gateway. Three of them came forward to meet us. In a moment I distinguished Shaw; Henry Chatillon followed, with his face of manly simplicity and frankness, and Deslauriers came last, with a broad grin of welcome. The meeting was not on either side one of mere ceremony. For my own part, the change was a most agreeable one, from the society of savages and men little better than savages, to that of my gallant and high-minded companion, and our noble-hearted guide. My appearance was equally welcome to Shaw, who was beginning to entertain some very uncomfortable surmises concerning me.

Bordeaux greeted me cordially, and shouted to the cook. This functionary was a new acquisition, having lately come from Fort Pierre with the trading wagons. Whatever skill he might have boasted, he had not the most promising materials to exercise it upon. He set before me, however, a breakfast of biscuit, coffee, and salt pork. It seemed like a new phase of existence, to be seated once more on a bench, with a knife and fork, a plate and teacup, and something resembling a table before me. The coffee seemed delicious, and the bread was a most welcome novelty, since for three weeks I had tasted scarcely anything but meat, and that for 5 the most part without salt. The meal also had the relish of good company, for opposite to me sat Shaw in elegant dishabille. If one is anxious thoroughly to appreciate the value of a congenial companion, he has only to spend a few weeks by himself in an Ogillallah village. And if he can contrive 10 to add to his seclusion a debilitating and somewhat critical illness, his perceptions upon this subject will be rendered considerably more vivid.

Shaw had been two or three weeks at the fort. I found him established in his old quarters, — a large apartment 15 usually occupied by the absent *bourgeois*. In one corner was a soft pile of excellent buffalo-robes, and here I lay down. Shaw brought me three books.

" Here," said he, " is your Shakespeare and Byron, and here is the Old Testament, which has as much poetry in it 20 as the other two put together."

I chose the worst of the three, and for the greater part of that day I lay on the buffalo-robes, fairly revelling in the creations of that resplendent genius which has achieved no more signal triumph than that of half beguiling us to forget the unmanly character of its possessor.

CHAPTER XX

THE LONELY JOURNEY

On the day of my arrival at Fort Laramie, Shaw and I were lounging on two buffalo-robes in the large apartment hospitably assigned to us; Henry Chatillon also was present, busy about the harness and weapons, which had been brought into the room, and two or three Indians were crouching on the floor, eying us with their fixed, unwavering gaze.

"I have been well off here," said Shaw, "in all respects but one; there is no good *shongsasha* to be had for love or money."

I gave him a small leather bag containing some of excellent quality, which I had brought from the Black Hills. "Now, Henry," said he, "hand me Papin's chopping-board, or give it to that Indian, and let him cut the mixture; they understand it better than any white man."

The Indian, without saying a word, mixed the bark and the tobacco in due proportions, filled the pipe, and lighted it. This done, my companion and I proceeded to deliberate on our future course of proceeding; first, however, Shaw acquainted me with some incidents which had occurred at the fort during my absence.

About a week before, four men had arrived from beyond the mountains: Sublette, Reddick, and two others. Just before reaching the fort, they had met a large party of Indians, chiefly young men. All of them belonged to the village of our old friend Smoke, who, with his whole band of adherents, professed the greatest friendship for the whites. The travellers therefore approached and began to converse without the least suspicion. Suddenly, however, their bridles

257

were seized, and they were ordered to dismount. Instead of
complying, they lashed their horses, and broke away from
the Indians. As they galloped off, they heard a yell behind
them, with a burst of derisive laughter, and the reports of
several guns. None of them were hurt, though Reddick's
bridle-rein was cut by a bullet within an inch of his hand.
After this taste of Indian manners, they felt for the moment
no disposition to encounter farther risks. They intended to
pursue the route southward along the foot of the mountains
to Bent's Fort; and as our plans coincided with theirs, they
proposed to join forces. Finding, however, that I did not
return, they grew impatient of inaction, forgot their late
danger, and set out without us, promising to wait our arrival at Bent's Fort. From thence we were to make the long
journey to the settlements in company, as the path was not
a little dangerous, being infested by hostile Pawnees and
Camanches.

We expected, on reaching Bent's Fort, to find there still
another reinforcement. A young Kentuckian had come out
to the mountains with Russel's party of California emigrants.
One of his chief objects, as he gave out, was to kill an Indian;
an exploit which he afterwards succeeded in achieving, much
to the jeopardy of ourselves, and others who had to pass
through the country of the dead Pawnee's enraged relatives.
Having become disgusted with his emigrant associates, he
left them, and had some time before set out with a party of
companions for the head of the Arkansas. He left us a letter,
to say that he would wait until we arrived at Bent's Fort,
and accompany us thence to the settlements. When, however,
he came to the fort, he found there a party of forty men
about to make the homeward journey, and wisely preferred
to avail himself of so strong an escort. Sublette and his companions also joined this company; so that on reaching Bent's
Fort, some six weeks after, we found ourselves deserted by
our allies and thrown once more upon our own resources.

On the fourth of August, early in the afternoon, we bade a final adieu to the hospitable gateway of Fort Laramie. Again Shaw and I were riding side by side on the prairie. For the first fifty miles we had companions with us: Troché, a trapper, and Rouville, a nondescript in the employ of the Fur Company, who were going to join the trader Bisonette at his encampment near the head of Horse Creek. We rode only six or eight miles that afternoon before we came to a little brook traversing the barren prairie. All along its course grew copses of young wild-cherry trees, loaded with ripe fruit, and almost concealing the gliding thread of water with their dense growth. Here we encamped; and being too indolent to pitch our tent, we flung our saddles on the ground, spread a pair of buffalo-robes, lay down upon them, and began to smoke. Meanwhile Deslauriers busied himself with his frying-pan, and Raymond stood guard over the band of grazing horses. Deslauriers had an active assistant in Rouville, who professed great skill in the culinary art, and, seizing upon a fork, began to lend his aid in cooking supper. Indeed, according to his own belief, Rouville was a man of universal knowledge, and he lost no opportunity to display his manifold accomplishments. He had been a circus-rider at St. Louis, and once he rode round Fort Laramie on his head, to the utter bewilderment of the Indians. He was also noted as the wit of the fort; and as he had considerable humor and abundant vivacity, he contributed more that night to the liveliness of the camp than all the rest of the party put together. At one instant he would kneel by Deslauriers, instructing him in the true method of frying antelope-steaks, then he would come and seat himself at our side, dilating upon the correct fashion of braiding up a horse's tail, telling apocryphal stories how he had killed a buffalo bull with a knife, having first cut off his tail when at full speed, or relating whimsical anecdotes of the *bourgeois* Papin. At last he snatched up a volume of Shakespeare

that was lying on the grass, and halted and stumbled through
a line or two to prove that he could read. He went gambol-
ling about the camp, chattering like some frolicsome ape; and
whatever he was doing at one moment, the presumption
5 was a sure one that he would not be doing it the next. His
companion Troché sat silently on the grass, not speaking a
word, but keeping a vigilant eye on a very ugly little Utah
squaw, of whom he was extremely jealous.

On the next day we travelled farther, crossing the wide
10 sterile basin called "Goché's Hole." Towards night we became involved among ravines; and being unable to find
water, our journey was protracted to a very late hour. On
the next morning we had to pass a long line of bluffs, whose
raw sides, wrought upon by rains and storms, were of a
15 ghastly whiteness most oppressive to the sight. As we
ascended a gap in these hills, the way was marked by huge
footprints, like those of a human giant. They were the
tracks of the grizzly bear, of which we had also seen abundance on the day before. Immediately after this we were
20 crossing a barren plain, spreading in long and gentle undulations to the horizon. Though the sun was bright, there
was a light haze in the atmosphere. The distant hills assumed strange, distorted forms in the mirage, and the edge
of the horizon was continually changing its aspect. Shaw
25 and I were riding together, and Henry Chatillon was a few
rods before us, when he stopped his horse suddenly, and
turning round with the peculiar earnest expression which
he always wore when excited, called us to come forward.
We galloped to his side. Henry pointed towards a black
30 speck on the grey swell of the prairie, apparently about a
mile off. "It must be a bear," said he; "come, now we
shall all have some sport. Better fun to fight him than to
fight an old buffalo bull; grizzly bear so strong and smart."

So we all galloped forward together, prepared for a hard
fight; for these bears, though clumsy in appearance, are

incredibly fierce and active. The swell of the prairie concealed the black object from our view. Immediately after it appeared again. But now it seemed very near to us; and as we looked at it in astonishment, it suddenly separated into two parts, each of which took wing and flew away. We stopped our horses and looked at Henry, whose face exhibited a curious mixture of mirth and mortification. His eye had been so completely deceived by the peculiar atmosphere that he had mistaken two large crows at the distance of fifty rods for a grizzly bear a mile off. To the journey's end Henry never heard the last of the grizzly bear with wings.

In the afternoon we came to the foot of a considerable hill. As we ascended it, Rouville began to ask questions concerning our condition and prospects at home, and Shaw was edifying him with an account of an imaginary wife and child, to which he listened with implicit faith. Reaching the top of the hill, we saw the windings of Horse Creek on the plains below us, and a little on the left we could distinguish the camp of Bisonette among the trees and copses along the course of the stream. Rouville's face assumed just then a ludicrously blank expression. We inquired what was the matter; when it appeared that Bisonette had sent him from this place to Fort Laramie with the sole object of bringing back a supply of tobacco. Our rattlebrain friend, from the time of his reaching the fort up to the present moment, had entirely forgotten the object of his journey, and had ridden a dangerous hundred miles for nothing. Descending to Horse Creek, we forded it, and on the opposite bank a solitary Indian sat on horseback under a tree. He said nothing, but turned and led the way towards the camp. Bisonette had made choice of an admirable position. The stream, with its thick growth of trees, enclosed on three sides a wide green meadow, where about forty Dahcotah lodges were pitched in a circle, and beyond them a few lodges of the friendly Shiennes. Bisonette himself lived in

the Indian manner. Riding up to his lodge, we found him
seated at the head of it, surrounded by various appliances
of comfort not common on the prairie. His squaw was near
him, and rosy children were scrambling about in printed
5 calico gowns; Paul Dorion, also, with his leathery face and
old white capote, was seated in the lodge, together with
Antoine Le Rouge, a half-breed Pawnee, Sibille, a trader,
and several other white men.

"It will do you no harm," said Bisonette, "to stay here
10 with us for a day or two, before you start for the Pueblo."

We accepted the invitation, and pitched our tent on a rising ground above the camp and close to the trees. Bisonette
soon invited us to a feast, and we suffered abundance of the
same sort of attention from his Indian associates. The
15 reader may possibly recollect that when I joined the Indian
village, beyond the Black Hills, I found that a few families
were absent, having declined to pass the mountains along
with the rest. The Indians in Bisonette's camp consisted
of these very families, and many of them came to me that
20 evening to inquire after their relatives and friends. They
were not a little mortified to learn that while they, from
their own timidity and indolence, were almost in a starving
condition, the rest of the village had provided their lodges
for the next season, laid in a great stock of provisions, and
25 were living in abundance. Bisonette's companions had been
sustaining themselves for some time on wild cherries, which
the squaws pounded, stones and all, and spread on buffalo-
robes to dry in the sun; they were then eaten without
farther preparation, or used as an ingredient in various
30 delectable compounds.

On the next day, the camp was in commotion with a new
arrival. A single Indian had come with his family from the
Arkansas. As he passed among the lodges, he put on an expression of unusual dignity and importance, and gave out
that he had brought great news to tell the whites. Soon

after the squaws had pitched his lodge, he sent his little son
to invite all the white men and all the more distinguished
Indians to a feast. The guests arrived and sat wedged together, shoulder to shoulder, within the hot and suffocat-
ing lodge. The Stabber, for that was our entertainer's
name, had killed an old buffalo bull on his way. This veteran's boiled tripe, tougher than leather, formed the main
item of the repast. For the rest, it consisted of wild cherries
and grease boiled together in a large copper kettle. The
feast was distributed, and for a moment all was silent, stren-
uous exertion; then each guest, though with one or two exceptions, turned his wooden dish bottom upwards to prove
that he had done full justice to his entertainer's hospitality.
The Stabber next produced his chopping-board, on which he
prepared the mixture for smoking, and filled several pipes,
which circulated among the company. This done, he seated
himself upright on his couch, and began with much gesticulation to tell his story. I will not repeat his childish jargon.
It was so entangled, like the greater part of an Indian's
stories, with absurd and contradictory details, that it was
almost impossible to disengage from it a single particle of
truth. All that we could gather was the following : —

He had been on the Arkansas, and there he had seen six
great war-parties of whites. He had never believed before
that the whole world contained half so many white men.
They all had large horses, long knives, and short rifles, and
some of them were dressed alike in the most splendid war-
dresses he had ever seen. From this account it was clear
that bodies of dragoons and perhaps also of volunteer cav-
alry had passed up the Arkansas. The Stabber had also seen
a great many of the white lodges of the Meneaska, drawn by
their long-horned buffalo. These could be nothing else than
covered ox-wagons, used, no doubt, in transporting stores
for the troops. Soon after seeing this, our host had met
an Indian who had lately come from among the Camanches,

who had told him that all the Mexicans had gone out to
a great buffalo hunt; that the Americans had hid themselves in a ravine; and that when the Mexicans had shot
away all their arrows, the Americans fired their guns, raised
their war-whoop, rushed out, and killed them all. We could
only infer from this, that war had been declared with Mexico, and a battle fought in which the Americans were victorious. When, some weeks after, we arrived at the Pueblo,
we heard of General Kearney's march up the Arkansas, and
of General Taylor's victories at Matamoras.

As the sun was setting that evening a crowd gathered on
the plain by the side of our tent, to try the speed of their
horses. These were of every shape, size, and color. Some
came from California, some from the States, some from
among the mountains, and some from the wild bands of the
prairie. They were of every hue, white, black, red, and gray,
or mottled and clouded with a strange variety of colors.
They all had a wild and startled look, very different from
the sober aspect of a well-bred city steed. Those most noted
for swiftness and spirit were decorated with eagle feathers
dangling from their manes and tails. Fifty or sixty Dahcotah were present, wrapped from head to foot in their heavy
robes of whitened hide. There were also a considerable
number of the Shiennes, many of whom wore gaudy Mexican ponchos, swathed around their shoulders, but leaving
the right arm bare. Mingled among the crowd of Indians
was a number of Canadians, chiefly in the employ of Bisonette, — men whose home is the wilderness, and who love
the camp-fire better than the domestic hearth. They are contented and happy in the midst of hardship, privation, and
danger. Their cheerfulness and gayety is irrepressible, and
no people on earth understand better how "to daff the
world aside and bid it pass." Besides these, were two or
three half-breeds, a race of rather extraordinary composi-
tion, being according to the common saying half Indian,

half white man, and half devil. Antoine Le Rouge was the
most conspicuous among them, with his loose trousers and
fluttering calico shirt. A handkerchief was bound round his
head to confine his black snaky hair, and his small eyes
twinkled beneath it with a mischievous lustre. He had a
fine cream-colored horse, whose speed he must needs try
along with the rest. So he threw off the rude high-peaked
saddle, and substituting a piece of buffalo-robe, leaped
lightly into his seat. The space was cleared, the word was
given, and he and his Indian rival darted out like lightning
from among the crowd, each stretching forward over his
horse's neck and plying his heavy Indian whip with might
and main. A moment, and both were lost in the gloom; but
Antoine soon came riding back victorious, exultingly patting
the neck of his quivering and panting horse.

About midnight, as I lay asleep, wrapped in a buffalo-
robe on the ground by the side of our cart, Raymond came
and woke me. Something, he said, was going forward which
I would like to see. Looking down into the camp, I saw on the
farther side of it a great number of Indians gathered about
a fire, the bright glare of which made them visible through
the thick darkness; while from the midst proceeded a loud,
measured chant which would have killed Paganini outright,
broken occasionally by a burst of sharp yells. I gathered
the robe around me, for the night was cold, and walked
down to the spot. The dark throng of Indians was so dense
that they almost intercepted the light of the flame. As I
was pushing among them with little ceremony, a chief interposed himself, and I was given to understand that a white
man must not approach the scene of their solemnities too
closely. By passing round to the other side where there
was a little opening in the crowd, I could see clearly what
was going forward, without intruding my unhallowed presence into the inner circle. The society of the " Strong
Hearts " were engaged in one of their dances. The " Strong

Hearts" are a warlike association, comprising men of both the Dahcotah and Shienne nations, and entirely composed, or supposed to be so, of young braves of the highest mettle. Its fundamental principle is the admirable one of never re-
5 treating from any enterprise once begun. All these Indian associations have a tutelary spirit. That of the Strong Hearts is embodied in the fox, an animal which white men would hardly have selected for a similar purpose, though his subtle character agrees well enough with an Indian's
10 notions of what is honorable in warfare. The dancers were circling round and round the fire, each figure brightly illumined at one moment by the yellow light, and at the next drawn in blackest shadow as it passed between the flame and the spectator. They would imitate with the most ludi-
15 crous exactness the motions and voice of their sly patron the fox. Then a startling yell would be given. Many other warriors would leap into the ring, and with faces upturned towards the starless sky, they would all stamp, and whoop, and brandish their weapons like so many frantic devils.

20 We remained here till the next afternoon. My companion and I with our three attendants then set out for the Pueblo, a distance of three hundred miles, and we supposed the journey would occupy about a fortnight. During this time we all hoped that we might not meet a single human
25 being, for should we encounter any, they would in all probability be enemies, in whose eyes our rifles would be our only passports. For the first two days nothing worth mentioning took place. On the third morning, however, an untoward incident occurred. We were encamped by the side
30 of a little brook in an extensive hollow of the plain. Deslauriers was up long before daylight, and before he began to prepare breakfast he turned loose all the horses, as in duty bound. There was a cold mist clinging close to the ground, and by the time the rest of us were awake the animals were invisible. It was only after a long and anxious

search that we could discover by their tracks the direction
they had taken. They had all set off for Fort Laramie, following the guidance of a mutinous old mule, and though
many of them were hobbled, they travelled three miles
before they could be overtaken and driven back. 5

For two or three days, we were passing over an arid
desert. The only vegetation was a few tufts of short grass,
dried and shrivelled by the heat. There was abundance of
strange insects and reptiles. Huge crickets, black and bottle
green, and wingless grasshoppers of the most extravagant di- 10
mensions, were tumbling about our horses' feet, and lizards
without number darting like lightning among the tufts of
grass. The most curious animal, however, was that commonly called the horned-frog. I caught one of them and
consigned him to the care of Deslauriers, who tied him up 15
in a moccason. About a month after this, I examined the
prisoner's condition, and finding him still lively and active,
I provided him with a cage of buffalo-hide, which was hung
up in the cart. In this manner he arrived safely at the settlements. From thence he travelled the whole way to Boston, 20
packed closely in a trunk, being regaled with fresh air regularly every night. When he reached his destination he
was deposited under a glass case, where he sat for some
months in great tranquillity, alternately dilating and con-
tracting his white throat to the admiration of his visitors. 25
At length, one morning about the middle of winter, he gave
up the ghost, and he now occupies a bottle of alcohol in the
Agassiz Museum. His death was attributed to starvation, a
very probable conclusion, since for six months he had taken
no food whatever, though the sympathy of his juvenile ad- 30
mirers had tempted his palate with a great variety of delicacies. We found also animals of a somewhat larger growth.
The number of prairie-dogs was astounding. Frequently the
hard and dry plain was thickly covered, for miles together,
with the little mounds which they make at the mouth of

their burrows, and small squeaking voices yelped at us, as
we passed along. The noses of the inhabitants were just
visible at the mouth of their holes, but no sooner was their
curiosity satisfied than they would instantly vanish. Some
of the bolder dogs — though in fact they are no dogs at all,
but little marmots rather smaller than a rabbit — would sit
yelping at us on the top of their mounds, jerking their tails
emphatically with every shrill cry they uttered. As the
danger drew nearer they would wheel about, toss their heels
into the air, and dive in a twinkling into their burrows.
Towards sunset, and especially if rain was threatening, the
whole community made their appearance above ground. We
saw them gathered in large knots around the burrow of
some favorite citizen. There they would all sit erect, their
tails spread out on the ground, and their paws hanging
down before their white breasts, chattering and squeaking
with the utmost vivacity upon some topic of common interest, while the proprietor of the burrow sat on the top of his
mound, looking down with a complacent countenance on the
enjoyment of his guests. Meanwhile, others ran about from
burrow to burrow, as if on some errand of the last importance to their subterranean commonwealth. The snakes are
apparently the prairie-dog's worst enemies; at least I think
too well of the latter to suppose that they associate on
friendly terms with these slimy intruders, which may be
seen at all times basking among their holes, into which they
always retreat when disturbed. Small owls, with wise and
grave countenances, also make their abode with the prairie-
dogs, though on what terms they live together I could never
ascertain.

On the fifth day after leaving Bisonette's camp, we saw,
late in the afternoon, what we supposed to be a considerable
stream, but on approaching it, we found to our mortification
nothing but a dry bed of sand, into which the water had
sunk and disappeared. We separated, some riding in one

direction and some in another, along its course. Still we found no traces of water, not even so much as a wet spot in the sand. The old cotton-wood trees that grew along the bank, lamentably abused by lightning and tempest, were withering with the drought, and on the dead limbs, at the summit of the tallest, half a dozen crows were hoarsely cawing, like birds of evil omen. We had no alternative but to keep on. There was no water nearer than the South Fork of the Platte, about ten miles distant. We moved forward, angry and silent, over a desert as flat as the outspread ocean.

The sky had been obscured since the morning by thin mists and vapors, but now vast piles of clouds were gathered together in the west. They rose to a great height above the horizon, and looking up at them I distinguished one mass darker than the rest, and of a peculiar conical form. I happened to look again, and still could see it as before. At some moments it was dimly visible, at others its outline was sharp and distinct; but while the clouds around it were shifting, changing, and dissolving away, it still towered aloft in the midst of them, fixed and immovable. It must, thought I, be the summit of a mountain; and yet its height staggered me. My conclusion was right, however. It was Long's Peak, once believed to be one of the highest of the Rocky Mountain chain, though more recent discoveries have proved the contrary. The thickening gloom soon hid it from view, and we never saw it again, for on the following day, and for some time after, the air was so full of mist that the view of distant objects was entirely cut off.

It grew very late. Turning from our direct course, we made for the river at its nearest point, though in the utter darkness it was not easy to direct our way with much precision. Raymond rode on one side and Henry on the other. We heard each of them shouting that he had come upon a deep ravine. We steered at random between Scylla and Charybdis, and soon after became, as it seemed, inextricably involved with deep chasms all around us, while the darkness was such that we could not see a rod in any direction. We partially extricated ourselves by scrambling, cart and all, through a shallow ravine. We came next to a steep descent, down which we plunged without well knowing what was at the bottom. There was a great cracking of sticks and dry twigs. Over our heads were certain large shadowy objects; and in front something like the faint gleaming of a dark sheet of water. Raymond ran his horse against a tree; Henry alighted, and, feeling on the ground, declared that there was grass enough for the horses. Before taking off his saddle, each man led his own horses down to the water in the best way he could. Then picketing two or three of the evil-disposed, we turned the rest loose, and lay down among the dry sticks to sleep. In the morning we found ourselves close to the South Fork of the Platte, on a spot surrounded by bushes and rank grass. Compensating ourselves with a hearty breakfast for the ill-fare of the previous night, we set forward again on our journey. When only two or three rods from the camp, I saw Shaw stop his mule, level his gun, and fire at some object in the grass. Deslauriers next jumped forward, and began to dance about, belaboring the unseen enemy with a whip. Then he stooped down, and drew out of the grass by the neck an enormous rattlesnake, with his head completely shattered by Shaw's bullet. As Deslauriers held him out at arm's length with an exulting grin, his tail, which still kept slowly writhing about, almost touched the ground; and his body in the largest part was as thick as a stout man's arm. He had fourteen rattles, but the end of his tail was blunted, as if he could once have boasted of many more. From this time till we reached the Pueblo, we killed at least four or five of these snakes every day, as they lay coiled and rattling on the hot sand. Shaw was the St. Patrick of the party, and whenever he killed a snake he pulled off his tail and stored it away in his bullet-pouch, which was soon crammed with an edifying collection of rattles, great and small. Deslauriers with his whip also came in for a share of praise. A day or two after this, he triumphantly produced a small snake about a span and a half long, with one infant rattle at the end of his tail. 5

We forded the South Fork of the Platte. On its farther bank were the traces of a very large camp of Arapahoes. The ashes of some three hundred fires were visible among the scattered trees, together with the remains of sweating lodges, and all the other appurtenances of a permanent 10 camp. The place, however, had been for some months deserted. A few miles farther on we found more recent signs of Indians; the trail of two or three lodges, which had evidently passed the day before; every footprint was perfectly distinct in the dry, dusty soil. We noticed in particular the 15 track of one moccason, upon the sole of which its economical proprietor had placed a large patch. These signs gave us but little uneasiness, as the number of the warriors scarcely exceeded that of our own party. At noon we rested under the walls of a large fort, built in these solitudes some 20 years since by M. St. Vrain. It was now abandoned and fast falling into ruin. The walls of unbaked bricks were cracked from top to bottom. Our horses recoiled in terror from the neglected entrance, where the heavy gates were torn from their hinges and flung down. The area within was overgrown 25 with weeds, and the long ranges of apartments once occupied by the motley concourse of traders, Canadians, and squaws, were now miserably dilapidated. Twelve miles farther on, near the spot where we encamped, were the remains of another fort, standing in melancholy desertion and neglect. 30

Early on the following morning we made a startling discovery. We passed close by a large deserted encampment of Arapahoes. There were about fifty fires still smouldering on the ground, and it was evident from numerous signs that the Indians must have left the place within two hours of our reaching it. Their trail crossed our own, at right angles, and led in the direction of a line of hills, half a mile on our left. There were women and children in the party, which would have greatly diminished the danger of encountering 5 them. Henry Chatillon examined the encampment and the trail with a very professional and business-like air.

"Supposing we had met them, Henry?" said I.

"Why," said he, "we hold out our hands to them, and give them all we've got; they take away everything, and 10 then I believe they no kill us. Perhaps," added he, looking up with a quiet, unchanged face, "perhaps we no let them rob us. Maybe before they come near, we have a chance to get into a ravine, or under the bank of the river; then, you know, we fight them."

15 About noon on that day we reached Cherry Creek. Here was a great abundance of wild cherries, plums, gooseberries, and currants. The stream, however, like most of the others which we passed, was dried up with the heat, and we had to dig holes in the sand to find water for ourselves and our 20 horses. Two days after, we left the banks of the creek, which we had been following for some time, and began to cross the high dividing ridge which separates the waters of the Platte from those of the Arkansas. The scenery was altogether changed. In place of the burning plains, we passed 25 through rough and savage glens, and among hills crowned with a dreary growth of pines. We encamped among these solitudes on the night of the sixteenth of August. A tempest was threatening. The sun went down among volumes of jet-black cloud, edged with a bloody red. But in 30 spite of these portentous signs, we neglected to put up the tent, and, being extremely fatigued, lay down on the ground and fell asleep. The storm broke about midnight, and we pitched the tent amid darkness and confusion. In the morning all was fair again, and Pike's Peak, white with snow, was towering above the wilderness afar off.

We pushed through an extensive tract of pine woods. Large black-squirrels were leaping among the branches. From the farther edge of this forest we saw the prairie again, hollowed out before us into a vast basin, and about a mile in front we could discern a little black speck moving upon its surface. It could be nothing but a buffalo. Henry primed his rifle afresh and galloped forward. To the left of the animal was a low rocky mound, of which Henry availed himself in making his approach. After a short time we heard the faint report of the rifle. The bull, mortally wounded from a distance of nearly three hundred yards, ran wildly round and round in a circle. Shaw and I then galloped forward, and passing him as he ran, foaming with rage and pain, discharged our pistols into his side. Once or twice he rushed furiously upon us, but his strength was rapidly exhausted. Down he fell on his knees. For one instant he glared up at his enemies, with burning eyes, through his black tangled mane, and then rolled over on his side. Though gaunt and thin, he was larger and heavier than the largest ox. Foam and blood flowed together from his nostrils as he lay bellowing and pawing the ground, tearing up grass and earth with his hoofs. His sides rose and fell like a vast pair of bellows, the blood spouting up in jets from the bullet-holes. Suddenly his glaring eyes became like a lifeless jelly. He lay motionless on the ground. Henry stooped over him, and, making an incision with his knife, pronounced the meat too rank and tough for use; so, disappointed in our hopes of an addition to our stock of provisions, we rode away and left the carcass to the wolves.

In the afternoon we saw the mountains rising like a gigantic wall at no great distance on our right. "*Des sauvages! des sauvages!*" exclaimed Deslauriers, looking round with a frightened face, and pointing with his whip towards the foot of the mountains. In fact, we could see at a distance a number of little black specks, like horsemen in rapid motion.

Henry Chatillon, with Shaw and myself, galloped towards
them to reconnoitre, when to our amusement we saw the
supposed Arapahoes resolved into the black tops of some
pine-trees which grew along a ravine. The summits of these
pines, just visible above the verge of the prairie, and seeming to move as we ourselves were advancing, looked exactly
like a line of horsemen.

We encamped among ravines and hollows, through which
a little brook was foaming angrily. Before sunrise in the
morning the snow-covered mountains were beautifully tinged
with a delicate rose-color. A noble spectacle awaited us as
we moved forward. Six or eight miles on our right, Pike's
Peak and his giant brethren rose out of the level prairie, as
if springing from the bed of the ocean. From their summits
down to the plain below they were involved in a mantle of
clouds, in restless motion, as if urged by strong winds. For
one instant some snowy peak, towering in awful solitude,
would be disclosed to view. As the clouds broke along the
mountain, we could see the dreary forests, the tremendous
precipices, the white patches of snow, the gulfs and chasms
as black as night, all revealed for an instant, and then disappearing from the view.

On the day after, we had left the mountains at some
distance. A black cloud descended upon them, and a tremendous explosion of thunder followed, reverberating among
the precipices. In a few moments everything grew black,
and the rain poured down like a cataract. We got under an
old cotton-wood tree, which stood by the side of a stream,
and waited there till the rage of the torrent had passed.

The clouds opened at the point where they first had
gathered, and the whole sublime congregation of mountains
was bathed at once in warm sunshine. They seemed more
like some vision of eastern romance than like a reality of
that wilderness; all were melted together into a soft delicious blue, as voluptuous as the sky of Naples or the

transparent sea that washes the sunny cliffs of Capri. On the left the sky was still of an inky blackness; but two concentric rainbows stood in bright relief against it, while far in front the ragged clouds still streamed before the wind, and the retreating thunder muttered angrily. 5

Through that afternoon and the next morning we were passing down the banks of the stream, called "Boiling Spring Creek," from the boiling spring whose waters flow into it. When we stopped at noon, we were within six or eight miles of the Pueblo. Setting out again, we found by 10 the fresh tracks that a horseman had just been out to reconnoitre us; he had circled half round the camp, and then galloped back at full speed for the Pueblo. What made him so shy of us we could not conceive. After an hour's ride we reached the edge of a hill, from which a welcome sight 15 greeted us. The Arkansas ran along the valley below, among woods and groves, and closely nestled in the midst of wide corn-fields and green meadows, where cattle were grazing, rose the low mud walls of the Pueblo.

CHAPTER XXI

THE PUEBLO AND BENT'S FORT

We approached the gate of the Pueblo. It was a wretched species of fort, of most primitive construction, being nothing more than a large square enclosure, surrounded by a wall of mud, miserably cracked and dilapidated. The slender pickets
5 that surmounted it were half broken down, and the gate dangled on its wooden hinges so loosely that to open or shut it seemed likely to fling it down altogether. Two or three squalid Mexicans, with their broad hats, and their vile faces overgrown with hair, were lounging about the bank of the
10 river in front of it. They disappeared as they saw us approach; and as we rode up to the gate, a light active little figure came out to meet us. It was our old friend Richard. He had come from Fort Laramie on a trading expedition to Taos; but finding when he reached the Pueblo that the war
15 would prevent his going farther, he was quietly waiting till the conquest of the country should allow him to proceed. He seemed to feel bound to do the honors of the place. Shaking us warmly by the hand, he led the way into the area.

20 Here we saw his large Santa Fé wagons standing together. A few squaws and Spanish women, and a few Mexicans, as mean and miserable as the place itself, were lazily sauntering about. Richard conducted us to the state apartment of the Pueblo, a small mud room, very neatly finished, consid-
25 ering the material, and garnished with a crucifix, a looking-glass, a picture of the Virgin, and a rusty horse-pistol. There were no chairs, but instead of them a number of chests and boxes ranged about the room. There was another room

beyond, less sumptuously decorated, and here three or four
Spanish girls, one of them very pretty, were baking cakes
at a mud fire-place in the corner. They brought out a
poncho, which they spread upon the floor by way of table-
cloth. A supper, which seemed to us luxurious, was soon   5
laid out upon it, and folded buffalo-robes were placed around
it to receive the guests. Two or three Americans besides
ourselves were present. We sat down in Turkish fashion,
and began to ask the news. Richard told us that, about
three weeks before, General Kearney's army had left Bent's 10
Fort to march against Santa Fé; that when last heard from
they were approaching the defiles that led to the city. One
of the Americans produced a dingy newspaper, containing
an account of the battles of Palo Alto and Resaca de la
Palma. While we were discussing these matters, the door-   15
way was darkened by a tall, shambling fellow, who stood
with his hands in his pockets taking a leisurely survey of
the premises before he entered. He wore brown homespun
trousers, much too short for his legs, and a pistol and bowie-
knife stuck in his belt. His head and one eye were envel-   20
oped in a huge bandage of linen. Having completed his observations, he came slouching in, and sat down on a chest.
Eight or ten more of the same stamp followed, and very
coolly arranging themselves about the room, began to stare
at the company. We were forcibly reminded of the Oregon 25
emigrants, though these unwelcome visitors had a certain
glitter of the eye, and a compression of the lips, which distinguished them from our old acquaintances of the prairie.
They began to catechise us at once, inquiring whence we
had come, what we meant to do next, and what were our   30
prospects in life.

The man with the bandaged head had met with an untoward accident a few days before. He was going down to
the river to bring water, and was pushing through the
young willows which covered the low ground when he came

unawares upon a grizzly bear, which, having just eaten a
buffalo bull, had lain down to sleep off the meal. The bear
rose on his hind legs, and gave the intruder such a blow
with his paw that he laid his forehead entirely bare, clawed
5 off the front of his scalp, and narrowly missed one of his
eyes. Fortunately he was not in a very pugnacious mood,
being surfeited with his late meal. The man's companions,
who were close behind, raised a shout, and the bear walked
away, crushing down the willows in his leisurely retreat.

10   These men belonged to a party of Mormons, who, out of
a well-grounded fear of the other emigrants, had postponed
leaving the settlements until all the rest were gone. On account of this delay, they did not reach Fort Laramie until
it was too late to continue their journey to California.
15 Hearing that there was good land at the head of the Arkansas, they crossed over under the guidance of Richard, and
were now preparing to spend the winter at a spot about
half a mile from the Pueblo.

     When we took leave of Richard it was near sunset. Pass-
20 ing out of the gate, we could look down the little valley of
the Arkansas; a beautiful scene, and doubly so to our eyes,
so long accustomed to deserts and mountains. Tall woods
lined the river, with green meadows on either hand; and
high bluffs, quietly basking in the sunlight, flanked the
25 narrow valley. A Mexican on horseback was driving a herd
of cattle towards the gate, and our little white tent, which
the men had pitched under a tree in the meadow, made a
pleasing feature in the scene. When we reached it, we
found that Richard had sent a Mexican to bring us an
30 abundant supply of green corn and vegetables, and invite
us to help ourselves to whatever we wanted from the fields
around the Pueblo.

     The inhabitants were in daily apprehension of an inroad
from more formidable consumers than we. Every year, at
the time when the corn begins to ripen, the Arapahoes, to

the number of several thousands, come and encamp around
the Pueblo. The handful of white men, who are entirely
at the mercy of this swarm of barbarians, choose to make a
merit of necessity ; they come forward very cordially, shake
them by the hand, and tell them that the harvest is entirely   5
at their disposal. The Arapahoes take them at their word,
help themselves most liberally, and usually turn their horses
into the corn-fields afterwards. They have the foresight,
however, to leave enough of the crops untouched to serve
as an inducement for planting the fields again for their   10
benefit in the next spring.

The human race in this part of the world is separated
into three divisions, arranged in the order of their merits :
white men, Indians, and Mexicans ; to the latter of whom
the honorable title of " whites " is by no means conceded.   15

In spite of the warm sunset of that evening the next
morning was a dreary and cheerless one. It rained steadily,
clouds resting upon the very tree-tops. We crossed the
river to visit the Mormon settlement. As we passed through
the water, several trappers on horseback entered it from the   20
other side. Their buckskin frocks were soaked through by
the rain, and clung fast to their limbs with a most clammy
and uncomfortable look. The water was trickling down their
faces, and dropping from the ends of their rifles and from
the traps which each carried at the pommel of his saddle.   25
Horses and all, they had a disconsolate and woe-begone
appearance, which we could not help laughing at, forgetting
how often we ourselves had been in a similar plight.

After half an hour's riding, we saw the white wagons of
the Mormons drawn up among the trees. Axes were sound-   30
ing, trees falling, and log-huts rising along the edge of the
woods and upon the adjoining meadow. As we came up, the
Mormons left their work, seated themselves on the timber
around us, and began earnestly to discuss points of theol-
ogy, complain of the ill-usage they had received from the

"Gentiles," and sound a lamentation over the loss of their great temple of Nauvoo. After remaining with them an hour we rode back to our camp, happy that the settlements had been delivered from the presence of such blind and desperate fanatics.

On the following morning we left the Pueblo for Bent's Fort. The conduct of Raymond had lately been less satisfactory than before, and we had discharged him as soon as we arrived at the former place, so that the party, ourselves included, was now reduced to four. There was some uncertainty as to our future course. The trail between Bent's Fort and the settlements, a distance computed at six hundred miles, was at this time in a dangerous state; for since the passage of General Kearney's army, great numbers of hostile Indians, chiefly Pawnees and Camanches, had gathered about some parts of it. They became soon after so numerous and audacious that scarcely a single party, however large, passed between the fort and the frontier without some token of their hostility. The newspapers of the time sufficiently display this state of things. Many men were killed, and great numbers of horses and mules carried off. Not long since I met with a young man, who, during the autumn, came from Santa Fé to Bent's Fort, where he found a party of seventy men, who thought themselves too weak to go down to the settlements alone, and were waiting there for a reinforcement. Though this excessive timidity proves the ignorance of the men, it may also evince the state of alarm which prevailed in the country. When we were there in the month of August, the danger had not become so great. There was nothing very attractive in the neighborhood. We supposed, moreover, that we might wait there half the winter without finding any party to go down with us; for Sublette and the others whom we had relied upon had, as Richard told us, already left Bent's Fort. Thus far on our journey Fortune had kindly befriended us.

We resolved therefore to take advantage of her gracious mood, and trusting for a continuance of her favors, to set out with Henry and Deslauriers, and run the gantlet of the Indians in the best way we could.

Bent's Fort stands on the river, about seventy-five miles below the Pueblo. At noon of the third day we arrived within three or four miles of it, pitched our tent under a tree, hung our looking-glasses against its trunk, and having made our primitive toilet, rode towards the fort. We soon came in sight of it, for it is visible from a considerable distance, standing with its high clay walls in the midst of the scorching plains. It seemed as if a swarm of locusts had invaded the country. The grass for miles around was cropped close by the horses of General Kearney's soldiery. When we came to the fort, we found that not only had the horses eaten up the grass, but their owners had made way with the stores of the little trading post; so that we had great difficulty in procuring the few articles which we required for our homeward journey. The army was gone, the life and bustle passed away, and the fort was a scene of dull and lazy tranquillity. A few invalid officers and soldiers sauntered about the area, which was oppressively hot; for the glaring sun was reflected down upon it from the high white walls around. The proprietors were absent, and we were received by Mr. Holt, who had been left in charge of the fort. He invited us to dinner, where, to our admiration, we found a table laid with a white cloth, with castors in the middle, and chairs placed around it. This unwonted repast concluded, we rode back to our camp.

Here, as we lay smoking round the fire after supper, we saw through the dusk three men approaching from the direction of the fort. They rode up and seated themselves near us on the ground. The foremost was a tall, well-formed man, with a face and manner such as inspire confidence at once. He wore a broad hat of felt, slouching and tattered, and the rest of his attire consisted of a frock and leggins of buckskin, rubbed with the yellow clay found among the mountains. At the heel of one of his moccasons was buckled a huge iron spur, with a rowel five or six inches in diameter. His horse, which stood quietly looking over his head, had a rude Mexican saddle, covered with a shaggy bearskin, and furnished with a pair of wooden stirrups of preposterous size. The next man was a sprightly, active little fellow, about five feet and a quarter high, but very strong and compact. His face was swarthy as a Mexican's, and covered with a close, curly, black beard. An old, greasy, calico handkerchief was tied round his head, and his close buckskin dress was blackened and polished by grease and hard service. The last who came up was a large, strong man, dressed in the coarse homespun of the frontiers, who dragged his long limbs over the ground as if he were too lazy for the effort. He had a sleepy gray eye, a retreating chin, an open mouth, and a protruding upper lip, which gave him an air of exquisite indolence and helplessness. He was armed with an old United States yager, which redoubtable weapon, though he could never hit his mark with it, he was accustomed to cherish as the very sovereign of firearms.

The first two men belonged to a party who had just come from California, with a large band of horses, which they had sold at Bent's Fort. Munroe, the taller of the two, was from Iowa. He was an excellent fellow, open, warm-hearted, and intelligent. Jim Gurney, the short man, was a Boston sailor, who had come in a trading vessel to California, and taken the fancy to return across the continent. The journey had already made him an expert "mountain-man," and he presented the extraordinary phenomenon of a sailor who understood how to manage a horse. The third of our visitors, named Ellis, was a Missourian, who had come out with a party of Oregon emigrants, but having got as far as

Bridger's Fort, he had fallen home-sick, or, as Jim averred, love-sick. He thought proper therefore to join the California men, and return homeward in their company.

They now requested that they might unite with our party, and make the journey to the settlements in company 5 with us. We readily assented, for we liked the appearance of the first two men, and were very glad to gain so efficient a reinforcement. We told them to meet us on the next evening at a spot on the river-side, about six miles below the fort. Having smoked a pipe together, our new allies 10 left us, and we lay down to sleep.

CHAPTER XXII

TÊTE ROUGE, THE VOLUNTEER

The next morning, having directed Deslauriers to repair with his cart to the place of meeting, we came again to the fort to make some arrangements for the journey. After completing these we sat down under a sort of porch, to smoke with some Shienne Indians whom we found there. In a few minutes we saw an extraordinary little figure approach us in a military dress. He had a small, round countenance, garnished about the eyes with the kind of wrinkles commonly known as crow's feet, and surmounted by an abundant crop of red curls, with a little cap resting on the top of them. Altogether, he had the look of a man more conversant with mint-juleps and oyster suppers than with the hardships of prairie-service. He came up to us and entreated that we would take him home to the settlements, saying that unless he went with us he should have to stay all winter at the fort. We liked our petitioner's appearance so little that we excused ourselves from complying with his request. At this he begged us so hard to take pity on him, looked so disconsolate, and told so lamentable a story, that at last we consented, though not without many misgivings.

The rugged Anglo-Saxon of our new recruit's real name proved utterly unmanageable on the lips of our French attendants; and Henry Chatillon, after various abortive attempts to pronounce it, one day coolly christened him Tête Rouge, in honor of his red curls. He had at different times been clerk of a Mississippi steamboat, and agent in a trading establishment at Nauvoo, besides filling various other capacities, in all of which he had seen much more of

"life" than was good for him. In the spring, thinking that
a summer's campaign would be an agreeable recreation, he
had joined a company of St. Louis volunteers.

"There were three of us," said Tête Rouge, "me and
Bill Stephens and John Hopkins. We thought we would
just go out with the army, and when we had conquered the
country, we would get discharged and take our pay, you
know, and go down to Mexico. They say there's plenty of
fun going on there. Then we could go back to New Orleans
by way of Vera Cruz."

But Tête Rouge, like many a stouter volunteer, had reck-
oned without his host. Fighting Mexicans was a less amusing occupation than he had supposed, and his pleasure trip
was disagreeably interrupted by brain fever, which attacked
him when about halfway to Bent's Fort. He jolted along
through the rest of the journey in a baggage-wagon. When
they came to the fort he was taken out and left there, with
the rest of the sick. Bent's Fort does not supply the best
accommodations for an invalid. Tête Rouge's sick-chamber
was a little mud room, where he and a companion, attacked
by the same disease, were laid together, with nothing but a
buffalo-robe between them and the ground. The assistant-
surgeon's deputy visited them once a day and brought them
each a huge dose of calomel, the only medicine, according
to his surviving victim, with which he was acquainted.

Tête Rouge woke one morning, and turning to his companion, saw his eyes fixed upon the beams above with the glassy
stare of a dead man. At this the unfortunate volunteer lost
his senses outright. In spite of the doctor, however, he
eventually recovered; though between the brain fever and
the calomel, his mind, originally none of the strongest, was
so much shaken that it had not quite recovered its balance
when we came to the fort. In spite of the poor fellow's
tragic story, there was something so ludicrous in his appearance, and the whimsical contrast between his military dress

and his most unmilitary demeanor, that we could not help
smiling at them. We asked him if he had a gun. He said
they had taken it from him during his illness, and he had
not seen it since; but " perhaps," he observed, looking at
5 me with a beseeching air, " you will lend me one of your big
pistols if we should meet with any Indians." I next inquired
if he had a horse; he declared he had a magnificent one,
and at Shaw's request, a Mexican led him in for inspection.
He exhibited the outline of a good horse, but his eyes were
10 sunk in the sockets, and every one of his ribs could be
counted. There were certain marks too about his shoulders,
which could be accounted for by the circumstance that, during Tête Rouge's illness, his companions had seized upon
the insulted charger, and harnessed him to a cannon along
15 with the draft horses. To Tête Rouge's astonishment we
recommended him by all means to exchange the horse, if he
could, for a mule. Fortunately the people at the fort were
so anxious to get rid of him that they were willing to make
some sacrifice to effect the object, and he succeeded in
20 getting a tolerable mule in exchange for the broken-down
steed.

A man soon appeared at the gate, leading in the mule by
a cord, which he placed in the hands of Tête Rouge, who,
being somewhat afraid of his new acquisition, tried various
25 flatteries and blandishments to induce her to come forward.
The mule, knowing that she was expected to advance,
stopped short in consequence, and stood fast as a rock, looking straight forward with immovable composure. Being
stimulated by a blow from behind, she consented to move,
30 and walked nearly to the other side of the fort before she
stopped again. Hearing the bystanders laugh, Tête Rouge
plucked up spirit and tugged hard at the rope. The mule
jerked backward, spun herself round, and made a dash
for the gate. Tête Rouge, who clung manfully to the rope,
went whisking through the air for a few rods, when he let

go and stood with his mouth open, staring after the mule,
which galloped away over the prairie. She was soon caught
and brought back by a Mexican, who mounted a horse and
went in pursuit of her with his lasso.

Having thus displayed his capacities for prairie travel- 5
ling, Tête Rouge proceeded to supply himself with provisions
for the journey, and with this view applied to a quarter-
master's assistant who was in the fort. This official had a
face as sour as vinegar, being in a state of chronic indignation because he had been left behind the army. He was as 10
anxious as the rest to get rid of Tête Rouge. So, producing
a rusty key, he opened a low door which led to a half
subterranean apartment, into which the two disappeared
together. After some time they came out again, Tête Rouge
greatly embarrassed by a multiplicity of paper parcels con- 15
taining the different articles of his forty days' rations.
They were consigned to the care of Deslauriers, who about
that time passed by with the cart on his way to the appointed place of meeting with Munroe and his companions.

We next urged Tête Rouge to provide himself, if he could, 20
with a gun. He accordingly made earnest appeals to the
charity of various persons in the fort, but totally without
success,— a circumstance which did not greatly disturb us,
since in the event of a skirmish, he would be more apt to do
mischief to himself or his friends than to the enemy. When 25
all these arrangements were completed, we saddled our
horses, and were preparing to leave the fort, when looking
round we discovered that our new associate was in fresh
trouble. A man was holding the mule for him in the middle
of the fort, while he tried to put the saddle on her back, 30
but she kept stepping sideways and moving round and round
in a circle until he was almost in despair. It required some
assistance before all his difficulties could be overcome. At
length he clambered into the black war-saddle on which he
was to have carried terror into the ranks of the Mexicans.

"Get up," said Tête Rouge; "come now, go along, will you?"

The mule walked deliberately forward out of the gate. Her recent conduct had inspired him with so much awe that he never dared to touch her with his whip. We trotted forward towards the place of meeting; but before we had gone far, we saw that Tête Rouge's mule, who perfectly understood her rider, had stopped and was quietly grazing, in spite of his protestations, at some distance behind. So getting behind him, we drove him and the contumacious mule before us, until we could see through the twilight the gleaming of a distant fire. Munroe, Jim, and Ellis were lying around it; their saddles, packs, and weapons were scattered about, and their horses picketed near them. Deslauriers was there too with our little cart. Another fire was soon blazing. We invited our new allies to take a cup of coffee with us. When both the others had gone over to their side of the camp, Jim Gurney still stood by the blaze, puffing hard at his little black pipe, as short and weather-beaten as himself.

"Well," he said, "here are eight of us; we'll call it six — for them two boobies, Ellis over yonder, and that new man of yours, won't count for anything. We'll get through well enough, never fear for that, unless the Comanches happen to get foul of us."

CHAPTER XXIII

INDIAN ALARMS

We began our journey for the settlements on the twenty-seventh of August, and certainly a more ragamuffin caval-cade never was seen on the banks of the Upper Arkansas. Of the large and fine horses with which we had left the frontier in the spring, not one remained: we had supplied their place with the rough breed of the prairie, as hardy as mules and almost as ugly; we had also with us a number of the latter detestable animals. In spite of their strength and hardihood, several of the band were already worn down by hard service and hard fare, and as none of them were shod, they were fast becoming footsore. Every horse and mule had a cord of twisted bull-hide coiled about his neck, which by no means added to the beauty of his appearance. Our saddles and all our equipments were worn and battered, and our weapons had become dull and rusty. The dress of the riders corresponded with the dilapidated furniture of our horses, and of the whole party none made a more dis-reputable appearance than my friend and I. Shaw had for an upper garment an old red flannel shirt, flying open in front, and belted around him like a frock; while I, in absence of other clothing, was attired in a time-worn suit of buckskin.

Thus, happy and careless as so many beggars, we crept slowly from day to day along the monotonous banks of the Arkansas. Tête Rouge gave constant trouble, for he could never catch his mule, saddle her, or indeed do anything else without assistance. Every day he had some new ailment, real or imaginary, to complain of. At one moment he would be woe-begone and disconsolate, and at the next he would

be visited with a violent flow of spirits, to which he could
only give vent by incessant laughing, whistling, and telling stories. When other resources failed, we used to amuse
ourselves by tormenting him; a fair compensation for the
5 trouble he cost us. Tête Rouge rather enjoyed being laughed
at, for he was an odd compound of weakness, eccentricity,
and good-nature. He made a figure worthy of a painter as
he paced along before us, perched on the back of his mule,
and enveloped in a huge buffalo-robe coat, which some char-
10 itable person had given him at the fort. This extraordinary
garment, which would have contained two men of his size,
he chose, for some reason best known to himself, to wear
inside out, and he never took it off, even in the hottest
weather. It was fluttering all over with seams and tatters,
15 and the hide was so old and rotten that it broke out every
day in a new place. Just at the top of it a large pile of red
curls was visible, with his little cap set jauntily upon one
side, to give him a military air. His seat in the saddle was
no less remarkable than his person and equipment. He
20 pressed one leg close against his mule's side, and thrust the
other out at an angle of forty-five degrees. His trousers
were decorated with a military red stripe, of which he was
extremely vain; but being much too short, the whole length
of his boots was usually visible below them. His blanket,
25 loosely rolled up into a large bundle, dangled at the back of
his saddle, where he carried it tied with a string. Four or
five times a day it would fall to the ground. Every few
minutes he would drop his pipe, his knife, his flint and
steel, or a piece of tobacco, and scramble down to pick them
30 up. In doing this he would contrive to get in everybody's
way; and as most of the party were by no means remarkable for a fastidious choice of language, a storm of anath-
emas would be showered upon him, half in earnest and half
in jest, until Tête Rouge would declare that there was no
comfort in life, and that he never saw such fellows before.

Only a day or two after leaving Bent's Fort, Henry Chatillon rode forward to hunt, and took Ellis along with him. After they had been some time absent we saw them coming down the hill, driving three dragoon-horses, which had escaped from their owners on the march, or perhaps had given out and been abandoned. One of them was in tolerable condition, but the others were much emaciated and severely bitten by the wolves. Reduced as they were, we carried two of them to the settlements, and Henry exchanged the third with the Arapahoes for an excellent mule.

On the day after, when we had stopped to rest at noon, a long train of Santa Fé wagons came up and trailed slowly past us in their picturesque procession. They belonged to a trader named Magoffin, whose brother, with a number of other men, came and sat down with us on the grass. The news they brought was not of the most pleasing complexion. According to their accounts, the trail below was in a very dangerous state. They had repeatedly detected Indians prowling at night around their camps; and the large party which had left Bent's Fort a few weeks before us had been attacked, and a man named Swan, from Massachusetts, had been killed. His companions had buried the body; but when Magoffin found his grave, which was near a place called "The Caches," the Indians had dug up and scalped him, and the wolves had shockingly mangled his remains. As an offset to this intelligence, they gave us the welcome information that the buffalo were numerous at a few days' journey below.

On the next afternoon, as we moved along the bank of the river, we saw the white tops of wagons on the horizon. It was some hours before we met them, when they proved to be a train of clumsy ox-wagons, quite different from the rakish vehicles of the Santa Fé traders, and loaded with government stores for the troops. They all stopped, and

the drivers gathered around us in a crowd. Many of them
were mere boys, fresh from the plough. In respect to the
state of the trail, they confirmed all that the Santa Fé men had
told us. In passing between the Pawnee Fork and the Caches,
5 their sentinels had fired every night at real or imaginary
Indians. They said also that Ewing, a young Kentuckian
in the party that had gone down before us, had shot an
Indian who was prowling at evening about the camp. Some
of them advised us to turn back, and others to hasten for-
10 ward as fast as we could; but they all seemed in such a
state of feverish anxiety and so little capable of cool judgment, that we attached slight weight to what they said.
They next gave us a more definite piece of intelligence: a
large village of Arapahoes was encamped on the river below.
15 They represented them to be friendly; but some distinction
was to be made between a party of thirty men, travelling
with oxen, which are of no value in an Indian's eyes, and a
mere handful like ourselves, with a tempting band of mules
and horses.

20   Early in the afternoon of the next day, looking along the
horizon before us, we saw that at one point it was faintly
marked with pale indentations, like the teeth of a saw. The
distant lodges of the Arapahoes, rising between us and the
sky, caused this singular appearance. It wanted still two or
25 three hours of sunset when we came opposite their camp.
There were full two hundred lodges standing in the midst
of a grassy meadow at some distance beyond the river,
while for a mile around on both banks of the Arkansas were
scattered some fifteen hundred horses and mules, grazing
30 together in bands, or wandering singly about the prairie.
The whole were visible at once, for the vast expanse was
unbroken by hills, and there was not a tree or a bush to
intercept the view.

   Here and there walked an Indian, engaged in watching
the horses. No sooner did we see them than Tête Rouge

begged Deslauriers to stop the cart and hand him his military jacket, which was stowed away there. In this he invested himself, having for once laid the old buffalo-coat aside, assumed a martial posture in the saddle, set his cap over his left eye with an air of defiance, and earnestly entreated that somebody would lend him a gun or a pistol only for half an hour. Being called upon to explain these proceedings, Tête Rouge observed, that he knew from experience what effect the presence of a military man in his uniform always has upon the mind of an Indian, and he thought the Arapahoes ought to know that there was a soldier in the party.

Meeting Arapahoes here on the Arkansas was a very different thing from meeting the same Indians among their native mountains. There was another circumstance in our favor. General Kearney had seen them a few weeks before, as he came up the river with his army, and, renewing his threats of the previous year, he told them that if they ever again touched the hair of a white man's head he would exterminate their nation. This placed them for the time in an admirable frame of mind, and the effect of his menaces had not yet disappeared. I wished to see the village and its inhabitants. We thought it also our best policy to visit them openly, as if unsuspicious of any hostile design; and Shaw and I, with Henry Chatillon, prepared to cross the river. The rest of the party meanwhile moved forward as fast as they could, in order to get as far as possible from our suspicious neighbors before night came on.

The Arkansas at this point, and for several hundred miles below, is nothing but a broad sand-bed, over which glide a few scanty threads of water, now and then expanding into wide shallows. At several places, during the autumn, the water sinks into the sand and disappears altogether. At this season, were it not for the numerous quicksands, the river might be forded almost anywhere without difficulty, though its channel is often a quarter of a mile wide. Our horses jumped down the bank, and wading through the water, or galloping freely over the hard sand-beds, soon reached the other side. Here, as we were pushing through the tall grass, we saw several Indians not far off; one of them waited until we came up, and stood for some moments in perfect silence before us, looking at us askance with his little snake-like eyes. Henry explained by signs what we wanted, and the Indian, gathering his buffalo-robe about his shoulders, led the way towards the village without speaking a word.

The language of the Arapahoes is so difficult, and its pronunciation so harsh and guttural, that no white man, it is said, has ever been able to master it. Even Maxwell, the trader who has been most among them, is compelled to resort to the curious sign-language common to most of the prairie tribes. With this sign-language Henry Chatillon was perfectly acquainted.

Approaching the village, we found the ground strewn with piles of waste buffalo-meat in incredible quantities. The lodges were pitched in a circle. They resembled those of the Dahcotah in everything but cleanliness. Passing between two of them, we entered the great circular area of the camp, and instantly hundreds of Indians, men, women, and children, came flocking out of their habitations to look at us; at the same time, the dogs all around the village set up a discordant baying. Our Indian guide walked towards the lodge of the chief. Here we dismounted; and loosening the trail-ropes from our horses' necks, held them fast as we sat down before the entrance, with our rifles laid across our laps. The chief came out and shook us by the hand. He was a mean-looking fellow, very tall, thin-visaged, and sinewy, like the rest of the nation, and with scarcely a vestige of clothing. We had not been seated a moment before a multitude of Indians came crowding around us from every part of the village, and we were shut in by a dense wall of savage faces. Some of our visitors crouched around us on the ground; others sat behind them; others, stooping, looked over their heads; while many more stood behind, peering over each other's shoulders, to get a view of us. I looked in vain among this throng of faces to discover one manly or generous expression; all were wolfish, sinister, and malignant, and their complexions, as well as their features, unlike those of the Dahcotah, were exceedingly bad. The chief, who sat close to the entrance, called to a squaw within the lodge, who soon came out and placed a wooden bowl of meat before us. To our surprise, however, no pipe was offered. Having tasted of the meat as a matter of form, I began to open a bundle of presents, — tobacco, knives, vermilion, and other articles which I had brought with me. At this there was a grin on every countenance in the rapacious crowd; their eyes began to glitter, and long thin arms were eagerly stretched towards us on all sides to receive the gifts.

The Arapahoes set great value upon their shields, which they transmit carefully from father to son. I wished to get one of them; and displaying a large piece of scarlet cloth, together with some tobacco and a knife, I offered them to any one who would bring me what I wanted. After some delay a tolerable shield was produced. They were very anxious to know what we meant to do with it, and Henry told them that we were going to fight their enemies the Pawnees. This instantly produced a visible impression in our favor, which was increased by the distribution of the presents. Among these was a large paper of awls, a gift appropriate to the women; and as we were anxious to see the beauties of the Arapahoe village, Henry requested that they might be called to receive them. A warrior gave a shout, as if he were calling a pack of dogs together. The squaws, young and old, hags of eighty and girls of sixteen, came

running with screams and laughter out of the lodges; and
as the men gave way for them, they gathered round us and
stretched out their arms, grinning with delight, their native
ugliness considerably enhanced by the excitement of the
5 moment.

Mounting our horses, which during the whole interview
we had held close to us, we prepared to leave the Arapahoes.
The crowd fell back on each side, and stood looking on.
When we were half across the camp an idea occurred to us.
10 The Pawnees were probably in the neighborhood of the
Caches; we might tell the Arapahoes of this, and instigate
them to send down a war-party and cut them off, while we
ourselves could remain behind for a while and hunt the
buffalo. At first thought, this plan of setting our enemies
15 to destroy one another seemed to us a master-piece of policy;
but we immediately recollected that should we meet the
Arapahoe warriors on the river below, they might prove
quite as dangerous as the Pawnees themselves. So rejecting
our plan as soon as it presented itself, we passed out of the
20 village on the farther side. We urged our horses rapidly
through the tall grass, which rose to their necks. Several
Indians were walking through it at a distance, their heads
just visible above its waving surface. It bore a kind of seed,
as sweet and nutritious as oats; and our hungry horses, in
25 spite of whip and rein, could not resist the temptation of
snatching at this unwonted luxury as we passed along.
When about a mile from the village, I turned and looked
back over the undulating ocean of grass. The sun was just
set; the western sky was all in a glow, and sharply defined
30 against it, on the extreme verge of the plain, stood the
clustered lodges of the Arapahoe camp.

Reaching the bank of the river, we followed it for some
distance farther, until we discerned through the twilight the
white covering of our little cart on the opposite bank. When
we reached it we found a considerable number of Indians

there before us. Four or five of them were seated in a row
upon the ground, looking like so many half-starved vultures.
Tête Rouge, in his uniform, was holding a close colloquy
with another by the side of the cart. Finding his signs and
gesticulation of no avail, he tried to make the Indian under- 5
stand him by repeating English words very loudly and distinctly again and again. The Indian sat with his eye fixed
steadily upon him, and in spite of the rigid immobility of
his features, it was clear at a glance that he perfectly understood and despised his military companion. The exhibition 10
was more amusing than politic, and Tête Rouge was directed
to finish what he had to say as soon as possible. Thus re-
buked, he crept under the cart and sat down there; Henry
Chatillon stooped to look at him in his retirement, and
remarked in his quiet manner that an Indian would kill 15
ten such men and laugh all the time.

One by one our visitors arose and stalked away. As the
darkness thickened we were saluted by dismal sounds. The
wolves are incredibly numerous in this part of the country,
and the offal around the Arapahoe camp had drawn such 20
multitudes of them together that several hundreds were
howling in concert in our immediate neighborhood. There
was an island in the river, or rather an oasis in the midst
of the sands, at about the distance of a gun-shot, and here
they seemed to be gathered in the greatest numbers. A hor- 25
rible discord of low mournful wailings, mingled with ferocious howls, arose from it incessantly for several hours after
sunset. We could distinctly see the wolves running about
the prairie within a few rods of our fire, or bounding over
the sand-beds of the river and splashing through the water. 30
There was not the slightest danger from them, for they are
the greatest cowards on the prairie.

In respect to the human wolves in our neighborhood, we
felt much less at our ease. That night each man spread his
buffalo-robe upon the ground with his loaded rifle laid at

his side or clasped in his arms. Our horses were picketed
so close around us that one of them repeatedly stepped over
me as I lay. We were not in the habit of placing a guard,
but every man was anxious and watchful: there was little
5 sound sleeping in camp, and some one of the party was on
his feet during the greater part of the night. For myself,
I lay alternately waking and dozing until midnight. Tête
Rouge was reposing close to the river-bank, and about this
time, when half asleep and half awake, I was conscious that
10 he shifted his position and crept on all-fours under the cart.
Soon after I fell into a sound sleep, from which I was roused
by a hand shaking me by the shoulder. Looking up, I saw
Tête Rouge stooping over me with a pale face and dilated
eyes.

15 " What's the matter ? " said I.

Tête Rouge declared that as he lay on the river-bank,
something caught his eye which excited his suspicions. So
creeping under the cart for safety's sake, he sat there and
watched, when he saw two Indians, wrapped in white robes,
20 creep up the bank, seize upon two horses and lead them off.
He looked so frightened and told his story in such a discon-
nected manner that I did not believe him, and was unwilling to alarm the party. Still, it might be true, and in that
case the matter required instant attention. So, directing
25 Tête Rouge to show me which way the Indians had gone, I
took my rifle, in obedience to a thoughtless impulse, and left
the camp. I followed the river-bank for two or three hundred yards, listening and looking anxiously on every side.
In the dark prairie on the right I could discern nothing to
30 excite alarm ; and in the dusky bed of the river, a wolf was
bounding along in a manner which no Indian could imitate.
I returned to the camp, and when within sight of it, saw
that the whole party was aroused. Shaw called out to me
that he had counted the horses, and that every one of them
was in his place. Tête Rouge, being examined as to what

he had seen, only repeated his former story with many as-
severations, and insisted that two horses were certainly
carried off. At this Jim Gurney declared that he was crazy;
Tête Rouge indignantly denied the charge, on which Jim
appealed to us. As we declined to give our judgment on so
delicate a matter, the dispute grew hot between Tête Rouge
and his accuser, until he was directed to go to bed and not
alarm the camp again if he saw the whole Arapahoe village
coming.

CHAPTER XXIV

THE CHASE

The country before us was now thronged with buffalo, and a sketch of the manner of hunting them will not be out of place. There are two methods commonly practised, "running" and "approaching." The chase on horseback, which
5 goes by the name of "running," is the more violent and dashing mode of the two, that is to say, when the buffalo are in one of their wild moods; for otherwise it is tame enough. A practised and skilful hunter, well mounted, will sometimes kill five or six cows in a single chase, loading his
10 gun again and again as his horse rushes through the tumult. In attacking a small band of buffalo, or in separating a single animal from the herd and assailing it apart from the rest, there is less excitement and less danger. In fact, the animals are at times so stupid and lethargic that there is little sport
15 in killing them. With a bold and well-trained horse the hunter may ride so close to the buffalo that as they gallop side by side he may touch him with his hand; nor is there much danger in this as long as the buffalo's strength and breath continue unabated; but when he becomes tired and
20 can no longer run with ease, when his tongue lolls out and the foam flies from his jaws, then the hunter had better keep a more respectful distance; the distressed brute may turn upon him at any instant; and especially at the moment when he fires his gun. The horse then leaps aside, and the hunter
25 has need of a tenacious seat in the saddle, for if he is thrown to the ground there is no hope for him. When he sees his attack defeated, the buffalo resumes his flight, but if the shot is well directed he soon stops; for a few moments he stands still, then totters and falls heavily upon the prairie.

The chief difficulty in running buffalo, as it seems to me, is that of loading the gun or pistol at full gallop. Many hunters for convenience' sake carry three or four bullets in the mouth; the powder is poured down the muzzle of the piece, the bullet dropped in after it, the stock struck hard upon the pommel of the saddle, and the work is done. The danger of this is obvious. Should the blow on the pommel fail to send the bullet home, or should the bullet, in the act of aiming, start from its place and roll towards the muzzle, the gun would probably burst in discharging. Many a shattered hand and worse casualties besides have been the result of such an accident. To obviate it, some hunters make use of a ramrod, usually hung by a string from the neck, but this materially increases the difficulty of loading. The bows and arrows which the Indians use in running buffalo have many advantages over firearms, and even white men occasionally employ them.

The danger of the chase arises not so much from the on- set of the wounded animal as from the nature of the ground which the hunter must ride over. The prairie does not al- ways present a smooth, level, and uniform surface; very often it is broken with hills and hollows, intersected by ra- vines, and in the remoter parts studded by the stiff wild- sage bushes. The most formidable obstructions, however, are the burrows of wild animals, wolves, badgers, and par- ticularly prairie-dogs, with whose holes the ground for a very great extent is frequently honeycombed. In the blind- ness of the chase the hunter rushes over it unconscious of danger; his horse, at full career, thrusts his leg deep into one of the burrows; the bone snaps, the rider is hurled for- ward to the ground and probably killed. Yet accidents in buffalo running happen less frequently than one would sup- pose; in the recklessness of the chase, the hunter enjoys all the impunity of a drunken man, and may ride in safety over gullies and declivities, where, should he attempt to pass in his sober senses, he would infallibly break his neck.

The method of "approaching," being practised on foot,
has many advantages over that of "running"; in the former,
one neither breaks down his horse nor endangers his own
life; he must be cool, collected, and watchful; must understand the buffalo, observe the features of the country and
the course of the wind, and be well skilled in using the rifle.
The buffalo are strange animals; sometimes they are so
stupid and infatuated that a man may walk up to them in
full sight on the open prairie, and even shoot several of
their number before the rest will think it necessary to retreat. At another moment they will be so shy and wary
that in order to approach them the utmost skill, experience,
and judgment are necessary. Kit Carson, I believe, stands
pre-eminent in running buffalo; in approaching, no man
living can bear away the palm from Henry Chatillon.

After Tête Rouge had alarmed the camp, no farther disturbance occurred during the night. The Arapahoes did not
attempt mischief, or if they did the wakefulness of the party
deterred them from effecting their purpose. The next day
was one of activity and excitement, for about ten o'clock
the man in advance shouted the gladdening cry of *buffalo,
buffalo!* and in the hollow of the prairie just below us, a
band of bulls were grazing. The temptation was irresistible,
and Shaw and I rode down upon them. We were badly
mounted on our travelling horses, but by hard lashing we
overtook them, and Shaw, running alongside a bull, shot
into him both balls of his double-barrelled gun. Looking
round as I galloped by, I saw the bull in his mortal fury
rushing again and again upon his antagonist, whose horse
constantly leaped aside, and avoided the onset. My chase
was more protracted, but at length I ran close to the bull
and killed him with my pistols. Cutting off the tails of our
victims by way of trophy, we rejoined the party in about a
quarter of an hour after we had left it. Again and again that
morning rang out the same welcome cry of *buffalo, buffalo!*

Every few moments, in the broad meadows along the river, we saw bands of bulls, who, raising their shaggy heads, would gaze in stupid amazement at the approaching horsemen, and then breaking into a clumsy gallop, file off in a long line across the trail in front, towards the rising prairie on the left. At noon, the plain before us was alive with thousands of buffalo, — bulls, cows, and calves, — all moving rapidly as we drew near; and far off beyond the river the swelling prairie was darkened with them to the very horizon. The party was in gayer spirits than ever. We stopped for a nooning near a grove of trees by the river.

"Tongues and hump-ribs to-morrow," said Shaw, looking with contempt at the venison steaks which Deslauriers placed before us. Our meal finished, we lay down to sleep. A shout from Henry Chatillon aroused us, and we saw him standing on the cartwheel, stretching his tall figure to its full height, while he looked towards the prairie beyond the river. Following the direction of his eyes, we could clearly distinguish a large dark object, like the black shadow of a cloud, passing rapidly over swell after swell of the distant plain; behind it followed another of similar appearance, though smaller, moving more rapidly, and drawing closer and closer to the first. It was the hunters of the Arapahoe camp chasing a band of buffalo. Shaw and I caught and saddled our best horses, and went plunging through sand and water to the farther bank. We were too late. The hunters had already mingled with the herd, and the work of slaughter was nearly over. When we reached the ground we found it strewn far and near with numberless carcasses, while the remnants of the herd, scattered in all directions, were flying away in terror, and the Indians still rushing in pursuit. Many of the hunters, however, remained upon the spot, and among the rest was our yesterday's acquaintance, the chief of the village. He had alighted by the side of a cow, into which he had shot five or six arrows, and his

squaw, who had followed him on horseback to the hunt, was
giving him a draught of water from a canteen, purchased
or plundered from some volunteer soldier. Recrossing the
river, we overtook the party, who were already on their way.

5   We had gone scarcely a mile when we saw an imposing
spectacle. From the river-bank on the right, away over the
swelling prairie on the left, and in front as far as the eye
could reach, was one vast host of buffalo. The outskirts of
the herd were within a quarter of a mile. In many parts
10 they were crowded so densely together that in the distance
their rounded backs presented a surface of uniform blackness; but elsewhere they were more scattered, and from
amid the multitude rose little columns of dust where some
of them were rolling on the ground. Here and there a battle
15 was going forward among the bulls. We could distinctly
see them rushing against each other, and hear the clattering
of their horns and their hoarse bellowing. Shaw was riding
at some distance in advance, with Henry Chatillon; I saw
him stop and draw the leather covering from his gun. With
20 such a sight before us, but one thing could be thought of.
That morning I had used pistols in the chase. I had now a
mind to try the virtue of a gun. Deslauriers had one,
and I rode up to the side of the cart; there he sat under
the white covering, biting his pipe between his teeth and
25 grinning with excitement.

"Lend me your gun, Deslauriers."

"Oui, Monsieur, oui," said Deslauriers, tugging with
might and main to stop the mule, which seemed obstinately
bent on going forward. Then everything but his moccasons
30 disappeared as he crawled into the cart and pulled at the
gun to extricate it.

"Is it loaded?" I asked.

"Oui, bien chargé; you'll kill, mon bourgeois; yes, you'll
kill — c'est un bon fusil."

I handed him my rifle and rode forward to Shaw.

" Are you ready ? " he asked.

" Come on," said I.

" Keep down that hollow," said Henry, "and then they won't see you till you get close to them."

The hollow was a kind of wide ravine; it ran obliquely towards the buffalo, and we rode at a canter along the bottom until it became too shallow; then we bent close to our horses' necks, and, at last, finding that it could no longer conceal us, came out of it and rode directly towards the herd. It was within gunshot; before its outskirts, numerous grizzly old bulls were scattered, holding guard over their females. They glared at us in anger and astonishment, walked towards us a few yards, and then turning slowly round, retreated at a trot which afterwards broke into a clumsy gallop. In an instant the main body caught the alarm. The buffalo began to crowd away from the point towards which we were approaching, and a gap was opened in the side of the herd. We entered it, still restraining our excited horses. Every instant the tumult was thickening. The buffalo, pressing together in large bodies, crowded away from us on every hand. In front and on either side we could see dark columns and masses, half hidden by clouds of dust, rushing along in terror and confusion, and hear the tramp and clattering of ten thousand hoofs. That countless multitude of powerful brutes, ignorant of their own strength, were flying in a panic from the approach of two feeble horsemen. To remain quiet longer was impossible.

" Take that band on the left," said Shaw; " I 'll take these in front."

He sprang off, and I saw no more of him. A heavy Indian whip was fastened by a band to my wrist; I swung it into the air and lashed my horse's flank with all the strength of my arm. Away she darted, stretching close to the ground. I could see nothing but a cloud of dust before me, but I knew that it concealed a band of many hundreds of buffalo.

In a moment I was in the midst of the cloud, half suffocated by the dust and stunned by the trampling of the flying herd; but I was drunk with the chase and cared for nothing but the buffalo. Very soon a long dark mass became visible,
5 looming through the dust; then I could distinguish each bulky carcass, the hoofs flying out beneath, the short tails held rigidly erect. In a moment I was so close that I could have touched them with my gun. Suddenly, to my amazement, the hoofs were jerked upwards, the tails flourished in
10 the air, and amid a cloud of dust the buffalo seemed to sink into the earth before me. One vivid impression of that instant remains upon my mind. I remember looking down upon the backs of several buffalo dimly visible through the dust. We had run unawares upon a ravine. At that moment
15 I was not the most accurate judge of depth and width, but when I passed it on my return, I found it about twelve feet deep and not quite twice as wide at the bottom. It was impossible to stop; I would have done so gladly if I could; so, half sliding, half plunging, down went the little mare.
20 She came down on her knees in the loose sand at the bottom; I was pitched forward against her neck and nearly thrown over her head among the buffalo, who amid dust and confusion came tumbling in all around. The mare was on her feet in an instant and scrambling like a cat up the opposite side.
25 I thought for a moment that she would have fallen back and crushed me, but with a violent effort she clambered out and gained the hard prairie above. Glancing back, I saw the huge head of a bull clinging as it were by the forefeet at the edge of the dusty gulf. At length I was fairly among
30 the buffalo. They were less densely crowded than before, and I could see nothing but bulls, who always run at the rear of a herd to protect their females. As I passed among them they would lower their heads, and turning as they ran, try to gore my horse; but as they were already at full speed there was no force in their onset, and as Pauline ran faster

than they, they were always thrown behind her in the effort. I soon began to distinguish cows amid the throng. One just in front of me seemed to my liking, and I pushed close to her side. Dropping the reins, I fired, holding the muzzle of the gun within a foot of her shoulder. Quick as lightning she sprang at Pauline; the little mare dodged the attack, and I lost sight of the wounded animal amid the tumult. Immediately after, I selected another, and urging forward Pauline, shot into her both pistols in succession. For a while I kept her in view, but in attempting to load my gun, lost sight of her also in the confusion. Believing her to be mortally wounded and unable to keep up with the herd, I checked my horse. The crowd rushed onwards. The dust and tumult passed away, and on the prairie, far behind the rest, I saw a solitary buffalo galloping heavily. In a moment I and my victim were running side by side. My firearms were all empty, and I had in my pouch nothing but rifle bullets, too large for the pistols and too small for the gun. I loaded the gun, however, but as often as I levelled it to fire, the bullets would roll out of the muzzle and the gun returned only a report like a squib, as the powder harmlessly exploded. I rode in front of the buffalo and tried to turn her back; but her eyes glared, her mane bristled, and, lowering her head, she rushed at me with the utmost fierceness and activity. Again and again I rode before her, and again and again she repeated her furious charge. But little Pauline was in her element. She dodged her enemy at every rush, until at length the buffalo stood still, exhausted with her own efforts, her tongue lolling from her jaws.

Riding to a little distance, I dismounted, thinking to gather a handful of dry grass to serve the purpose of wadding, and load the gun at my leisure. No sooner were my feet on the ground than the buffalo came bounding in such a rage towards me that I jumped back again into the saddle with all possible despatch. After waiting a few minutes

more, I made an attempt to ride up and stab her with my
knife; but Pauline was near being gored in the attempt.
At length, bethinking me of the fringes at the seams of my
buckskin trousers, I jerked off a few of them, and, reloading
5 the gun, forced them down the barrel to keep the bullet in
its place; then approaching, I shot the wounded buffalo
through the heart. Sinking to her knees, she rolled over
lifeless on the prairie. To my astonishment, I found that,
instead of a cow, I had been slaughtering a stout yearling
10 bull. No longer wondering at his fierceness, I opened his
throat, and cutting out his tongue, tied it at the back of my
saddle. My mistake was one which a more experienced eye
than mine might easily make in the dust and confusion of
such a chase.

15 Then for the first time I had leisure to look at the scene
around me. The prairie in front was darkened with the retreating multitude, and on either hand the buffalo came filing up in endless columns from the low plains upon the
river. The Arkansas was three or four miles distant. I
20 turned and moved slowly towards it. A long time passed
before, far in the distance, I distinguished the white covering of the cart and the little black specks of horsemen before
and behind it. Drawing near, I recognized Shaw's elegant
tunic, the red flannel shirt, conspicuous far off. I overtook
25 the party, and asked him what success he had had. He had
assailed a fat cow, shot her with two bullets, and mortally
wounded her. But neither of us was prepared for the chase
that afternoon, and Shaw, like myself, had no spare bullets
in his pouch; so he abandoned the disabled animal to Henry
30 Chatillon, who followed, despatched her with his rifle, and
loaded his horse with the meat.

We encamped close to the river. The night was dark,
and as we lay down we could hear, mingled with the
howlings of wolves, the hoarse bellowing of the buffalo,
like the ocean beating upon a distant coast.

CHAPTER XXV

THE BUFFALO CAMP

No one in the camp was more active than Jim Gurney, and no one half so lazy as Ellis. Between these two there was a great antipathy. Ellis never stirred in the morning until he was compelled, but Jim was always on his feet before daybreak; and this morning as usual the sound of his voice awakened the party.

"Get up, you booby! up with you now, you're fit for nothing but eating and sleeping. Stop your grumbling and come out of that buffalo-robe, or I'll pull it off for you."

Jim's words were interspersed with numerous expletives, which gave them great additional effect. Ellis drawled out something in a nasal tone from among the folds of his buffalo-robe; then slowly disengaged himself, rose into a sitting posture, stretched his long arms, yawned hideously, and, finally raising his tall person erect, stood staring about him to all the four quarters of the horizon. Deslauriers's fire was soon blazing, and the horses and mules, loosened from their pickets, were feeding on the neighboring meadow. When we sat down to breakfast the prairie was still in the dusky light of morning; and as the sun rose we were mounted and on our way again.

"A white buffalo!" exclaimed Munroe.

"I'll have that fellow," said Shaw, "if I run my horse to death after him."

He threw the cover of his gun to Deslauriers and galloped out upon the prairie.

"Stop, Mr. Shaw, stop!" called out Henry Chatillon, "you'll run down your horse for nothing; it's only a white ox."

But Shaw was already out of hearing. The ox, which had no doubt strayed away from some of the government wagon trains, was standing beneath some low hills which bounded the plain in the distance. Not far from him a band of veri-
5 table buffalo bulls were grazing; and startled at Shaw's approach, they all broke into a run, and went scrambling up the hillsides to gain the high prairie above. One of them in his haste and terror involved himself in a fatal catas-trophe. Along the foot of the hills was a narrow strip of
10 deep marshy soil, into which the bull plunged and hope-lessly entangled himself. We all rode to the spot. The huge carcass was half sunk in the mud, which flowed to his very chin, and his shaggy mane was outspread upon the surface. As we came near, the bull began to struggle with convulsive
15 strength; he writhed to and fro, and in the energy of his fright and desperation would lift himself for a moment half out of the slough, while the reluctant mire returned a suck-ing sound as he strained to drag his limbs from its tenacious depths. We stimulated his exertions by getting behind him
20 and twisting his tail; nothing would do. There was clearly no hope for him. After every effort his heaving sides were more deeply imbedded, and the mire almost overflowed his nostrils; he lay still at length, and looking round at us with a furious eye, seemed to resign himself to his fate. Ellis
25 slowly dismounted, and, levelling his boasted yager, shot the old bull through the heart; then lazily climbed back again to his seat, pluming himself no doubt on having ac-tually killed a buffalo. That day the invincible yager drew blood for the first and last time during the whole journey.
30   The morning was a bright and gay one, and the air so clear that on the farthest horizon the outline of the pale blue prairie was sharply drawn against the sky. Shaw was in the mood for hunting; he rode in advance of the party, and before long we saw a file of bulls galloping at full speed upon a green swell of the prairie at some distance in front.

Shaw came scouring along behind them, arrayed in his red shirt, which looked very well in the distance; he gained fast on the fugitives, and as the foremost bull was disappearing behind the summit of the swell, we saw him in the act of assailing the hindmost; a smoke sprang from the muzzle of his gun and floated away before the wind like a little white cloud; the bull turned upon him, and just then the rising ground concealed them both from view.

We were moving forward until about noon, when we stopped by the side of the Arkansas. At that moment Shaw appeared riding slowly down the side of a distant hill; his horse was tired and jaded, and when he threw his saddle upon the ground, I observed that the tails of two bulls were dangling behind it. No sooner were the horses turned loose to feed than Henry, asking Munroe to go with him, took his rifle and walked quietly away. Shaw, Tête Rouge, and I sat down by the side of the cart to discuss the dinner which Deslauriers placed before us, and we had scarcely finished when we saw Munroe walking towards us along the riverbank. Henry, he said, had killed four fat cows, and had sent him back for horses to bring in the meat. Shaw took a horse for himself and another for Henry, and he and Munroe left the camp together. After a short absence all three of them came back, their horses loaded with the choicest parts of the meat. We kept two of the cows for ourselves, and gave the others to Munroe and his companions. Deslauriers seated himself on the grass before the pile of meat, and worked industriously for some time to cut it into thin broad sheets for drying, an art in which he had all the skill of an Indian squaw. Long before night, cords of raw hide were stretched around the camp, and the meat was hung upon them to dry in the sunshine and pure air of the prairie. Our California companions were less successful at the work; but they accomplished it after their own fashion, and their side of the camp was soon garnished in the same manner as our own.

We meant to remain at this place long enough to prepare provisions for our journey to the frontier, which, as we supposed, might occupy about a month. Had the distance been twice as great and the party ten times as large, the rifle of
5 Henry Chatillon would have supplied meat enough for the whole within two days; we were obliged to remain, however, until it should be dry enough for transportation; so we pitched our tent and made other arrangements for a permanent camp. The California men, who had no such shelter,
10 contented themselves with arranging their packs on the grass around their fire. In the mean time we had nothing to do but amuse ourselves. Our tent was within a rod of the river, if the broad sand-beds, with a scanty stream of water coursing here and there along their surface, deserve to be
15 dignified with the name of river. The vast flat plains on either side were almost on a level with the sandbeds, and they were bounded in the distance by low, monotonous hills, parallel to the course of the stream. All was one expanse of grass; there was no wood in view, except some trees and
20 stunted bushes upon two islands which rose from the wet sands of the river. Yet far from being dull and tame, the scene was often a wild and animated one; for twice a day, at sunrise and at noon, the buffalo came issuing from the hills, slowly advancing in their grave processions to drink
25 at the river. All our amusements were to be at their expense. An old buffalo bull is a brute of unparalleled ugliness. At first sight of him every feeling of pity vanishes. The cows are much smaller and of a gentler appearance, as becomes their sex. While in this camp we forebore to at-
30 tack them, leaving to Henry Chatillon, who could better judge their quality, the task of killing such as we wanted for use; but against the bulls we waged an unrelenting war. Thousands of them might be slaughtered without causing any detriment to the species, for their numbers greatly exceed those of the cows; it is the hides of the latter alone

which are used for the purposes of commerce and for making the lodges of the Indians; and the destruction among
them is therefore greatly disproportionate.

Our horses were tired, and we now usually hunted on
foot. While we were lying on the grass after dinner, smoking, talking, or laughing at Tête Rouge, one of us would
look up and observe, far out on the plains beyond the river,
certain black objects slowly approaching. He would inhale
a parting whiff from the pipe, then rising lazily, take his
rifle, which leaned against the cart, throw over his shoulder
the strap of his pouch and powder-horn, and with his moccasons in his hand, walk across the sand towards the opposite side of the river. This was very easy; for though the
sands were about a quarter of a mile wide, the water was
nowhere more than two feet deep. The farther bank was
about four or five feet high, and quite perpendicular, being
cut away by the water in spring. Tall grass grew along its
edge. Putting it aside with his hand, and cautiously looking through it, the hunter can discern the huge shaggy back
of the bull slowly swaying to and fro, as, with his clumsy,
swinging gait, he advances towards the water. The buffalo
have regular paths by which they come down to drink. Seeing at a glance along which of these his intended victim is
moving, the hunter crouches under the bank within fifteen
or twenty yards, it may be, of the point where the path
enters the river. Here he sits down quietly on the sand.
Listening intently, he hears the heavy, monotonous tread of
the approaching bull. The moment after, he sees a motion
among the long weeds and grass just at the spot where the
path is channelled through the bank. An enormous black
head is thrust out, the horns just visible amid the mass of
tangled mane. Half sliding, half plunging, down comes the
buffalo upon the river-bed below. He steps out in full sight
upon the sands. Just before him a runnel of water is gliding,
and he bends his head to drink. You may hear the water as

it gurgles down his capacious throat. He raises his head,
and the drops trickle from his wet beard. He stands with
an air of stupid abstraction, unconscious of the lurking
danger. Noiselessly the hunter cocks his rifle. As he sits
5 upon the sand, his knee is raised, and his elbow rests upon
it, that he may level his heavy weapon with a steadier aim.
The stock is at his shoulder; his eye ranges along the barrel.
Still he is in no haste to fire. The bull, with slow deliberation, begins his march over the sands to the other side.
10 He advances his foreleg, and exposes to view a small spot,
denuded of hair, just behind the point of his shoulder;
upon this the hunter brings the sight of his rifle to bear;
lightly and delicately his finger presses the hair-trigger.
The spiteful crack of the rifle responds to his touch, and
15 instantly in the middle of the bare spot appears a small red
dot. The buffalo shivers; death has overtaken him, he cannot tell from whence; still he does not fall, but walks
heavily forward, as if nothing had happened. Yet before
he has gone far out upon the sand, you see him stop; he
20 totters; his knees bend under him, and his head sinks forward to the ground. Then his whole vast bulk sways to one
side; he rolls over on the sand, and dies with a scarcely
perceptible struggle.

Waylaying the buffalo in this manner, and shooting them
25 as they come to water, is the easiest method of hunting
them. They may also be approached by crawling up ravines
or behind hills, or even over the open prairie. This is often
surprisingly easy; but at other times it requires the utmost
skill of the most experienced hunter. Henry Chatillon was
30 a man of extraordinary strength and hardihood; but I have
seen him return to camp quite exhausted with his efforts,
his limbs scratched and wounded, and his buckskin dress
stuck full of the thorns of the prickly-pear, among which he
had been crawling. Sometimes he would lie flat upon his face,
and drag himself along in this position for many rods together.

On the second day of our stay at this place, Henry went out for an afternoon hunt. Shaw and I remained in camp, until, observing some bulls approaching the water upon the other side of the river, we crossed over to attack them. They were so near, however, that before we could get under cover of the bank our appearance as we walked over the sands alarmed them. Turning round before coming within gun-shot, they began to move off to the right in a direction parallel to the river. I climbed up the bank and ran after them. They were walking swiftly, and before I could come within gun-shot distance they slowly wheeled about and faced me. Before they had turned far enough to see me I had fallen flat on my face. For a moment they stood and stared at the strange object upon the grass; then turning away, again they walked on as before; and I, rising immediately, ran once more in pursuit. Again they wheeled about, and again I fell prostrate. Repeating this three or four times, I came at length within a hundred yards of the fugitives, and as I saw them turning again, I sat down and levelled my rifle. The one in the centre was the largest I had ever seen. I shot him behind the shoulder. His two companions ran off. He attempted to follow, but soon came to a stand, and at length lay down as quietly as an ox chewing the cud. Cautiously approaching him, I saw by his dull and jelly-like eye that he was dead.

When I began the chase, the prairie was almost tenantless; but a great multitude of buffalo had suddenly thronged upon it, and looking up I saw within fifty rods a heavy, dark column stretching to the right and left as far as I could see. I walked towards them. My approach did not alarm them in the least. The column itself consisted almost entirely of cows and calves, but a great many old bulls were ranging about the prairie on its flank, and as I drew near they faced towards me with such a grim and ferocious look that I thought it best to proceed no farther. Indeed, I was

already within close rifle-shot of the column, and I sat down on the ground to watch their movements. Sometimes the whole would stand still, their heads all one way ; then they would trot forward, as if by a common impulse, their hoofs
5 and horns clattering together as they moved. I soon began to hear at a distance on the left the sharp reports of a rifle, again and again repeated ; and not long after, dull and heavy sounds succeeded, which I recognized as the familiar voice of Shaw's double-barrelled gun. When Henry's rifle
10 was at work there was always meat to be brought in. I went back across the river for a horse, and, returning, reached the spot where the hunters were standing. The buffalo were visible on the distant prairie. The living had retreated from the ground, but ten or twelve carcasses were
15 scattered in various directions. Henry, knife in hand, was stooping over a dead cow, cutting away the best and fattest of the meat.

When Shaw left me he had walked down for some distance under the river-bank to find another bull. At length
20 he saw the plains covered with the host of buffalo, and soon after heard the crack of Henry's rifle. Ascending the bank, he crawled through the grass, which for a rod or two from the river was very high and rank. He had not crawled far before to his astonishment he saw Henry standing erect
25 upon the prairie, almost surrounded by the buffalo. Henry was in his element. Quite unconscious that any one was looking at him, he stood at the full height of his tall figure, one hand resting upon his side, and the other arm leaning carelessly on the muzzle of his rifle. His eye was ranging
30 over the singular assemblage around him. Now and then he would select such a cow as suited him, level his rifle, and shoot her dead ; then quietly reloading, he would resume his former position. The buffalo seemed no more to regard his presence than if he were one of themselves ; the bulls were bellowing and butting at each other, or rolling about

in the dust. A group of buffalo would gather about the carcass of a dead cow, snuffing at her wounds; and sometimes they would come behind those that had not yet fallen, and endeavor to push them from the spot. Now and then some old bull would face towards Henry with an air of stupid amazement, but none seemed inclined to attack or fly from him. For some time Shaw lay among the grass, looking in surprise at this extraordinary sight; at length he crawled cautiously forward, and spoke in a low voice to Henry, who told him to rise and come on. Still the buffalo showed no sign of fear; they remained gathered about their dead companions. Henry had already killed as many cows as we wanted for use, and Shaw, kneeling behind one of the carcasses, shot five bulls before the rest thought it necessary to disperse.

The frequent stupidity and infatuation of the buffalo seems the more remarkable from the contrast it offers to their wildness and wariness at other times. Henry knew all their peculiarities; he had studied them as a scholar studies his books, and derived quite as much pleasure from the occupation. The buffalo were a kind of companions to him, and, as he said, he never felt alone when they were about him. He took great pride in his skill in hunting. He was one of the most modest of men; yet in the simplicity and frankness of his character, it was clear that he looked upon his pre-eminence in this respect as a thing too palpable and well established to be disputed. But whatever may have been his estimate of his own skill, it was rather below than above that which others placed upon it. The only time that I ever saw a shade of scorn darken his face was when two volunteer soldiers, who had just killed a buffalo for the first time, undertook to instruct him as to the best method of "approaching." Henry always seemed to think that he had a sort of prescriptive right to the buffalo, and to look upon them as something belonging to himself. Nothing excited

his indignation so much as any wanton destruction committed among the cows, and in his view shooting a calf was a
cardinal sin.

Henry Chatillon and Tête Rouge were of the same age;
5 that is, about thirty. Henry was twice as large, and about
six times as strong as Tête Rouge. Henry's face was roughened by winds and storms; Tête Rouge's was bloated by
sherry-cobblers and brandy-toddy. Henry talked of Indians
and buffalo; Tête Rouge of theatres and oyster-cellars.
10 Henry had led a life of hardship and privation; Tête
Rouge never had a whim which he would not gratify at the
first moment he was able. Henry moreover was the most
disinterested man I ever saw; while Tête Rouge, though
equally good-natured in his way, cared for nobody but him-
15 self. Yet we would not have lost him on any account; he
served the purpose of a jester in a feudal castle; our camp
would have been lifeless without him. For the past week
he had fattened in a most amazing manner; and, indeed,
this was not at all surprising, since his appetite was inordi-
20 nate. He was eating from morning till night; half the time
he would be at work cooking some private repast for himself, and he paid a visit to the coffee-pot eight or ten times
a day. His rueful and disconsolate face became jovial and
rubicund, his eyes stood out like a lobster's, and his spirits,
25 which before were sunk to the depths of despondency, were
now elated in proportion; all day he was singing, whistling,
laughing, and telling stories. Being mortally afraid of Jim
Gurney, he kept close in the neighborhood of our tent. As
he had seen an abundance of low fast life, and had a con-
30 siderable fund of humor, his anecdotes were extremely
amusing, especially since he never hesitated to place himself
in a ludicrous point of view, provided he could raise a laugh
by doing so. Tête Rouge, however, was sometimes rather
troublesome; he had an inveterate habit of pilfering provisions at all times of the day. He set ridicule at defiance,

and would never have given over his tricks, even if they
had drawn upon him the scorn of the whole party. Now
and then, indeed, something worse than laughter fell to his
share; on these occasions he would exhibit much contrition,
but half an hour after we would generally observe him   5
stealing round to the box at the back of the cart, and slyly
making off with the provisions which Deslauriers had laid
by for supper. He was fond of smoking; but having no
tobacco of his own, we used to provide him with as much
as he wanted, a small piece at a time. At first we gave him 10
half a pound together; but this experiment proved an entire
failure, for he invariably lost not only the tobacco, but the
knife intrusted to him for cutting it, and a few minutes after
he would come to us with many apologies and beg for more.

We had been two days at this camp, and some of the 15
meat was nearly fit for transportation, when a storm came
suddenly upon us. About sunset the whole sky grew as
black as ink, and the long grass at the edge of the river bent
and rose mournfully with the first gusts of the approaching
hurricane. Munroe and his two companions brought their 20
guns and placed them under cover of our tent. Having no
shelter for themselves, they built a fire of driftwood that
might have defied a cataract, and, wrapped in their buffalo-
robes, sat on the ground around it to bide the fury of the
storm. Deslauriers ensconced himself under the cover of 25
the cart. Shaw and I, together with Henry and Tête Rouge,
crowded into the little tent; but first of all the dried meat
was piled together, and well protected by buffalo-robes
pinned firmly to the ground. About nine o'clock the storm
broke amid absolute darkness; it blew a gale, and torrents 30
of rain roared over the boundless expanse of open prairie.
Our tent was filled with mist and spray beating through the
canvas, and saturating everything within. We could only distinguish each other at short intervals by the dazzling flashes
of lightning, which displayed the whole waste around us

with its momentary glare. We had our fears for the tent;
but for an hour or two it stood fast, until at length the cap
gave way before a furious blast; the pole tore through the
top, and in an instant we were half suffocated by the cold
5 and dripping folds of the canvas, which fell down upon us.
Seizing upon our guns, we placed them erect, in order to lift
the saturated cloth above our heads. In this agreeable situation, involved among wet blankets and buffalo-robes, we spent
several hours of the night, during which the storm would
10 not abate for a moment, but pelted down with merciless fury.
Before long the water gathered beneath us in a pool two or
three inches deep; so that for a considerable part of the
night we were partially immersed in a cold bath. In spite
of all this, Tête Rouge's flow of spirits did not fail him; he
15 laughed, whistled, and sang in defiance of the storm, and
that night paid off the long arrears of ridicule which he
owed us. While we lay in silence, enduring the infliction
with what philosophy we could muster, Tête Rouge, who
was intoxicated with animal spirits, cracked jokes at our
20 expense by the hour together. At about three o'clock in the
morning, preferring "the tyranny of the open night" to
such a wretched shelter, we crawled out from beneath the
fallen canvas. The wind had abated, but the rain fell steadily. The fire of the California men still blazed amid the
25 darkness, and we joined them as they sat around it. We
made ready some hot coffee by way of refreshment; but
when some of the party sought to replenish their cups, it
was found that Tête Rouge, having disposed of his own
share, had privately abstracted the coffee-pot and drunk
30 the rest of the contents out of the spout.

In the morning, to our great joy, an unclouded sun rose
upon the prairie. We presented a rather laughable appearance, for the cold and clammy buckskin, saturated with
water, clung fast to our limbs. The light wind and warm
sunshine soon dried it again, and then we were all encased

in armor of intolerable stiffness. Roaming all day over
the prairie and shooting two or three bulls, were scarcely
enough to restore the stiffened leather to its usual pliancy.

Besides Henry Chatillon, Shaw and I were the only hunters in the party. Munroe this morning made an attempt 5
to run a buffalo, but his horse could not come up to the
game. Shaw went out with him, and being better mounted,
soon found himself in the midst of the herd. Seeing nothing
but cows and calves around him, he checked his horse. An
old bull came galloping on the open prairie at some dis- 10
tance behind, and turning, Shaw rode across his path, levelling his gun as he passed, and shooting him through the
shoulder into the heart.

A great flock of buzzards was usually soaring about a few
trees that stood on the island just below our camp. Through- 15
out the whole of yesterday we had noticed an eagle among
them; to-day he was still there; and Tête Rouge, declaring
that he would kill the bird of America, borrowed Deslauriers's gun and set out on his unpatriotic mission. As might
have been expected, the eagle suffered no harm at his hands. 20
He soon returned, saying that he could not find him, but
had shot a buzzard instead. Being required to produce the
bird in proof of his assertion, he said he believed that he
was not quite dead, but he must be hurt, from the swiftness
with which he flew off. 25

"If you want," said Tête Rouge, "I'll go and get one of
his feathers; I knocked off plenty of them when I shot him."

Just opposite our camp, was another island covered with
bushes, and behind it was a deep pool of water, while two
or three considerable streams coursed over the sand not far 30
off. I was bathing at this place in the afternoon when a
white wolf, larger than the largest Newfoundland dog, ran
out from behind the point of the island, and galloped leisurely over the sand not half a stone's-throw distant. I could
plainly see his red eyes and the bristles about his snout; he

was an ugly scoundrel, with a bushy tail, a large head, and a most repulsive countenance. Having neither rifle to shoot nor stone to pelt him with, I was looking after some missile for his benefit, when the report of a gun came from the camp, and the ball threw up the sand just beyond him; at this he gave a slight jump, and stretched away so swiftly that he soon dwindled into a mere speck on the distant sand-beds. The number of carcasses that by this time were lying about the neighboring prairie summoned the wolves from every quarter; the spot where Shaw and Henry had hunted together soon became their favorite resort, for here about a dozen dead buffalo were fermenting under the hot sun. I used often to go over the river and watch them at their meal. By lying under the bank it was easy to get a full view of them. There were three different kinds: the white wolves and the gray wolves, both very large, and besides these the small prairie wolves, not much bigger than spaniels. They would howl and fight in a crowd around a single car-cass, yet they were so watchful, and their senses so acute, that I never was able to crawl within a fair shooting dis-tance; whenever I attempted it, they would all scatter at once and glide silently away through the tall grass. The air above this spot was always full of turkey-buzzards or black vultures; whenever the wolves left a carcass they would de-scend upon it, and cover it so densely that a rifle bullet shot at random among the gormandizing crowd would generally strike down two or three of them. These birds would often sail by scores just above our camp, their broad black wings seeming half transparent as they expanded them against the bright sky. The wolves and the buzzards thickened about us every hour, and two or three eagles also came to the feast. I killed a bull within rifle-shot of the camp; that night the wolves made a fearful howling close at hand, and in the morning the carcass was completely hollowed out by these voracious feeders.

After remaining four days at this camp we prepared to leave it. We had for our own part about five hundred pounds of dried meat, and the California men had prepared some three hundred more; this consisted of the fattest and choicest parts of eight or nine cows, a small quantity only being taken from each, and the rest abandoned to the wolves. The pack animals were laden, the horses saddled, and the mules harnessed to the cart. Even Tête Rouge was ready at last, and slowly moving from the ground, we resumed our journey eastward. When we had advanced about a mile, Shaw missed a valuable hunting-knife, and turned back in search of it, thinking that he had left it at the camp. The day was dark and gloomy. The ashes of the fires were still smoking by the river-side; the grass around them was trampled down by men and horses, and strewn with all the litter of a camp. Our departure had been a gathering signal to the birds and beasts of prey. Scores of wolves were prowling about the smouldering fires, while multitudes were roaming over the neighboring prairie; they all fled as Shaw approached, some running over the sand-beds and some over the grassy plains. The vultures in great clouds were soaring overhead, and the dead bull near the camp was completely blackened by the flock that had alighted upon it; they flapped their broad wings, and stretched upwards their crested heads and long skinny necks, fearing to remain, yet reluctant to leave their disgusting feast. As he searched about the fires he saw the wolves seated on the hills waiting for his departure. Having looked in vain for his knife, he mounted again, and left the wolves and the vultures to banquet undisturbed.

CHAPTER XXVI

DOWN THE ARKANSAS

In the summer of 1846, the wild and lonely banks of the Upper Arkansas beheld for the first time the passage of an army. General Kearney, on his march to Santa Fé, adopted this route in preference to the old trail of the Cimarron. When we were on the Arkansas, the main body of the troops had already passed on; Price's Missouri regiment, however, was still on its way, having left the frontier much later than the rest; and about this time we began to meet one or two companies at a time moving along the trail. No men ever embarked upon a military expedition with a greater love for the work before them than the Missourians; but if discipline and subordination are the criterion of merit, they were worthless soldiers indeed. Yet when their exploits have rung through all America, it would be absurd to deny that they were excellent irregular troops. Their victories were gained in the teeth of every established precedent of warfare; and were owing to a combination of military qualities in the men themselves. Doniphan's regiment marched through New Mexico more like a band of free companions than like the paid soldiers of a modern government. When General Taylor complimented him on his success at Sacramento and elsewhere, the colonel's reply very well illustrates the relations which subsisted between the officers and men of his command.

"I don't know anything of the manœuvres. The boys kept coming to me, to let them charge; and when I saw a good opportunity, I told them they might go. They were off like a shot, and that's all I know about it."

The backwoods lawyer was better fitted to conciliate the good-will than to command the obedience of his men. There were many serving under him who both from character and education could better have held command than he.

At the battle of Sacramento his frontiersmen fought under every disadvantage. The Mexicans had chosen their position; they were drawn up across the valley that led to their native city of Chihuahua; their whole front was covered by intrenchments and defended by batteries, and they outnumbered the invaders five to one. An eagle flew over the Americans, and a deep murmur rose along their lines. The enemy's batteries opened; long they remained under fire, but when at length the word was given, they shouted and ran forward. In one of the divisions, when midway to the enemy a drunken officer ordered a halt; the exasperated men hesitated to obey.

"Forward, boys!" cried a private from the ranks; and the Americans rushed like tigers upon the enemy. Four hundred Mexicans were slain upon the spot, and the rest fled, scattering over the plain like sheep. The standards, cannon, and baggage were taken, and among the rest a wagon laden with cords, which the Mexicans, in the fulness of their confidence, had made ready for tying the American prisoners.

Doniphan's volunteers, who gained this victory, passed up with the main army; but Price's soldiers, whom we now met, were men from the same neighborhood, precisely similar in character, manners, and appearance. One morning, as we were descending upon a wide meadow, where we meant to rest for an hour or two, we saw a body of horsemen approaching at a distance. In order to find water, we were obliged to turn aside to the river-bank, a full half-mile from the trail. Here we put up a kind of awning, and spreading buffalo-robes on the ground, Shaw and I sat down to smoke.

"We are going to catch it now," said Shaw; "look at
those fellows; there'll be no peace for us here."

And in truth about half the volunteers had straggled
away from the line of march, and were riding over the
meadow towards us.

"How are you?" said the first who came up, alighting
from his horse and throwing himself upon the ground. The
rest followed close, and a score of them soon gathered about
us, some lying at full length and some sitting on horseback.
They all belonged to a company raised in St. Louis. There
were some ruffian faces among them, and some haggard with
debauchery; but on the whole they were extremely good-
looking men, superior beyond measure to the ordinary rank
and file of an army. Except that they were booted to the
knees, they wore their belts and military trappings over the
ordinary dress of citizens. Besides their swords and holster
pistols, they carried slung from their saddles the excellent
Springfield carbines, loaded at the breech. They inquired
the character of our party, and were anxious to know the
prospect of killing buffalo, and the chance that their horses
would stand the journey to Santa Fé. All this was well
enough, but a moment after a worse visitation came upon us.

"How are you, strangers? whar are you going and whar
are you from?" said a fellow, who came trotting up with
an old straw hat on his head. He was dressed in the coars-
est brown homespun cloth. His face was rather sallow from
fever-and-ague, and his tall figure, though strong and sinewy,
had a lean, angular look, which, together with his boorish
seat on horseback, gave him an appearance anything but
graceful. More of the same stamp were close behind him.
Their company was raised in one of the frontier counties,
and we soon had abundant evidence of their rustic breeding;
they came crowding round by scores, pushing between our
first visitors, and staring at us with unabashed faces.

"Are you the captain?" asked one fellow.

"What's your business out here?" asked another.

"Whar do you live when you're to home?" said a third.

"I reckon you're traders," surmised a fourth; and to crown the whole, one of them came confidentially to my side and inquired in a low voice, "What's your partner's name?" 5

As each new-comer repeated the same questions, the nuisance became intolerable. Our military visitors were soon disgusted at the concise nature of our replies, and we could overhear them muttering curses. While we sat smoking, not in the best imaginable humor, Tête Rouge's tongue 10 was not idle. He never forgot his military character, and during the whole interview he was incessantly busy among his fellow-soldiers. At length we placed him on the ground before us, and told him that he might play the part of spokesman. Tête Rouge was delighted, and we soon had 15 the satisfaction of seeing him gabble at such a rate that the torrent of questions was in a great measure diverted from us. A little while after, a cannon with four horses came lumbering up behind the crowd; and the driver, who was perched on one of the animals, stretching his neck so as 20 to look over the rest of the men, called out, —

"Whar are you from, and what's your business?"

The captain of one of the companies was among our visitors, drawn by the same curiosity that had attracted his men. Unless their faces belied them, not a few in the 25 crowd might with great advantage have changed places with their commander.

"Well, men," said he, lazily, rising from the ground where he had been lounging, "it's getting late; I reckon we'd better be moving." 30

"I shan't start yet, anyhow," said one fellow, who was lying half asleep with his head resting on his arm.

"Don't be in a hurry, captain," added the lieutenant.

"Well, have it your own way; we'll wait a while longer," replied the obsequious commander.

At length, however, our visitors went straggling away as they had come, and we, to our great relief, were left alone again.

No one was more relieved than Deslauriers by the departure of the volunteers; for dinner was getting colder every moment. He spread a well-whitened buffalo-hide upon the grass, placed in the middle the juicy hump of a fat cow, ranged around it the tin plates and cups, and then announced that all was ready. Tête Rouge, with his usual alacrity on such occasions, was the first to take his seat. In his former capacity of steamboat clerk, he had learned to prefix the honorary *Mister* to everybody's name, whether of high or low degree; so Jim Gurney was Mr. Gurney, Henry was Mr. Henry, and even Deslauriers, for the first time in his life, heard himself addressed as Mr. Deslauriers. This did not prevent his conceiving a violent enmity against Tête Rouge, who, in his futile though praiseworthy attempts to make himself useful, used always to intermeddle with cooking the dinners. Deslauriers's disposition knew no medium between smiles and sunshine and a downright tornado of wrath; he said nothing to Tête Rouge, but his wrongs rankled in his breast. Tête Rouge had taken his place at dinner; it was his happiest moment; he sat enveloped in the old buffalo-coat, sleeves turned up in preparation for the work, and his short legs crossed on the grass before him; he had a cup of coffee by his side and his knife ready in his hand, and while he looked upon the fat hump-ribs, his eyes dilated with anticipation. Deslauriers sat opposite to him, and the rest of us by this time had taken our seats.

"How is this, Deslauriers? You have n't given us bread enough."

At this Deslauriers's placid face flew into a paroxysm of contortions. He grinned with wrath, chattered, gesticulated, and hurled forth a volley of incoherent words in broken English at the astonished Tête Rouge. It was just possible

to make out that he was accusing him of having stolen and
eaten four large cakes which had been laid by for dinner.
Tête Rouge, confounded at this sudden attack, stared at his
assailant for a moment in dumb amazement, with mouth and
eyes wide open. At last he found speech, and protested that 5
the accusation was false; and that he could not conceive
how he had offended Mr. Deslauriers, or provoked him to
use such ungentlemanly expressions. The tempest of words
raged with such fury that nothing else could be heard. But
Tête Rouge, from his greater command of English, had a 10
manifest advantage over Deslauriers, who, after sputtering
and grimacing for a while, found his words quite inadequate
to the expression of his wrath. He jumped up and vanished,
jerking out between his teeth one furious *sacré enfant de
garce!* a Canadian title of honor, made doubly emphatic 15
by being usually applied together with a cut of the whip
to refractory mules and horses.

The next morning we saw an old buffalo bull escorting
his cow with two small calves over the prairie. Close behind came four or five large white wolves, sneaking stealthily 20
through the long meadow-grass, and watching for the moment when one of the children should chance to lag behind
his parents. The old bull kept well on his guard, and faced
about now and then to keep the prowling ruffians at a
distance. 25

As we approached our nooning-place, we saw five or six
buffalo standing at the summit of a tall bluff. Trotting
forward to the spot where we meant to stop, I flung off
my saddle and turned my horse loose. By making a circuit
under cover of some rising ground, I reached the foot of 30
the bluff unnoticed, and climbed up its steep side. Lying
under the brow of the declivity, I prepared to fire at the
buffalo, who stood on the flat surface above, not five yards
distant. The gleaming rifle-barrel levelled over the edge
caught their notice, and they turned and ran. Close as they

were, it was impossible to kill them when in that position,
and stepping upon the summit, I pursued them over the
high arid table-land. It was extremely rugged and broken;
a great sandy ravine was channelled through it, with smaller
5 ravines entering on each side, like tributary streams. The
buffalo scattered, and I soon lost sight of most of them as
they scuttled away through the sandy chasms; a bull and
a cow alone kept in view. For a while they ran along the
edge of the great ravine, appearing and disappearing as they
10 dived into some chasm and again emerged from it. At last
they stretched out upon the broad prairie, — a plain nearly
flat and almost devoid of verdure, for every short grass-blade
was dried and shrivelled by the glaring sun. Now and then
the old bull would face towards me; whenever he did so I
15 fell to the ground and lay motionless. In this manner I
chased them for about two miles, until at length I heard in
front a deep, hoarse bellowing. A moment after, a band of
about a hundred bulls, before hidden by a slight swell of
the plain, came at once into view. The fugitives ran towards
20 them. Instead of mingling with the band, as I expected,
they passed directly through, and continued their flight.
At this I gave up the chase, crawled to within gun-shot of
the bulls, and sat down on the ground to watch them. My
presence did not disturb them in the least. They were not
25 feeding, for there was nothing to eat; but they seemed to
have chosen the parched and scorching desert as their play-
ground. Some were rolling on the ground amid a cloud of
dust; others, with a hoarse rumbling bellow, were butting
their large heads together, while many stood motionless, as
30 if quite inanimate. Except their monstrous growth of tangled
grizzly mane, they had no hair; for their old coat had fallen
off in the spring, and their new one had not as yet appeared.
Sometimes an old bull would step forward, and gaze at me
with a grim and stupid countenance; then he would turn
and butt his next neighbor; then he would lie down and

roll over in the dust, kicking his hoofs in the air. When
satisfied with this amusement, he would jerk his head and
shoulders upward, and resting on his forelegs, stare at me
in this position, half blinded by his mane, and his face
covered with dirt; then up he would spring upon all fours, 5
shake his dusty sides, turn half round, and stand with his
beard touching the ground, in an attitude of profound abstraction, as if reflecting on his puerile conduct. "You are
too ugly to live," thought I; and aiming at the ugliest, I
shot three of them in succession. The rest were not at all 10
discomposed at this; they kept on bellowing, butting, and
rolling on the ground as before. Henry Chatillon always
cautioned us to keep perfectly quiet in the presence of a
wounded buffalo, for any movement is apt to excite him to
make an attack; so I sat still upon the ground, loading and 15
firing with as little motion as possible. While I was thus
employed, a spectator made his appearance: a little antelope came running up to within fifty yards; and there it
stood, its slender neck arched, its small horns thrown back,
and its large dark eyes gazing on me with a look of eager 20
curiosity. By the side of the shaggy and brutish monsters
before me, it seemed like some lovely young girl in a den of
robbers or a nest of bearded pirates. The buffalo looked
uglier than ever. "Here goes for another of you," thought
I, feeling in my pouch for a percussion-cap. Not a percussion- 25
cap was there. My good rifle was useless as an old iron bar.
One of the wounded bulls had not yet fallen, and I waited
for some time, hoping every moment that his strength
would fail him. He still stood firm, looking grimly at me,
and, disregarding Henry's advice, I rose and walked away. 30
Many of the bulls turned and looked at me, but the wounded
brute made no attack. I soon came upon a deep ravine which
would give me shelter in case of emergency; so I turned
round and threw a stone at the bulls. They received it with
the utmost indifference. Feeling myself insulted at their

refusal to be frightened, I swung my hat, shouted, and
made a show of running towards them; at this they
crowded together and galloped off, leaving their dead and
wounded upon the field. As I moved towards the camp I
saw the last survivor totter and fall dead. My speed in returning was wonderfully quickened by the reflection that
the Pawnees were abroad, and that I was defenceless in case
of meeting with an enemy. I saw no living thing, however,
except two or three squalid old bulls scrambling among
the sand-hills that flanked the great ravine. When I reached
camp the party were nearly ready for the afternoon move.

We encamped that evening at a short distance from the
river-bank. About midnight, as we all lay asleep on the
ground, the man nearest to me, gently reaching out his hand,
touched my shoulder, and cautioned me at the same time
not to move. It was bright starlight. Opening my eyes and
slightly turning, I saw a large white wolf moving stealthily
around the embers of our fire, with his nose close to the
ground. Disengaging my hand from the blanket, I drew
the cover from my rifle, which lay close at my side; the
motion alarmed the wolf, and with long leaps he bounded out
of the camp. Jumping up, I fired after him, when he was
about thirty yards distant; the melancholy hum of the
bullet sounded far away through the night. At the sharp
report, so suddenly breaking upon the stillness, all the men
sprang up.

"You've killed him," said one of them.

"No, I haven't," said I; "there he goes, running along
the river."

"Then there's two of them. Don't you see that one lying
out yonder?"

We went out to it, and instead of a dead white wolf,
found the bleached skull of a buffalo. I had missed my
mark, and, what was worse, had grossly violated a standing
law of the prairie. When in a dangerous part of the country,

it is considered highly imprudent to fire a gun after encamping, lest the report should reach the ears of Indians.

The horses were saddled in the morning, and the last man
had lighted his pipe at the dying ashes of the fire. The
beauty of the day enlivened us all. Even Ellis felt its influence, and occasionally made a remark as we rode along,
and Jim Gurney told endless stories of his cruisings in the
United States service. The buffalo were abundant, and at
length a large band of them went running up the hills on
the left.

"Too good a chance to lose," said Shaw. We lashed our
horses and galloped after them. Shaw killed one with each
barrel of his gun. I separated another from the herd and
shot him. The small bullet of the rifle-pistol striking too
far back did not immediately take effect, and the bull ran
on with unabated speed. Again and again I snapped the
remaining pistol at him. I primed it afresh three or four
times, and each time it missed fire, for the touch-hole was
clogged up. Returning it to the holster, I began to load the
empty pistol, still galloping by the side of the bull. By this
time he had grown desperate. The foam flew from his jaws
and his tongue lolled out. Before the pistol was loaded he
sprang upon me, and followed up his attack with a furious
rush. The only alternative was to run away or be killed.
I took to flight, and the bull, bristling with fury, pursued
me closely. The pistol was soon ready, and then looking
back I saw his head five or six yards behind my horse's tail.
To fire at it would be useless, for a bullet flattens against
the adamantine skull of a buffalo bull. Inclining my body
to the left, I turned my horse in that direction as sharply
as his speed would permit. The bull, rushing blindly on
with great force and weight, did not turn so quickly. As I
looked back, his neck and shoulder were exposed to view;
and, turning in the saddle, I shot a bullet through them
obliquely into his vitals. He gave over the chase and soon

fell to the ground. An English tourist represents a situation
like this as one of imminent danger : this is a mistake ; the
bull never pursues long, and the horse must be wretched
indeed that cannot keep out of his way for two or three
5 minutes.

We were now come to a part of the country where we
were bound in common prudence to use every possible precaution. We mounted guard at night, each man standing
in his turn ; and no one ever slept without drawing his rifle
10 close to his side or folding it with him in his blanket. One
morning our vigilance was stimulated by finding traces of a
large Camanche encampment. Fortunately for us, however,
it had been abandoned nearly a week. On the next evening
we found the ashes of a recent fire, which gave us at the
15 time some uneasiness. At length we reached the Caches, a
place of dangerous repute ; and it had a most dangerous
appearance, consisting of sand-hills everywhere broken by
ravines and deep chasms. Here we found the grave of Swan,
killed at this place, probably by the Pawnees, two or three
20 weeks before. His remains, more than once violated by the
Indians and the wolves, were suffered at length to remain
undisturbed in their wild burial-place.

For several days we met detached companies of Price's
regiment. Horses would often break loose at night from
25 their camps. One afternoon we picked up three of these
stragglers quietly grazing along the river. After we came
to camp that evening, Jim Gurney brought news that more
of them were in sight. It was nearly dark, and a cold, drizzling rain had set in ; but we all turned out, and after an
30 hour's chase nine horses were caught and brought in. One
of them was equipped with saddle and bridle ; pistols were
hanging at the pommel of the saddle, a carbine was slung
at its side, and a blanket rolled up behind it. In the morning, as we resumed our journey, our cavalcade presented a
much more imposing appearance than ever before. We kept

on till the afternoon, when, far behind, three horsemen appeared on the horizon. Coming on at a hand-gallop, they soon overtook us, and claimed all the horses as belonging to themselves and others of their company. They were of course given up, very much to the mortification of Ellis and Jim Gurney.

Our own horses now showed signs of fatigue, and we resolved to give them half a day's rest. We stopped at noon at a grassy spot by the river. After dinner Shaw and Henry went out to hunt; and while the men lounged about the camp, I lay down to read in the shadow of the cart. Looking up, I saw a bull grazing alone on the prairie more than a mile distant, and taking my rifle I walked towards him. As I came near, I crawled upon the ground until I approached to within a hundred yards; here I sat down upon the grass and waited till he should turn himself into a proper position to receive his death-wound. He was a grim old veteran. His loves and his battles were over for that season, and now, gaunt and war-worn, he had withdrawn from the herd to graze by himself and recruit his exhausted strength. He was miserably emaciated; his mane was all in tatters; his hide was bare and rough as an elephant's, and covered with dried patches of the mud in which he had been wallowing. He showed all his ribs whenever he moved. He looked like some grizzly old ruffian grown gray in blood and violence, and scowling on all the world from his misanthropic seclusion. The old savage looked up when I first approached, and gave me a fierce stare; then he fell to grazing again with an air of contemptuous indifference. The moment after, as if suddenly recollecting himself, he threw up his head, faced quickly about, and to my amazement came at a rapid trot directly towards me. I was strongly impelled to get up and run, but this would have been very dangerous. Sitting quite still, I aimed, as he came on, at the thin part of the skull above the nose, hoping that the shot might have the

effect of turning him. After he had passed over about three-
quarters of the distance between us, I was on the point
of firing, when, to my great satisfaction, he stopped short.
I had full opportunity of studying his countenance; his
whole front was covered with a huge mass of coarse matted
hair, which hung so low that nothing but his two forefeet
were visible beneath it; his short thick horns were blunted
and split to the very roots in his various battles, and across
his nose and forehead were two or three large white scars,
which gave him a grim, and at the same time a whimsical,
appearance. It seemed to me that he stood there motionless
for a full quarter of an hour staring at me through the
tangled locks of his mane. For my part, I remained as quiet
as he, and looked quite as hard. I felt greatly inclined to
come to terms with him. " My friend," thought I, " if you 'll
let me off, I 'll let you off." At length he seemed to have
abandoned any hostile design. Very slowly and deliberately
he began to turn about; little by little his side came into
view, all beplastered with mud. It was a tempting sight. I
forgot my prudent intentions, and fired my rifle; a pistol
would have served at that distance. The old bull spun round
like a top, and galloped away over the prairie. He ran some
distance, and even ascended a considerable hill, before he
lay down and died. After shooting another bull among the
hills, I went back to camp.

At noon, on the fourteenth of September, a very large
Santa Fé caravan came up. The plain was covered with the
long files of their white-topped wagons, the close black car-
riages in which the traders travel and sleep, large droves of
mules and horses, and men on horseback and on foot. They
all stopped on the meadow near us. Our diminutive cart
and handful of men made but an insignificant figure by the
side of their wide and bustling camp. Tête Rouge went to
visit them, and soon came back with half a dozen biscuit in
one hand, and a bottle of brandy in the other. I inquired

where he got them. "Oh," said Tête Rouge, "I know some
of the traders. Dr. Dobbs is there, besides." I asked who
Dr. Dobbs might be. "One of our St. Louis doctors," replied Tête Rouge. For two days past I had been severely attacked by the same disorder which had so greatly reduced my
strength when at the mountains; at this time I was suffering
not a little from pain and weakness. Tête Rouge, in answer
to my inquiries, declared that Dr. Dobbs was a physician of
the first standing. Without at all believing him, I resolved
to consult this eminent practitioner. Walking over to the
camp, I found him lying sound asleep under one of the
wagons. He offered in his own person but indifferent evidence of his skill, for it was five months since I had seen so
cadaverous a face. His hat had fallen off, and his yellow
hair was all in disorder; one of his arms supplied the place
of a pillow; his trousers were wrinkled halfway up to his
knees, and he was covered with little bits of grass and straw
upon which he had rolled in his uneasy slumber. A Mexican stood near, and I made him a sign to touch the doctor.
Up sprang the learned Dobbs, and sitting upright rubbed
his eyes and looked about him in bewilderment. I regretted
the necessity of disturbing him, and said I had come to ask
professional advice.

"Your system, sir, is in a disordered state," said he,
solemnly, after a short examination.

I inquired what might be the particular species of disorder.

"Evidently a morbid action of the liver," replied the
medical man; "I will give you a prescription."

Repairing to the back of one of the covered wagons, he
scrambled in; for a moment I could see nothing of him
but his boots. At length he produced a box which he had
extracted from some dark recess within, and, opening it,
presented me with a folded paper. "What is it?" said I.
"Calomel," said the doctor.

Under the circumstances I would have taken almost anything. There was not enough to do me much harm, and it might possibly do good; so at camp that night I took the poison instead of supper.

5   That camp is worthy of notice. The traders warned us not to follow the main trail along the river, "unless," as one of them observed, "you want to have your throats cut!" The river at this place makes a bend; and a smaller trail, known as "the Ridge-path," leads directly across the prairie

10 from point to point, a distance of sixty or seventy miles.

We followed this trail, and after travelling seven or eight miles, came to a small stream, where we encamped. Our position was not chosen with much forethought or military skill. The water was in a deep hollow, with steep, high

15 banks; on the grassy bottom of this hollow we picketed our horses, while we ourselves encamped upon the barren prairie just above. The opportunity was admirable either for driving off our horses or attacking us. After dark, as Tête Rouge was sitting at supper, we observed him pointing with

20 a face of speechless horror over the shoulder of Henry, who was opposite to him. Aloof amid the darkness appeared a gigantic black apparition, solemnly swaying to and fro as it advanced steadily upon us. Henry, half vexed and half amused, jumped up, spread out his arms, and shouted. The

25 invader was an old buffalo bull, who, with characteristic stupidity, was walking directly into camp. It cost some shouting and swinging of hats before we could bring him first to a halt and then to a rapid retreat.

The moon was full and bright; but as the black clouds

30 chased rapidly over it, we were at one moment in light and at the next in darkness. As the evening advanced, a thunder-storm came up and struck us with such violence that the tent would have been blown over if we had not interposed the cart to break the force of the wind. At length it subsided to a steady rain. I lay awake through nearly the whole

night, listening to its dull patter upon the canvas above.
The moisture, which filled the tent and trickled from everything in it, did not add to the comfort of the situation.
About twelve o'clock Shaw went out to stand guard amid
the rain and pitchy darkness. Munroe was also on the alert. 5
When about two hours had passed, Shaw came silently in,
and, touching Henry, called to him in a low, quick voice to
come out. "What is it?" I asked. "Indians, I believe,"
whispered Shaw; "but lie still; I'll call you if there's a
fight." 10

He and Henry went out together. I took the cover from
my rifle, put a fresh percussion-cap upon it, and then, being
in much pain, lay down again. In about five minutes Shaw
returned. "All right," he said, as he lay down to sleep.
Henry was now standing guard in his place. He told me in 15
the morning the particulars of the alarm. Munroe's watchful eye had discovered some dark objects down in the hollow, among the horses, like men creeping on all-fours. Lying flat on their faces, he and Shaw crawled to the edge of
the bank, and were soon convinced that these dark objects 20
were Indians. Shaw silently withdrew to call Henry, and
they all lay watching in the same position. Henry's eye is
one of the best on the prairie. He detected after a while the
true nature of the intruders; they were nothing but wolves
creeping among the horses. 25

It is very singular that, when picketed near a camp,
horses seldom show any fear of such an intrusion. The
wolves appear to have no other object than that of gnawing
the trail-ropes of raw hide by which the animals are secured.
Several times in the course of the journey my horse's trail- 30
rope was bitten in two by these nocturnal visitors.

CHAPTER XXVII

THE SETTLEMENTS

The next day was extremely hot, and we rode from morning till night without seeing a tree, a bush, or a drop of water. Our horses and mules suffered much more than we, but as sunset approached, they pricked up their ears and 5 mended their pace. Water was not far off. When we came to the descent of the broad shallow valley where it lay, an unlooked-for sight awaited us. The stream glistened at the bottom, and along its banks were pitched a multitude of tents, while hundreds of cattle were feeding over the mead- 10 ows. Bodies of troops, both horse and foot, and long trains of wagons, with men, women, and children, were moving over the opposite ridge and descending the broad declivity before us. These were the Mormon battalion in the service of government, together with a considerable number of 15 Missouri Volunteers. The Mormons were to be paid off in California, and they were allowed to bring with them their families and property. There was something very striking in the half military, half-patriarchal appearance of these armed fanatics, thus on their way with their wives and children, to 20 found, it might be, a Mormon empire in California. We were much more astonished than pleased at the sight before us. In order to find an unoccupied camping-ground, we were obliged to pass a quarter of a mile up the stream, and here we were soon beset by a swarm of Mormons and Missourians. 25 The United States officer in command of the whole came also to visit us, and remained some time at our camp.

In the morning the country was covered with mist. We were always early risers, but before we were ready, the voices of men driving in the cattle sounded all around us. As we passed above their camp, we saw through the obscurity that the tents were falling, and the ranks rapidly forming; and, mingled with the cries of women and children, the rolling of the Mormon drums and the clear blast of their trumpets sounded through the mist.

From that time to the journey's end, we met almost every day long trains of government wagons, laden with stores for the troops, crawling at a snail's pace towards Santa Fé.

Tête Rouge had a mortal antipathy to danger, but one evening he achieved an adventure more perilous than had befallen any man in the party. The day after we left the Ridge-path we encamped close to the river, and at sunset saw a train of wagons encamping on the trail, about three miles off. Though we saw them distinctly, our little cart, as it afterwards proved, entirely escaped their notice. For some days Tête Rouge had been longing for a dram of whiskey. So, resolving to improve the present opportunity, he mounted his horse " James," which he had obtained from the volunteers in exchange for his mule, slung his canteen over his shoulder, and set out in search of his favorite liquor. Some hours passed without his returning. We thought that he was lost, or perhaps that some stray Indian had snapped him up. While the rest fell asleep I remained on guard. Late at night a tremulous voice saluted me from the darkness, and Tête Rouge and James soon became visible, advancing towards the camp. Tête Rouge was in much agitation and big with important tidings. Sitting down on the shaft of the cart, he told the following story : —

When he left the camp he had no idea, he said, how late it was. By the time he approached the wagoners it was perfectly dark ; and as he saw them all sitting around their fires within the circle of wagons, their guns laid by their sides, he thought he might as well give warning of his approach, in order to prevent a disagreeable mistake. Raising

his voice to the highest pitch, he screamed out in prolonged accents, "*Camp ahoy!*" This eccentric salutation produced anything but the desired effect. Hearing such hideous sounds proceeding from the outer darkness, the wagoners
5　thought that the whole Pawnee nation were upon them. Up they sprang, wild with terror. Each man snatched his gun; some stood behind the wagons; some threw themselves flat on the ground, and in an instant twenty cocked muskets were levelled full at the horrified Tête Rouge, who just
10　then began to be visible through the gloom.

"Thar they come," cried the master wagoner; "fire, fire, shoot that feller."

"No, no!" screamed Tête Rouge, in an ecstasy of fright; "don't fire, don't; I'm a friend, I'm an American citizen!"
15　"You're a friend, be you?" cried a gruff voice from the wagons; "then what are you yellin' out thar for like a wild Injun? Come along up here if you're a man."

"Keep your guns p'inted at him," added the master wagoner; "maybe he's a decoy, like."
20　Tête Rouge in utter bewilderment made his approach, with the gaping muzzles of the muskets still before his eyes. He succeeded at last in explaining his true character, and the Missourians admitted him into camp. He got no whiskey; but as he represented himself as a great invalid, and suffer-
25　ing much from coarse fare, they made up a contribution for him of rice, biscuit, and sugar from their own rations.

In the morning at breakfast, Tête Rouge once more related this story. We hardly knew how much of it to believe, though after some cross-questioning we failed to discover
30　any flaw in the narrative. Passing by the wagoners' camp, they confirmed Tête Rouge's account in every particular.

"I wouldn't have been in that feller's place," said one of them, "for the biggest heap of money in Missouri."

A day or two after, we had an adventure of another sort with a party of wagoners. Henry and I rode forward to hunt. After that day there was no probability that we should meet with buffalo, and we were anxious to kill one, for a supply of fresh meat. They were so wild that we hunted all the morning in vain, but at noon as we approached Cow Creek we saw a large band feeding near its margin. Cow Creek is densely lined with trees which intercept the view beyond, and it runs, as we afterwards found, at the bottom of a deep trench. We approached by riding along the bottom of a ravine. When we were near enough, I held the horses while Henry crept towards the buffalo. I saw him take his seat within shooting distance, prepare his rifle, and look about to select his victim. The death of a fat cow seemed certain, when suddenly a great smoke and a rattling volley of musketry rose from the bed of the creek. A score of long-legged Missourians leaped out from among the trees and ran after the buffalo, who one and all took to their heels and vanished. These fellows had crawled up the bed of the creek to within a hundred yards of the game. Never was there a fairer chance for a shot. They were good marksmen; all cracked away at once, and yet not a buffalo fell. In fact, the animal is so tenacious of life that it requires no little knowledge of anatomy to kill it, and it is very seldom that a novice succeeds in his first attempt at approaching. The balked Missourians were excessively mortified, especially when Henry told them that if they had kept quiet he would have killed meat enough in ten minutes to feed their whole party. Our friends, who were at no great distance, hearing the fusillade, thought that the Indians had fired the volley for our benefit. Shaw came galloping on to reconnoitre and learn if we were yet among the living.

At Cow Creek we found the welcome novelty of ripe grapes and plums, which grew there in abundance. At the Little Arkansas, not much farther on, we saw the last buffalo, a miserable old bull, roaming over the prairie melancholy and alone.

From this time forward the character of the county was
changing every day. We had left behind us the great arid
deserts, meagrely covered by the tufted buffalo-grass, with
its pale green hue and its short shrivelled blades. The plains
5 before us were carpeted with rich herbage sprinkled with
flowers. In place of buffalo we found plenty of prairie-hens,
and bagged them by dozens without leaving the trail. In
three or four days we saw before us the forests and meadows
of Council Grove. It seemed like a new sensation as we
10 rode beneath the resounding arches of these noble woods,
— ash, oak, elm, maple, and hickory, festooned with enormous grape-vines, purple with fruit. The shouts of our
scattered party, and now and then the report of a rifle,
rang through the breathless stillness of the forest. We rode
15 out again with regret into the broad light of the open
prairie. Little more than a hundred miles now separated us
from the frontier settlements. The whole intervening country
was a succession of green prairies, rising in broad swells and
relieved by trees clustering like an oasis around some spring,
20 or following the course of a stream along some fertile hollow. These are the prairies of the poet and the novelist. We
had left danger behind us. Nothing was to be feared from
the Indians of this region, the Sacs and Foxes, Kanzas and
Osages. We had met with rare good fortune. Although for
25 five months we had been travelling with an insufficient force
through a country where we were at any moment liable to
depredation, not a single animal had been stolen from us,
and our only loss had been one old mule bitten to death by
a rattlesnake. Three weeks after we reached the frontier,
30 the Pawnees and the Camanches began a regular series of
hostilities on the Arkansas trail, killing men and driving
off horses. They attacked, without exception, every party,
large or small, that passed during the next six months.

Diamond Spring, Rock Creek, Elder Grove, and other
'camping places besides, were passed in quick succession.

At Rock Creek we found a train of government provision-wagons under the charge of an emaciated old man in his seventy-first year. Some restless American devil had driven him into the wilderness at a time of life when he should have been seated at his fireside with his grandchildren on his knees. I am convinced that he never returned; he was complaining that night of a disease, the wasting effects of which upon a younger and stronger man, I myself had proved from severe experience. Long before this no doubt the wolves have howled their moonlight carnival over the old man's attenuated remains.

Not long after we came to a small trail leading to Fort Leavenworth, distant but one day's journey. Tête Rouge here took leave of us. He was anxious to go to the fort in order to receive payment for his valuable military services. So he and his horse James, after an affectionate farewell, set out together, with what provisions they could conveniently carry, including a large quantity of brown sugar. On a cheerless rainy evening we came to our last 'camping ground.

In the morning we mounted once more. In spite of the dreary rain of yesterday, there never was a brighter autumnal morning than that on which we returned to the settlements. We were passing through the country of the half-civilized Shawanoes. It was a beautiful alternation of fertile plains and groves just tinged with the hues of autumn, while close beneath them nestled the log-houses of the Indian farmers. Every field and meadow bespoke the exuberant fertility of the soil. The maize stood rustling in the wind, ripe and dry, its shining yellow ears thrust out between the gaping husks. Squashes and huge yellow pumpkins lay basking in the sun in the midst of their brown and shrivelled leaves. Robins and blackbirds flew about the fences, and everything betokened our near approach to home and civilization. The forests that border the Missouri soon rose before us, and we entered the wide tract of bushes which forms their outskirts.

We had passed the same road on our outward journey in the spring, but its aspect was now totally changed. The young wild apple-trees, then flushed with their fragrant blossoms, were hung thickly with ruddy fruit. Tall grass grew by the
5 roadside in place of tender shoots just peeping from the warm and oozy soil. The vines were laden with purple grapes, and the slender twigs of the swamp maple, then tasselled with their clusters of small red flowers, now hung out a gorgeous display of leaves stained by the frost with
10 burning crimson. On every side we saw tokens of maturity and decay where all had before been fresh with opening life. We entered the forest, checkered, as we passed along, by the bright spots of sunlight that fell between the opening boughs. On either side rich masses of foliage al-
15 most excluded the sun, though here and there its rays could find their way down, striking through the broad leaves and lighting them with a pure transparent green. Squirrels barked at us from the trees; coveys of young partridges ran rustling over the fallen leaves, and the golden oriole,
20 the blue-jay, and the flaming red-bird darted among the shadowy branches. We hailed these sights and sounds of beauty by no means with unmingled pleasure. Many and powerful as were the attractions of the settlements, we looked back regretfully to the wilderness behind us.

25   At length we saw the roof of a white man's dwelling between the opening trees. A few moments after, we were riding over the miserable log-bridge that led into West-port. Westport had beheld strange scenes, but a rougher-looking troop than ours, with our worn equipments and
30 broken-down horses, was never seen even there. We passed the well-remembered tavern, Boone's grocery, and old Vogel's dram-shop, and encamped on a meadow beyond. Here we were soon visited by a number of people who came to purchase our horses and equipments. This matter disposed of, we hired a wagon and drove to Kanzas landing. Here we

were again received under the hospitable roof of our old friend Colonel Chick, and seated under his porch, we looked down once more on the eddies of the Missouri.

Deslauriers made his appearance in the morning, strangely transformed by a hat, a coat, and a razor. His little log-house was among the woods not far off. It seems he had meditated giving a ball in honor of his return, and had consulted Henry Chatillon, as to whether it would do to invite his *bourgeois*. Henry expressed his entire conviction that we would not take it amiss, and the invitation was now proffered accordingly, Deslauriers adding as a special inducement that Antoine Lajeunesse was to play the fiddle. We told him we would certainly come, but before evening the arrival of a steamboat from Fort Leavenworth prevented our being present at the expected festivities. Deslauriers was on the rock at the landing-place, waiting to take leave of us.

"Adieu! mes bourgeois, adieu! adieu!" he cried, as the boat put off; "when you go another time to de Rocky Montagnes I will go with you; yes, I will go!"

He accompanied this assurance by jumping about, swinging his hat, and grinning from ear to ear. As the boat rounded a distant point, the last object that met our eyes was Deslauriers still lifting his hat and skipping about the rock. We had taken leave of Munroe and Jim Gurney at Westport, and Henry Chatillon went down in the boat with us.

The passage to St. Louis occupied eight days, during about a third of which time we were fast aground on sandbars. We passed the steamer "Amelia" crowded with a roaring crew of disbanded volunteers, swearing, drinking, gambling, and fighting. At length one evening we reached the crowded levee of St. Louis. Repairing to the Planters' House, we caused diligent search to be made for our trunks, which were at length discovered stowed away in the farthest

corner of the store-room. In the morning, transformed
by the magic of the tailor's art, we hardly recognized each
other.

On the evening before our departure, Henry Chatillon
came to our rooms at the Planters' House to take leave of
us. No one who met him in the streets of St. Louis would
have taken him for a hunter fresh from the Rocky Mountains. He was very neatly and simply dressed in a suit of
dark cloth; for although since his sixteenth year he had
scarcely been for a month together among the abodes of
men, he had a native good taste which always led him to
pay great attention to his personal appearance. His tall
athletic figure with its easy flexible motions appeared to
advantage in his present dress; and his fine face, though
roughened by a thousand storms, was not at all out of keeping with it. He had served us with a fidelity and zeal beyond all praise. We took leave of him with regret; and
unless his changing features, as he shook us by the hand,
belied him, the feeling on his part was no less than on ours.
Shaw had given him a horse at Westport. My rifle, an excellent piece, which he had always been fond of using, is
now in his hands, and perhaps at this moment its sharp
voice is startling the echoes of the Rocky Mountains. On
the next morning we left town, and after a fortnight of railroads, coaches, and steamboats, saw once more the familiar
features of home.

NOTES

xxxii 9 **woman's rights:** of which, at least as far as the suffrage is concerned, Parkman was a sturdy, though courteous, opponent.

xxxii 30 **I went ... to prepare for a literary undertaking:** the series of historical works (see Introduction).

xxxii 32 **inexorable circumstances:** Parkman's eye trouble (see Introduction).

xxxvi 18 **Mr. Remington:** Frederick Remington, who also is now gone (1861–1909).

1 1 **St. Louis:** founded as a post of the French fur trade in 1764 by Laclede, and named after Louis IX, the patron saint of the reigning king, Louis XV. It became the emporium of the American fur trade, and winter rendezvous of representatives of fur companies and free trappers operating in the Rockies. See Parkman, *The Conspiracy of Pontiac*, II, 257, 258; Chittenden, *Fur Trade*, I, 97. — 3 **Oregon and California ... Santa Fé:** see Introduction. — 8 **Steamboats ... passing up the Missouri:** the first navigation of the Missouri by steam was in 1819, when the *Independence* left St. Louis on the Mississippi for Franklin, Missouri. For an account of the annual voyages of the early Missouri steamboats from St. Louis in the interests of the fur trade, see Chittenden, *Fur Trade*, I, 35 ff.

2 7 **"mountain men":** the name given to the trappers in the Rockies, as distinct from those trappers who used to hunt afoot in the lowland forests (*coureurs de bois*, bushrangers), and those who followed the streams in canoes (*voyageurs;* see page 98, line 9).

3 2 **Independence:** "Independence, ... five miles east of Kansas City, was laid out in 1827, and by 1831 had become the western rendezvous both for the Santa Fé and the Oregon traffic. Its early settlers were chiefly Tennesseeans and Kentuckians. It was connected with the Mormon migration of 1831–1833." — Editor's note to *Commerce of the Prairies*, E. W. T., XIX, 189.

"Independence and Westport, just south of the Missouri's great bend to the east, were the gateway of the earliest regular travel and traffic across the plains. These towns are now the suburbs of Kansas City. . . . The old Santa Fé trail led by these settlements. From these points, too, the fur-trading companies conducted expeditions annually to . . . beyond the Rocky Mountains."— *Quarterly of Oregon Hist. Soc.*, Vol. I, *The Oregon Trail*, p. 354. — 8 **Spaniards:** from the Mexican provinces ; New Mexico was a part of Old Mexico, and the home almost exclusively of Spanish Americans till after the Mexican War (1846–1848). — 28 **Westport :** see preceding note.

4 31 **"Kentucky fellows " :** see note to page 5.

5 25 **choice of leaders :** see Introduction.

6 11 **the various motives :** see Introduction. Parkman is writing before the days of the gold fever, when one motive was supreme.

8 9 **Fort Leavenworth :** near the mouth of the Little Platte ; for many years the most westerly military post of the United States ; established, according to orders from the army, in 1827 by Colonel (later General) Leavenworth. — 10 **the dragoons in their expedition of last summer:** see pages 216, 217. — 22 **Daniel Boone:** "Backwoodsman of Kentucky," whose fame even Byron echoed in *Don Juan ;* born in Pennsylvania in 1734, and dying in Missouri in 1820.

10 20 *"Sacré enfant de garce" :* a mild equivalent in English would be "confounded son of a gun " ; *garce* is literally a coarse term for a degraded woman. — 33 **Jean Baptiste :** a nickname for a French Canadian. — 35 *bourgeois :* as a term in the fur trade it meant the manager of the frontier trading post or fur-trading expedition, who "conducted his business with an almost military discipline." See page 64. But it was loosely used of any one in authority. See Parkman, *Pontiac*, I, 295 ; and Chittenden, *Fur Trade*, I, 52.

11 4 **Fur Company :** see Introduction.

12 15 **"lope " :** an easy, cantering gait, characteristic of the mustang. — 34 **Kanzas Indian :** for Kansas, now officially spelled Kansa, Indian. "We saw here [on the Kansas river] the first village of Kanzas Indians. Their huts are made of poles and bark, and are about sixteen feet wide, by thirty long, and eight high. The ends are perpendicular, but the sides joining with the roof in a gradual curve, make the whole very nearly in the shape of the half of a circular cylinder." *Quarterly of Oregon Hist. Soc.*, Vol. VII, *Route Across the Rocky Mountains*, p. 68.

13 19 **bows and arrows :** the Plains Indians were at this time only partially armed with the rifle, though the Iroquois of New York and the Algonquian of New England and Canada had been deft in its use already in the seventeenth century. — 28 **fording**: a dangling participle. How would you correct it? — 33 **Methodist Shawanoe Mission**: one of the earliest of the Protestant missions on "the last American Frontier." Catholic missions, notably Spanish, had long before penetrated the Indian country of the Far West, primarily in what was then Spanish territory. The Shawnee had been removed west of the Mississippi after the War of 1812, in which they had borne a part, fighting against Clark and Wayne in Ohio. Tecumseh was a Shawnee.

14 6 **the Shawanoes**: "The Shawnees [Shawnee] have made considerable advancement towards civilization [i.e. in their new home]. Many of them have good farms and comfortable houses. Some of them are good mechanics, and most of them speak the English language tolerably well." *Quarterly of Oregon Hist. Soc.*, Vol. VII, *Route Across the Rocky Mountains*, p. 65.

15 15 **Hendrick**: after a great Mohawk war chief, famous in the "Old French War" for sagacity and corpulence. — 20 **Pontiac**: after the great chief of that name. See note to **130** 2. — 24 **Ogillallah**: see Introduction. Now spelled Oglala.

18 33 **"jump off"**: "jumping-off place" is a phrase of frequent occurrence in journals of early western travel, to designate the starting point on the frontier.

19 2 **General Kearney**: see pages 216, 217, and Introduction. — 12 **the expedition against Santa Fé**: see Introduction.

21 1 *pukwi* **lodges**: probably lodges made of rush mats, an ordinary type of summer dwelling among the Potawatomi.

23 9 **sixteen to the pound calibre**: for the meaning of this technical term, cf. "It [i.e. the backwoodsman's rifle] was generally bored out . . . to carry a ball of seventy, more rarely of thirty or forty, to the pound." — Roosevelt, *Winning of the West*, I, 149. — 18 **principles of Blackstone's Commentaries**: Parkman is thinking of his recent deliverance from the Harvard Law School, where, as his letters hint to us, Blackstone (the English jurist whose work was long a textbook) had pestered him not a little. — 25 **the trail of several companies of dragoons, who last summer had made an expedition under Colonel Kearney to Fort Laramie**: see pages 216, 217, and note to **89** 2. — 27 **the grand trail of the Oregon emigrants up the Platte**: see Introduction and map. The route along the Platte enabled them to find water and fodder for their horses and cattle.

24 12 **Mazeppa:** the hero of Byron's poem of that name, from which Parkman takes the verses that follow (see *Selections from Byron* in Standard English Classics).

25 19 *sacrés:* curses; a coinage of Parkman's after the use of *sacré* (cursed) in the imprecation "*sacré enfant de garce*" (see note to **10** 20).

28 20 **the "great American desert," — those barren wastes:** the old geographies actually represented this region as a desert like the Sahara; and so it appeared to the imaginations of our fathers. It is now populous with tumultuous cities and opulent farms.

30 10 **"catch up":** hitch up.

33 14 **the St. Joseph's trail:** see map, and page 47, line 2. — **Fort Laramie:** see page 89, line 2, and note.

34 4 **St. Joseph:** "Beginning in 1844 Saint Joseph, then a thriving border town, situated on the river some fifty miles to the north of the first jumping off places, became an important fitting out place [for emigrants]." — *Quarterly of Oregon Hist. Soc.*, Vol. I, *The Oregon Trail*, p. 354. — 5 **Mormons:** the Mormons arose under Joseph Smith in western New York state in 1830. After several years in Kirtland, Ohio, and one year in Far West, Missouri, they founded Nauvoo, Illinois, in 1839, which had a population of fifteen thousand by 1841. Smith was assassinated in 1844, and Nauvoo was shortly after abandoned for a home farther west. Led by Brigham Young, on over South Pass along the Oregon trail went the mighty host of the Lord, and established in 1847, at a safe distance from the persecutions of the Gentiles, a city by the Great Salt Lake. The importance of this Mormon city in the history of "the last American frontier" has not been sufficiently recognized.

34 9 **"Latter Day Saints":** still used as the name of the Mormon sect.

41 17 "*Voulez-vous du souper, tout de suite?*": "Do you want supper right away?" — 18 "*Sous la charette*": "under the cart." *Charette* should be spelled *charrette*.

42 21 **to admiration:** note the slightly archaic meaning.

43 15 **"The livelong day he had not spoke":** I have not found the source of this line.

45 35 **the story of Mahomet and the refractory mountain:** according to that story, Mahomet, after summoning the mountain in vain, declared with some presence of mind and truth, "If the mountain will not come to Mahomet, Mahomet will go to the mountain."

47 2 **the St. Joseph trail . . . near its junction with the old legiti-mate trail of the Oregon emigrants:** see map.

50 24 **their captain:** see Introduction.

56 22 **prickly pears:** see page 61, line 21, and page 148, line 30.

59 13 **capotes:** heavy hooded cloaks thrown over the shoulders, worn by the trappers in cold weather.

60 4 *bois de vache:* "cow wood," the French-Canadian term for buffalo chips, or buffalo dung. It was often used for fuel in the absence of wood (see Palmer's account, *E. W. T.*, XXX, 48).

63 14 **A flourishing colony of prairie-dogs:** for a picture of such a colony see Gregg, *Commerce of the Prairies*, in *E. W. T.*, XX, 278.

73 1 **my note-book:** *The Oregon Trail* was based on notebooks kept during the trip, according to Parkman's usual custom.

74 2 **"the South Fork of the Platte":** see map.

79 8 *"Avance donc!"* "go ahead!" "get up!" (see page 23, line 13).

80 28 **Scott's Bluff:** a little this side of Fort Laramie (see map).

83 28 **Macbeth's witches:** see the first scene of Shakespeare's *Macbeth.*

85 13 **the Black Hills:** "To the trapper, the Black Hills were the best known [of the Rocky Mountain regions], as they were the nearest mountains that he was wont to frequent. . . . The name is now restricted to the mass of mountains enclosed by the two Forks of the Cheyenne river in the modern states of Wyoming and South Dakota, but it had a far broader application in early times." — Chittenden, *Fur Trade*, II, 735. Parkman's "Black Hills" are those mountains in southeastern Wyoming, between the Medicine Bow and the North Platte. The flat country between the Medicine Bow and Parkman's "Black Hills" was Laramie Plains. See our map, but especially the map to Frémont's *Expedition*, Washington, 1845, a book apparently used by Parkman in planning his trip (see page 205, line 18, and note).

86 26 **an Indian medicine-bag:** a pouch, often elaborately worked, containing nondescript articles (varying according to the superstitions of the owner), supposed to possess properties that bring health and good luck. It was often slung over the shoulders by a baldric and worn at medicine dances.

87 8 *shongsasha:* red willow bark (see page 175, line 19).

88 34 *impending:* etymological sense.

89 1 **Looking back :** a dangling participle. Correct it. — 2 **Fort Laramie :** "Fort Lauramie belongs to the American Fur Company, and is built for a protection against the Indians. The occupants of the fort, who have been long there, being mostly French and having wives of the Sioux, do not apprehend any danger. The fort is built of Dobies (unburnt bricks). A wall of six feet in thickness and fifteen in height, encloses an area of one hundred and fifty feet square. Within and around the wall, are the buildings, constructed of the same material. These are a Trading House, Ware Houses for storing goods and skins, Shops and Dwellings for the traders and men. In the centre is a large open area." — *Quarterly of Oregon Hist. Soc.*, Vol. VII, *Route Across the Rocky Mountains*, p. 78.

There is a picture of Fort Laramie as it looked in 1842, opposite p. 78 of Paxson's *Last American Frontier*. Shortly after Parkman was there in 1846, it was converted by the United States into a military post, chiefly as a protection to emigrants. — 11 *engagés :* employees, an old French-Canadian term applied in the fur trade, especially to the common hired hands engaged at Montreal, Michilimackinac, and St. Louis. Cf. Chittenden, *Fur Trade*, I, 58.

90 10 **subsequent proceedings :** see page 103.

91 5 **the extreme outposts . . . about seven hundred miles to the eastward :** i.e. at Fort Leavenworth (see note to **8** 9).

92 30 **" great medicine " :** Parkman tells in his *Histories* of a band of warriors who, hanging the Jesuits' crosses around their necks, went out to victorious slaughter, and ever after maintained that the Christians' symbol of salvation was " great war medicine." Anything mysterious was to the Indian " great medicine."

95 11 **the traveller Catlin :** George Catlin (1796–1872), who was for eight years " amongst the wildest tribes of Indians in North America," and published accounts of his observations, once widely read. He seems to have been rather an accurate portrayer of externals than a penetrating critic of Indian character. His drawings have often been reproduced in later works. Catlinite, or pipestone, the clay from which the Indians carved their pipe bowls, is named after him.

98 9 *voyageur :* see note to **2** 7. — 14 **Monterey and Buena Vista :** Taylor defeated the Mexicans in a three days' battle, on September 21–23, 1846, at Monterey, in northern Mexico ; and on February 23, 1847, at Buena Vista with scarcely four thousand men, he put to rout the twenty thousand under Santa Anna.

100 17 *Meneaska:* white men. — 24 **them:** illogical pronominal reference ; the antecedent is grammatically singular.

103 8 **Laramie Plains:** see note to **85** 13. — 28 **"La Bonté's Camp":** evidently on the site of the La Bonté (temporary) trading post at the mouth of La Bonté creek on the Platte beyond Fort Laramie (see page 150).

105 11 **ties . . . between the sexes:** the French trappers were from the earliest days peculiarly given to such alliances, and often became veritable Indians themselves. See the description of Reynal on next page. — 23 **the same disorder that occasioned such heavy losses to the army on the Rio Grande:** apparently the dysentery, destined later to occasion still heavier losses in the armies of the Civil War.

112 13 **like the cowl of a Capuchin friar:** Parkman is not making a conventional comparison ; he had already been in Rome, and, though still in the early twenties, he compassed in experience something of the life both by the Tiber and by the Platte. — 22 **Irving's "Astoria":** an account by Washington Irving of John Jacob Astor's short-lived fur-trading post (1811–1813) at the mouth of the Columbia River. Published in 1836.

116 11 **General Kearney, on his late return from California :** after the taking of Santa Fé (see Introduction).

117 11 **Fort Pierre :** a famous old post of the fur trade on the upper Missouri (see map). There was a cross-country trail connecting it with Fort Laramie.

119 27 **"free trapper" :** a trapper unattached to any of the fur companies, the hardiest and most picturesque hunter of the Old West. Cf. Irving's *Adventures of Captain Bonneville*, published in 1837.

123 6 *traineau:* see page 95, line 32.

130 2 **King Philip :** chief of the Wampanoag Indians, in the uprising against the New England colonists (1675–1676). — 2 **Pontiac :** the great chief of the Ottawa, who organized and prosecuted the Indian war on the western frontier (1763–1764). See Parkman's *Conspiracy of Pontiac.* — **Tecumseh :** the revolted chief of the Shawnee, whose army was defeated by General Harrison at Tippecanoe in 1811. Tecumseh was not at Tippecanoe in person. He joined the British and was slain at the battle of the Thames in 1813.

131 19 **the "Parks" :** North, Middle, and South Parks, the principal open valleys in the Rockies of Colorado, in which are the sources of the North Platte, Grand, and South Platte respectively. — 25 **When the buffalo are extinct**: within forty years Parkman's prophecy of the passing of the buffalo was practically fulfilled. The Indian himself, in his slaughter of the cows (see page 313, line 2), was partially responsible ; but the white man, especially after the opening up of the transcontinental railroads, proved the buffalo's murrain. During one period of three years in the seventies he killed at least five million merely for their hides, to say nothing of those he killed for pleasure.

138 4 **every gift among the Indians**: hence the proverbial expression, "Indian giver," a common taunt among youngsters.

139 35 *pommes blanches:* literally "white apples," small white roots eaten by the Indians, sometimes called "swan apples."

140 25 **Salvator**: Salvator Rosa, a famous Italian painter of the Neapolitan school. Died at Rome 1673.

141 3 **the Pythian Apollo**: a marble statue of Apollo, the Greek sun god, in the act of slaying the Python with his arrow, stands in the Belvedere ("Fair-view") room of the Vatican gallery at Rome. Byron describes it vividly in *Childe Harold*, Canto IV, 161. — 5 **West**: Benjamin West, an American painter, famous for his historical and battle pieces. Among his Indian studies are his work in oil, "Penn's Treaty with the Indians," and his work in pencil illustrating a contemporary account of the battle at Bushy Run in 1763. He died in 1820. — 6 **a Mohawk!**: the Mohawk were one of the five tribes of the dreaded Iroquois of north-central New York.

154 25 **looking from them**: a dangling participle.

166 3 **impended**: etymological sense. Cf. "impending," page 88, line 34. — 34 **Gros-Ventre**: French, big belly. Explain why so many names of Indian tribes and bands are French. The Grosventres were a tribe of Siouan stock, also called Minitaree, living in villages contiguous to the Mandan on the upper Missouri.

174 4 **Shienne**: a spelling of "Cheyenne."

187 13 **Taos**: an old Spanish town in New Mexico (see map) ; originally an Indian pueblo, and still in part a prominent pueblo settlement. — **Santa Fé**: chief city of the old northern province of Mexico (founded, according to scholars, in 1605), and terminal of the American Santa Fé trade (see map and Introduction). — 16 **Nez Percé mission**: a Catholic mission to the Nez Percé Indians far away in the Oregon country. *Nez Percé* is French for "pierced nose."

194 6 *pemmican :* from the Cree language : *pimmi*, meat ; *kon*, fat. — 7 *wasna:* more accurately, dried meat and cherries (sometimes with the stones) pulverized together and usually mixed into melted tallow, which, hardening, preserved the preparation indefinitely. It was a staple on journeys, apparently often in the form of soup. The modern pemmican, used especially on Arctic voyages, though differing in some minor ingredients, is essentially similar.

204 21 **Sancho Panza:** the pompous squire of Don Quixote, in Cervantes's romance of that name.

205 18 **"Fremont's Expedition"**: J. C. Frémont (1813–1890), "the Pathfinder," was sent out by the United States to explore west of the Missouri ; on the first expedition (1842) he explored to South Pass in the Rockies ; on the second (1843–1844) he penetrated to Oregon and northern California.

207 13 **a lineal descent from bears, wolves:** an Indian clan — to be distinguished from a tribe — was constituted by lineal descent from some one animal (occasionally object), and the effigy mounds (bears, deer, etc.) of the Mississippi valley, especially numerous around the lakes of Madison, Wisconsin, are silent but eloquent witnesses of this ancient belief, a belief (totemism) all but universal among primitive peoples. It may be mentioned that all the earthworks of aboriginal America, whether effigy, burial, or defensive, are of Indian origin. "The mysterious race of mound-builders" existed only in the heads of ignorant dreamers.

209 12 **descending the Arkansas on the trail of General Kearney's army:** see Introduction ; also page 264, line 9, and page 277, line 10. Note that Parkman is speaking of his return to Fort Leavenworth over the course that Kearney had taken a few weeks before from Fort Leavenworth for Santa Fé.

216 11 **Colonel Kearney left Fort Leavenworth . . . marched to Fort Laramie, passed along the foot of the mountains [the Rockies] to Bent's Fort, and then, turning eastward again, returned to the point whence he set out:** this was practically Parkman's route also. For Bent's Fort see note to **258** 10. — 16 **Sweetwater:** a small tributary of the North Platte, arising in South Pass. The Oregon trail followed its course.

223 29 **fraternities:** the existence of such fraternities has been questioned by some later students of Indian customs, who seem not to have remembered this testimony of an eyewitness (see page 265, line 34). Cf. W. J. Hoffman's account of the cult societies of the Menomini Indians in the *Fourteenth Annual Report of the Bureau of Ethnology*, pp. 66–161.

227 23 **After having ridden:** a dangling gerund.

232 34 **with his witch-hazel rod:** a form of divination; held in the hand, the rod was supposed to point downward when the diviner reached a spot where gold, a spring of water, or the like, was hidden in the ground.

245 9 *nom de guerre:* assumed name.

251 8 **Descending:** a dangling participle.

255 31 **Fort Pierre:** see map and note to **117** 11.

258 10 **Bent's Fort:** see map and page 281, line 5. Bent's Fort, on one branch of the Santa Fé trail, five hundred and thirty miles from Independence, was "the great crossroads station of the south-west. The north and south route between the Platte river country and Santa Fé, and the east and west route up the Arkansas and into the mountains, found this their most natural trading point." — Chittenden, *Fur Trade*, II, 543. Bent was of a well-known St. Louis family in the first half of the nineteenth century.

259 2 **adieu to . . . Fort Laramie:** a trail had been worn by the dragoons of Fort Leavenworth from Fort Laramie, through St. Vrain's, crossing the South Platte at Cherry Creek, past Boiling Springs, on to Bent's Fort; this is the route Parkman was now about to traverse.

262 10 **the Pueblo:** see map, and page 276, lines 1 ff.

264 9 **General Kearney's march up the Arkansas:** see Introduction; also page 209, line 12, and page 277, line 10. — 10 **General Taylor's victories at Matamoras:** Matamoras, near the mouth of the Rio Grande, was occupied by Taylor, May 18, 1846. — 25 **ponchos:** a poncho is "a kind of cloak worn by the Spanish Americans, like a blanket with a slit in the middle for the head." — Webster's *New International*. — 32 **"to daff the world aside":** see Shakespeare, *1 Henry IV*, IV, i.

265 23 **Paganini:** an Italian violinist, famous in Parkman's boyhood (1782–1840). — 34 **The society of the "Strong Hearts":** see page 223, line 29.

267 28 **Agassiz Museum:** at Harvard University, named after the great naturalist, Louis Agassiz (1807–1873), a professor at that school.

269 8 **South Fork of the Platte:** see map. — 23 **Long's Peak:** see map. Long was an early government explorer. — 34 **Scylla and Charybdis:** the monsters fabled to be on opposite shores of the Straits of Messina, between Italy and Sicily, each equally a terror to mariners.

270 34 **St. Patrick:** who is reputed to have driven all the snakes out of Ireland.

271 20 **the walls of a large fort, built . . . by M. St. Vrain:** see map. Note how many of the names one meets in this early western country betray the wide activity of the old French trappers and traders of Canada or the country along the Mississippi, the Louisiana of the eighteenth century, settled from France and Canada. Ceran St. Vrain, who died in 1818, was of a well-known St. Louis family, when St. Louis was the emporium of the fur trade.

272 34 **Pike's Peak:** see map. As Parkman tells us on page 274, they finally passed within six or eight miles of the mountain. Pike was an early government explorer.

273 31 *"Des sauvages!":* "the savages!"

277 10 **three weeks before, General Kearney's army had left Bent's Fort to march against Santa Fé:** see Introduction. — 14 **the battles of Palo Alto and Resaca de la Palma:** fought at the beginning of the Mexican War, respectively on May 8 and 9, 1846, by which Taylor's army drove the Mexicans across the Rio Grande. Taylor, advancing, captured Monterey in northern Mexico after a three days' battle, September 21–23.

280 2 **Nauvoo:** see note to **34** 5.

282 20 **yager:** obviously the same word as "yager" (from German, *Jaeger*, a hunter), which means a member of a special body of infantry in the German army. Explain how the meaning in the text might have come about. — 29 **had come in a trading vessel to California:** around Cape Horn, the regular route before the development of the transcontinental trails. For a classic example of the sailor making shift in the backwoods, see Cowper's *Pathfinder*.

283 1 **Bridger's Fort:** a trading post, the first important stopping place of the emigrants on the Oregon trail after their journey through South Pass (see map).

284 25 **Tête Rouge:** "Red Head."

285 12 **Fighting Mexicans was a less amusing occupation than he had supposed:** compare the similar disillusion of Birdofredum

Sawin as manifested in his letters from the front (Lowell, *Biglow Papers*, first series).

291 13 **a long train of Santa Fé wagons:** Parkman was now traversing the branch of the Santa Fé trail that followed the Upper Arkansas to Bent's Fort. "The old trail of the Cimarron" branched off near The Caches (see map). — 25 **"The Caches":** see map. There were several other places in the fur-trading regions bearing this name. A cache was a large hole in the ground in which a fur trader stored such merchandise, provisions, and effects as he was for the time being unable to carry with him. It was protected from water within, and when it was closed up, all traces of its existence were carefully obliterated, usually by building a camp fire over it. But a cache would sometimes be discovered, especially by Indians and wolves. The traders usually respected the caches of their colleagues.

292 4 **Pawnee Fork:** see map.

293 16 **General Kearney . . . renewing his threats of the previous year:** see pages 216, 217. Kearney's expedition to Fort Laramie in 1845 and his expedition against Santa Fé in 1846 must be kept distinct.

294 16 **sign-language:** "We may suppose that at first only signs most natural and expressive were used. By-and-by other signs were introduced, always conventional, but becoming more and more arbitrary, until there resulted a means of communication almost as perfect as if each understood and spoke the oral language of the other . . . used in its completeness only by the Plains Indians." — Dodge, *Our Wild Indians*, p. 380.

302 13 **Kit Carson:** "trapper, guide, soldier, and Indian agent" (1809–1868). Though his national reputation was gained in the days of the Overland Mail, a number of years after the date of Parkman's trip, he was already known through his services as guide to Frémont.

304 33 *"Oui, bien chargé . . . c'est un bon fusil":* "yes, well loaded . . . it's a good gun."

322 14 **By lying:** a dangling gerund. How would you correct it?

324 4 **the old trail of the Cimarron:** for a considerable distance the regular Santa Fé trail went along the Cimarron river. This is the trail shown on our map. Note that Parkman is still on the branch trail between Bent's Fort and The Caches.

325 5 **the battle of Sacramento:** fought in northern Mexico, February 28, 1847.

329 14 *sacré enfant de garce!:* see note to **10** 20.

334 15 **the Caches:** see page 291, line 25, and note.

338 8 **a smaller trail, known as "the Ridge-path":** short cuts such as this were not uncommon both on the Oregon and the Santa Fé trail.

344 9 **Council Grove:** one hundred and fifty miles from Independence ; here the Santa Fé traders organized their caravans (see Introduction).